In the Realm of the Senses

A Materialist Theory of Seeing and Feeling

In the Realm of the Senses

A Materialist Theory of Seeing and Feeling

Stuart Walton

zero books

Winchester, UK
Washington, USA

First published by Zero Books, 2016
Zero Books is an imprint of John Hunt Publishing Ltd., Laurel House, Station Approach,
Alresford, Hants, SO24 9JH, UK
office1@jhpbooks.net
www.johnhuntpublishing.com
www.zero-books.net

For distributor details and how to order please visit the 'Ordering' section on our website.

ISBN: 978 1 78279 051 8
Library of Congress Control Number: 2015935793

A CIP catalogue record for this book is available from the British Library.

Design: Stuart Davies

Printed and bound by CPI Group (UK) Ltd, Croydon, CR0 4YY, UK

CONTENTS

for Joshua Wong

Preface

Two conflicting narratives of human sensuality and sensibility have come to dominate philosophy since the European enlightenments. One insists that the senses have been freed from their imprisonment in the adjacent cells of theology and rationalism, and released back into the open air in which the human species first emerged as a species. The other laments the damage done to sensible apprehension, and all sensitivity, by a world that has ravaged the fragile senses through over-stimulation and abuse, just as the bodies of industrial workers were left in ruins by the exigencies of mechanised production and then mechanised war. The one current has bred lyric rhapsodies down to our own day, in which whatever depredations unreconciled life has visited on the vulnerable individual have been, and may be, compensated by a restored sensual alertness to the gorgeous world, to the sudden appearance of bashful snowdrops in the stony rubbish, the exquisite regret in the cello concerto, the scent of vanilla. Its counterpart has been trained alike by conservative ethics and ideological critique into an urgent refusal of the variant slaveries of hedonistic sensualism and of the commodity economy of consumer society.

The present work aims to break the unwitting compact into which these complementary traditions have locked the life of the senses. A continuing tussle for ascendancy between the mind and the body, which every philosophical era imagines itself to have settled, while helplessly perpetuating it, has the invariable result of according victory to one or the other competitor, despite every solemn avowal of their interdependence. If the current vogue is once again to insist that everything in thought, up to the airiest abstractions, is a product of the digestive system or of sexual desire, not a blush is spared for the apparent triumphalism implicit in the notion. A bodiless thought that conceived itself as untrammelled by the physiological eventually issued in mass murder, but its reaction-formation in the shape of discourses of the body, in the era since the European dictatorships, has only more securely harnessed philosophy to the once redundant idea of transcendental apperception, the postulate that the world is nothing other than what the individual sensate body experiences it to be.

Nothing is to be gained by blasting away one side or the other of the frozen dialectic of mind and body, intellect and sensuality. Similarly, turning away from propositional thought towards the speculations of neuroscience, with which contemporary philosophy has discovered a boundless fascination, does nothing other than repeat the manoeuvre by which thought surrendered itself to pontifical authority in the scholastic ages. Instead, a thinking must be attempted that remains sensitive to what there is of each in either, for good or ill as the matter may be. The task undertaken by Adorno's late work, '[t]o use the strength of the subject to break through the fallacy of constitutive subjectivity,'[1] is the guiding principle here. By refusing alike the superstitious materialising of abstract concepts to which nominalism and the linguistic current in twentieth century thought did homage, no less than the spiritualising of matterinbody culture and present-day obscurantist sensualism, the following text is an attempt to reinvest materialism with a practice that would again honour it.

The opening section maps the philosophical territory, tracing the routes by which the sensual life became absorbed in vulgar materialism at the expense of the mind, and looks for ways in which the two parties to the contest of the physical and the mental might be reconciled amid the din of global technology. Following on is a sequential consideration of each of the five classical senses in their applications, in which historical excursions into their development and the course of their fate in modern experience will help to illuminate what has been done to human beings spiritually through each of these five corporeal channels. A short meditation on the alleged sixth sense, while not hospitable to the practical consequences of defeating the sensory life by mystically supplementing it, at least acknowledges the yearning for a solution to the predicament in which modern sensibility finds itself.

The senses are the first means by which reality has its way with the new born. If the life ahead is to be at all intelligible, let alone do even the most minimal justice to its latest participant, the senses each of them is born with must become integrally constitutive of them. The conflict between mind and body is a mere distraction, compared to the struggle for active disposition over the sensory capacities waged between each individual gifted with them and a world that wants them for its own.

Stuart Walton
February 2015

Part One

Theory of the Senses

The Senses in Materialism

The realm of the senses, in which humanity has allegedly dwelt ever since its spiritual craft capsized in rough seas, has proved not to be the isle of the blessed that it might have seemed. A first attempt to introduce the mind and the body, strangers since Plato, to each other might have followed on from the iconoclasm of the Enlightenment had not the age of reason only succeeded in replacing the immortal soul with the rapacious intellect. From amid all the talk of the transcendent subject in Kant and Hegel, and conceived in part against it, emerged the individual sanctified in the firestorm of his emotions, young Werther thrilled to the brim with raging jealousy, and then, more peaceably, the dreaming solitary bewitched by birdsong, surrendering to the unhinging potency of laudanum, or just surprised by daffodils. The sights and sounds and scents of Romantic nature opened an alternative world, but led precisely nowhere when it was revealed that nature itself had just contingently come to be, extrapolating itself by exactly the same principle – selection of the fittest by ruthless discarding of the inadequate – by which the entirety of economic relations were informed. A world-historical attempt to give dialectical cognition a materialist turn, freeing the whole of society through the agency of its most downtrodden elements, resulted in a political apparatus of paranoid surveillance and a state that refused to wither away, while psychoanalysis brought forth the heir to the Platonic *daimon*, the Christian soul and the Cartesian *cogito* in the form of the individual ego, enchained by neurotic repression, the evidence for which played out in his head each night when he fell asleep.

If the life of the senses had been wholly or severely curtailed by the currents of theology and philosophy up to the first great crisis of imperialism, the twentieth century saw it finally burst its bounds. The official version of cultural history insists that, since the art nouveau era, human sensual life has been released to its full potential: the explosion of entertainment media based on moving pictures, the revaluation of decadence from a moral category to a statement of defiant individualism, the availability of varieties of sexual experience and a teeming pharmacopoeia of intoxicants, not to mention the kinds of sensual assault endured in the trenches of Flanders and the aerial bombing of densely populated cities, have flooded human consciousness with the very experience the disembodied mind once alternately dreamed about and dreaded. But just as the thinking subject once constructed fortifications around itself from which it gained a commanding view of external reality – or, where reality got in the way, the supreme Being of the ontologists – the feeling subject now appears cast adrift on a torrent of sensory data, incapable of reconnecting it to something like reflective thinking. Moreover, if there is a preponderance of sensuality in contemporary life, as both thoroughgoing sensualists and old-fashioned moralists insist, it appears to run in surprisingly narrow channels. Throughout both halves of the world, human beings appear strikingly similar in their musical tastes, in their predilections for visual entertainment, in the demands they make of their physical relationships, and in what they eat and drink. It is as though the search for a single unitary deity, long since abandoned by an ecumenical theology with more scrupulous manners than primal monotheism, in favour of a single common ancestor of *Homo sapiens*, has taken the syncretising urge to its final extreme by providing a single *table d'hôte* menu of sensual diversions. Thus has globalisation, striding triumphantly over the fallen ranks of 'workers of the world', found a final way to unite recalcitrant humanity.

To posit a materialist theory of the senses, in light of the classical tradition, may appear a tautology. The bodily senses are surely the means by which the lineaments of the material world are delivered to consciousness, leaving the mind free to dwell on higher things. In Plato's tripartite system in the fourth book of the *Republic,* reflection on metaphysical matters takes place in the head, while the heart pumps out distracting emotions, and the stomach and genitals call raucously to be satiated. The soul, chafing for the time being, as the infamous metaphor has it, in the dungeon of the flesh, flies free in ecstasy at the moment of death, but is not entirely prevented meanwhile from contemplation of perfection, which is how it knows there must be a beyond. It not only inextinguishably survives the physical body, it also pre-exists it, so that the corporeal life of each individual is a momentary sojourn in an entrammelling state, in which it is weighed down by feelings and appetites, but whose pathos consists in its never quite forgetting that it will return to a flawless realm of transcendence. How, therefore, can a study of the senses be anything other than materialist? What this study intends, however, is precisely that reconnection of the material and the metaphysical that Plato disdains. If, on his own view, an access of negative emotion or the privations of hunger and bodily insufficiency are distractions for the life of the soul, then the soul must require a minimum level of material amenity for its efficient functioning. There can be no higher life for the malnourished, or as Brecht put it, 'Bread first, then morals!' It will be the contention of a reformed materialism, though, that it isn't simply a question of the physical sustenance of the body providing for the elevated operations of the mind, but that those very operations are themselves generated by the way sensory inputs are converted into mental activity. The 'seeing and feeling' of the title are to be understood in both applications: as the application of the physical senses of sight, touch and so on, and also as the operation of metaphysical cognition in understanding and experiencing. This project is imbued with all the ethical urgency that two millennia of regarding the body as a dungeon have produced in the shape of unimaginable suffering.

Just as an intellectual life cleansed of the dirt-marks of physicality prepared the way for radical inhumanity, however, so too a sensuous life lived for its own delectable sake too often collapsed into irrationalism. The moments where the Romantic poets succumb to the 'Ah!' of inarticulate wonder, the onslaughts of opium and absinthe that signed cognition's excuse-note for the Symbolists and *décadents*, are the moments at which the spirit has nothing more to offer to a world that saw its victory thereby confirmed in them. The natural world has always offered apparent means of escape through altered consciousness, the more so where its clients viewed the alteration of consciousness as nothing more than mere escape. Romanticism aspired to liberate the individual spirit through unmediated sensuous contact with nature, including its own nature, but may always have kept the laudanum bottle to hand for when the piping of nightingales palled. An encounter with the sublime rendered in poetry that aimed to reproduce it through its own verbal resources produced a doubled effect, liberating the individual consciousness from the tyranny of reason, the better that others could exercise their own rationality on it in teasing out its cryptic allusiveness. Its programme was to recast an overly instrumentalised reason via the *qualia* of nature, the very medium in which Palaeolithic consciousness first struggled to acquire reason. When it surrendered wholesale to social realism in the documentary novels and paintings of the Victorian era, it once more accepted its traditional role as light relief, in the form of the lyrical passages that intervene in Dickens and Zola between the consumptive expiring of street-urchins. Romantic art had sought to transcend the decorative element that inhered in even the greatest works, precisely by making the decorative tendency turn dynamic. It rescinded the Aristotelian verdict on tragedy, that its frightfulness usefully exorcised radical dissatisfaction with life, in the interest of maintaining social stability. In the productions of Sturm und Drang, Goethean *Empfindsamkeit*,

Gothic horror and the wanderer poised on the lip of the abyss, it hoped to provoke emotional and sensual response for the sake of glorifying unmediated nature, removing the aesthetic once more to a realm outside society, at the very moment at which society, in the urban dawn of industrialisation, was already turning its back on nature.

Making a virtue of necessity, most of the plethora of early modernist art movements celebrated the de-organicising of human life in the automated age. If the rhythms of the mass-production assembly-line had been innervated by urban workers, evicting the cyclical pulse of the seasons to install the linear processual character of a life that consisted in repeating one fragmented bit of the system over and over, perhaps there might turn out to be something paradoxically liberating in the transformation. Constructivism and futurism envisioned the world as the gigantic apparatus it already was, in which human beings, precisely by surrendering their chaotic inner natures to its iron mechanisms, would find a higher purpose. On the conviction that there was strength in number, mass production brought with it mass entertainment and mass politics, to suit the ambience of the urban crowd, where psychoanalytic rumour had it that self-alienation was rampant. The self, however, had delivered nothing but inwardness and despair along with the occasional gasp of ravishment, while crowds were capable of breaching the ramparts of privilege, making institutions quake on their medieval foundations, shedding tears *en masse* unashamedly as Queen Christina went to her exile, revelling in the collective thrill of apostasy at the bonfires of books. These were gusts of sensuality that the solitary had never known.

There might never have been any need for collective sensuality had the solitary version of it not miscarried. Barely more than a generation after the repining Keats had dreamed himself back to the primordial Garden on the nightingale's trill, the search for a lost Eden provided a prospectus for the American

Transcendental movement of the 1830s and 1840s. Ralph Waldo Emerson issued a call to the rising generation 'to look at the world with new eyes', investing the whole of nature not with evidence of the Trinitarian God, but with a freebooting pantheistic spirituality in tune with the rugged individualism of the American frontier. In 1845, Henry David Thoreau embarked on his own two-year return to Edenic innocence at Walden Pond in Massachusetts, where he built himself a small shack to live in. Although the journey into the woods wasn't exactly the disappearance into the wilderness that later imagination has fancied (it was less than two miles away from the family home in Concord), Thoreau pursued the experiment itself with a thoroughgoing rigour, hoeing beans, chopping wood, baking bread. The rural idyll is intermittently penetrated by civilisation in the form of the freight locomotives that clatter by at intervals, their whistles shrieking, along the Fitchburg railroad a little way to the south. But far from wrecking the bucolic tranquillity, the trains only serve to sharpen his hearing to all the other sounds that the natural world has to offer. Cows low melodiously or disconsolately, whip-poor-wills sing, owls scream their eldritch laments, dogs bark at distant passing wagons, bull-frogs croak in Aristophanic chorus, and in the mornings, the sunrise is greeted by the reveillant crowing of cockerels, shrill and clear in the uninhabited density, yet never so piercing to the acclimatised writer as ever to wake him up.

For whom else, though, do the cowbells toll? The romantic and transcendentalist retreat is a private enterprise of the spirit, not available to all. If you can afford the extended eco-break, or don't mind subsisting in genteel poverty, you can really start to live again. Animating the sensual awakenings of both sickly British poet and rough-hewn American philosopher is a more or less explicit challenge to society's work ethic. Those freight trains carrying merchandise to the cities are provisioning a way of life so hectically caught up in itself that it has lost contact with the natural world that supplies it. But this remains a privileged view, and it is perhaps just because it no longer comes naturally to those whom labour has permanently reduced to the 'dull opiate' state Keats tries to shake off, or for whom a wander in the woods might at best be a way of beguiling a summertime Sunday afternoon, that its celebration in poetry and memoir comes to be so highly valued. Thoreau's account in particular is replete with waves of ironic self-awareness. The entrancing sounds of the wood are heightened once the screaming trains have faded into the distance, but the whole enterprise of writing about them, as the 'Sounds' chapter of *Walden* candidly grants, is a second-order reflection merely of the sensuous verity of actually living among them.

Transcendentalism knew perfectly well that its fatal flaw was its solipsism. There were already too many human beings, even in the antebellum United States, for all of them to retreat to isolated shacks in the woods. If the sensual life were only available to privileged individuals, the rest could at best only experience it vicariously through their odes and journals. It still put its trust wholeheartedly, though, in a naive pastoralism. The only sensuous experience that mattered was immanent to the natural world, the marginalisation of which produced the dead-eyed legions Engels saw pouring out of the factory gates. The urban avant-garde of the twentieth century's first decades would have none of this, wagering on the hammer-blows of automation and the racket and drunkenness of the streets over the dull stupefaction of the countryside. Modernist painting fumigated the last vestiges of pastoralism from the visual arts, outshouting the turbid landscapes of the 1870s with the jostle of the city boulevards, turning from the gaiety of boating-parties on the river to the morbid physiognomies of drinkers. If absinthe frazzled the nerves, they had at least been used. Neurasthenia, much in vogue by then in the consulting-rooms, was better than stagnation. The often overlooked hinge on which twentieth century painting swung open was the fauvist moment, which incandesced and fizzled in barely a year, but by applying the electric shrillness of the city lights to the village squares and distant hills of rural France, saw off the last of a senescent post-impressionism.

The attempts to recuperate the sensual life that unite the cult of sensibility of the late-eighteenth century, the Romantic generation and the American transcendentalist movement were driven by the desire to overturn once and for all the prolonged despite in which western thought had held it, according to which the senses were the corporeal appendages to a soul, an intellect, a psyche, forever yearning to be unleashed from them. Sophocles in old age said that the loss of sexual desire was like being unchained from a lunatic. On this view, which passed from the Platonic dialogues almost unedited into the canons of the Christian church, the sensual life wavers uncertainly between squalor and concupiscence, the vulgarity of the various appetites and the careless morals into which they lead, the body supplying its own incriminating evidence of the fact by its combining the functions of excretion and generation in the one set of organs. By the later medieval era, the epithet 'sensual' had begun to float between a neutral reference to the operations of physical sensation, the 'sensual life' denoting simply what is perceptible by the senses, and a more distinctly pejorative usage, in currency by the late-fifteenth century, as meaning lewd or unchaste. Sensual persons, then, are those who are absorbed in the life of the senses to the detriment of moral, intellectual or spiritual interests, to the ecclesiastical courts excessively worldly or profane individuals, a danger to themselves and to others. 'These be they who separate themselves, sensual,' declares the New Testament Book of Jude, 'having not the Spirit.' And what this reflects is the inescapable notion that to be aware of the sensual life to an undue extent is to have fallen prey to its gratification. Milton's *Comus* (1634), barely able to choose among the ravening bestiary from which comparisons for drunkards may be drawn –

are they wolves, bears, leopards, tigers, pigs or goats? – fairly suppurates with righteous disgust:

And they, so perfect is their misery,
Not once perceive their foul disfigurement,
But boast themselves more comely than before,
And all their friends and native home forget,
To roll with pleasure in a sensual sty.

Pigs then. 'No gratification, however sensual, can, of itself, be esteemed vicious,'[1] claimed Hume in the following century, raising an Enlightenment protest against the puritanical view, but sensuality would take a lot of disentangling by then from its corrupting implication in excess. When 'sensualism' achieved coinage as a philosophical belief in the Romantic era, in both Georgian Britain and Napoleonic France, it already applied both to the elevated theoretical doctrine that the senses were the sole source of knowledge, and more basely to actual addiction to sensual indulgence.

If the senses were nothing other than luxurious ways of receiving information about their surroundings, then these pioneering movements would have been little more than explorations in heightened consciousness, in the manner of experiments with hallucinogens. What they attempted, rather, was a reconstruction of the modern soul by restitution of the sensual organs, and in this respect they already had an intricate understanding of the mutually informing relationships between sensation, perception and decision.

As the brain receives sensations from the world around it, it processes them into perceptions, which are in turn the basis of human cognition. It doesn't just see, hear, feel, smell and taste external reality; it interprets it. And it needs to interpret it because reality supplies the information on which its rational and irrational decisions are based. The brain makes ordering and prioritising decisions all the time about its environment, so that it is possible for it not to perceive what it senses. Consciousness can see without noticing, hear without listening, and so on. It is capable of arriving at one summary perception from an array of different sensations, but also, conversely, can build a number of perceptions from a single sensation. These may be competing hypotheses, or distinct alternative ways of looking at the same thing. It is also possible to perceive something that isn't directly offered to the senses, either because the brain, faced with incomplete information, fills in the gaps on the basis of what it is used to perceiving, or through the automatic exercise of intuition. 'Perceptions,' says a neuroscientist, 'are the brain's educated guesses about what the combined senses are telling it, and as such they will almost always depend on interactions between different modalities.'[2] There is a distinction, and an important one, between pure and simple sensation and cognitive perception, and it is in the interstices of that distinction that the brain can be tricked by such ruses as optical illusions, or exercises in perceptual distraction. More sinisterly, however, the sensual faculties can be deadened by habit into only ever experiencing the world in the same few ways.

By the turn of the twentieth century, interest in the functioning of the senses had been largely bequeathed to science. Deep investigations into the ways in which the brain could be deceived by sense-impressions took the place of the opportune luxuries of intoxicants and the natural world. Descartes had postulated that if the senses could fool the intellect, as they did in dreams, optical and auditory illusions and so forth, then basing an entire epistemology on the information they delivered, as both science and philosophy were inclined to do, might be seen as a thoroughly risky venture. 'Whatever I have up till now accepted as most true I have acquired either from the senses or through the senses,' he writes in the *Meditations on First Philosophy* (1641). 'But from time to time I have found that the senses deceive, and it is prudent never to trust completely those who have deceived us even once.'[3] The now notorious experiments of Ivan Pavlov and his assistant Ivan Tolochinov in 1901, by which the theory of conditional reflex was arrived at, established that dogs could be induced to salivate at the prospect of being fed, when nothing other than visual, auditory or tactile triggers were presented to them. Stimuli ranged from the famous bell to tuning-forks and whistles, metronomes and electric shocks, while what prompted the elaboration of the theory in the first place was the dogs' drooling reaction to the mere appearance in their lab coats of the scientists. These and similar experiments were also performed on children, who could be trained to salivate, or snap their mouths open, like the dogs, in expectation of being given a biscuit. If physiological reflexes could be manipulated in this way, inducing the brain to expect a reward before there was any concrete evidence of it, then the life of the senses was perhaps as ignobly misleading as Platonism and Christian theology had always held it to be.

In the same period that Pavlov and Tolochinov were inserting cannulae into children's cheeks to watch them slaver, a more refined exploration of the same psychic mechanisms was driving in the United States the earliest efforts of the nascent advertising industry to ground its own practices in solid theory. The Bible of commercial enterprise was Walter Dill Scott's *The Psychology of Advertising*, first published in 1913, but going through successive editions. Scott advocated sedulous study of the latest psychology, particularly the then newly fashionable psychology of adolescence and youth, in order to attain maximum behavioural impact. Advertisements would henceforth no longer give straightforward descriptive accounts of the product's properties, but would attempt, either explicitly or covertly, to create the need for it via the manipulation of deep impulses such as self-image and peer pressure:

> *We have instinctive responses to act for the preservation and furtherance of (1) our bodies, clothes, homes, personal property and family … (2) ourselves as we exist in the minds of others; (3) our mental faculties. We have seen that to secure action along these lines it is not necessary to show the value of such action or the necessity of it, but merely to present the proper stimulus, and the action is forthcoming immediately.*[4]

George Orwell would call it 'rattling the stick in the swill bucket'.

Advertising had begun to rely supremely on visual imagery, promoting highly idealised lifestyles and identities, which could implicitly be purchased along with the products themselves. At exactly the moment that the development of moving pictures was introducing a mass audience to what would be the twentieth century's most dynamic art form, advertising was able to capitalise on the deceptive three-dimensionality of film to create lasting and memorable images for its products. What was possibly the first ever cinema ad in the United States, for Admiral cigarettes, made in 1897, shows a group of four men sitting next to a giant cigarette pack. Suddenly, a woman in naval uniform bursts through the pack, and gaily distributes cigarettes to the men. They light up and then unroll a large banner printed with words that, a century later, would have become a shameful confession: 'WE ALL SMOKE'. An ad for Shredded Wheat, produced in 1904, consists of no more action than a husband and wife sitting at a table with a box of cereal between them. The woman takes a shredded-wheat biscuit out of the pack and hands it to her companion, who wolfs it down with relish. Print ads for these products would once have made extensive discursive claims for their benefits, typically their health-promoting or therapeutic qualities, but with the development of moving pictures, nothing more was needed, at least in the early days, than to show people like the spectators themselves consuming the products. The sight alone of somebody else smoking or eating was thought enough of a trigger to make the viewer wish to do the same. Combine those images with strong cultural reinforcements, via the depiction of attractive, healthy-looking people leading something like the lifestyle the viewer fancied for herself, and a recurring desire for particular products could be cemented into her psyche. The coming of sound film in 1929 only deepened the psychological compact. At the same time, the perceived exhortatory power of motion-picture advertising had had a noticeable effect on the styling of its print counterpart, which by the 1920s had begun to rely much less on textual information, and much more on image-driven messages.

If there is a disturbing aspect to the way sensual life has become so malleable in the modern era, it is because traditionally the senses were not thought of as being tools for others to use in quite this way. In the earliest surviving written analysis of the senses, in Book II of the *De Anima*, composed in the mid-fourth century BC, Aristotle prefaces his descriptions of the five senses by remarking that sense-perceptions have a twofold function, what he calls their actual and potential operations. The actual functioning of a sense refers to the way it is actively, consciously used to investigate an object or an environment, whereas the senses in their potential, or as he says dormant, state go on registering the world around us whether we pay attention to the information they are supplying us or not. What the manipulation of the senses in modern times appears to add to the two Aristotelian valences is a third meaning. In the Pavlovian experiments and in contemporary advertising, the subjective consciousness is not just neutrally taking in sense-impressions from the outside world; it is actually responding to the deliberate action on its senses of tendentious agencies that want it to respond in a certain way, by thinking certain thoughts, or formulating certain desires.

A clue to the debasement of the sensual life in western thinking lies in the extended consideration of the senses in the *De*

Anima. Aristotle defines each sense as 'the recipient of the perceived forms without their matter.'[5] He uses the image of an impression created in wax by a signet-ring. The image registered is the exact form of the ring, regardless of whether the ring itself is made of bronze or gold. In other words, the operation of the senses can divulge the colours, the flavours, the sounds of things, 'but not as they are said to be each of these things, but as they are of a certain kind.'[6] In other words, it is a matter of indifference in each case what the substance is; what matter is its essential quality. It is as if all the senses deliver to the mind is the surface impression of each thing, the attributes that any idiot can determine, whereas true understanding lies in something much deeper. What each object is in itself is what is most important to know, and while some of those essences are apprehensible to the physical senses – the infusoria swarming under the microscope lens, the pulsing of distant stars in the telescope – other immutable laws of the physical world are not. Who could ever point to the force of gravity? Nobody has ever seen it, and yet Newtonian physics has established its existence. And is there not something more profound in the molecular composition of the objects in question, as distinct from the whistling of wind in the flue, or the flaring of sunlight off the sparkling sea, which chance moments of perception are available to anybody in possession of their sensual faculties? Is it not the very effects of the sensual world that disguise their true nature? Do they not distract, beguile, ravish or otherwise impress with their sweetness and strangeness and unfathomable sorcery? Is not the evidence of the senses prior to a rigorous and proper understanding of the world, which, once attained, is the passport to maturity, to an adulthood of humankind in which the sensual elements can be left behind? If so, then progression to the older and more knowledgeable self is a matter of transcending the senses, not to the extent that they cease to function, but in a manner that allows the self to privilege what it theoretically knows over what it might sensually enjoy. Essence and appearance are thereby posited as the opposed aspects of every phenomenon, providing philosophy's route-map to the Kantian things-in-themselves, Hegel's Absolute Spirit, Heidegger's Being.

The official name for doing as far as possible without sensual things was asceticism, the fabled austerity according to which Socrates declared, on casting a jaundiced eye over a laden market-stall, that there were such a lot of things he didn't need. To Plato and Aristotle too, what is immaterial is always more elevated, a verdict that early Christianity ratifies in its elaboration of the rule-bound monastic life. Asceticism could only derive its truth, however, from its antagonistic relation to the lineaments of sensuality, otherwise it was nothing other than old-fashioned deprivation, the condition under which the greater part of humanity has permanently lived down to the information age. If asceticism, which may indeed offer the proverbial quiet space that the universal bustle has all but drowned out, is not conceived on the model of an inversion of everyday enjoyment, its dignity is undermined by its being cast as the respectable version of that enjoyment, as what Adorno calls 'authorised fulfilment'. In that case, it deludes itself into thinking that it is good for the soul, much as the medieval midwife might have smothered one twin, the better that the other might be nurtured.

The preference for the non-sensual was erected on the principle that the higher things, the Eternal Ideas, were more durable, whereas what one physically saw and touched was sooner or later lost to transience. If training one's soul on the imperishable offered some kind of succour amid universal fungibility, it failed the adept inasmuch as it conjured out of his own fungible existence an enforced reconciliation with the way things were, at the expense of any notion of how they may come to be. A state of being that hasn't happened yet cannot by definition partake of the nature of an eternal verity. Thus does idealism, understood in its everyday usage as the yearning towards a perfect state, in fact comprise only an accommodation with the pre-existent. Moreover, sensual experience is not merely transient. It is, in a literal sense, unreal. On the basis of it, the mind forms its opinions of the world, but sense-perception is for Plato only at best the illusory apparatus by which, paradoxically enough, the mind arrives at true knowledge. According to the *Theaetetus*, concrete perception serves as a rope-bridge slung across the chasm that separates the individual's vulnerable encampment in the present world from the stable terrain of the eternal. Once negotiated, it can be discarded. It may well be that without the sight of beautiful things, humans would gain no access to the concept of beauty itself, but the beauty of flowers and sunny days and boys' faces withers away, whereas the ideal itself endures. Seeking to rescue the corporeal individual from the encumbrances of materiality, however, Platonic asceticism, in briskly expunging the comfort of the corporeal from an existence already mortgaged to suffering, thereby breaking its resistance to suffering, only managed to break its heart.

The charge under which the ascetic life obtained its conviction against sensualism, that a life of hedonistic self-indulgence was lived at the expense of responsibility towards others, backfired when it became clear that self-denial was no more capable of promoting goodwill towards men than was stuffing one's face. Indeed, as many of the early hagiographies attest, extravagant acts of self-abnegation – through starvation, stylitism, mortifying of the flesh – often appear the *dernier cri* of self-indulgence, hard to reconcile anyway with the duty of *agape*, either towards oneself or to the world at large. The practice of human fellowship is primarily modelled on the idea of a convivium of like-minded souls, freely partaking together of what social and spiritual nourishment there might be. On that basis, it discovers its motivation to help others in darker times. The refusal of sensual sustenance, by contrast, must effectively begin with the abrogation of communal solidarity, for fear that the intermingling of sensate bodies and minds might produce enjoyment. Where, in any case, did the joyous return of the Platonic soul to the realm of the sempiternal learn the form of its ecstatic release, if not from the ecstatic releases available to mortality itself? If there must be a realm of the ideal, on the principle that philosophers wouldn't be able to conceive of it if it didn't exist – the doctrine that would eventually furnish St Anselm with the ontological proof of God – then there must also be something better than mere satisfaction about the sensual life, or the senses wouldn't have managed to point the way to it.

The physical world apprehensible to the senses gains its portal into the metaphysical by virtue of the fact that many of the attributes of concrete objects are not, properly considered, physical essences. In what sense is redness, despite its being the effect of a particular reflection of light on to the retina, a physical attribute rather than an idea? The mechanisms of perception of the physical, for all that they are in themselves physiological, do not have to do with tangible physical substances with true spatial extension, as in the Cartesian definition. Plato in the *Phaedrus* isolates beauty as the only one of the Forms that is also a sensory experience, unlike, say, truth or wisdom or courage, but beauty is no more a physical entity in itself than is red. These attributes are, however, what invest metaphysical ideas with their concrete reality in the physical world, as a modern metaphysician explains: 'Colour, beauty, virtue, and other forms of value could ... be excluded from such a world on the grounds that they are not purely *physical* features of things. That is what creates the metaphysical problem: if the world is exclusively physical, how can colour or beauty or any other nonphysical feature be fitted into the world as it is independently of us?'[7] Just as metaphysical notions are rooted in the concrete, so too are concrete phenomena thereby granted access to the domain of intellection. The ascetic conception that would quarantine the spiritual from the physical by casting the latter as the locus of temptation falters before the reminder that beauty, which derives its metaphoric force in beautiful thoughts and beautiful wisdom from the beautiful body, or even from beautiful music, refuses to be cast as malevolent. The hiatus between the two realms, which preoccupied Thomas Mann for much of his career, is the poorly policed border where one territory is permanently open to the other, where the physical is capable of moving in and taking up possession in the spirit.

For the time being, in the early twenty-first century, what science appears to want to know most of all about the senses is the effect of their abolition. What happens to human beings when they are deprived of their physical senses is a question that has mightily preoccupied experimental psychologists since the Second World War. During the global paranoia that marked the Cold War, the subject was pursued with obsessive interest on both sides of the ideological divide, not least as, long before the worldwide return of physical torture, it appeared to offer an alternative methodology for coercive interrogation. Investigations in sensory deprivation have most recently been put to use in punitive contexts such as Guantánamo Bay. They also ran parallel to research into the effects of hallucinogenic drugs such as LSD, itself considered as a potential agent for breaking down the resistance of enemy personnel under questioning. When the Sandoz laboratory in Switzerland, owners of the patent for lysergic acid diethylamide 25, cut off its supply to the CIA in protest at the unethical uses to which it was being put, interest in the psychic effects of sensory deprivation grew. What studies repeatedly showed was that, if healthy subjects were isolated in an environment impermeable to outside sense-impressions, their responses would gradually begin to mimic the cognitive and perceptual effects of hallucinogenic substances, or dissociative psychotic states such as schizophrenia.

The subject has always had strong pop-cultural traction too.

Paddy Chayefsky's 1978 novel *Altered States,* filmed by Ken Russell in 1980, is premised on the idea that, if somebody stayed in the flotation tank for long enough, he would eventually regress hallucinogenically to a primordial genetic state, entering the tank as William Hurt and coming out as *Homo erectus*. In the story, the dramatic effect is guaranteed by combining isolation with the ingestion of psychotropic mushrooms, procured from the Toltec people in Mexico. The results are predictably, if fancifully, dramatic. Flotation tanks have since become an item of furniture at upmarket spas. They don't involve complete sensory deprivation, but the atmosphere of bobbing about on water in a darkened room offers a mental calm that mythically transports the customer back to a state of intra-uterine bliss.

Hallucinatory states can be induced remarkably easily without chemical intervention. A study in 2004 in which subjects with healthy vision were blindfolded for four days found that most had begun seeing things at the end of day one. Sleep deprivation for a couple of nights brings on perceptual disturbances that typically begin in the peripheral visual field and drift towards the centre. Until comparatively recently, however, it had been thought that the process was a gradual one, building up over a period of hours or even days. This assumption was comprehensively overturned by a study undertaken at University College London in 2009, in which a group of nineteen non-psychotic subjects were put in an anechoic chamber with no visual or auditory inputs, and asked to record their responses. Eleven of the participants reported hallucinogenic episodes: unfamiliar faces or random objects drifted into view, accompanied by a descent into melancholy, mild paranoia, or illusory effects in those of their senses, such as smell, that hadn't been neutralised. Almost all felt that something 'very special or important' had happened to them during the experiment, with two even becoming aware of an 'evil presence' in the room with them. The unexpected aspect of these findings was that the volunteers were enclosed in the chamber not for an hour or two, as in previous investigations, but for fifteen minutes.

The brain, deprived of external stimulation in the visual cortex, supplies its own images, projecting outwards what would normally remain buried at the subconscious level. A metaphysically minded researcher might have assured the two most suggestible subjects of the experiment that the evil presence they intuited was nothing more than the world itself, experienced without the mediating influence of ordinary sense-perception. Undistracted by being able to see or hear anything, the individual mind is thrown back on its own resources, but is the disturbed consciousness thus produced a true consciousness of external reality, now disentangled from the untrustworthy phantasms in which the *cogito* is enmeshed, or does it simply represent a pointless partial imitation of psychosis?

If the effects of radical sensory deprivation suggest anything, it may well be that the less extreme deprivation of the senses to which postmodern experience has been widely subjected has had a proportionately destabilising impact on individual lives. The mass commodification of life under global market conditions, the bureaucratisation of desire and wish-fulfilment by the culture industry, which insists all the more earnestly in the era of electronic communications than it did when it only had cinema and television at its disposal that it is simply supplying the prevailing currents of demand, have encouraged people to imagine that a golden age of possibility has dawned. 'Do you know what I do about unhappiness?' the rich businessman asks Janet Leigh in *Psycho* (1960), wafting $40,000 in her face. 'I buy it off.' And indeed much of the happiness the sensual life might deliver is today only available to those with the resources to pay for it. That there may yet, however, be an intensity of experience outside present conditions is hardly suspected by anybody, partly because they haven't the resources anyway, and partly because nobody believes any such outside could exist. Hence the exponential growth in fantasy worlds and wizards. The human spirit will not be sustained on a regimen of heteronomously imposed imagination, however, but by the imaginative mobilisation of its own innate potentialities, which have been fraudulently refashioned for it as fantasy. At the outermost limits of what it can see and feel lie the means of its liberation, not in the ever-narrowing confines of the immediately apparent. Far from promoting a retreat into solipsism, which is more the preferred technique of the internet age, the resensualisation of life holds the power to reconnect living beings to each other. In nothing else can the indefinitely postponed dawn of universal transfiguration consist. The one-eyed man may be king in the land of the blind, but only the blind can overthrow him.

The Senses in Captivity

The life of the senses, ostensibly liberated from the tyranny of mind ever since the modern mind was forced to acknowledge its own vital immersion in them, remains everywhere in chains. If the discovery of evolution put paid to the fallacy that the rational intellect raised humanity above the bestial, it nonetheless came too late to mitigate the deformation that the mind had already inflicted on the sensory body, which men and women shared with the unthinking beasts. Once intellect was the means by which the great-souled and high-minded were separated from the mass, its own intracellular division was replicated between intellect itself and the senses, the biological seniority of which counted for nothing when the uncultivated had nothing else to fall back on. The developed intellect of the classical eras tolerated just as much of sensory capability as was necessary to inform it about the physical world, but its own metaphysical productions, like the Platonic Ideas, scorned the trash of the material world as soon as it had discarded it, yearning instead to inhabit a realm of pure ideation that would pay as little heed to concrete externality as the brain itself paid to the failing body, lacerated by injury or disintegrating towards extinction. Dividing itself off from the mundane, intellect created the division of labour, a division that not even the Anglo-Irish empiricism of the seventeenth century, fixing Cartesian rationality in its sights, felt compelled to ameliorate. Locke nowhere insisted, as Leibniz claimed, that there was nothing in the mind that was not first present in the senses, since the mind itself was capable of operating at a reflexive remove from the somatic evidence it received through the sensorium, producing its own ideas through reflecting on its own operations. In refusing Descartes' innate ideas, the immanent conceptual logic by which all human beings interpreted the world, Locke's *Essay* reclassified them under the analogical rubric of 'internal sense', with the proviso only that children and idiots were not party to them. In the post-Darwinian epoch, the intellect was tethered fast to its origins in the senses, like a metropolitan plutocrat being forcibly reminded of his humble provincial beginnings, so that what was reflected in the mind was what the body had experienced, even – and especially – where it had most convinced itself that what it contained was pure immediacy. The result has been a withered materialism of neither the dialectical nor the historical variety, but one that takes its cue from a sensory life almost entirely subjected to the exchange principle under which all must live, as though the physical in its brute materiality were enough to compensate for the persistent longing the mind feels that the world might after all be induced to yield some deeper meaning.

The body wants what the mind cannot deliver, while the mind oscillates between wanting to be freed of its own exertions in the body's pleasure and granted the licence to disregard the body when it fails. There may be no going back to the tripartite model of the intellect, emotions and appetites in Plato, or of the methodological separation, in philosophy at least, between the physics and the metaphysics of Aristotle, nor to the mind-body dualism of Descartes' meditations, for all that it isn't quite the rigidly demarcated structure that subsequent reputation would have it, but nor does a static materialism that lashes the two together as in a three-legged race do anything to liberate either term. There have been moments in the past century of critical theory when contentions over the exact nature of the interfusing of mind and body within each individual have recalled the fourth century dispute between miaphysite and dyophysite theories of the human and the divine in Christ. Fastening the intellectual to the somatic does not automatically weight everything in favour of the somatic, although post-structuralist and later theories of the body often give the impression that abstract notions such as compassion are less interesting than the genitals. There is a moment of the non-corporeal within the corporeal, just as much as, if not more than, there is a memory of physical discomfiture in the ethical. Materialism earned its spurs by charging at the idealist notions that had shackled human beings to their physical conditions, by disregarding them and so leaving them intact, but the moment of its victory could no more be prolonged than can any revolutionary upheaval, which must always give way to a morning after in which the task of new construction must begin. The ascendancy of the corporeal moment in the dyophysite version of the mind-body problem was expected to liberate the mind from the *naïveté* of the sententious, but has only succeeded in subjecting the contents of mental experience to naïve physicality. Nothing that cannot be explained in terms of concrete immediacy slips through the theoretical net, which has resulted in the fashion for phenomenological sensory histories that attempt to delineate, albeit through the distrusted conceptual currency of language, how the early modern world smelt and felt, as well as in poetic tracts that seek to reorient alienated modern consciousness, by urging it to turn its disinfected senses on the unnoticed beauty of the world, in spite of its giving every impression of having annihilated it. It was precisely in accordance with its own concept that the mind once construed what beauty there was, since neither the lilies nor Solomon looked glorious until perceived as such. The cultural history of such perception became the terrain on which the battle between mind and body was fought, but the truce that an unreflective materialism declared between them, by leaving all the spoils on the latter's side, has been nothing of the sort. Intellective understanding is robbed of its efficacy by having its nose rubbed in its own bodily secretions, just as much as its own imperious dignity was fatuous when it didn't imagine it needed a body. An enlightenment that proceeds from concrete experience still needs its intellective moment if it is to do justice to that experience, otherwise enlightenment itself would have betrayed its own principle. Philosophical insight depends in its innermost function on a reality that it takes as its theme, and its challenge in the most recent era has been to recouple itself to physical reality in order to fulfil the only task worthy of it. That it has chosen to subordinate itself to the sensory realm, without which it had frozen into sterile speculative metaphysics in the time of the Scholastics, has only created a variant kind of heteronomy, under which it labours as under the edicts of the medieval church. The latest attempt at liberating thought by refocusing it on the sensual has failed, not because the sensory realm is the veil of illusion that the rationalist intellect saw in it, behind which the true essences lay concealed, but because in a disenchanted world the sensual is illusion itself, saturated as it is with the falsehood that reified social relations have projected into it. Against the aerated conceits of theoretical philosophy, which flopped in the project of compensating people for the faultiness of the immediate world, by training their gaze instead to the distant horizon, an unphilosophical materialism has offered only the miserable solace of whatever there is in the vicinity, which is just what prompted metaphysical speculation in the first place.

If the quarantining of mind and body from each other in classical thought sanctioned the autarchy of the mind, a sanction that grew increasingly clandestine with the waning of antique theology, their prescribed cohabitation in vulgar materialism, which resembles the planned communal living of the Stalinist era, tended to grant the body the owner-occupier's role. The body, all but anaesthetised to external sensation in Platonic idealism, recovered some feeling in its extremities in the age of empiricism, when the rationalising labour of the mind was reconnected to the somatic. Nonetheless, the relationship remained unequal. What the body perceived was the raw material for cognition, which then transformed it into an idea of itself. Objectivity entered the philosophical purview in Locke and Kant, but on the understanding that the subjective remained aprioristic, that there could be no objective world without the subjective apprehension of it. The subject, implicitly, remains an empty shell until traces of the objective are precipitated in it through its senses, making it something like a constitutional monarch whose executive power is belied by its subordination to the overarching state. Only when the dialectical method refined in Hegel's *Phenomenology* turned its attention fully towards the objective did the materialist version of dialectics emerge, but even then with the proviso that the objective was the physically rooted foundation of a theory of knowledge that had the effect of giving fresh legitimacy to subjective experience. What remains behind when cognition has apprised itself of the facts of consciousness is sheer inert matter, its residual character bearing witness to the fact that cognition has not fully understood it after all. The only basis of cognition is the material, but the material in some measure resists it, since it is never entirely available to the senses, which are its route of transmission to the intellect. Sensation can only apply its perceptual energies to whatever is in front of it or around it – the rest is an epistemological token – and sensation is temporally and historically conditioned through and through. Rationality cannot elude the persistently nagging intimation that the sense-impressions just are in themselves what the rational intellect credits itself with finding in them. The body already knows what the mind reassures it that it knows about it.

The traditional antagonism between subject and object in philosophy replicated itself in the mind-body dualism, with the mind as subject and the body the conduit for the objective, despite the fact that sensation is itself deeply imbricated with subjectivity. In the object-world, the individual body is the only object that is both object and subject. The fact that the antagonism has persisted even into the era of miaphysite materialism gives evidence not of the truth after all of the Platonic hierarchy, but of the unreconciled state of subjectivity in the present world. Consciousness draws its material from a state of being already saturated with the character of bad objectivity, in which relations between individuals, as in the Marxist theory of commodity fetishism, have taken on the nature of relations between things. Just so have the relations between people and things themselves become a relation between things. When one's neighbour is as much a thing as oneself, some oppressed solidarity might emerge; when the subject is no more than another object in the presence of actual objects, true subjecthood fades to an anthropological memory. Sensation that would tear the wrappings off mummified consciousness cannot be gleaned by a consciousness that all too readily coalesces with the world around it, as though it had to take it for its own, no matter what. But nor can a false reconciliation between subjective perception and objective existence obviate the need to preserve the ancient categories of speculative thought. Suspended as they are between cognition and raw externality, the physical senses could, for all their much-noted gullibility, still be the honest mediators between self and world, holding the two parties at the objectifying distance necessary to sustain the possibility of genuine rapprochement, in a world in which subjectivity could properly feel at home. If the mundane fate that Erasmus feared would expose the fragility of his own thought – 'I am afraid that the world may ultimately carry the day' – is to be avoided, only unsparing self-reflection on their own co-optation by an anything but hospitable world will fit a sensually based thought for the task.

That we should be concerned with a 'materialist theory' of sensuality seems to speak a certain pleonasm. The question presses itself again: How could a theory of the senses be anything other?

To begin with, the classic statement of the corporeal roots of intellectual existence, according to the empirical tradition in Locke, Berkeley and Hume, has the effect of dematerialising concrete experience by sublating it in the form of the contents of intellectual consciousness. Once sense-impressions have served their purpose in the construction of the metaphysical, they cease to matter. At the outset of materialist dialectics, this had the effect of nudging philosophy in the direction of a pre-psychological subjectivism. Whatever individuals were made to feel by the object-world must contain the truth of the matter, a nominalist posture that didn't survive the Marxian account of alienation, which stated that the laws of objective value, and not their own predilections, structured the lives of human beings. Individual perception is true to the extent that it reflects prevailing conditions, but fails in its power of insight for exactly the same reason. Inasmuch as the route of escape from such heteronomous perception lay in mental activity that transformed the rough sense-data into rational propositions, it thereby spiritualised them, leaving behind their physical integuments as remnants of the non-identical. If the apprehensible world of particulars that the senses perceive is not to become fuel for the universality of socialised consciousness to consume, the universal and particular must somehow be mutually mediating. The universal mental categories to which the sense-impressions are subjugated are the product of a ruthlessly integrating society, which pays lip-service to individuality even as it stamps it out wherever it threatens to take root. To note that concepts have their origins in the physical is entirely compatible with a transcendental model of the subject after the Kantian manner, a question of basic genealogy, much as succeeding generations would come to celebrate the astonishing intellectual advances that humanity has achieved since the days of *Homo habilis*.

The empirical version of the formation of consciousness does not allow for the reciprocal two-way process in which the products of a somatically based idealism then re-influence and recondition the sense-impressions. Existence was to structure cognition and then withdraw, as though it didn't itself then reflect the cognition it had thus supplied. When Locke speaks of the mind reflecting upon itself, he unwittingly preserves the prioristic function of cognitive understanding that empiricism thought to put to flight. The somatic realm provides the concepts, which are then reflected not back into the somatic realm but into themselves. This absence of a properly dialectical, mutually conditioning equation is what accounts for the reifying of the senses in modern experience. It isn't that the material world is transformed smoothly into the mind's conceptions, which are in turn used to smooth down the material world in accordance with them, but that there are elements of each in each, which asymmetrically mediate each other, and without which the mind ignores the unpredictable evidence of the senses, while the sensory faculties register only what they are told to.

Modern sense-theory, for all its ostensible celebration of the sensuous dynamism of the physical, has tended nonetheless to conceive the objects of sense as elements of inert materiality, resistant to any other operation than simple apperception, and thus as abstractions of themselves. All the activity between self and world takes place on the mind's side of the transaction. Since antiquity, the mind has been nothing if not an active process by which, with the by no means indispensable aid of external entities, it becomes itself, becomes 'I'. The 'I' in such a construction might be looking at a window. At the most basic level, it is simply sensibly registering the physical attributes of the window, doing no more than an infant would. At the first level of mental conception, it defines the object before it as a window by comparing to other such windows it has encountered. It knows what the function of the window is, what it is made of, how to operate it, how to maintain it, and it knows a little of its history. Following on from that, the mind is also capable of thinking about the window as a notion *in abstracto*. It might imagine an alternative design for a window, how it might be incorporated differently into the wall of which it forms part, what poetic metaphors it might sustain, and so forth. In other words, the mind, having conceptualised the physical object, wishes to do something with that conception, perhaps as a prelude to doing something physically such as opening the window, but perhaps also just as a moment in thinking. A static materialism leaves the matter there, with both the original window and the notional window sublimely indifferent towards one another, whereas a materialism worthy of the name allows that there is still something about the window that has not been absorbed into the successive stages of the mind's activity, even as that activity has redeemed itself from being just another reflection of whatever there is.

Histories of the senses, evoking the sights and smells of the ancient world or the cities at the dawn of the industrial era, have attempted to acknowledge the temporality of the sensual, much as social history in the past century introduced subjectivity into the Victorian chronicles of events whose impersonal sweep had barely altered since Gibbon. What they have mostly done, however, is to sensualise history, whereas what a true, subjectively oriented account of experience needs is the historicising of sense. Popular philosophy, with its ahistorical prattle about 'what it means to be human', has elided the historically conditioned and historically mutilated nature of consciousness, which no more had a single paramount meaning in the epoch of the religious wars than it does in the age of people-trafficking. The ways of sensing circumambient reality have changed as that reality has changed, and most of all in accordance with the ways in which society wishes its clients to use their senses on what it puts before them. In his late work on historiography, Siegfried Kracauer argued that what prevents history from becoming a science is that something new is always happening in it, much of which fails to conform to the established laws, modelled on the immutable laws of physics, and which then have to be rewritten as a consequence. There cannot be a pre-emptive law of something unpredictable, the very principle of which Newtonian science consigned to the realms of mere contingency. Even in the contemporary oxymoron of 'chaos theory', the contingent is ground under the homogenising millstone of an, albeit disputed, explication. What happens in human affairs, however, including the perception of those affairs themselves, continues in part to escape what a global scientific historiography expects of it. The same holds true for the senses. New things are happening to the senses all the time, but people are conditioned to see them as further examples of the eternal, in the obverse process to that by which the culture industry aims to offer its clients more of the same in the guise of the new. A theoretical account of seeing and feeling in the present age dispenses at its peril with an innervated awareness of how seeing and feeling are products of that age, of how the age itself just is the way reality is seen and felt by those whose consciousness constitutes it.

What is offered to the senses now is imbued with an artificial instrumentalised materialism, in which the raw sensuality of nature and the external is forced into ideologically motivated functions. The astonishing sights promised by the package holiday; the compilation CDs that offer to encapsulate and summarise an era, of recent history or of one's own life; the smell of baking and coffee-roasting in the supermarket, which are intended to conjure the fugitive artisanal world that the supermarket made it its mission to destroy; the taste of something authentic, iconic or heritage-laden in the locally sourced but interchangeable offerings of brasserie, bistro, restaurant and pub menus; the social habit of embracing that over-compensates with theatrical hugs for the frozen atomism into which sociality has solidified are the remnants of a sensual life that industrial society gave up, more or less willingly, when it turned itself to the task of endless productivity, the reproduction of social conditions themselves. Every aspect of the social is mechanised, digitised, the transparency of permanent accessibility itself the opaque screen that separates human beings from their own freedom and from each other. Freedom in the eighteenth century variant was circumscribed by historical contingency, but contingency itself was still the obverse of that necessity under which an unleashed subjectivity ought to guarantee freedom and the rights of man. Today's freedom is circumscribed by a historical necessity that has done its level best to abolish contingency through rational planning, casting aside with the vagaries of chance the sensual responses that were their applicable medium. It was both the asset and the liability of the senses that they were various, just as it was of all the body's functions, in the Cartesian conception. If the body was anatomisable into its constituent parts, the soul was one and indivisible, and that asymmetry is what in itself gave rise to internal perceptual error. 'Descartes's letter to the Princess Elizabeth [stated]: "everyone feels that he is a single person". But feelings were not enough, as Descartes was able to demonstrate through his attempt at anatomising body and soul, where one entity (body) was shown to be divisible, whilst the other (soul) resisted any attempt at fragmentation.'[8] The array of sense-impressions is just what the mind attempts to synthesise into a unitary concept, thereby negating the polyvalent variousness of sensation, as though rational cognition were a matter of taking care of the pounds after all rather than the pence. The perceptions in themselves are not enough, but must submit themselves to a ratification that then has no further need of them in each instance. Notwithstanding the attempt to make the senses the hypostasis of a richer experience of life, in the Romantic movement and its distant descendants in the era of post-war liberalism, this is the legacy to which theories of the senses are still subject, the more so to the extent that they conceive the sensual life as a holiday from the dreary task-mastering of the intellect. Empiricism at least accorded them their preliminary role in what the intellect got up to.

The strata of mental experience that, according to the refutation of empiricism, grow hydroponically in consciousness without the need for any nutritive rooting in practical experience, would have precisely nothing to say to practical experience, if it were not for the fact that their roots keep showing all too tellingly. What Leibniz in the *Nouvelles Essais* (1705), in obstinate defence of Descartes contra Locke, calls the 'innate ideas' are what intelligence supposedly establishes for itself, without regard to the external realm. Kant would later call them 'intellectual intuitions'. 'Now the soul comprises being, substance, unity, identity, cause, perception, reason, and many other notions which the senses cannot give.'[9] He accepts Locke's version to the extent that 'the source of a good part of ideas [is to be found] in the spirit's reflection upon its own nature'. In its self-mediation, reflection convicts the sense-impressions of their fatally mediated, and thus deceptive, character. External sensible objects cannot speak directly to the soul; God is the only external force that can do that, transcendently by way of the soul's immanent reflection. For the late-scholastic rationalist tradition in which Leibniz wrote, the self-sustaining nature of first principles floats free of the empirical evidence that would, by grounding them, tether them down to a world nonetheless patronised as entirely perfect as far as it goes. It scarcely notices that the ideas the soul arrives at are still ideas of *things*, most of which have sensible properties. What is perception with nothing to perceive? What is the substance of the substanceless? In a reversal of what the empirical impulse would increasingly insist, as its distrust of idealism deepened, it was precisely the most nebulous thought-forms that reflected the phenomena of concrete reality, while insights into absolute being, the noumena, were the most piercingly illuminated. '[D]istinct ideas are a representation of God ... confused ideas are a representation of the universe.'[10] This logic proceeds from the apprehension of temporality. A perceived world is always changing, as are the registers of perception itself – one's eyesight fails, one's ears become stuffed up, a cold blocks the nasal passages – whereas the mind offers access to the immutable. That the immutable is made to include the idea of perception itself hardly occasions a blush. Its idea of perception is as purely objectless as is its idea of causation, the principle overmastering any empirical manifestation of it, so that even though in its burnished perfection it might have become the hypostasis of a perfect world, it turns out to be a mere ornament, standing aloofly above a reality nonetheless teeming with perceivable things. The materialist turn given to idealism in the nineteenth century, the attempt ultimately to do away with philosophy's abstractions, failed in its determination to wash away the idealist residue that still clung to the material objects like a musty smell. In certain quarters, it licensed an idealist materialism, now wedded to linguistics rather than internal intuition. British logical positivism, offshoot of the verificationist approach imported with the arrival of the Vienna Circle in England between the wars, doomed Anglo-Saxon philosophy to a tiresomely analytical temper, which it wouldn't forgo until it decided it could no longer afford to ignore the voguishness of Parisian deconstruction in the 1980s. It was in essence nothing other than the reprise of Cartesian cognitive inquiry, liberated from the theological lip-service of the seventeenth century, the more comprehensively to surrender itself to the fetish of scientific rigour. Its professorial ethereality – 'How do I know this chair I'm sitting on exists?' – invited nothing better than the student's insolence: 'Well, let's try kicking it from under you. See if that helps.'

The turn back to the senses that modern experience has cultivated, from the age of post-war sexual liberation to the present, has predominantly hoped to find in sensuality a moment of the irrational, a respite from the iron cage of logic, as though the senses, like the emotions, were to be fenced off in their own enclosure where a voracious rationality couldn't get at them. Anthemic writing such as that of Diane Ackerman, which tries valiantly enough to re-objectify the objects of sense, so that the reader might sense them anew and say to herself as in the song, 'What a wonderful world', for all its yielding to an ideological acceptance of the given, expresses something of the precious temporality of sensuous experience, but at the cost of suggesting precisely that it is only momentary. The bursts of pleasure to be found in the sudden chirrup of birdsong or the scent of Chanel are the stabs of consciousness that intervene, if consciousness is adequately sensitive, to penetrate the numbing effect of the rest of quotidian reality. A fully material sense-theory demands to know what the rest of consciousness consists in if the sensory moments are only delicious little blips in it. There is, to be sure, an implied soft critique in sensory theory that present social relations are to blame for the etiolation of the senses, though the proposition is never pursued, just because the heightening of the senses is feebly postulated as the antidote to it. On this model, sensory apprehension is structured like emotional response, a sudden exogamous incursion into rational consciousness, which rationality sooner or later smothers. To be sure, much sensory experience has precisely that character, like sudden shafts of sunlight piercing the overcast sky, but the fetishizing of those moments in such theory only allows rationality's clouds to roll back once they are done. In any case, the opposition between sensuality and rationality represents the frozen persistence of

Leibnizian dualism. Sense-impressions would only seem irrational if there were no time to think about them, but all sensing takes place in time, and time itself is a primary object of the senses. Their evocational power, consecrated since Proust, to transport the individual to another phase of life is only limited by the fact that the journey on offer is always a return ticket. It is a physiologically grounded commonplace to associate the sense of smell particularly with nostalgia, but all the senses are routinely recruited by the nostalgia industry, which has anyway anaesthetised the pain that its yearning for homecoming originally comported. The ache of turning back is felt to consist partly in the irretrievability of the past, and partly in the yearning one feels for the person one was, somebody younger, more vigorous, more receptive to experience, despite the fact that experience itself might have proved sufficient to let one see that the pathos of the younger self was its barely formed understanding of experience, the very experience that now forms the objective prism through which the younger self is glimpsed.

Having relegated the senses to the disreputable nether regions of the body, despite the fact that four of the five have their functionality in the same head that housed the intellectual faculty, classical philosophy sold the pass to a sterile hedonism. Conceived in opposition to the mental life, the life of the senses in the festive worldview of Aristippus resembles nothing more dignified than adolescent refusal of anything that requires effort. The Cynic school of Diogenes is its morbid antipode, its chief proponent openly surrendering existence to ungarnished frugality and the honest scavenging of beasts. Beasts indeed are what humankind is reduced to if there is nothing other than the essentials of subsistence, as King Lear complains when chafing under the austerity imposed on him by the wicked daughters. 'Our basest beggars / Are in the poorest thing superfluous' (II:iv). But just so is sensuality made only the fragmentary consolation in a life otherwise given over to the so-called higher things. Only in the post-Romantic era did sensuality, released from its founding obligation as the motor-force of the cult of sensualism, stand a chance of being anything more than just the defiance of intellectuality. For Ludwig Feuerbach, the object of thought, including humanity itself, is given only by the senses, having acquired exactly that immediacy that Leibniz granted only to the apprehension of God. While the argument sought to claim the epistemic high ground from abstract conceptualising, what it missed, as Marx readily pointed out in siding with Hegel on this question, was that sensual perception is itself subject to the mental labour by which human consciousness produces itself. Hegel the arch-idealist had posited sense-certainty and the natural life to be integral components of the historical process, because they function collectively in the development of society, whereas for Feuerbach they remain the individual moments that far less reflective intelligences than his have boiled them down to in later eras. If sense-certainty were capable alone of illuminating humanity's place in the world, it would suffice only to compel it to divulge what it knows, like an interrogated captive, regardless of what practical application such knowledge might then be put to, but it is just that application that constitutes both history and the philosophical conceptions that men have of it. The tender immediacy of love-relationships between a fully reconciled I and You, which Feuerbach set over against abstract thought, offers no surer route to direct knowledge than the Hegelian Absolute Spirit that he indicted. The lover's touch, far from being the means by which a restless search for meaning could be pacified, provokes one of its most querulous demands.

Materialist thought of the nineteenth century would turn promptly to the historicity of sensory being. The senses are not only developed and refined but mutilated and deformed in social history, depending on one's social rank. Charles Fourier shuddered at the malodorous racket in which the poorest strata of society were forced to live, but pointed also to the dulling of the senses in bourgeois experience, which was obsessed with the accumulation of capital, the ultimate means of humankind's alienation from its own nature. Marx too is eloquent on the injury done to sensory life by conditions in the Victorian factories, which are only the most recent accretion to the geological layers built on the sense-organs by social history: 'the *forming* of the five senses is a labour of the entire history of the world down to the present.'[11] The refinement of the senses in advanced societies, and in the more educated strata of those societies, is what makes them into a subjective capacity of certain human beings, rather than their simply being biological aptitudes. In this way, they become specifically human traits, because they are empowered to see the object-world transformed into humanly purposed phenomena. The trained eye can appreciate the contours of a triumphantly airborne female form in the *Winged Victory of Samothrace*; for the untrained, it is merely a block of hacked marble, and for the idiot, nothing more than an indecipherable shape among other indecipherable shapes. The humanising of nature prepares the development of the senses, which gain their functional refinement through adaptation to a world progressively constructed for human purposes: 'the objectification of the human essence, both in its theoretical and practical aspects, is required to make man's *sense human,* as well as to create the *human sense* corresponding to the entire wealth of human and natural substance.'[12] At their highest level of development, the senses, in producing a new form of social being, produce a new variety of human need. A sensory consciousness that can see the beauty in aesthetic forms, appreciate the greatest music, the finest cuisine and so on, cannot regress to an earlier state of being once natural history has turned its perception into necessity. 'All history is the history of preparing and developing "man" to become the object of *sensuous* consciousness,' Marx writes, 'and turning the requirements of "man as man" into his needs ... The *rich* human being is simultaneously the human being *in need of* a totality of human manifestations of life – the man in whom his own realisation exists as an inner necessity, as *need* .'[13] It is the denial of such necessity, either in the poverty-stricken life of the industrial worker, or in the obsessive hoarding of the capitalist, for whom every trip to the theatre and every grand dinner forgone is another accrual of capital reserves, that produces a society alienated from its own resources and its own potential. While even a materialist philosophy continued to treat these as theoretical problems, as opposed to practical exigencies that affected the political life of societies, it would fail to gain true insight into them.

Marx's argument stands in direct refutation of the current of austerity that marked one particular strand of the socialist tradition since its precursor in the ascetic Rousseau. While a dewy-eyed belief in the purity of the peasant's existence as being closer to nature, with all its enriching calamities, pestilences and scarcities, elevates dire necessity to the level of programmatic virtue, it refuses the gaudy products of civilisation, including a philosophy that can afford to turn up its nose at philosophy, in favour of the dignity of want. The entire French Enlightenment was preoccupied with the degree to which refined civility was a corrupting influence, even while its benefits were greedily gobbled up, and the Rousseau whose printed works included a diatribe against the printing-press, for spreading fanciful ideas, lived on milk and cheese, fruits and roots, and the country wine of meagre smallholdings, the coarser the better. To the economic and philosophic Marx, such asceticism is a wilfully perverse effort of self-alienation. Feuerbach conceived humanity as the self-alienation of nature in a species that viewed nature as a hostile force to be dominated, but Rousseauian frugality, as with the entire cult of simplicity, plain living, vegetarianism and Spartan austerity, represents the self-alienation of humanity from its own sensuous history. As a recoil from the luxury of aristocratic *décadence* in France, it had its political rationale – the irrefragably pure Saint-Just advocated a bread-and-water diet, supplemented by a little milk, as perfectly sufficient for children of the Revolutionary generation – but it fatally painted the sensual life itself as black as the sins of the oppressors. If Marx's economics can be criticised as harbouring a fully developed theory of production and exchange, but as lacking an equally fully articulated theory of consumption, the austerity tradition in socialism had tried energetically to pre-empt one. Having subjected the sensual life to heartless suppression in the grim working conditions of the urban labourers, capitalism offered them the compensation of a world remade as a gigantic bazaar, in which economic demand would be managed by manipulation of the sensory lives of workers as consumers, consuming the mass-produced artefacts they had themselves in many cases manufactured, and which were now transformed from the end-result of alienated labour into the visually and tactilely covetable displays in the department-stores, none of the earliest of which managed to seduce the elderly Marx into a theory of them. Nonetheless, if the history of consumer society in the past and present centuries has been one of the progressive beguilement of the sensory faculties, in the interest of initiating its clients into the ceaseless dance of exchange, there is still more of hope than of diagnostic apposition in David Howes' assertion that because 'the life of the senses is not separate from the life of the mind ... procuring and consuming food and other commodities can themselves be a form of critical analysis.'[14] The examples given of such critical analysis are gay men collecting Ken and Barbie dolls, and American youngsters using the Kool-Aid drink as a hair-dye. If this is as critical as modern consumerism gets, the manufacturing corporations have little to fear. Ironic re-contextualising is more a way of eluding critical appraisal than facilitating it, and even where application of actual critical faculties is enjoined, in consumer assessment and supermarket websites where everything can be given a star rating or a mark out of ten, the convocation of consumers' views only serves to assure the corporations that there are many willing participants in the game who are prepared to give their consultancy services for free, as an extra bonus to having paid for the commodity itself in the first place.

The subjective turn in philosophy that the laws of synthetic judgment in Kant bequeathed it obliged it to live with the corporeal being whether it liked it or not. When philosophy became a mood, a *Weltanschauung*, rather than a system of knowledge, it couldn't help but find its resources in the category of individual experience and its psychological effects. Schopenhauer's world-conspectus derives its morbid vitality from the theory of the ubiquity of suffering, to which he was practically the first since the classical tragedians to pay heed. The perpetual disappointment and dismay to which the mass of humanity is subject has its roots in the somatic fragility of the body, which protests its own irreducible quiddity against a world that may as well be nothing more than a stage-set. Misery is the only constant, the trans-subjective hypostasis that underlies all experience and all thought. Struggling free of a philosophy that appeared, despite his early enthusiasm for it, to offer only repinement into the passivity of eastern mysticism, Nietzsche turned against the negative in Schopenhauer in order to greet the eternal return of experience, the crucifying pain as well as the droplets of ecstasy, with a yelp of gratitude. The individual body is still the seat of thought, its predilections the basis of the cultural development of peoples, but it could be trained by, among other things, dietetic principles to produce the archetype of a world-changing consciousness. A period of vegetarianism might flush the German soul of the lumbering ponderousness with which meat, dumplings and beer have afflicted it, much as it did his momentarily, as long as one wasn't tempted to elevate it to the status of a religion. Vegetarians have much in common with socialists and others who would like to elevate humankind by paradoxically reducing it to the herd mentality of collectivities. Unsuspected histories of social evolution could be unearthed more through nutritional study, or by enquiring into the universal inclination for intoxicants, than they can through the vapid retailing of currents of thought, theological disputes, critical events, and the deeds of the marionettes whom historiography has dignified as the great.

Phenomenology represented the explicit attempt to throw out once and for all the nominalism inherent in all prior speculative thought, and return philosophy to the one realm it might reasonably say something about, the concrete existent. Its objectification of the phenomena, however, put them at the service of the intentionality it posited as the root of all sensory consciousness. Every perception proceeded from a will to perceive, which was itself exonerated from being another of the phenomena. It lacked both a social and historical dimension, but placed its faith in the ordering power of conceptual logic, to which the famous 'things themselves' were expected to genuflect. In time, it ossified into pure ontology, the skeletal Being that haunts Heidegger's theoretical edifice, and which he had no wish to clothe with flesh. A body is the last thing required by what he called his phenomenology of the quotidian, for all that there could scarcely be anything more obviously 'everyday' than the physical body everybody inhabits. The 'always-already' note in Heidegger's existentialism, the intuited peculiarity of *Geworfenheit*, that 'thrownness' that seems to characterise all awareness, which makes of ontic subjects the projectiles of a mysterious force that has preceded them, pulls the carpet from under any present sensory impulses to which it might be subject, and on which it might reflect.

> *What we 'first' hear is never noises or complexes of sounds, but the creaking waggon, the motor-cycle. We hear the column on the march, the north wind, the woodpecker tapping, the fire crackling.*

> *It requires a very artificial and complicated frame of mind to 'hear' a 'pure noise'. The fact that motor-cycles and waggons are what we proximally hear is the phenomenal evidence that in every case Dasein, as Being-in-the-world, already dwells alongside what is ready-to-hand within-the-world; it certainly does not dwell proximally alongside 'sensations'; nor would it first have to give shape to the swirl of sensations to provide a springboard from which the subject leaps off and finally arrives at a 'world'. Dasein, as essentially understanding, is proximally alongside what is understood.*[15]

And yet one hears mysterious noises all the time. Unfathomable phenomena present themselves to the modern sensorium as a condition of its being thrown into a world it hasn't made. What Maurice Merleau-Ponty would call the 'habitual body' was the natural state of *Dasein* or Being in the phenomenologies of the last century. It was an amalgam of learned consciousness and muscle-memories that carried its bearer through the life into which it had been flung, and which only encountered other such beings in a zone outside the historical moment.

Variously qualified as sexed, injurable, critical, organless, multivalent, polysemic, inscribed, indeterminate and post-human, bodies are thickly crowded into the organon of contemporary theory like commuters on an underground train. Embodiment is the operative concept by which cognitive processes are referred to the corporeal being in which they arise, its overall state of health and hormonal disposition, what point in the circadian cycle it currently occupies, and so forth, as well as to the environment in which it finds itself. Much of this work draws on the computer analogies with which the neurological sciences are obsessed, with the brain conceived as hardware on which a variety of software programs generated by reality and the body's response to it are run. The theory of situated cognition, a belated form of the behaviourism of the mid-twentieth century, states that consciousness is continuously remoulded by the flow of experience or, in vulgar English, bears the imprint of whatever last sat on it, rather than being, as empiricism thought, an accretion of learned knowledge formed by the ephemera of experience sedimenting themselves to form a subjectivity.

In a society in which everything presented to sensory consciousness has been preformed, in recognition of the fact that consciousness can no longer trust itself to apprehend the phenomena for itself, subjective experience has worn thin. Lashed together into the false unity that bureaucratic administration has created for its own convenience, men and women are exposed to the worst form of collectivity since the chanting of fascist mobs became bad manners. The subject's awareness of its conditions would only stand a chance of objectifying itself if it could discern the means of an objectification that didn't immediately become its entire support-system. Moments of spontaneous responsiveness congeal into the temperaments that crude psychology attributes to them, vivacious or melancholy, naive or phlegmatic. A belated species of humoral classification sees only the fixed identity of each individual, who remains at the mercy of the disposition that nature has randomly conferred on them, as though nothing in subjectivity had ever become, but had only sprung fully formed into being. Although personality is invested with the false objectivity that the object-world itself has taken on, each individual's response to his sense-impressions is nonetheless seen as entirely arbitrary. When a monument to a departed controversial national leader is erected, people's individual reactions to it are seen as purely a matter of aesthetico-political taste, whereas the statue itself is a pure disinterested phenomenon, a piece of deftly sculpted bronze, but a subjective experience that had had the courage of its convictions restored to it would perceive the ideological intent behind the work, the fraudulent universality with which artistic means had been appropriated for the furtherance of a mythical social unity. Any criticism is held to derive either from the grinding of well-honed axes – as it frequently does, to be sure – or from the kind of ill-bred tactlessness that fails to see the *faux pas* in speaking ill of the dead, even though the dead herself may have spoken nothing but ill of them while she lived. The life of the senses is similarly hypnotised: its responses are only the contingent manifestations of psychological proclivities, where they differ from each other at all, but where they converge in the mass, they become the objective legitimation in human form of an inhuman world. Every piece of external authority welcomed into the self as something like the self, or, as on Facebook, as something that induces the self to hit 'Like', is another progression of its own alienation from itself. Rather than having been fashioned by its own ingenuity, it has been bought off the peg. To postmodern theory in its psychoanalytic mood, there is nothing especially disturbing about this; it's just the way things are. 'The self consists precisely in the distance that separates self from itself, and in the return to self that crosses that distance by recklessly hurling itself across it.'[16] But what is this 'return to self' that a reckless hurling achieves? The first half of the proposition acknowledges the Lacanian gap between the self and its significations, the lacuna that in itself precisely is the self, but the second half is a strange projectile wish-fulfilment in which, like Baron Münchhausen pulling himself out of the quagmire by his own pigtail, the self leaps over its own actual bodily and psychic existence and returns to a mythical originary self, the one that existed prior to, or apart from, the self that had become constituted by its self-distance. In materialist terms, the distance between the self and itself is the index of the self's estrangement from itself by ideology, by its having internalised the concealed gap inherent in everything that presents itself as a unified spectacle. The self's dissolution in the collectivities of bureaucracy and of the culture industry is no less real for the official mendacity that a wealth of consumer choice reflects the glorious variety of individual preference: 'To each his own!'

Wilful exercise of the senses might well be the antidote to the boredom that people everywhere say they feel, were it not for the fact that the mental lassitude under which they chafe is frequently experienced by the bored as the result of external circumstances, to which they have become haplessly subjected. In this state, they look to others to rescue them from their own passivity. Boredom is the objective correlative of free time, which nobody knows how to fill for themselves, now that leisure has taken on the homogeneous features of organised work. A day at the theme-park, an hour's pointless exertion at the gym, the dragooning of people into large collectives by the holiday industry all help to fill the horrifying absence that unsupervised time, once the blissful retreat from back-breaking or mind-numbing labour, threatens. The voguish notion that boredom is good because it furnishes the conditions in which one might eventually do something creative discounts the intimation of extraneous force bored people feel, as much as it does the conviction of their own inner emptiness. In any case, it is just as easy to argue the opposite, that boredom facilitates the pretext for war. Bored people want to be entertained; they don't want to entertain themselves. They announce their arrival in online chat-rooms by declaring they are bored, as though somebody else might take pity on them and offer to send round a troupe of jugglers. When adjured to think of some way of diverting themselves, they only look hopeless, reacting to the conventional charge that they lack imagination with the inarticulate conviction that in a half-decent world, they wouldn't have to amuse themselves. In this, they might be right. The bored individual thinking up something that might occupy him is like the lonely child having to play games by himself, thrown back on his own resources where external resources are in short supply. To ask the sensory life to supply this lack is to yoke it to the extraneous ends it rejects even as it serves them. The favourite films and music that light life up on better days are tainted to mediocrity by being made to counteract mediocrity medicinally. Only a strengthened sense of one's own self can dispel boredom, and only then where its strength isn't enacted at the expense of others. Among the internal senses that neuroscience now posits as supplementary to the externally oriented physical ones is proprioception, the sense of one's own being, its disposition in the space that it inhabits. In its moments of greatest reconciliation with the world, the self distributes its own self-awareness innocently throughout the world, a demeanour that was once the index of healthy psychology. Tonio Kröger watches one of the two beloveds of his youth walk into a dance-hall in the company of the other:

> *Hans Hansen was just as he had always been. He was wearing his reefer jacket with the gold buttons and with the broad blue collar hanging out over his back; in his free hand he held his sailor's cap with its short ribbons, carelessly dangling it to and fro ... [A]s if in defiance of all and sundry, [he] turned his head straight towards the table, and his steely blue eyes inspected each member of the company in turn, with a challenging and slightly contemptuous air; he even let go of Ingeborg's hand and swung his cap more vigorously to and fro, to show what a fine fellow he was.*[17]

Even the slight contempt was forgivable in the last era before everybody started behaving the same way.

The engagement of the senses as means of distraction should, like all escapism, arouse the gravest suspicion. Not only does the question arise of what it is perception is being distracted from, but the abused functionality to which sensual life is thereby reduced has the effect only of reifying sensory response, not animating it. In aesthetics, the senses are what each recipient uses to construe the substrate of meaning, intentional or otherwise, from the work of art, the means by which its implicit critique of the way of the world is articulated. Degraded to the level of mere entertainment, the senses are bewitched into a state of passive consent, becoming the means by which the individual becomes only a plaything of industrial forces disguised as culture. Popular genres and products that were once explicitly directed at children, such as circus clowning, practical jokes, novelty songs, baggy clothing suitable for pre-schoolers, salty snacks and sweets, all the way to the current mania for animation films, are now packaged for their elders too, since their elders' senses have atrophied through their being presumed too stupid to understand anything more demanding, and the continuities between sensory data and understanding have been severed anyway. Behaving like children has acquired a precarious dignity for adults presented with no other choice, in the idiotic belief that regression to a state of presumed innocence enables a liberation of the spirit. Yearning to be free of the constricting rigidity of a rationalised society, consciousness reverses into infantile irrationalism, and reaches for its rattle if provoked into self-consciousness of its own humiliation. It sees in the childhood state only exemption from the adult responsibilities of which a ruthlessly administered world is only too happy to relieve it, in secular misconstrual of Christianity's counsel to become like children, which intended the inquiring receptivity and the open mind of childhood, not its blissful ignorance. Attractions that are 'fun for adults and kids alike' betray both, by plaguing the kids with the fun-stopping presence of adults, and inducing adults to forget that their own entertainment was once precisely what they were able to do once the kids had gone to bed. A futuristic funhouse at an amusement park in Queensland invites customers to 'challenge your senses and ignite your imagination', its sales-patter strenuously referencing the banned hallucinogenic drugs – 'a chemical-free trip into other dimensions of your imagination that explodes your senses' – that the kids haven't tried yet and most of the adults have only read about. The thrill officially consists in risking mental damage, the laser-light displays and 'ultra-groovy music' advertised as 'mind-blowing', 'mind-warping', the promised sensory overload, once the aetiology of neurasthenia and nervous breakdowns, also borrowing its analogical power from the world of substance-addiction. 'It's a unique experience that leaves you wanting more. Many visitors return again and again' [infinitygc.com.au]. The claim that the senses, by being mercilessly bombarded with external stimuli, could be the means to destroy the mind could have supplied a dystopian fable to Wells or Huxley, but passes unquestioned in the context of contemporary entertainment, with such disappointed voices as there are only raised to protest that, despite the claims made for the attraction, they emerged from it still fully in possession of their faculties.

In Freud's standard structural model of consciousness, it is the job of the ego, among other duties, to represent the sense-impressions it receives of the external world to the id, the half-submerged life of the unruly passions. The ego is a detached fragment of the id that breaks off in early development to negotiate with reality on the remaining id's behalf, at once reining it in and protecting it from itself. 'The ego has taken over the task of representing the external world for the id, and so of saving it,' Freud writes in a late summary, 'for the id, blindly striving to gratify its instincts in complete disregard of the superior strength of outside forces, could not otherwise escape annihilation.'[18] What the ego perceives of externality, it subjects to the process of thought, the intermediate factor between desire and action, which is compounded of the sedimented traces of experience in memory. On the one hand, it knows what is best for the organism, while on the other, being continuously solicited by the instincts to lay aside such knowledge in the interest of gratification. On the occasions that it surrenders to the id, the superego then informs it of its error by means of guilt-feelings. The problem is that, as Freud puts it, 'the poor ego ... has to serve three harsh masters, and has to do its best to reconcile the claims and demands of all three.'[19] The instinctual drives of the id try to beguile it into loosing itself from its rational chains, even while the superego warns it of the consequences. The third harsh master is nothing other than the external world itself, which far from pointing the way to the rational choice in each situation, or supplying the occasions for the ego's self-realisation, throws both temptation and frustration in its path. What the ego is saddled with is the task of constructing a false harmony out of the competing incommensurable influences at work on it, and its failure to do so is the constitutive substance of every personality. In a telling concession, Freud waves aside the various attempts of mysticism at bypassing the normal functioning of the ego and the id, reading meanings directly into reality by a reconfiguration of the perceptual systems of consciousness, but then admits in the next breath that psychoanalysis, in its treatment of the enfeebled ego, adopts essentially the same methodology. 'For [its] object is to strengthen the ego, to make it more independent of the superego, to widen its field of vision, and so to extend its organisation that it can take over new portions of the id. Where id was, there shall ego be. It is reclamation work, like the draining of the Zuyder Zee.'[20] The present-day project of liberating sensuality from the restraining trammels of the rational aims at short-circuiting the relations between ego and id in Freud's structural model, but its conceptual weakness is that it needs the very sense-data that the ego delivers to the id in order to spring the former from its imprisonment. Freud's own metaphor, in *The Ego and the Id* (1923), of the horse and rider illustrates the instinctual force of the id as a beast of superior strength, which can nonetheless be brought under the rider's control and encouraged to move in a particular direction. If it succeeds in throwing the rider, it only gallops off into the surrounding country, of which it has no knowledge, so that it soon becomes lost or injured. Cutting the senses free of their symbiotic relation to thought is to do the same. It leaves both without foundation, a prospect that ought to invest all the talk of mind-blowing sensory overload with its properly sinister character.

The grotesquely exaggerated forms that sense-objects take on in an allegedly sensualist world strip them of the contingency in which human beings once, mythically or otherwise, found something that spoke to their own nature, and reinvest them with the authentically Gorgon-like stare of the mythological, of something projected out from humanity that human knowledge has now decisively cast off. A perfect emblem of them is the overdeveloped or cosmetically reconfigured body, in which physiology itself becomes the means of the body's own alienation from itself. Enormously muscled men, and women with pneumatic breast and lip implants, look like imperfect replicants designed by an alien race still at the elementary stage in their study of the human species. Their contours no longer resemble the human form at all, but rather that of primitive objects at the critical point in prehistory when they ceased to be purely functional and began taking on stylised artistic forms. Nobody knows what to do with an artificially plasticised body other than look at it in a state of repulsed fascination. Blown up into its own caricature, it absolves both its owner and his or her admirers from anything other than an aestheticised relation to it, and in an era when erotic relations have been cryogenically suspended, stands in for the spontaneous physical impulse that the suddenly noticed protrusion of breasts or muscles once warmly prompted. Nothing, as the moralising cliché has it, is left to the imagination, which can instead be rusticated into a state of semi-retirement. At the dawn of the motion-picture industry, a continuing debate was fomented about whether a filmed version of a novel didn't inevitably traduce the original work. Cinema audiences who would never have got through a Thomas Hardy novel satisfy themselves with a condensed and predigested version of it, which exempts the viewer not only from the labour of reading, but also the laborious exertion of the imagination required to bring the narrative action to life in his mind. Its ready-made appearance on the screen was thus all the more comforting, in that he could partake of the classics without feeling nakedly exposed to them. Although the debate quickly grew sterile as a means of marking off true connoisseurs from philistines, it has some structural homology with the ideological mood of sensualism, which also offers to free its clients from the drudgery of conceptualising what only needs to be seen and felt. The integrative labour of interpretation, to be sure, always reduces the multi-functional work of the sensory apparatus to a unitary perception, in which the responses of two or more, sometimes all five, of the sensory registers is processed into a single proposition. When that proposition then takes its place in a cognative thought-process, what results is a synthesis of a synthesis, the remoteness of which from concrete externality is what sensualism, with some justification, criticises. Its own solution to the aridity of rational intellection, however, pulls up at the first fence, leaving sensate consciousness with nothing more than the raw data of the object-world, which are never the neutral phenomena of natural science that a naive sensualism wants them to be. In the case of popular cultural media, the raw data are never so raw that they haven't already been marinated according to the industry's secret recipe. Rather than spoiling the fun, an energised critical consciousness might look to the underlying ideological content of popular entertainment, and find its own liberation in seeing the monstrously distended and hypertrophic forms of cultural sense-objects for what they are.

If sensory stimulations are the holiday from critical consciousness, a life totally given over to them denudes them of their festive character, because there is nothing then to throw them into relief. Who does actually live only in the senses? The nearest thing to it is a deliberate self-enfeeblement in which the exigencies of external circumstance are the things one can hardly bear thinking about, a self-deceiving late version of Nietzschean free-spiritedness, but with exactly the opposite effect to what Nietzsche intended. A pious cult of sensualism, such as that recommended in the hedonistic current that followed the liberation of aesthetic forms in the early years of the last century, turned desperate after the Great War, when layers of social affectation and the gaily borne drunkenness that became a personal style themselves scarcely survived the first economic crisis. Ruthless political order soon swept them away altogether as the capering frivolity they undoubtedly largely were. The hope in such visions of sensuousness was that the unmediated sensory faculties, were they at all still capable of such functioning, would reconnect humanity to the natural, to those natural impulses that would provide a reconciled access to the natural world. The attempt failed because the natural world itself turned out to have become only the adjunct to thoroughly socialised consciousness, which needed it only as the occasional picturesque backdrop to its own self-absorbed bustle, but also because the only stance towards the natural that would have stood any chance of breathing life back into it was one in which it became exactly the image of human fate, not the ornamental relief from it. Verlaine turned the conventional image of rain as a representation of sadness into an active interrogation: 'Il pleure dans mon coeur / Comme il pleut sur la ville; / Quelle est cette langueur / Qui pénètre mon coeur? // O bruit doux de la pluie / Par terre et sur les toits! / Pour un coeur qui s'ennuie / O le chant de la pluie!'[21] ('There are tears in my heart / As it rains on the town; / What is this languor / That pierces my heart? // O sweet sound of the rain / On earth and roofs! / For a heart that sickens / O the song of the rain', translation mine). It isn't that the downpour induces a reflective moment; it is itself the reflection of the poet's own ambivalent reflectiveness. Such moments recur throughout the history of modern painting, when the natural and man-made worlds are made to turn eloquent of the lack of reconciliation in human affairs. In Giorgio de Chirico's *The Soothsayer's Recompense* (1913), a marble statue of the soothsayer reclines on its plinth amid the lengthening frozen shadows cast by Romanesque arches, while the world of human commerce chuffs invisibly by in the background on a steam-train, its white plume rising above a brick wall. What there is in the foreground is also of human construct, but is the decayed remnant of a deceased urban culture, alienated entirely now from the bustling world of rail freight. Dispositions of shadow and light are all that are left to animate the uninhabited interiors of Vilhelm Hammershøi, each one trapped in grey aspic, stiller than the still lives they otherwise resemble. When human figures do appear, they quickly ossify into objects homogeneous with their surroundings, standing with their backs to the viewer in the middle of the room, caught in the act of forgetting what they were about to do. A young man leans in the corner looking into a book, as motionless and incidental as a hat stand (*Interior with Young Man Reading*, 1898). The great entropy proposed by Clausius in the 1860s has brought everything to rest. 'We must not fear daylight,' Magritte suggested, 'just because it almost always illuminates a miserable world,' repeatedly cloaking his street of house fronts in crepuscular gloom beneath a bland blue sky. Edward Hopper's pairs and solitaries go about their business, standing on the front steps in the sun, tending the gas-station on a deserted road, raking the leaves, leafing through a magazine on the train while the countryside glides by unnoticed, unremarkable figures shrouded in an air of placid defeat. Images of detachment in modern figurative art, from self and from others, of the world from the self, confront their spectators with the evidence of their own isolation, a mood in which the immaterial seems to flash up from every concrete phenomenon, as readily intuitable as the mythological and religious symbolism of classical painting once was. The shadows are no longer the poetic image of darkening spirits; they are darkened spirits made manifest.

'God made everything out of nothing,' said Paul Valéry, 'but the nothingness shows through.' Turning to the world of sensual objects for relief from the rain-sodden emptiness of the heart, modern consciousness finds that the objects themselves, like the people behind the profile pictures on dating sites, look in reality nothing like their images. The cheerless notion that what you see is what you get, by which people try to pretend they have nothing to hide, as though under police interrogation, expresses exactly the opposite of the truth. What outward appearance seems to promise turns out to be unavailable, whereas what you get, in a society that places a premium on looks as never before, is what you don't see, the nothing at the heart of things, the 'life with a hole in it', as Philip Larkin called it in the title of a brilliant late poem, borrowing its acerbity from the advertising slogan of a brand of peppermints that made a virtue of their having a bit missing. It is as though the Kantian noumenon, the metaphysical centre of the concrete that perception cannot penetrate, stands revealed after all, only not as its spiritual essence but its hollow void. Tearing the layers off the pungent-smelling onion, Peer Gynt discovers it has no centre any more than his own life has had. Everything is a trick, as he who has dedicated life to the haphazard pursuit of sensory stimuli rather than organic attachments to others, to human community, and a world that hasn't earned his loyalty, should know. 'Life, as they say, plays with cards up its sleeve; but when one snatches at them, they've disappeared, and one grips something else – or else nothing at all.'[22] And yet, rather than surrender the terrain to a cheaply constructed nihilism, what critical consciousness demands is that the essence of phenomena be not nothing but something, the true nature of the object as against the implicit critique that refuses to be satisfied with what there is on the surface. Classical philosophy's error was to posit the essence as something immutable, something breathed on by the divine, which would be the same eternally for all human beings, whereas if it were to have any commensurability at all with the human, it would be because each object contained within itself something different for each of its perceivers. The objective and subjective are bound together in a mutually conditioning process, but an atomised society encourages its members to imagine their own perceptual cognition, over which it has otherwise cast a hypnotic spell, as sovereign, instead of reading into the objects that confront them the evidence of their own vulnerability. A contemporary index of the myopia that obscures critical vision is the popularity of bite-sized quotations about life. Such quotation is hardly ever other than the appeal to higher authority, an external sanction for what one might have tried imperfectly to grasp for oneself. Twitter accounts that are nothing but quotations from some favoured authority – Nietzsche quotes, Socrates quotes – without the perceived need for any form of exegesis convict themselves of their own lack of the wisdom they hope to find encapsulated in the utterances of the great, unless some vestigial wisdom attaches of course to their having chosen the quotation in the first place. Thought itself surrenders to the exchange principle when fragments of it can be dispensed like free tasting samples. There is a universal preference for eternal verities couched in the imperative – 'Live your life as though you were borrowing it from someone else' – which resemble the exhortatory exclamations of state propaganda in the former communist bloc. 'Vigorously struggle to attain the grain quota!' The tone of ordering others about convinces the recycler of such platitudes that he has himself attained enough insight to dispense unsought advice to others, while the object-world into which insight is most urgently required remains unbroached.

Not the smallest reason for the failure of address between self and world is that the objects themselves have assumed the threatening dimension of monstrosity. On the Beaufort scale of sensory stimulation, everything aspires to the condition of a hurricane. As in the Queensland attraction, visual entertainments are designed as mind-blowing spectacles to distract attention from their lack of substantive content. Every minor half-occasion is now marked with a firework display. Music has to be loud enough to drown conversation in case people discover they haven't really got anything to say to each other, while they sit at public tables eating food overladen with red-hot spice and lactic fat. A whole industry of mechanical and electrical appliances exists to supplement the lost sense of touch that has impoverished sexual relations and turned them into skilled labour. The bombastic mode, rightly distrusted in public discourse and grandiloquent prose, is forgiven when it invests the physical world, as though people are being encouraged to habituate themselves early to the inevitable eventual weakening of their faculties in later life, when large-print books will be needed for those who still want books, their atrophied taste buds will need to take everything with plenty of mustard, and everybody around them will need to speak up. It goes without saying that, in the prevailing climate, subtlety and delicacy are the apologetic qualities of things that go off at half-cock, that fail to offer people their money's worth or, in the American saying, don't give enough bang for the buck. The soft and the quiet, the unostentatious, are shunned because they appear to require too much concentration, one's resources of which have often been fully extorted by labour, and for the unbearable arrogance with which such modes seem not to feel the need to compete. As so often, advertising represents the distilled essence of this as of many other cultural tendencies, with its increasingly strident irruption into every context of life, its disruptive insolence as widely resented as it is nonetheless widely attended to. Attempting to mimic the unforeseen delight prompted by unexpected gifts, or the sudden intervention in a quiet soporific day of the jangling ice-cream van, it only turns the joy of the unforeseen into a lethal ambush. Alone among the senses, only smell has resisted the acromegaly that has deformed all the others. Strong smells, even ostensibly pleasant ones, seem to emanate too much from the organic life that the exaggerations of sense-stimuli have otherwise managed to leave behind. The stronger something smells, the more it carries the suggestion of something rotting, as though odour were always the warning-note of a putrefaction that might bear disease and infection. Smells linger in one's clothing, on the skin and in the hair, often resistant to ablution, an affront to hygiene. Disputes between neighbours can as easily arise from offensive odours as from too much noise, and not just of refuse. Nobody likes smelling other people's cooking, especially at times of day when they themselves don't need to eat. It is incumbent on everybody to smell of as little as possible – even the olfactory masks of deodorants and perfumes can be thought too strong – so that nobody is distracted from the assaults to which their other senses are readily sacrificed.

The Senses in Solitude

Sensuality could only liberate the subject incarcerated by the functionalism of social existence if it recognised that the subject is just as imprisoned within itself as it within society. The various cults of self-expression, from Romanticism to the intoxicant heydays of the post-war era, have been predicated on a naive subjectivism that imagines that consciousness can cut its bonds to functionality simply by ignoring them, or by reinterpreting its captivity as freedom. Its own relation to the sensual world, however, is not one of imperiously passing in review all that earth has to offer, as one moves from one masterpiece to the next in the art museum, but is a mutually binding relation in which the self is no more and no less than another of the objects, conditioned by the historical layers of meaning deposited in them, reified by the sterile functionality to which the exchange principle has reduced them. The sensual objects are shot through to the core with temporality, which sensualism can no more elide than the apostles of hallucinogenic creativity could stay high on their choice of intoxicant. Sensory consciousness cannot open an escape-hatch out of reality, for the reason that it is this reality in itself, variously interpreted. Standing on the shore with the open sea stretching calmly before it towards the imagined horizon it thinks it sees an emblem of the inscrutable future. It imagines it perceives something of its own insignificance in the contemplation of the pitch-dark heavens and the multitude of other worlds. What it sees is its immersion in its own subjectivity, for which the same boundless ocean and the same night sky are not the elemental timeless objectivities to which it opens itself, thereby setting itself free, but the petrified reflections of its own situatedness in social and cultural time. The solitude to which sensualism has always found itself attracted, and for which it was accused of solipsism by both rationalised society and the apostles of its overthrow, is itself historically mediated in its innermost being. Solitude fancies itself to be a state of pure isolation, not recognising that it can only ever be an apartness from something, which something characterises it down to its nerve-endings. The getting away from it all that travel agents promise is only fulfillable if the travellers hold before them the 'it all' that they have escaped from, as was indicated by those picture-postcards that, in gloating to the recipients back home how he had banished all thought of work, only announced that it was still uppermost in the sender's mind. Solitary sensuality deceives itself that what it most wants is to be mentally removed, by physical means, from the bad immediate, whereas what would truly delight everyone the world over would be to be reconciled to the good immediate through true proximity.

Each new day dawns, as does each successive epoch in

conventional historiography, with the possibility that it might provide the awakening subject with the freedom to do something, to become something other, and closes just as surely with the chill comfort that it has at least spared him from something, that he is at least still alive. The grim circularity of which conventional linear time is invisibly comprised cheats him of the possibility that the straight road ahead might just branch off into interesting detours, entrapping him instead within a temporal going round in circles, a humourless parody of the cyclical time of the ancients, when the seasonal cycle precisely held out the hope implicit in everything beginning again, renewed. Instead, the course of history declines such an accommodation, which it would only yield under the utopian conditions in which historical time, the time of successive disasters, was arrested by having a materialist spanner thrown into its works, an insight of Walter Benjamin's theses on history. 'A historical materialist cannot do without the notion of a present which is not a transition, but in which time stands still and has come to a stop.'[23] Sensuality and its external stimulations are ideologically posited as the interruption to the endless circularity secreted in linear time, as though repeatedly offering oneself up to the same amusements were not in itself part and parcel of the dreary treadmill. The compulsion to repeat, identified by psychoanalysis as a key aspect of neurotic behaviour, ought to be as monotonous as turning up at the office every day, but marks out its own sacrosanct zone by convincing itself of its own atemporality. What the suppressed instincts keep demanding, according to Freud, appears to be entirely resistant to the temporal dimension, and the same is true of the repressed material in neurosis, which never changes, even though everything about the ego's interactions with external reality subjects it to a process of continuous gradual transformation. The repressed, however, is only a moment of congealed temporality, set solid at the point of its earliest denial. In the same way, the sensory life is just what is frozen into a static caricature of itself in vulgar materialism, an eternal verity turned to stone, while reified consciousness is helplessly subject to the vicissitudes of whatever happens next. It would only be when what happens next could be made to reflect the entirety of an awakened human will that sensuality itself would, like Galatea, be liberated from the stone.

The Senses in the Ideal

A congenial quartet of people sit at lunch under a parasol, on a restaurant terrace perched on a promontory above the Mediterranean. Despite its being mid-November, the sunny day is as benign as July at its best back home. The sapphire-blue sea rushes and retreats in whispers on the shingle below. Bracing-fresh shellfish and heaps of leafy salad are accompanied by limpid white wine, its clean crispness mingling with the ozone tang of the air. Light breaths of breeze blow along bare arms. Peaceable conversation flows. The scene engages all the senses in a state of contentment, like the reconciliation for which one yearns in more troubled conditions. It needs neither to become a snapshot of an irrecoverable idyll, nor be the model to which all future contentment would henceforth direct itself. While such moments as these are more easily come by on holiday, they tempt unreconciled consciousness to think that holidays from it are the answer to its chafing, but a holiday is always precisely that, an interlude in daily life that leaves daily life itself unchanged, a miserable hulk in the middle distance to which one must inevitably return. Consciousness thereby lets itself be talked out of the transformation of its everyday conditions that would render vacations once again a pleasurable option instead of dire necessity. Not for nothing does the vacationing impulse often falter in later life, as though experience had finally suggested that physically removing oneself wasn't the solution, though nobody has explained that to the elderly constituency for whom the cruise industry caters, and who may well have come to a late serenity in which tottering about on deck in a gentle swell is quite as agreeable as pottering in the garden at home. The old adage that you cannot in any case find escape in travel, for the reason that you always take yourself and your history with you, was partly true in that it gestured towards the vanity of fleeing one's life by going away, but balanced its sage advice with the countervailing hopelessness that, since staying at home could hardly be any better, to dream of escape at all was out of the question.

The truth content of the sensualist-hedonist tradition lay in its contention that the life of the senses found its mother tongue in the articulation of desire. Sensuality was intimately linked to volition, or ought to be. Instead, in the industrial world, sensual life was ruthlessly exposed to every kind of abuse, which consumer society has only perpetuated in more subtle forms by offering complex gratifications of the sensual life it has otherwise systematically benumbed. Under the official ideology of choice, the choices anybody might make are predetermined. Visits to cultural sites are packaged as 'experiences': the 'VIP Experience' at Warwick Castle includes a 'Birds of Prey Experience', a belated existential language that already hopes, before anybody has even bought a ticket, that their lives will be somehow importantly marked by the encounter [warwick-castle.com/plan/vip-experiences.aspx]. If elective affinities are not to be found in the sensual world any longer, the next best recourse would be to remarkable sensual modalities that arose by chance, spontaneously, but exactly nothing can be left to chance in consumerism. Everybody must identify with whatever the marketing department wishes to sell next. The institution of Black Friday, originating in the United States as a day when retailers, out of the goodness of their hearts ostensibly, offer substantial reductions on goods for one day in the lead-up to Christmas, is parodically named because the retailers are supposedly offering to make a loss, but deserves its name more darkly for the atrocious contempt with which consumers are treated like packs of slavering dogs. In Britain, the tussles and fist-fights that break out in the stores have in many places become a matter for the police, who might profitably turn their attention to the assistants dangling the perfume-sets and coffee-machines over the heads of the baying mob. The civil unrest promoted by businesses, which never act otherwise than in accordance with their own sphere of interests, has created a perfect image of the mobilisation of volition in late capitalist economics. Whether anybody genuinely wants a new coffee-machine is a secondary matter compared to the fact that the new one is being sold at a third of its original price, which was in itself a carefully calculated fraud to begin with, and that everybody else wants it. Estelle Reiner's line from *When Harry Met Sally* (1989), in response to Meg Ryan's faked orgasm in Katz's Deli, 'I'll have what she's having', is the expression of what all consumers want from the society conceived in their name, the promise of an extravagant sensory pleasure that everybody else obligingly fakes, *pour encourager les autres*, but also to persuade themselves that they have got what they paid for. In one of his talks for children on German radio in 1930, Benjamin suggested to his young listeners that when you fully understand something such as a commodity, see through it from every angle, you no longer need to have it, as though the old proverb that said to understand all is to forgive all might productively be reformulated to state that to understand everything is to refuse everything:

> *the more someone understands something and*
> *the more he knows of a particular kind of beauty –*
> *whether it's flowers, books, clothing, or toys – the*
> *more he can rejoice in everything that he knows and*
> *sees, and the less he's fixated on possessing it, buying it*
> *himself, or receiving it as a gift.*[24]

The challenge to the sensual life is to plot a course around the manipulated acquisitive urge in consumerism that doesn't come to grief on the rocks of ascetic renunciation. Books may not have been Benjamin's most prudent example, in that unlike the other commodities he instances, they cannot be fully known without at least temporary possession. The frisson prompted by looking into an unfamiliar book at the children's library, one that already lured him in with the suggestive snatches of its prose that flickered out of the riffled pages, promised a small boy that a universe of things he didn't know still lay in wait. Consumer goods, including books themselves today, which have the same extravagant claims plastered over their covers as electrical retailers make for what are known as home entertainment systems, would like to appropriate even a fraction of this quietly proffered enticement, and can only achieve it by lying in order to create the myth of their own indispensability, a myth that stands exposed when they fall apart after a certain period of use. Cunningly, Benjamin ends his talk by telling the children that they 'must now explain this to your parents', even at the implicit risk of their parents so internalising the lesson that they will be empowered to resist raiding the Christmas toy-displays for their children.

The ascetic temper has always stood ready to counteract the blandishments of sensual delight, on the time-worn principle that an excess of such delight is ruinous. Kant's short article 'On Stupefying Oneself by the Excessive Use of Food or Drink' barely troubles itself to raise a discursive argument against the gluttons and drunkards: 'A human being who is drunk is like a mere animal, not to be treated as a human being ... It is obvious that putting oneself in such a state violates a duty to oneself.'[25] The truth of the matter is demonstrated by the fact that the intimations of happiness, strength and freedom from care that intoxicants provide, by which they 'arouse imagination to an *active* play of representations,'[26] are followed by the after-effects of dejection and weakness, which are always to be granted the axiomatic final say in the matter. The question turns, as so often in the moralistics of intoxication, on the exquisite difficulty in pinpointing the borderline between enjoyment and excess: 'But who can determine the *measure* for someone who is quite ready to pass into a condition in which he no longer has clear eyes for *measuring*?'[27] Luring its victims into precisely such incapacity for measuring, while officially abjuring all greed other than that of private capital accumulation, the credit economy of consumer society introduces them to a world of debt bondage. Excesses of food and drink may be officially beyond the pale on health grounds, which even Kant refused to allow had anything to do with the matter, but there are mountains of other commodities on which to spend the bank's money. All that is solid may indeed melt into air, as Marx and Engels put it, but only after you have bought it on credit. Once demythologised by acquisition from the realm of the eternal to that of mortal decay, consumer goods look like the detritus the corporations always knew them to be. The same fate awaits the sensory stimulations to which hedonism appeals for relief from the metaphysical, continually blowing them up again like half-deflated balloons, at a party from which everybody else has already begun to drift away.

Reclamation of the Senses

What is to be done? The question had better be asked, if reflection on the deformation of the sensory life is not to subside into flat surrender to present conditions, where such surrender can as easily take the form of unreflective sensualism as of narrow-minded conformity. All that has materially changed since Debord observed that a crucial characteristic of the spectacle society is that all dialogue between the spectacle and its clients is strictly prohibited is that, in a micro-electronic and digital world, the spectacle has become exponentially more spectacular, and its consumers more brutally isolated than ever in their absorption in it, isolated from each other and from their own inner nature. At a silent disco, the dancers each wear headphones relaying their own choice of music, in apparent freedom from the tyranny of a single DJ. The common purpose that once marked the innocently gratuitous activity of dancing together has thereby been removed as a last superfluous evidence of solidarity. In the arena of political activism, which has been driven back to the most overtly repressive societies, where it is as barbarically punished as ever, an alleged quiescence has overcome the rising generations in the affluent countries, reflected in the relative paucity, compared to two generations ago, of establishment political parties that offer even the most modest critique of established social conditions. Debt bondage has created states of economic emergency reflected in the immiseration of populations that once enjoyed at least the rudiments of state welfare, while the processes of representative liberal democracy have atrophied to an amorphous, purely discursive form that cannot compete with the tides of self-expression on the internet, and have resulted in progressive disengagement from electoral procedures that resemble nothing deeper than pantomime. Practical politics is no longer about ideas, only about the self-presentation of the parties as institutional structures. The advent of televised debates among the principal party leaders in the UK in 2010 produced hardly anything more apposite than purely sensory responses: the colours of their ties were analysed, their physiognomies compared, the agitation or serenity of their personal demeanours when under attack were scrutinised, with the result that the slander once levelled at women, that they only voted for the most handsome male candidate rather than bother their heads with trying to understand the issues, has become scandalously true of the entire electorate.

Such figures of dissent as there have been in recent times, manifested in anti-capitalist protests and symbolic actions in as close proximity to international summits as the security apparatus will permit, have reflected a faint oppositional impulse, but too often serve only to remind the system of its boundless liberality in permitting the occasional bat squeak of dissent to penetrate the roar of material and ideological productivity. The events of 2011, which saw both the origins of the international Occupy movement and a wave of rioting in British cities, showed up the traditional structures of dissent as futility incarnate. No purpose other than squalid opportunist acquisitiveness lay behind the British civil disturbances, while Occupy demonstrated that, while it was perfectly possible still to foment a state of administrative inconvenience in public places, it used to be a good idea when activism was fuelled by ideas. The repeated objection of the London occupiers to the accusation that they had no clue what they wanted to see happen, and therefore no notion as to how they would know when they had won, other than that the world might become nicer by virtue of their living in tents on the street and going about in comedy masks, was that the whole process was a heuristic one, that they would know what they wanted once they had all had time to think about it. A strategy of acting first and thinking later is what has subjected the anciently embattled relations between theory and praxis to their reified etiolation, and resulted only in sustaining the status quo ante, where it hasn't relapsed, through the triumph of contentless activism, into barbarity. A protester with precisely nothing to say is capitalism's dream protester, as was acknowledged by the Bank of England's executive director for financial stability, a purely ideological job title if ever there was, who generously paid tribute to the demonstrators in October 2012 by saying they had stressed the importance to bankers and politicians of eradicating inequality: 'If I am right and a new leaf is being turned, then Occupy will have played a key role in this fledgling financial reformation.'[28] There has been precious little evidence of it since, but perhaps these are still early days.

A philosophy that only turned its gaze away from a degraded

material reality might easily stand accused of spiritual complicity with those whose official hatred of western materialism has turned murderously dogmatic. It would be impotent both before vulgar materialism and the adepts of its annihilation. That such annihilation remains only an absolutist myth is evidenced by the preferred means of materiality's extinction, the chopping off of heads, enraged idealism's helpless protest against materiality since the Jacobin terror, the hope that removing the thinking brain from the body to which it is shackled, incidentally destroying the whole misguided organism along the way, would separate reason from sensuality once and for all. The sentence against materialism can only be carried out materially, through a cultic addiction to killing, which it inherited as much from what passes for the judicial system in the old autocracies, upon which the capitalist economies have long bestowed their favour, as from a puritanical interpretation of the apparatus of belief in which it is officially rooted. Only materiality will keep having the last word. Every excised clitoris is offered a standing rebuke by the very next girl to be born with one. In any case, the apostles of puritanical asceticism have not scrupled to do without the paraphernalia of capitalist acquisition, from personal music systems and American-made weapons to the video-recorders on which the decapitations are captured. Without its deep entrenchment in the material world, fundamentalism would not know what it was vainly trying to extinguish, and the austerity of its revulsion is in part a regressive reaction-formation against its own intolerable entanglement in materiality. Much as societies that had officially progressed beyond the bourgeois historical era still needed the figure of bourgeois complacency to cathect the fury of the masses, as in the China of the Cultural Revolution, so militant fundamentalism must ever torment itself anew with the ubiquity of materialist ignorance, the state of apartness from the divine that manifests itself in such practices as displaying one's adornments. That the compulsive display of adornments is indeed one of the sicknesses of a reified materiality hardly licenses savage murder, but nor does the doomed project of material annihilation help the adept to recognise that overcoming the universal subjection to materiality requires the reformation of the ideal in a deeper critical consciousness than nihilistic rejectionism can furnish. Just as political praxis turns to pointless collusion without embeddedness in theory, and theory itself fades to sterility without a continuous address of the practical circumstances it wishes to change, and from the soil of which, despite its own distaste, it must draw its nourishment, just so does a refusal of materiality only stand a chance of altering a stubbornly concrete world if it first sees it for what it is by seeing through it, which is to say exercising its sensory faculties in accordance with its own tirelessly objectifying logic, rather than offering them to the beguilement of blood-drenched video-games, or their objective realisation as videoed executions.

The advice, meanwhile, that allowing the senses free rein through their carefully calculated stimulation, expressed in certain currents within critical theory, as much as in the various approaches of New Age spirituality and the rather less spiritual business of the aromatherapy industry, could help free socialised human beings from the prison of instrumental rationality is the counsel of despair. Cultivating pleasure for its own sake in a regression to the pre-rational or semi-rational state may feel like the defeat of rationality, but is all the more a regression for that reason. The failure of self-realisation in the adult state, for which in present conditions the adult is scarcely to be blamed, is what occasions it. In opening itself to an imagined cornucopia of sensual ecstasies, which ecstasies are overwhelmingly the stock-in-trade of consumer society anyway, it presumes itself to be gaining a world of possibility, and fails to see that its own true fulfilment is what it has ascetically renounced. For the sake of self-delusion, it takes sense-impressions alone, divorced from any apprehension of their historical meanings, to be the antidote to history's nightmare. These impulses can turn inward, as much as lunging outward, for solace in a sensualised life. Daubing the surface of the body with tattoos is among the ways that, by referring back to supposedly primeval times, one uncouples oneself from present decorum, and makes oneself the spectacle that life obstinately refuses to be. Foolish diets founded on the myths of detoxification and inner purity enable both the thrill of renunciation itself, willingly giving oneself over to a rule-bound regimen whose only dignity, when compared to every other regimen, is that the dieter has adopted the rules by choice, and the concomitant feeling that at the end of all the grim privation awaits a state of renewed zest for life, which has done nothing in the meantime to reform the panoply of regimens to which it expects her to submit. The online profiles of dating websites offer, just as astrology did, only more scientifically, to subject the principle of bitter chance that otherwise governs the founding of relationships to something like a bureaucratic sorting procedure, with everybody classified and potentially matched up according to what music and movies they like, or whether they unvaryingly prefer to penetrate or be penetrated, in a voluntaristic form of the mating protocols that Stalinist rationalisation prescribed for Soviet workers. Sex reduced to nothing more than the slaking of a physical urge, what Lenin contemptuously called the 'glass of water theory', vainly tries to free sexuality from its basis in material conditions, to which it proposes itself as the relief, and instead only subordinates erotic consciousness to the functional dictates of a biology for which it is anything but an end in itself. The late linguistic metamorphosis in English of the word 'orgasm' into an intransitive verb – 'Our sex advice guru explains how to orgasm more effectively' – serves notice that coming, once a point of heightened satisfaction on the continuum of corporeality, has become the functional *telos* of an act that is required, like a business contract, to have a satisfactory outcome for both partners.

At the dawn of scientific-philosophical investigation of the senses, Aristotle observed that sense-perception existed both in actuality and in potentiality. There is the active sense that human beings use when they look at an object to discern its properties, and there is the potential state in which it passively sees without remarking, but either way, the organism is changed by perception. '[P]erception arises ... in the animal's being moved and affected – for it is held to be a kind of alteration.'[29] For a moment, the human animal allows into itself something that is not like itself, but which, as a component henceforth of its knowledge of the world, becomes homogeneous with it because it is now partly constitutive of it. '[I]n being affected it becomes like what has acted on it.'[30] What Aristotle could scarcely anticipate is the degree to which the concrete sense-objects would become the means by which an external agency would directly manipulate the means of perception to engineer changes in the soul of the perceiver. Failing eventually to speak directly to the soul in the theological structures, it would harness elements of the sensory world to force an entry where enlightenment thinking had threatened to deny it access. The phenomena of the physical world are the means by which thinking recognises its anchorage in the real, and with the regression of consciousness under industrial relations of production, the vulnerable senses, shell-shocked by modernity, were laid open to the machinations of a functionalised world. It is the task of thinking at the present hour to interrupt the spinning mechanism that binds it to the thoughtless reproduction of whatever is, and to which unreflective sensualism would unwittingly condemn it, not by thought's fancying itself above all base materiality, but by exercising such a firm objectifying grip on it as would snap its chains. Today, any thought at all can only be its enemy. Critical thinking should stiffen its own sinews by reminding itself that it was only through massive world-historical exertion that it was placed in its present subjection to material conditions. The consciousness that comes with such thinking is hardly easy, any more than the ugly truth of the matter is easy on the eye, but whatever sorrow it incurs stands a chance of washing the scales from its eyes, and thereby turning to happiness. A world in which everything could be seen for what it is would be illuminated by the rising sun of a perception that thought had renewed, a perception absolved from the need to keep disabusing itself of what it perceives, its fierce unsparing light emanating from the only thing visible on the boundless precious earth that wouldn't demand to be looked at.

Part Two:

Application of the Senses

Chapter One

Sight

To see is to forget the name of the thing one sees. Paul Valéry

Founding the Senses in Philosophy

The preoccupation of modern philosophy with the problem of consciousness, in which what its antecedents knew as the soul has become a function of synaptic transmissions in the brain, contains a retroactive moment that it has not wholly avowed. Investigations into when and how the evolutionary leap occurred have given place to the more proleptic excitements of what implications for humanity may lie in the potential of external technologies to manipulate human awareness, emotional response and volition. If the scientific temperament urged on metaphysical reflection by such inquiries chimes harmoniously with a naive reductive materialism in full spate, as it assuredly does, and the question of what makes a person an individual can be wrested at last from the grasp of moonstruck speculation, then all to the good. But where does it leave the status of a world that existed before consciousness, either the consciousness of the species or that of its countless individual members? With the development of conceptual awareness came the origins of communication and social behaviour, and the beginning of human history, the inauguration of measurable time. History itself, however, grew out of the Nilotic ooze, which teemed with as much sensual life as does the modern metropolis.

Exactly what status the primordial world has for historical consciousness is a matter that hasn't unduly troubled it. Philosophy's own history is the developing history of subjecthood, the divergent accounts of a reality differently constituted at different moments in the human story, but always of the objective element in which the human subject finds itself. Even where it has turned back to the world of things, as in positivism and phenomenology, they are still things that the individual apprehends. That the world long predates human facticity is as discounted in philosophies of consciousness as it was in the various creation myths. However consciousness began though – whether it arose through the evolution of bestial groaning into a rudimentary communicative language, or under the socialising influence of cooperative behaviour, or when such cooperation produced emotional empathy between individuals in the group or, more fancifully, when encounters with psychotropic materials produced the first self-reflexiveness in cognition – however it began, consciousness couldn't have happened without its first having something to be aware that it was aware of. Experiments in sensory deprivation invariably find that the brain, famished of external stimuli, will create a hallucinatory world for itself in the soundless dark of the laboratory chamber. There is no pure subjectivity, not even here, but the subject insists on its own mediation by an external ontic world, of which it desires only to be a component, albeit the crowning component of a world it conjures or remakes in its own image. The senses are its gateway to such a world, and have evolved not as mere passive recording instruments of an external reality, but as tools that have enabled the human species to construct reality according to its own purposes. To be sure, what there is in the phenomenal world is increasingly what human beings have put there, much of which takes on the character of unfathomable second nature in the capitalist era, though even that is not entirely resistant to appropriation by the emotional and symbolic investments of individuals. Nonetheless, the fact that there is this antecedent reality is what colluded in the development of consciousness, and what would eventually lead, precisely *as development*, to the species turning its consciousness on itself.

The notion that there is a mutable, heuristic quality to sensory knowledge only began to receive its full philosophical due in the aftermath of evolutionary theory. Even the European enlightenment, in its deistic temper, had continued to acknowledge the existence of unchanging *noumena* beneath the surface layers of the objects that furnished the world. After the bourgeois revolutions and the rapid development of a business economy, by which the middle strata remodelled the social contract, it proved possible to fold the *noumena* away in a drawer. Georg Simmel, reflecting in 1889 on the ideational flux ushered in by mature capitalism, states, 'If now experience is being increasingly stressed as the only means of knowing, rather than the absolute and a priori knowledge that was striven for in previous times, then this implies the transformation of a cognitive substance that was required to be valid for all times into one that is capable of continual modification, increase and correction.'[1] By the time he was writing, such 'absolute and a priori knowledge' was itself one of the foundational myths of idealism, against which the malleable cognitive substance of modernity was conceived. A century and more before evolution was posited, the Enlightenment had its own versions of the development of consciousness that were already sufficiently supple not to need the postulate of prioristic knowledge, and on the eminently practical grounds that, had such knowledge existed, there would have been no need for the history of ideas. For the late Vico of the *Nuova Scienza* (1725), the human faculty for *ingenium*, the intellective habit of fashioning the world through sensory perception, as opposed to merely seeing it for what it irreducibly is, already points to the probable origins of knowledge in an account that is properly mythical in that, for all its speculative nature, it might well be true. Primeval beings interpreted the raging of thunderstorms as having been sent by an all-powerful god, and then went on to believe in the god their own creative faculties had generated. In so doing, they saw the storm-convulsed sky as though for the first time, projecting their own inner bodily responses to the violence of the storm on to the sky itself, which roars and weeps as they do, its fulgurations those of their own eyes flashing in panic. Their own terror, reflected in the sky, provokes the consciousness of a terrifying sky-god, whose very existence, prompting fresh terror in its own right, completes the threefold metaphoric process. Knowledge is as much a constructive enterprise according to Vico as it is for Simmel, but what binds the two theories most securely is that knowledge has no basis other than in the pre-existent. It arises heteronomously from what there is. Such temptation as there was to dispute this is what Vico's origin-myth itself disputes. One of Malebranche's interlocutors at the outset of their *Dialogues on Metaphysics* (1688) urges the other to agree on the need to shut themselves away in his study for their discussion, so as to 'take leave of this enchanting scene which casts its spell on our senses and by its variety proves too distracting.'[2] The other's ready assent sounds the note of the even more fanatical ascetic: 'I am disgusted with all that I see in this material and sensuous world, since I have heard you speak of another world full of intelligible beauty.'[3] They draw the curtain to shut out the disgusting world, but tellingly resolve against making the room utterly pitch-black. 'Darkness affects our senses just as much as light... at the present hour it might cause some uneasiness and fear in our imaginations.'[4] The thought is an uncanny prefiguration of Hegel's *Logic* – 'In absolute clearness there is seen just as much, and as little, as in absolute darkness'[5] – but the required conditions are a minimal degree of illumination without the intervention of external phenomena, which only trip off the imaginative passions into which the mind all too easily repines, like a schoolchild spotting something amusing through the classroom window during the tedium of a lesson. 'Reject... all that has come into your mind by means of the senses. Silence the imagination.'[6] In this, Malebranche proves his mettle as the zealous epigone of Descartes, whose consignment of the mind and body to their respective domains imaged that departmentalisation of knowledge that the early modern university had achieved. Intellectual enquiry is a cloistral matter only compromised by the world's paraphernalia, from which some gesture of retreat, however imperfect, is required, as acknowledged in the hopeless vow of self-denial that opens the *Third Meditation*. 'I will shut my eyes, stop my ears, and withdraw all my senses. I will eliminate from my thoughts all images of bodily things, or rather, since this is hardly possible, I will regard all such images as vacuous, false and worthless.'[7] The oath of allegiance to pure intellect undermines itself by its enunciation in such credal solemnity. If bodily things will impinge, they will have to be somehow falsified, a *coup d'esprit* that announces its own falsehood in the very act of convicting the concrete of being false. This act of force is the final verdict of failure on classical rationalism's attempt to make the one realm the vassal of the other, the view more germane to a slaveholding society. 'Most profitless is it,' says Philo of Alexandria in the first century AD, 'that the Mind should listen to Sense-perception, and not Sense-perception to Mind, for it is always right that the superior should rule and the inferior be ruled.'[8] The same point obtained, of course, between men, the creatures of intellect and reason, and women, perpetual playthings of sensuality.

Shutting out the visible world, or pretending it wasn't real, in order to engage in pure thought raised the question of what it was that thinking was intended to be the thinking of. If the world of phenomena and their appearances was only a mere distraction from the sublimity of meditation on immaterial essences, the immaterial essences bore a heavy responsibility to amount to something. Everything in being, even the ethereal elements such as air and light, possessed material existence, which is what made it apparent to the senses. One might meditate upon moral qualities such as hope or compassion, but it would prove as impossible not to train these cogitations on mental actualisations that were paradigmatic of them. Only the unknowable – God or the infinite – provided grounds for true substanceless reflection, and its stubborn uncognisability tended to cauterise the very act of thinking itself. The tone of Cartesian dualism harmonises unwittingly with the contentless meditation of an eastern mysticism of which it knew nothing, the attempt to wash the screen of the mind to such a pristine blankness that it ceased to be mind at all. Where sense-material did break in, its means of apprehension could be denied: 'I now know that even bodies are not strictly perceived by the senses or the faculty of imagination but by the intellect alone,' Descartes famously pronounced, 'and that this perception derives not from their being touched or seen but from their being understood.'[9] A fastidious horror of nature allows the perceiving consciousness to bypass the operation of the sense-organs entirely. What gives the objects meaning is their processing by the cognitive faculty. The inkwell is not an inkwell until I perceive it as such, which is as true for me, its user, as it was for whoever made it to that purpose. That I can see it and touch it and smell it are entirely incidental to its ontic presence, which I grasp by means of my conceptual apprehension. 'The world is my representation,' Schopenhauer begins, retrieving the thought from Descartes and Berkeley, pleased to find it also in the vedantic philosophy of ancient India, but not quite according the declaration its true emphasis, which lay not in the concluding substantive, but in the personal pronoun. 'Die Welt ist *meine* Vorstellung,' not yours, not everybody's, not God's, but mine. If the world is both will and representation, there is will too in the representing. By the time subjective idealism was ready to give way to the science of psychology in the later nineteenth century, such mathematically terse equivalences had evaporated into a cloud of multiple subjectivities, and the attendant realisation that some residue in the object always escapes the concept.

Prior Status of Sight

At its inception, philosophy took as its theme what it could see. The dimensions of the visible world formed its boundaries, the relations of objects to each other in space made a structure for it, and their material qualities – their sizes, shapes, textures, temperature, and so forth – became the grammar of descriptive thinking. There would be some attempt, in the Platonic academy notably, to insist that the lineaments of the physical world were the ephemera among which the soul dwelt, the latter being the proper focus of speculative thought, but already by the time of Aristotle's metaphysics, Greek thought was conceding that the external world was what generated the metaphysical concepts, that knowledge had properly to concern itself with what there is. His principal work on the senses forms part of the treatise entitled *De Anima (Peri psuches/On The Soul)*. The soul is itself formed by what it senses of objective reality, which obeys its own internal laws, the entirety of which intellectual inquiry might eventually hope to uncover. Any notion that the Aristotelian turn in antique philosophy obviated the need for meditation on spiritual essences, however, is quickly dispelled by a survey of the course that subsequent philosophy took. For Kant, the external object itself had a kind of soul, the *Ding an sich* (thing-in-itself). Hegel's substance-become-subject grasps at the Absolute Knowing that the realm of phenomenal appearance doesn't readily yield up. To Heidegger, the ontological world is a mass of visible manifestations of the ontical, pure Being, *Dasein*. The theological mode is never far behind metaphysical cogitation; like Time's winged chariot hurrying near, it is the impulsive force in Kierkegaard, and in the twentieth century, it still informs the critical contention in Martin Buber, in *The Eclipse of God* (1952), that Greek philosophy was responsible for inaugurating the hegemony of sight over the other senses, resulting in that opticising of philosophy in which, as though the Plato of the *Timaeus* never spoke, the visible world became *the* world. 'The object of this visual thought is the universal as existence or as a reality higher than existence. Philosophy is grounded on the presupposition that one sees the absolute in universals.'[10] However much of a misreading of Plato this may be, the salient point is the seeing, which is what supposedly convicts western metaphysics of the attitude of static contemplation.

Buber is on surer ground imputing this temperament to Aristotle than to Plato, but even in the case of the former, at least in the *De Anima,* there is no axiomatic assumption that sight prevails over all. 'That which is the object of sight is the visible,'[11] Aristotle declares, locating its essence in the attribute of colour. That which has colour is visible, its colour indeed being the manifestation of its visibility, what causes it to be visible in itself. The medium that makes the visible available to sight is light, although there are things, such as fire and certain luminous fish, that are visible in the dark. There is a sublime tautology in this: what we can see is visible, its visibility allowing us to see it. Visibility is a constitutive feature of most objects in the world, which is what makes sight possible in living creatures, the external world's visibility having implicitly produced the formation of the eye. There is no trace of the hegemonising of sight Buber detects here, not least because sight, like the other senses, is in itself reflexive. The senses sense themselves sensing; the eye sees itself seeing. In these famously nebulous passages from the third book of the *De Anima,* Aristotle gives the impression of coming tantalisingly close to, but stopping short of, the early-modern conception of (self-)consciousness in Descartes: 'it is quite clear that perceiving by sight is *not* some single thing. For when we are not seeing, it is by *sight* that we discern ... darkness and light.'[12] When the object is removed from sight, after all, it remains in the mind's eye, the imagination's version of the sense-organs. The reflexivity of sense-perception partakes of precisely the mechanism of dialogical becoming that Buber opposes to static contemplation. Contemplation is anything but static for Aristotle. Defining perception as the reception of Form (*eidos*) without Matter (*hyle*), he suggests that what the senses take delivery of are the qualities of sense-objects, without the specificity of the objects themselves, the second-order nature of perception owing some structural homology to the Platonic distinction in the *Republic* between the painting of a bed and an actual bed, which latter in itself is but a single metonymic exemplar of the concept 'bed'. If the Platonic-Aristotelian *eidos* seems to prepare the way for the Kantian thing-in-itself, it nonetheless forms the engine-fuel of cognition through perception, whereas for Kant himself, the thing-in-itself is what is unknowable precisely because it isn't available to sensory consciousness. Not that that does anything to prevent him from hailing sight as the 'noblest' of the senses – where touch is the 'coarsest' – because, for him, it comes closest to pure intuition, enabling an immediate representation of the phenomenal world without the consciousness of sensation, a pure refusal of the Aristotelian model. Only when the senses are over-stimulated, such as by a loud abrasive voice, or the emergence from a dark room into bright sunshine, does consciousness become aware of their functioning; where they are left in peace to operate at normal intensity, there is little or no consciousness of perception, and the objects they fix on remain elements of the cognition of external reality, instead of being internalised into subjective representations.

To the philosophical current, opening with the *De Anima*, that was prepared to be more hospitable to the encroachments of the senses on knowledge, has lain the charge, in the postmodern era, of over-privileging vision, to the extent indeed that, even where it imagines itself doing without the sensual life, it conceptualises its own mental operations as a form of seeing. '[F]rom the very outset,' Hannah Arendt says, 'in formal philosophy, thinking has been thought of in terms of seeing... The predominance of sight is so deeply embedded in Greek speech, and therefore in our conceptual language, that we seldom find any consideration bestowed on it, as though it belonged among things too obvious to be noticed.'[13] She dates the shift of emphasis in contemporary thought to Bergson and the linguistic turn, the theoretical knowledge of contemplation giving place to speech, the hermeneutics of the word, a transition from *nous* to *logos*. The movement from conceptual knowledge to the practical concretion of the verbal belatedly reiterates the corresponding turn in the theatrical styles of antiquity from the total sensuous experience of ancient Greek drama to the representational forms that achieved precedence in the great tragedians.[14] When tragedy was born out of the spirit of music, as Nietzsche tells it, it retained the imperative to deal with negative emotions, but in an objectifying mode that encouraged the audience to contemplate its didactic mission. The transformation was lost on Plato, who still saw in it only emotional muck-stirring, agitation for its own sake, and although the *Poetics* of Aristotle was in one sense the attempt to recuperate for the theatre, contra Plato, the Aeschylean goal of learning through experiencing, a dramatic version of Simmel's continual cognitive modification, two millennia *avant la lettre*, Aristotle had nonetheless aligned himself with the strictures of the master in suggesting that the effect of *dianoia*, thinking things through, is what dignifies the later theatre over the direct acoustical-melodic impact of its precursor. Contemplative distancing of the audience, who now viewed the calamitous events reported in the play as they would a painting, took the place of the unmediated inculcation of emotion by means of re-enactment. They learned from what they saw out there, rather than what they felt inside, precisely as spectators rather than participants. When what was predominantly the musical conjuration of emotion became a matter of attending to propositional argument in verbal form, the means of expiation for the uncivilised passions changed from expending them through undergoing them to purifying them through metaphysical abstraction. The point of looking on rather than taking part is that one is unmoved, detached, self-possessed, independent, autarchic, but precisely not involved or carried away. Knowledge becomes something one observes, as opposed to something that happens to one, the product of cogitation rather than experience. Torn between beguilement of the sensual life and the imperative for knowledge, Aristotle does after all postulate vision as the honorary sense that can bridge the chasm, by introducing the *Metaphysics* thus:

> *All men by nature desire to know. An indication of this is the delight we take in our senses; for even apart from their usefulness they are loved for themselves; and above all others the sense of sight. For not only with a view to action, but even when we are not going to do anything, we prefer seeing (one might say) to everything else. The reason is that this, most of all the senses, makes us know and brings to light many differences between things.*[15]

Sight is the favourite sense because, more than any of the others, it is the one that helps human beings to know their world. There are more things to see than there are to hear, touch, taste or smell, although whether simply looking at a beautiful landscape is quite as directly, voluptuously ravishing as smelling the pungent over-ripeness of a summer afternoon may be doubted. Because there is more to see, though, there is more for the visual faculty to teach the intellect than the other senses can command, and who would rather go blind than deaf, if there were to be any choice in the matter? The question, which remains unaddressed for now at the outset of this work on the unseen, is whether seeing things automatically provides access to knowledge of them. Even if there were no optical illusions, there would still be the sight of, say, electrical circuitry or motor-engines to those who have no understanding of their operations, and there would still be the willingness, imprinted since humans emerged from the caves, to see things that they didn't understand. The modern technological desire to produce video recordings of ghosts is less a desire to prove to sceptics that such phenomena exist than to produce a permanent record of their inexplicability. Aristotle's construction of sight as heuristic reaches back to primitive times: the visual environments of early humans, in their nomadic phase, constantly changed, as their transhumance took them from one fertile area to the next, but once they began to settle, they became used to seeing only the same surroundings, so that they had to create visual variety for themselves in the architecture of their dwellings, their artefacts, and in the shapes and spatial extensions of their cities. If looking facilitates knowing, then in these circumstances the knowledge it produced was tautologically of what humans had fashioned for themselves, at least until the social elites surrounded themselves with visual demonstrations of alienated power or gorgeous mystery.

The beginning of knowledge, as Aristotle's opening paragraph concludes, is differentiation, perceiving distinctions between and among things. By distinguishing one thing from another in the external world, the senses teach the mind analytical intelligence. They also teach it evaluative judgment, in that one thing is always better than another, the same with people, and if there has been a tradition in thought that sight is less prone to discriminative judgments than the other senses, it is one that Simmel at least contradicts. For him, seeing is entirely subjective, whereas hearing is not always so. The sound of another person's speech refers the hearer to the objective linguistic values of what they say, but what he sees when he looks at them is entirely his own subjective impression of them. Never is the act of looking more alertly engaged than in looking at another person, when something of oneself is revealed in looking appraisingly at the other, one's sympathy for his plight as much as one's distaste at his guilt. Simmel subscribes to the enframing view of sight. Whereas hearing offers temporal access to the consciousness of another in the time of its enactment, their appearance presents to the onlooker the congealed, fully formed pastness of their being, so that what can be heard of a person reveals their transient, shifting mental states, whereas what can be seen offers the more permanent record of who they are, and for this reason Simmel holds that what is heard is more readily imprinted on memory than what is seen. None of which appears to take into account the fact that the senses are generally engaged in concert with each other, the various messages supplementing and complicating each other, so that what consciousness receives is the three-dimensional view. Time and again, throughout philosophical history, the senses are treated as though they each functioned in turn, one by one, like the various sound-settings on a music system, being themselves subject to the same discriminative classification by which they enable metaphysical thought in Aristotle's observation. But it is the synaesthetic nature of the sensorium that makes evaluative judgment more complex than it might otherwise be, a point that Simmel contends by suggesting that perceptual acuity tends to fade with cultural development, as the subjective element rises. The individual sees less, even as he knows more confidently what he likes and dislikes, but it turns out that this confidence is borne not of the dulling of acuity after all, but of the supplementation of seeing by the other senses. Simmel's man of culture becomes more adept and sensitive at shorter distances, as is evidenced by the crucial role of smell – a short-distance sense – in the social appraisal of the other. Smelling people is more intimate than seeing or hearing them because it involves taking them into one's body, breathing them in, an observation that recalls Nietzsche's olfactory distaste for certain social types, and which, in an aside weeping with historical irony in 1907, is what explains 'the often vague aversion between Germanic peoples and Jews.'[16] Like many another theorist of the senses, Simmel maintains that there are more unpleasant odours than there are pleasant ones, which point he considers peculiar to the sense of smell, but the negative impressions of the senses generally are what furnish the mind with both its critical edge and its capacity for unhappiness. If it hadn't felt pain, seen its baby emerge stillborn, heard the cries of the dying, tasted the bitterness of lethally poisonous plants, and smelled the putrefaction of the departed, the anthropoid would never have learned the privilege of misery.

First Access to the Phenomenal

The traditional hierarchy of the senses, like many another hierarchy, was always worth abandoning, but without sacrificing the ordinal principle by which sight was treated first. Sight is the primary means by which the external world comes to consciousness. Finding itself in an unknown environment, the brain takes the measure of it firstly by what the organism sees. There may be sounds and smells as well, but it is visual information that provides its inaugural purchase on what there is around it. An unfamiliar sound may remain unfamiliar for the time being, just as a mysterious odour may not be identified, but what is perceived in the visual cortex is subjected to instantaneous analysis by consciousness. The phenomenal world must first disclose itself by the way it looks. Plato already teaches in the myth of the Cave that what we see is a mere projection, the illusory manifestation only of the ideal form it represents. But if it even only represents the ideal form, does the shadow on the wall not nevertheless have some veridical ontology of its own? If it points the way to the real, in what sense is it illusory? The fault lay already, at philosophy's outset, in positing the visual as indicative of something else, which remained hidden. At its most naïve, the tendency resulted in an impulse to classify reality according to orders of mimetic significance. The medieval doctrine of signatures – the hopeless belief that if a plant has kidney-shaped leaves, it will be good for curing renal ailments –

already sounds like a belated final wager on Mother Nature's wisdom. Conversely, if it were true, as Jakob Böhme still hoped as late as 1621, it would happily confirm that the inner nature of things declined to remain concealed. It wouldn't have to be teased out; it would explode forth, as everything in nature helplessly divulged itself to presence: 'there is nothing that is created or born in nature, but it also manifests its internal form externally, for the internal continually labours or works itself forth to manifestation' (*Signatura Rerum*, I:15). The self-disclosure of all things should theoretically be available to universal sight, but there are none so blind as those who fail to see, or who truculently persist in allowing that the visual messages things throw out can be ambiguous. Barely twenty years later, Descartes would speak up for these latter in the *Meditations*. What is present to sight can be highly deceptive, as witness the famous stick half-submerged in water, which looks bent when it isn't. All one can be securely in possession of is what goes on in the mind, the ground of all cognition, for even if the mind is deceived, there is still some objective entity that is being deceived. The representations of the external world that the mind conceives are transmuted essences of the phenomena that the perceiving being notices, but they lie on the other side of an unbridgeable chasm from the phenomena themselves. Wax, which had served very durably as the philosopher's exemplum since classical Athens, is once more pressed into service. In the *De Anima*, it was the substance into which a ring might be imprinted, in order to produce only a simulacrum that would tell us nothing about the ring itself. Descartes ratifies the point, but makes it even more primarily one about wax itself. Its outward form – its colour, shape, texture, the intensity of its smell – are all susceptible to change in different physical circumstances. What wax is in itself can therefore only be known by the mind. Its form precisely doesn't declare its true nature.

Nonetheless, the primordial belief persists into the era of

hallucinogenic experience and sensory deprivation that it is the mind which is more likely to be deceivable than the physical senses. If ideas were enough, in the Cartesian sense, they would be even more readily transmissible than they doubtless are. 'I'll believe it when I see it,' declares the thorough-going sceptic, whose patron saint in the Christian tradition is Thomas Didymus. The pathos of St Thomas's story (John 20: 24-29) is that his scepticism begins as the most steadfast loyalty, as he prudentially refuses to succumb to precisely those false prophets of whom the living master had warned. When his error is allayed by the risen Christ, he learns that it is blessed not to have seen and yet to believe, for all that that applies to none of the others present, who have all already seen him (and who had themselves anyway declined to believe Mary Magdalene). In popular perception, the story has been transfigured into the observation that there is just something obtuse about insisting on material evidence, particularly when it comes to founding a faith-system on a notion such as bodily resurrection, but also for many another account of the improbable, and yet it is finally the material evidence presented to his senses of sight and touch that has convinced him. There must be some value in physical evidence, even to the theological tradition, otherwise there would have been no point in Jesus repeatedly reappearing to his associates in the period after the crucifixion, and no imperishable ecclesiastical tradition of holy relics. The interpretation of Thomas's scepticism as a condemnation of doubt grates not only against scepticism itself, but against the purport of the scripture. Thomas doesn't stand condemned for his doubt, any more than the others did, and yet his hesitancy has passed into popular wisdom as an index of failure, as though all doubt were inadvisable or even foolish. Thus do conspiracy theorists of all kinds encourage us to 'keep an open mind'.

The irony is that an open mind, not in the sense of infantile credulity, but in the sense of one that hasn't arrogated to itself the proprietary rights to the interpretation of sense-data, the primary materials of which it then discards, is exactly what would help humanity out of its alienated condition. Dependent in the last degree on the physiological operations of the senses, the mind in its ascendancy over the material realm convinces itself that physiology is after all beneath it, or is at best an element that can be subsequently reimported into its own concepts. A postmodern philosophy obsessed with bodily functions, no less than a communitarian ethics of vulnerable bodies after the manner of Levinas, requires the category of the corporeal as crucially as Hegel required the dialectic of master and servant. The body, reined to critical theory's chariot, served in the post-1968 period as the draught-animal that would try to tug it out of the mud of a philosophy inclined to return to speculative maundering, once the final attempt to unite theory and practice blew up on the Parisian barricades. In still positing the body as a concept, philosophy did no more than recast physicality in the mind's idealistic coinage, elevating the lumbar agonies and ventral rumblings in Schopenhauer, not to mention the less outlandish bits of sex in Sade and Bataille, into part of its common currency. The effect was to train the sense-perceptions, the somatic underpinnings of cognition, into impersonating themselves. In discourses of the body, the penis behaves just like a real penis.

The reputation of sight has suffered grievously in contemporary discursive thought. It is either the autarchic tyrant of the various specular regimes to which modern institutions have been sworn, in medicine, penal policy and state surveillance, or it is the gullible faculty by which Debord's society of the spectacle has desubstantialised the global culture industry's clients into flabby plasticine. Much is made of the worldwide passivity induced by universal staring at screens, which in their ever-increasing multifunctionality have licensed a surrender of conceptualising thought to the conceptualisations offered by culture's administrators. Writing in an era when screens were filled only with stylised text and the figures of profit-and-loss accounts, Adorno commented that '[t]he computer – which thinking wants to make its own equal and to whose greater glory it would like nothing better than to eliminate itself – is the bankruptcy petition of consciousness in the face of a reality which at the present stage is not given visually but functionally, an abstraction in itself.'[17] Elaboration of the technology in the internet era, which has precisely completed the functionalization of the visual, has seemed only to confirm the verdict. In a strict sense, though, the images offered to human consumption everywhere are not about visual apprehension, but have become the instrumental apparatus by which the prevailing culture recruits subjectivity to its own purposes. If sight is, above all, the sense whose messages are processed and interpreted most autonomically, it was always likely to be the sense most helplessly susceptible to ideology. To notice the alternately commanding and importuning tone in everything from the messages in shop-windows to the ads that the computer, by obediently reporting its user's web navigation habits to advertisers, already assumes he will want to look at, is to take a small, possibly decisive step towards paranoid delusion, one from which the individual consciousness absolves itself by diagnosing it as precisely that, a delusion. The painful lesson taught by experience, that fulfilment depends on things not always turning out exactly the same way every time, is soothingly swabbed away by what the internet calls 'behavioural advertising'. Having enjoyed something once, there is no reason not to enjoy it a thousand times again. If a less overtly totalitarian version of Orwell's stamping boot could be imagined, one might figure the imminent future as a human face being stuffed with fried chicken while staring rapturously at a screen relaying an ad for fried chicken – forever.

The jostling for attention with which culture visually confronts the subject, and which the subject mistakes for the inexhaustible fecundity of novelty, is predicated more and more on the spectacular. But whereas in Baudrillard's theory, society has become entirely a matter of an illusory spectacle, so that the individual subject yearns for a taste of the authentic, according to Debord the spectacle just is all too real, because it is the visible evidence that life and its fluid social relations have been negated. The spectacle gestures towards another world implicitly going on just around the corner, where people could have access to everything if they so chose, but which often contains just enough of a minatory element that they feel they are perhaps better off where they are. Television's preoccupation with congenital abnormalities and unusual psychological conditions allows viewers to stare pruriently, in a way forbidden to them as children, the testaments of the affected serving both as tributes to the human spirit's indomitability and as encouragements to be thankful for one's own normality. If the now traditional notion that enthusiasm for commodities in the spectacle society has replaced the spiritual transports of the religious eras, itself a re-materialisation of Marx and Engels' 'All that is solid melts into air', the obsession with bodily malformation is the secular version of the veneration of bloodied relics and the preserved body-parts of the saints. The feeling is promoted that, to be worth looking at, things have to be unusual, striking, outstanding in some way, although since this applies to virtually everything on display, the concept of the outstanding has tended to shrivel. Medieval churches, at least until the Lutheran age, didn't stint on profuse decoration, the iridescence of stained glass, the magnificences of scale, the better to impress on the faithful that it was worth training their sights above present circumstances, to a state in which sin, not to mention its causes, might be sluiced away. Where it aims for the transcendental and misses the note, the culture industry settles instead for the atmosphere of the crowded town square on market day, or the clattering hubbub of the travelling fair on opening night, with something to see in whichever direction you turn, the intention being to reconcile its clients to the present faulty world, reconceived as a teeming utopia. What is missing is the heterogeneity that gave the market and the fair their festive air of a break from the common round. Under the myth of a protean array, today's merchandise all looks the same, and is all informed by the same impulse. 'Something is provided for all,' Adorno and Horkheimer write, 'so that none may escape.'[18] The production of commodities is cyclical: as each one supplants its predecessor as the indispensable new model, it has to be promoted in exactly the same terms as the one it supersedes, and which was produced by the same agency under the same immiserating conditions. Only an idiot would still be using the very product the agency was declaring last year to be the *dernier cri* of advanced technology, while the gloss of novelty the new one bears will just as surely be tarnished to refuse by next year's more sophisticated successor. If no communication is encouraged between consumers, who must ideally remain in the condition of isolation in which their screens maroon them, neither is any permitted between the monadic individual and the spectacle. The system, says Debord, is 'a circular production of isolation.'[19]

A measure of permeability has overcome the visible and invisible realms, which were once securely distinct from each other. It was the job of the latter to compensate individuals for the disappointments of the former, with the proviso that the immaterial could always be symbolically gestured at in concrete reality: the aforementioned church architecture, gargoyles and misericords, devotional processions and carnival parades, weeping effigies and bleeding relics. Secular society supplemented these theological appropriations of the other-worldly with its own repertoire of ghostly apparitions and poltergeists, wailing women and whey-faced children, acts of psychokinesis, the ectoplasmic effusions of seances and, in the post-war world, night skies refulgent with the lights of flying saucers. In a culture where everything must look sensational, and moreover where almost everybody possesses the private means of capturing uncanny events on video, posting them on the internet for everybody else's doubting scrutiny, supernatural manifestations no longer seem as compelling. UFO sightings have fallen sharply from their post-war spate in the 1980s, when in the wake of *Close Encounters of the Third Kind* (1977), the arrival of friendly space aliens seemed poised to deliver humanity from the Cold War. In fact, they were a product of the global standoff, in that western defence establishments talked many of them up as a distraction from the prototype aircraft testing in which they were actually engaged.

What these countervailing influences have brought about in postmodern society is the wrong kind of scepticism. A large element of rationalist doubt has always accompanied interest in the paranormal, driven primarily by cultural and, latterly, technological factors, but underlying that doubt itself is the growing uncertainty with which people evaluate anything. The constant bombardment of messages from ubiquitous screens has bred in them an overdeveloped receptivity. Notwithstanding that, there is virtually nobody who doesn't secretly know that they are being cheated. Nothing ever quite lives up to its billing. Grandiose claims framed in the hysterical superlative – 'the most terrifying movie ever made!', 'the convulsively funniest novel I've read all year!', 'the most fun you can have with your clothes on!' – carry within them the seeds of their own refutations. So pervasive are these ingrained responses that it comes to seem as though there is nothing that isn't part of the scam. True scepticism lies not in the refusal to believe in the *bona fides* of anything, but in the suspension of belief, the opposite of what the naturalistic theatre tried to instil in its audiences. Its contemporary mutation takes the form of playing along with the racket, because there seems no alternative, while privately knowing that it can't deliver what it promises. In this cast of mind, somebody's hyperventilating tale of a translucent wraith seen drifting about the stately home, or the disembodied footsteps that clatter up and down the stairs when everyone is tucked up in bed, is neither more nor less believable than the prognostications of weather forecasters. The dignity of spooky stories once lay in their rank improbability overcoming the reflex of incredulity. If they could never be proved, neither could they ever be disproved – other than by pointing to the laws of physics, an alienating language spoken by experts who couldn't conceal their contempt for ordinary gullibility. Now that so much of what the culture of the spectacle propounds sparks the same response, the laws of physics have no greater claim to finality in the matter than do poorly produced video-hoaxes on YouTube.

The *Paranormal Activity* film franchise, and other examples of the already threadbare genre known as 'found footage', represents an attempt to restore the reputation of video technology from its spoilsport status to what it was once hoped it would be, a means of verifying uncanny goings-on by recording the proof of them. At a deeper level, it reflects another salient fact about visual consciousness, namely its enmeshment in temporality. In the second film of the series, the viewer watches over and over the rotation of nocturnal scenes on the CCTV monitors, outside and inside the house, scanning the screen vigilantly for the slightest indication of movement or change, and is periodically rewarded with the shock of a spontaneously falling saucepan. While serving the interest of suspense, the technique reminds its audience of the pure receptivity that the visual realm requires of human beings before they can begin to interpret it, and also that the interpretations, once arrived at, are only ever provisional and contingent on whatever happens next, which must be interpreted anew. Sight is the most industrious sense, because its conclusions are never conclusions. Even those who are constrained to stay at home all the time, or those whose lives alternate between home and a monotonous workplace with nothing in between, can't be sure that the way things look now is the way they will look tomorrow, when incremental changes, however tiny, will have altered them. If the idle scepticism that spectacle culture has bred in people were able or at all inclined to defend itself, it would adduce something like the contingent fluidity of the visual world in its self-exoneration. Its ceaseless mendacities reflect the unreliability of perceptual habit, which wants to root itself securely in an idealised cognizance, but which must contend instead with uncertainty and flux. All too easily, however, modern philosophical scepticism turned hermeneutic instability into willed *naïveté*, as when the Wittgenstein of the *Philosophical Investigations* asks how we can really know whether somebody is in pain. Are its external manifestations, the grimacing and screaming, enough, or would we require some kind of penetrating X-ray vision, by which we might look inside the writhing individual and see it for ourselves? Notwithstanding the degraded rationality that might dismiss the screams of pain's victims as insufficient proof, a Cambridge Fellow's version of theology's sin against the Holy Ghost, in the case of the millions who suffer at the hands of others, the question could perhaps be answered by pointing not to the sufferers' contortions, but to the intentions of their persecutors.

Sensible and Intelligent Cognition

In the section on the 'transcendental unity of apperception' in the *Critique of Pure Reason*, Kant establishes a model of the relationship between the external world and the thinking consciousness as one of harmonious correspondence, in contradistinction to their conception as mutually estranged realms in Descartes. As the intellect matures through infancy and childhood, it develops the ability to interpret the objects and processes of the world around it in accordance with the *a priori* faculty of intuition, which functions both sensibly, in response to the information the physical senses convey to it, and intellectually, with regard to abstract ideas and concepts. The chicken-or-egg question as to which precedes which is summarily dispatched by Kant, along with any positing of an intermediate compromise position between the two. It can't be that experience constructs conceptual understanding, because the intellectual categories in which concepts arise are themselves given *a priori*; they do not depend on elements of the material world to set them in motion. What makes much more sense is that it is the conceptual faculty itself that generates experience of the material, which would only be a sort of bubbling primordial soup without it. There are two types of cognition – sensible and intellectual – producing what he terms figurative and intellectual synthesis, namely, physical and mental objects of consciousness, but they are both brought under the transcendental unity of the faculty for conceptual understanding. Even the non-concrete objects achieve a kind of metaphorical – in the Kantian terminology, intuitive – understanding within the mind. Geometrical figures such as lines and circles are pictured in the mind when it thinks of them. The notion of time as a linear continuum is imaged in the literal guise of a line. The most complex notion of all, which will be richly elaborated by Hegel, is that intellectual intuition is capable of contemplating itself as an object of cognition, and not necessarily with the aid of a mirror. In other words, there is in the act of synthesis by which the mind apprehends and processes the world a kind of inner visuality that corresponds to the information received directly by the optical nerves, and to which even the blind can bear witness. At the same time, there is a cogitative element to it, an 'I think', which accompanies all the representations that the mind makes of the information it receives, and which is to be defined as a spontaneously arising self-consciousness. It applies itself freely to the empirical world, but it doesn't depend on the empirical world for its generation. Once again, it is conceptual intuition that structures experience, and not the other way round.

For all that Kant maintains the position consistently through the *Critique*, an antinomy arises in his characterisation of the opposing argument. In the section on the 'Analytic of Concepts', he states that the conceptual understanding is innately present in consciousness: 'this representation, *I think*, is an act of *spontaneity*; that is to say, it cannot be regarded as belonging to sensibility.'[20] Shortly after, however, in emphasising again that the categories of conceptual understanding are independent of experience, he claims that '[t]he assertion of an empirical origin would attribute to them a sort of *generatio aequivoca* [spontaneous generation],'[21] but this sounds precisely like the spontaneous character with which his own thinking invests them. Whoever, opposing Kant, insisted that experience did generate the conceptual categories would hardly be arguing that they arose spontaneously – nothing can be spontaneously generated *by* something without collapsing into a contradiction in terms – but that they are derived precisely from the empirical world. But *how* derived? Kant would riposte. What causative relation is there between experience and the development of a faculty for categorising it? Why, for example, do experiencing humans develop it and not experiencing animals? Even if that point remains mysterious, however, including to the empiricist himself, it can scarcely be less mysterious than the spontaneously arising conceptual faculty in which Kant believes. The faculty, innately present from infancy, develops as the individual matures, but pre-exists its conscious experience of the material world. In the era before the *Origin of Species*, the implantation of such a faculty made more sense than it would when, humanity having come finally to consciousness of its evolutionary origins, the notion of innate conceptual capability would seem once again like a matter of exactly that spontaneous generation that Kant abjures.

According to the *Critique of Pure Reason*, everything the mind knows about the world depends on what the senses deliver to it, but only to the extent that it is subjected to intuitive understanding about its properties, its extension in space and duration in time, and that understanding in turn to conceptual thinking, the elements of which are the thought-forms to which intuitively grasped objects are submitted. The functions of sensibility and conceptual intellection are as vital as each other, neither one having precedence, and inasmuch as their functions are not interchangeable, they are to be considered as separate and distinct entities. What the system fails to account for, the lacuna with which it fed the development of German idealism that was to follow, is that the conceptual understanding is itself part of the reality that it claims to interpret. If it is given *a priori*, as Kant postulates, while the material of the sensual world comes to it only *a posteriori*, it is at risk of beginning always with a contentless thought, which in the terms of his own transcendental logic, would be a vacancy. 'Thoughts without content are empty; intuitions without concepts, blind.'[22] He insists on the interdependence of the elements of knowledge, and yet the system can't account for the fact that, in translating it into the forms of conceptual thinking, the mind forgoes something of the particularity of the object itself. Indeed, its particularity, the way it affects the subject in his thinking consciousness, is precisely what might deceive the thinker about its true nature. The rose looks red, but that may only be a trick of the light. Saturn's rings, viewed through a telescope, look head-on like a pair of handles attached to its sides. If the observer accepted the evidence of his senses thus implicitly as telling him something about the nature of the object in itself, he would fall into grievous error. In some sense, then, the objects of perception have to be carefully removed from the phenomenal world, so as to be subjected to the laboratory analysis that is conceptual thinking, in order that they may be studied more closely and known more comprehensively. That something is always left behind in this process is one of the pitfalls of pure logical deduction, the point of correction Hegel will offer to the Kantian system, and yet what the senses alone tell us about an object is, as Kant stated, no more than aesthetics.

By these lights, the culture of the spectacle has achieved great strides in the aestheticisation of experience. It would like its clients to be permanently astonished, an attitude of impotent reactivity faithfully reproduced every time somebody describes even the most unremarkable of propositions as 'amazing'. Even what might be truly amazing, the life filmed by the cameras of natural history programming, which now miss nothing, even down to the cellular level, is presented as, and therefore can't help looking like, artistic video, and is scored as such, the swelling orchestra explaining the majesty of the swelling ocean, the tootling piccolo the touching absurdity of the bird hopping about in search of a mate. During the Cold War standoff, what mattered was the protean array of the western cultural market-place, as distinct from the grey paucity of socialism, but with the disintegration of those rules of engagement, mere profusion no longer sufficed. A minty mouthwash has to propel its user into a state of gasping exhilaration, something like being on banned stimulants, so that the viewer is suffused with an envy that won't let him do without it. The aura of consumption, which was only conspicuous in Veblen's theory among the well-to-do, where its display functioned to energise economic aspiration, is now more obviously democratised, in that even those who can't afford an open-topped sports car can at least swill their mouths with something that will make them feel as though they're on drugs, a better experience anyway. The faculty for understanding such stimuli, as Kant would have conceived it, certainly now pre-exists the stimuli themselves, with the result that people are ready to see objects of utility bathed in the other-worldly light of the fantastical, even where utility once derived its use-value from its very banality.

Reification of Vision

A development in camera technology consists of a device that anticipates the user's wish and takes the picture for her, in case she isn't quick enough to capture it, or only realises how beautiful the countryside looked once she is driving out of it. In the mania to capture every moment as a visual record, in images that too often fall short of what one felt when one had the impulse to turn the spiritually perishable into the concrete, so as not to let it perish, people look to give tangible ballast to their faulty memories, and invest the flatly objective world with the character of their own enriching subjectivity. As soon as photographic technology was privately conceived as a means of neutrally recording reality, as distinct from throwing fresh angles on it, which happened all too early in its career, it became less than it could have been. Now that the camera assumes it knows what you will later want to look at, the technology has given up on subjectifying the objective, and instead become another means of objectifying the subject, who is no longer even called on to press the button. It may at least bring back something of the quiver of anticipatory surprise one used to feel when seeing photographs was a matter of collecting them from the developer's, when one couldn't open them quickly enough, but is no guarantee against the concomitant disappointment that often greeted the over-exposed, poorly framed images of what had been the magical week in Salzburg. Landscapes look like theatre scenery, glorious buildings appear as mere backdrop, the faces of one's nearest and dearest are caught in cruel grimaces and with menacing smirks that one never catches in real life. The simple-minded adage that the camera never lies was formulated against a mass of evidence to the contrary, as a means of reconciling the subject to its alienation by faulty technology, and in any case, if its function was to reveal the unexpected truth, the fact that the truth was so often uglier than one hoped made it something of a Pandora's box.

The objects of visuality endure in the thinking subject by virtue of the ephemerality that photography would like to abolish as imperfect. As the gaze sweeps over the view, it selects and processes its successive perceptions – the wooded hills, the distant harbour, the spires, the serried rooftops, the thicknesses of cloud conspiring to hide the feeble sun – which all shuttle through the interior consciousness like slides through a projector. The attention is arrested by a man getting out of a car with an unwieldy parcel under his arm, concentrating for a moment before flowing on again. A traveller notices what he can in an unknown environment, which may not look at all similar if he should ever happen to come here again, and on his return to the familiarity of home, finds that what he thought of with the wrong metaphor as the viscerally familiar, now looks subtly optically altered. Consciousness is no less subjective when it is receiving messages directly transmitted through the sensory faculties than when it contemplates its circumstances purely conceptually. The sights it sees carry associations for it of other sights, remind it of other experiences, transforming a reality in which the traces of something cognate from sense-memory vestigially linger, often without rational connection, into the material of its own subjecthood. A modernist literary aesthetic initiated by Proust is predicated on this insight, making from interior monologue a technical means for establishing the radical otherness of its characters, despite the fact that at one level the points of interest in a stream of consciousness are often precisely those moments in which the reader recognises his own transfigured responses. If the techniques of modernist literature and the cinema invite their audiences to identify with the central characters, they simultaneously distance them by making too obvious an attempt to excavate elements of psychological familiarity from them as markers of their truthfulness. The sentimental passages in the Victorian novel, often derided by a philistinism that considers the heart-wrenching deaths of the destitute to undermine the astringent critique to which destitution itself is subjected, were constitutive of the guarantee that literature could transcend its own flatly didactic status. They were the last survival in narrative art of the cult of sensibility that drenched the late-eighteenth century in convulsive misery from *Werther* onwards, but put to the polemical use of social critique. A more jaundiced view has it that such devices are where the infantility of English narratology most obviously convicts itself, even in the midst of what has conventionally been conceived as its golden age, in that its plots only evoke a simple-minded wish to conform to the ethical imperative of justice, which doesn't emerge dynamically from within the situations themselves, but is only statically imposed on them from above:

> *Any type of conflict or diversity – whether of interests, ideas, ethical options, or erotic preferences – is removed from the realm of the questionable and translated into the fairy-tale-juridical opposition of 'right' and 'wrong'. Once this path has been taken, evaluation and comment become superfluous because, just like in court, one need only ascertain the truth and judgment comes naturally. As an English juridical commonplace puts it: 'Justice is as simple as truth'.*[23]

The notion that justice might be simple, for all that it usually isn't, is anathema to an analysis that prefers conceptual rationality to the ocular evidence of injustice, which all too easily convokes the embarrassing simplicity of sympathy. Sympathising with the characters, that totem of bourgeois aesthetics scorned by Brecht as an impediment to objective understanding, at least raised the possibility, however chimerical, that one might come to hate the course of a world that had used them so roughly, whereas the attempt to inveigle the reader or viewer inside the character's consciousness always risked hardening his response to their fate, just because they didn't necessarily react to it as he would, and might turn out to be too weak or misguided to avoid it, while the attempt to repulse the spectator's involvement, by recourse to the famous *Verfremdungseffekt*, only reduced the characters to laboratory specimens. The intriguing moments in Brecht are those, such as when Mother Courage sings a threnody to Kattrin, the last of her children to be slaughtered, when official alienation is softened by something resembling pathos, a narrative trope that Soviet cinematography refused to do without. To presume that the viewer can only feel compassion for a character's suffering if he could imagine it happening to himself is to presume too little. For narrative art to be true to its conception, it must find a way of transcending the subjectifications of sensory consciousness, dissolving the ego, if only momentarily, in the intimation that there is a world beyond the imperatives of its own self-preservation.

If the spectacle culture of the post-war era has usurped from traditional aesthetics, which with the exception of music always involves the eye, the methodology of making its commodities stand out from the world around them – 'Look at *this*!' – art itself has surrendered to a certain spectacularisation. Postmodernist works inherited the concern with their own formal means from the conceptual art of the 1950s and 1960s, itself the logical outcome of a process that began with the foregrounding of light-effects in late impressionism. In the portraits of Rembrandt and the technique of *chiaroscuro*, the dialogue of light and shadow is used to create a definite mood, but doesn't occlude the manifest subject of the work. In Monet, the effects of light are to be enjoyed in themselves, hence the almost Warholian indifference of the subject-matter – haystacks, lily-pads, the Giverny bridge. Eventually, the transition from subject to substance became the objectivisation of the materials themselves – paint itself and its textures, fields of colour – in full abstraction. Much contemporary work utilises the single-shot technique of advertising, its visual point made at a glance, for all that its underlying tendencies might be straining for a deeper articulacy. Video art all too obviously replicates the strategies of the broadcast media, which long ago absorbed the montage technique of early avant-garde cinema. However formally advanced postmodernist art has become, it still has difficulty freeing itself from the ancient heritage of aesthetics in imposing a subjective lens on reality, rather than being the passive receptacle of it. Even a work whose content is nothing other than a wash of colour, or a blank canvas, or a video-screen full of squiggling interference, is saying something, often despite itself, about the imperfect world from which it arises. Its only way of avoiding its own deictic function would be not to exist in the first place. Aesthetics has been the primary means by which humanity has contested the inadequacy of what there already is, as is witnessed by the antique myths about art as the arena of human competition with the gods. Arachne's tapestry shames Athena, who slashes her face in repayment. The mellifluous piping of Marsyas outdoes Apollo, for which audacity he is bound to a tree and flayed alive. Icarus plunges to the sea when the sun burns away the wings his father built him. The insolence of Babel is rewarded with the confusion of tongues. Art connotes the production of ingenuity, of superior skill, an improvement on the pre-existent, and cannot be suffered to go unpunished. It insults the original Creator by offering something more than he did, hence the theological ban on images, which could even less withstand the talents of a Michelangelo than it could the child's enchantment by the names printed below the rows of colours in his paint box.

Tyranny of Vision

The alleged imperiousness of vision, the far-reaching, sweeping inclusivity that was chalked up to its honour by classical philosophy and then damned as an unwanted interference in Cartesianism, has persisted into current sensory theory, where it plays the same role of dominant malignancy as does the male in critiques of patriarchy, the white European imperium in postcolonial studies, and so forth. Vision decrees the panoptical surveillance of the Benthamite penal institution, the intrusions of the totalitarian state, the objectifying possessiveness of the male gaze, the specular regimes of bureaucracy and the medieval church, Napoleon's demand for a picture of the whole of society down to its humblest dregs, the scrutinising attentions of clinicians, anatomists, vivisectors, security-officers, border-guards, CCTV. It whets the insatiable appetite of spectators in the gladiatorial arena, the theatre, the sports stadium, the mass rally, the pillory, the gibbet, the hunt, the pogrom, the peep-show, the strip-club, down to the universal screens of the present era. Alain Badiou says that cinema is essentially pornographic in that it 'shows everything,'[24] shows it to a demanding gaze that wants only to see, where seeing reigns supreme over all other sensing and over thinking. What is missing from this static analysis is any recognition of the spellbinding effect its technologisation had on vision. Not only the new ways of seeing, but the kinds of messages that were relayed through these means, readily accepted as the properties essential to them, transformed ocular consciousness at a historical moment when there was more to see than ever before. It became harder for people to look at the unconfected worlds of nature and ordinary human affairs as they were used to, because their vision was not being actively beguiled as it was in the media spectacle. In 'The Work of Art in the Age of Its Mechanical Reproducibility' (1936), Benjamin attributes the loss of aura in visual art to the moment it became possible to reproduce and disseminate it in mass form, the cheap print and the colour postcard representing little inert shards of the real presence of the original artefact, but it is admittedly hard to say exactly how far back the attempt to entrance vision itself can be traced. The tricks it was possible to play with ostensibly neutral recording technologies such as photography were themselves preceded by dioramas, the phantasmagorias that entertained Kant and Hegel, the development of visual perspective in painting, the stained-glass windows, the palaces, temples and colossi of antiquity, a gigantic statue of Helios bestriding the entrance to the harbour at Rhodes, in heroic anticipation of DW Griffith. Art itself, including monumental architecture, tomb statuary, the decorated drinking vessel, the Magdalenian spear-thrower in the form of a mammoth carved from a reindeer antler,[25] is the primary attempt to beguile the sense of vision. Barely has the proscription on graven images been etched into the stone than the rage of Moses at the insolent sight of the golden calf, erected to keep the Israelites happy in his absence, provokes him to smash the tablets in fury. The interdiction is always already contravened, not least because the making of such images was precisely what was thought to permit glimpses into the beyond of the present world, for all that its institution is intended to prevent merely material figurations of the unknowable. Even the twentieth century's most universally saturating technologies, culminating in television, shared cognate roots with late-Victorian spiritualism. Guglielmo Marconi's wireless telegraph opened up the possibility of conducting conversations between continents. A box from which disembodied voices spoke of the doings of the world outside was soon a standard feature of the home. Moving-picture shows brought new dimensions of light, emotion and psychological acuity to dramatic production, and at the precise moment that the cinema was able to add sound to its pictures, television added pictures to radio. Spiritualists seized on the concept of wireless transmission as providing supporting evidence of their own age-old advocacy of the power of mind over matter, of telepathy, seeing not just a homology but a precise homogeneity between spiritual emanations and what were termed 'electrical rays'. Nor was it a case of spiritualists versus scientists. They were often the same people. Two of the British pioneers of optical media, William Crookes and Oliver Lodge, were successive presidents of the Society for Psychical Research, and believed as adamantly in ectoplasm as they did in cathode rays. 'Television', and the equivalent German term *Fernsehen,* were each coined significantly earlier than the technology that bears their names, 'remote seeing' having been the work of mediums and mesmerists before it was the stock-in-trade of the BBC and ARD. It remains impossible to locate the origins of TV in one single domain of knowledge, since it was not invented to serve a pre-existing need, but came about because of investigations into ways of amplifying ethereal or, as they would properly come to be termed, electrical signals from the beyond, occultist researches being a principal driver of the technology, as Stefan Andriopolous has reported. 'The interactions betweem occultism, the natural sciences, and technology point ... to a mutually constitutive relationship in which psychic and technical television render each other imaginable.'[26] Lamenting the tardiness of attempts to make these connections as early as 1899, the German spiritualist Carl du Prel sought to make the correspondences explicit: 'Valuable time was lost because it was thought that occultism had nothing to do with technology, whereas in truth, it contains the very philosophy of technology.'[27] The link that roped human creativity to freelance forms of belief remains continuous down to the modern era. Representational visual forms are as dangerous as witchcraft, all art as demonically possessive as voodoo. Early verdicts on TV as a form of home entertainment didn't fail to stress its balefully hypnotic nature, the charge once levelled at everything from the golden calf to the Gothic novel.

The culture of the Renaissance repealed theology's image-ban once and for all, and in so doing, paved the way for the progressive visualisation of the transcendent. There is an unbroken line of descent from the Sistine ceiling to the magic lantern. Far from being banned, images are now all but compulsory, and yet even at their most compromised, caught in the webs of global commerce or barking incoherently for attention in the cultural marketplace, they refer as the great altarpieces once did to a realm beyond the immediately visible, in the dimness of which something better, which once earned its makers the envious chastisement of the gods they tried to honour, still phosphoresces.

Conditioning of Vision

If the Kantian version of a sensory consciousness unaware of its own functioning feels more convincing in a society founded on the desensitising effects of mass administration, it remains the case that neither of the polar opposites of his and Aristotle's accounts takes cognisance of the social conditioning that produces particular modes of sense-perception in the first place. At whatever level it functions, the question persists as to whether the universal looking going on in contemporary society is also a universal seeing.

Every mass entertainment medium since the cinematograph has been convicted of duping the masses, initially by a conservative temperament that affects concern about the intellectual standards of a working populace in whose intellect it doesn't otherwise exhibit any interest, and later by an oppositionist mentality that sees in it a means of bribing them into apathy. Prior to the mass media, minority media were suspected of much the same tendencies: the riotous entertainment offered by the Gothic novel in the late-eighteenth and early-nineteenth centuries was held to be pernicious enough in western Europe that warnings were sounded in Germany about the dangers of *Lesesucht*, 'reading addiction'. The problem with entertainments is that they might distract the simple-minded from getting on with their work; on the other hand, their value is that they might distract them from noticing how dull and thankless their work is. They fulfil both functions of course, and there is a conservative case for arguing that both functions are equally important. Moreover, it remains an unenviable task to persuade the citizens of mass society that the diversions of an earlier age might have been preferable, when work occupied more of people's waking hours, and what was left in the time before bed was concentrating, by candlelight or fire, on the pursuit of a handicraft whose laborious technical demands themselves imitated the structure of labour.

Leisure, which once meant freedom from obligation, a condition in which one was permitted to do nothing, now denotes an alternative activity. All time, whether ostensibly free or not, has to be filled up, by the oxymoron of 'leisure activities', if by nothing else. Under the imperative that leisure must be as little like work as possible, it takes on the character of idiocy, predominantly the idiocy of staring at something and being amused by it. The film industry once prescribed a modest range of generic attitudes to which the movies catered: as well as hilarity, there were fear and anxiety, erotic attraction and visceral repulsion, and the tides of sympathetic emotion. These have gradually coalesced under the rubric of hilarity, so that there is nothing that can't be made funny in the interest of entertainment. Of all the things work isn't, the thing it most obviously isn't is funny. When Beckett famously said that nothing was funnier than unhappiness, he expressed something more piquant about the nature of humour than about unhappiness. Faced with the repellent, the impulse to 'laugh it up' reassures the audiences that nothing in the menacing world has power over them, for all that their reduction to the status of helpless infants being tickled is the distilled essence of powerlessness. Hilarity is the antonym of the boredom that Kant considered a subsidiary adjunct to actual pain, and which everybody superstitiously fears while surrendering to it daily. The visual sense is instrumentalised as the pre-eminent escape-route from tedium; compared to stimulating the taste faculty through appetiteless consumption, the sense of sight seems inexhaustible. Its mesmerising is the aim of everything that is delivered through one increasingly multi-functional screen: TV, films, games, the internet, virtual dating, occasional reading and – the imperative that overrides all these – advertising.

Advertising is founded on the wager that the eyes are, in Diane Ackerman's Buberesque formulation, 'the great monopolists of our senses,'[28] which is why it has taken on an increasingly peremptory distractive quality. Television introduced to declining cinema audiences, who had been used to focusing their attention on the ninety uninterrupted minutes of a film screening, the notion that broadcasts could be subdivided into gradually smaller segments by commercial messages, some of which were paying for the programmes they were interrupting. Advertising on websites employs animated figures that bounce about, rapidly sequenced audio-video clips, often expanding to take over the whole screen if the cursor is, almost unavoidably, accidentally clicked on it. Not content with their peripheral positioning, ads are now permitted to appear halfway through the text of a news item, so that as the user scrolls down, an inset screen opens up and plays a video before closing up again and permitting continuation of the text, which could hardly be more irrelevant now. The visual interplay of advertising takes on the mutually reflexive structure of medieval theology, in which the supplicant trained faithful eyes on an invisible God, who saw him in merciless transparency. Not content with making consumers stare at its advertising, a monopoly retailer has installed hidden cameras that take snapshots of the shoppers, so that the information already being gathered about their purchases, instead of being merely generically analysed by product, can now be matched up to a visual analysis that construes them in terms of their social type, age group, and so forth – all for the purposes of being able to advertise to them in a more personally focused way. There is both tyranny and pathos in this, in that the piercingly surveillant corporate eye that demands to know everything it can about its clients is reduced to the level of absurd subterfuges to find out about them the information they don't voluntarily submit. The lone outsider in the schoolyard couldn't be bullied half as efficiently if her tormentors didn't know that much about her; the retailers, by contrast, know what she is anonymously interested in through her purchases, and now want to enrich their knowledge by adding her physiognomy, as in the case of a criminal profile, to her actions. Where direct appeals to consumers through junk-mail and cold-calling fails through arousing resentment, impersonal advertising has to bear the ever weightier responsibility of influencing their behaviour. Human communication, on the internet most of all, is repurposed where possible into a commercial transaction, the insistent attempt by somebody to sell something to somebody else. Even at the apogee of its hubris in the entrepreneurial nineteenth century, the era that set the potential bounds of monopoly capitalism wider and wider still, the economic order that would come to gain hegemony over the whole of humankind scarcely dreamed that it could invest all relations between human beings with the nature of the transactions on which its own edifice was founded. What accounted for the lacunae in its influence over them was their leisure-time, but it was precisely in their leisure-time that they were free to buy, within the reach of their pecuniary ability, and where that failed, it would be supplied by the almost limitless extension of credit, the most lifelike chimera of personal freedom ever produced under the spell of economic dependency. Even given the possibility that advertising may very well not work most of the time, and thereby fails to sustain the crude behaviourism on which its psychological procedures are premised, the worldwide industry consecrated to it continues to flourish. Since consumers are less and less disposed to walk out in the world and see what there is, its attention-seeking strategies have grown correspondingly desperate in their invasiveness. The world's merchandise is delivered to their appraisal through one small screen, homogenising acquisitive desire by its enframing function, where once market-stalls and the shop-windows of the great city boulevards competed with each other in spatial extension, each display requiring another few steps to encounter. The nineteenthcentury glassed arcades and earliest department stores of Paris and London invested shopping with the aura of boundless possibility, making of the place of purchase a haven from the danger and weather of the streets, and permitting the aimless strolling of Benjamin's *flâneur*, who could dally amid the displays in an ecstasy of non-committal looking, but window-shopping is older still than that. In the eighteenth century, commercial premises in the metropolis began to be designed with broad glass frontages for the purpose of displaying the wares that might tempt a passer-by, giving 'shopping' – the verb form derives from the same era – the nature of a chance encounter, where previously the buyer had made a beeline to a place of business for something he specifically wanted. The shopkeeper lived behind or above the room in which he conducted his trade, and opened when his domestic circumstances permitted, rather than in accord with a schedule of regular hours. Following on from the efforts of street-criers and handbills, supplemented with notices in the public prints, shop windows made a direct visual appeal to the passing stroller. They addressed themselves, as advertising used to, to the lounger and loiterer, the loafer and saunterer, to those with time to stop and look, and allow desires to be precipitated in them like pearls. The German novelist Sophie von La Roche, perambulating Oxford Street in London in 1785, keenly took in the cornucopia:

> First one passes a watchmaker's, then a silk or fan store, now a silversmith's, a china or glass shop. The spirit booths are particularly tempting, for the English are in any case fond of strong drink. Here crystal flasks of every shape and form are exhibited: each one has a light behind it which makes all the

> different coloured spirits sparkle ... Just as alluring are the confectioners and fruiterers, where, behind the handsome glass windows, pyramids of pineapples, figs, grapes, oranges and all manner of fruits are on show.[29]

The cleanliness and neatness of the displays, even in a butcher's, where 'the goods were spread on snow-white cloths ... [with] no blood anywhere, no dirt,' strike her forcefully. Mercantile display has been refined already to a high aesthetic pitch in the global centre of capitalism: 'absolutely everything one can think of is neatly, attractively displayed, and in such abundance of choice as almost to make one greedy.'[30] The moral scruple is crucial, and is what will permit the rich in the modern era to bemoan the greed of the lower orders, as though they fail to see what is anyway untrue, that there is only so much to go around. The dialectics of acquisitive desire are held in the left critical tradition to create unfulfillable needs in people, and so help make them unhappy, the unhappiness compounded when they become aware of the spectacle of the better-off satisfying their every whim. But conspicuous consumption had existed since Athens, and was enough the subject of ecclesiastical concern that sumptuary laws were formulated against it throughout Europe in both Christian persuasions. Nobody would linger by laden market-stalls if all they did was remind them of what they couldn't have; they also assisted the individual in the process of her own self-definition, in the sense that, if she could, she would have this carriage-clock rather than that one. Envy might be morally suspect, but ambition never was, at least until ambition itself was co-opted as a commodity by television talent-shows. In this way, however, even though desire for unattainable commodities might not have resulted in mass dissatisfaction, it nonetheless helped to turn the visual world into a world of unmediated images, which then itself solidified into ideology. Exactly because what they wanted was as concretely unavailable to them as utopia, people's relation to it, and thereby to their own desire, froze into abstract reification. Where they didn't know what they wanted, the market offered them an external semblance of it, and the mass entertainment media of the twentieth century deepened the longing for commodities into an idealised yearning for the lifestyle and the looks that went with them. There is nothing inherently perverse in people wanting things, nor even perhaps in being persuaded to want something they hadn't previously known about, but the elaboration into a system of the urge to accumulate, which at the personal level had its origin in nothing more sinister than the instinct to make provision against the lean times, much as families preserved food for the winter, became as an economic principle the means of alienating them from those very survival instincts. The same holds for the business mogul who, despite having enriched his family beyond the dreams of surfeit by relentless acquisition, still wants more, but inasmuch as their life has been underwritten by those in whose own the stain of lean times stubbornly refuses to wash out, alienation has assumed the dimensions of economic evil.

Mediation of Vision

Is there such a thing as an unmediated visual image? It seems unlikely. In the course of a reflection on television, based on findings from the very first era of its dissemination into the American home, Adorno has this to say, contrasting it with its parent medium, radio: 'Whereas certainly the sense of hearing is in many respects more "archaic" than that of sight, which is devoted to the world of things, nonetheless the language of images, which escapes the mediation of the concept, is more primitive than the language of words.'[31] The same Adorno will insist elsewhere that all consciousness is socially and economically conditioned, and sight must after all be as conditioned as the other senses, arguably more so in that it is the primary sense to which the culture industry and advertising media appeal.

Pierre Bourdieu, opening his study of aesthetic taste, affirms that 'the "eye" is a product of history reproduced by education.'[32] Their conceptual mediation may have been preformed by such conditioning, but even when the audience sees the images that are beamed at it in the ways it is intended to, the images are being fed through the mediating filters of desire or revulsion, as the product promotion or the story dictate, and it frequently occurs anyway that even the most acquiescent sensibilities are provoked to read images against the grain, laughing uproariously at the pop star who imagines she looks daringly outrageous, or finding some sympathy with the emotionally frigid mother who finally walks out on her male family in the wake of a long bereavement, because she can no longer bear their emotional incontinence.

The kingdom of the visible is at once a tyranny and a hall of mirrors. Even if Buber, Arendt and others were right, and philosophy had over-privileged the hard-edged ocular realm at the expense of the soap-bubbles of inwardness, the visible does not of itself represent the transcendence of the material over the ideal. Just as the Aristotelian eye sees itself seeing, so does the eye of mass society. It is possible to look at the distant horizon and know perfectly well that there isn't a point in space at which the sky swoops down and touches the sea, despite what the eye insists, and it is possible to look at all images of the ideal and know that their very imaging is what announces their unreality. The Emerald City of Oz is a dreamland run by a charlatan in exile. The alternative worlds that might lurk down the rabbit-hole, through the looking-glass, at the back of the wardrobe, among the Himalayan peaks in Shangri-La, on an island where an enormous ape waits to redeem his isolation through love, among the interstellar wastes where the astronauts of the future will routinely boldly go, are bestowed with their chimerical aura precisely by the visualisation that illustrations and cinematography conferred on them. If what isn't real can be seen, then the reader, the filmgoer, can see it isn't real. Nothing but this lay behind the ban on images. The Judaic, Lutheran or Islamic instinct to preserve the numinous in non-figuration may have been sounder than the Ecce Homo of the Catholic visual art tradition, the muscular agonies of the crowning with thorns in Caravaggio, its blood-droplets of passive surrender in Guido Reni, sacrificing the noumenon of suffering to anatomical actuality. It isn't that nothing that can be seen is real; it's that the ways in which what isn't real can be made visible become the breath's mist on the mirror, by which what is real and invisible is obscured.

The self-overcoming of perceptual and cognitive error is what invests modern thought with its dynamism, on the anthropological model that Nietzsche proposes in *The Gay Science* (1882):

> *Through immense periods of time, the intellect produced nothing but errors; some of them turned out to be useful and species-preserving; those who hit upon or inherited them fought their fight for themselves and their progeny with greater luck. Such erroneous articles of faith, which were passed on by inheritance further and further, and finally almost became part of the basic endowment of the species, are, for example: that there are enduring things; that there are identical things; that there are things, kinds of material, bodies; that a thing is what it appears to be; that our will is free; that what is good for me is also good in and for itself. Only very late did the deniers and doubters of such propositions emerge; only very late did truth emerge as the weakest form of knowledge. It seemed that one was unable to live with it; that our organism was geared for its opposite: all its higher functions, the perceptions of sense and generally every kind of sensation worked with those basic errors that had been incorporated since time immemorial.*[33]

What the intellect and perceptions lived with throughout the greater part of human history was the often entirely useful consequence of error, of faults in the production of knowledge that had become foundationally constitutive of human understanding. Indeed, in some sense, understanding just is a question of lucky error. When the scientific pioneers of the various European enlightenments began to resolve incorrect thinking, the result was a disenchantment of the world that the greater part of society, trained to the theological trust invoked by Descartes, that a God who could be presumed to be above deceit directly implanted true knowledge through the perceptions, was at first unable to cope with. To Nietzsche, this was scarcely surprising. The voracity of the rational spirit's impulse to consume and digest knowledge – which it comes to call the truth – is what leads to identity-thinking, the false and ultimately ideological claim that everything in the world precisely fits its concept. Human beings should not want to know everything, or see everything naked, like the impudent Egyptian youth lifting the veil of the statue of Isis to lay bare her omniscience to his hungry gaze. They should rather attempt a return to the consciousness of the Greeks, whose responsiveness to the world's appearances taught them precisely about the appearances, not the putative inner essences. 'They knew how to *live*: what is needed for that is to stop bravely at the surface, the fold, the skin; to worship appearance, to believe in shapes, tones, words – in the whole Olympus of appearance! Those Greeks were superficial – *out of profundity!*'[34] The free thinkers, the daredevils of Nietzsche's raciest imaginary, are really artists. Read in dim light, the point may seem a rhapsodic anticipation of Adorno's contention in *Negative Dialectics* that the twin poles of a non-identitarian philosophy would be 'cogency and play,' but although it contains an element of the aesthetic, it is incumbent on philosophy to empty itself of the aesthetic, 'to sublimate the aesthetic into the real, by cogent insights ... Its affinity to art does not entitle it to borrow from art, least of all by virtue of the intuitions which barbarians take for the prerogatives of art.'[35] Free spirits might try to apprehend life by snatching its gorgeous fruits from the sensuous realm, but philosophy can only keep faith with its own substance 'by refusing to clutch at any immediate thing.'[36]

True human freedom would only be attainable for Nietzsche by means of somehow quelling the tireless work of memory. Triggered through our sensory faculties, its activations are as likely to result in anguish as in joy. Hope depends on being able to forget the possibility of disappointment, the alternative being a spiritual dyspepsia in which the soul is hampered, even immobilised, by its own ton-weight of undigested recollection. Seeing should thus be a disciplined activity, a seeing that aims at overcoming its own associations so that everything may be looked at anew. Only so can the eternal recurrence that he preaches be welcomed ecstatically. Not that such seeing should be a matter of wide-eyed infantility: cynicism, commended in a late letter to his critical champion Georg Brandes as 'the highest elevation you will find anywhere on earth,'[37] will be indispensable to correct the ingrained habits of scientific seeing. 'I was the first to discover the truth,' Nietzsche insists in his final text, *Ecce Homo*, 'because I was the first to see – to smell – lies for what they are.'[38] In all perception is an emotional species-memory that could reawaken the enchantment of the world if it weren't shouted down by the 'sober realists', whose only version of reality is the one they see before them. True knowing, by contrast, contains an intoxicating moment, by which it refers back to primordial fear, wish-fulfilment and so on, to which believers in realism are immune, since they are '*incapable* of drunkenness', deaf to the seductiveness of life. The doctrine is bitterly antithetical to notions of the slow accretion of wisdom through the progress of propositional knowledge, the gnarled accumulations of intellectual time moving at glacial pace, expressed in Henry James' conservative profundity that 'it takes an endless amount of history to make even a little tradition.'[39]

It must be possible to see through a faulty reality, otherwise faulty reality wouldn't be so assiduously designed to fool people. The multifarious ways that living creatures have evolved to deceive their predators suggests that deception is one of the indispensable tricks necessary to self-preservation, but the level of intrication and what looks like creativity in the detail of it far surpasses the requirements of camouflage. Natural mimicry in the lepidoptera with which he had a lifetime fascination led Nabokov to insist on a transcendent element in such mimetic design, an excess over the immanent need for immediate self-protection, which excess found its echo for him in the entrancing excess of the aesthetic itself:

> *'Natural selection' in the Darwinian sense, could not explain the miraculous coincidence of imitative aspect and imitative behaviour, nor one could appeal to the theory of the 'struggle for life' when a protective device was carried to a point of mimetic subtlety, exuberance, and luxury far in excess of a predator's power of appreciation. I discovered in nature the nonutilitarian delights that I sought in art. Both were a form of magic, both were a game of intricate enchantment and deception.*[40]

The incommensurate element, by which representation has its own techniques for the recording of reality, and which are common to all depiction, was recognised at the very outset of visual art's grasp at verisimilitude, as when Leonardo confesses that 'those who want to produce a deceptively real imitation of nature must not copy nature, but deceive the observer.'[41] In the famous tale in Pliny the Elder's *Naturalis Historiae* of the painting competition between Zeuxis and Parrhasios, the former concedes the victory to his rival, because whereas his own painting of grapes had deceived the birds into swooping down to peck at them, he had himself been deceived into asking Parrhasios to draw aside the curtain and reveal his own painting, not seeing that the curtain itself was the painting. In the 1964 seminar, Lacan glosses the story to say that, whereas the birds might be fooled by a superficial appearance, the human gaze is always lured to the notion of an indefinable something beyond or behind the appearance. The action of the gaze lures the eye as sense-organ into looking for some subjacent reality beneath the phenomenon, pulling it into a dialectical tension that is sharpened by the fact that there is precisely nothing behind it, only a lack. The experience of that lack structures the aesthetic faculty as much as it structures sexual response. Art's effect isn't in leading the spectator to a hidden reality; it just is the lure, the play, what Nabokov calls the 'deception', itself.

> *From the outset, we see, in the dialectic of the eye and the gaze, that there is no coincidence, but, on the contrary, a lure. When, in love, I solicit a look, what is profoundly unsatisfying and always missing is that – You never look at me from the place from which I see you. Conversely, what I look at is never what I wish to see.*[42]

The onlooker must be fooled by the artist into thinking that what he sees is the real thing, since the real thing itself is unavailable to vision. In the pre-eminent means of such fooling – the laws of linear perspective – the viewer is deceived into thinking that the river behind them is further away than the figures seated on the grass with their picnic in the foreground, even though they are all painted on the same two-dimensional plane. Additionally, there must be something else about the scene that isn't readily present to the eye, its interior meaning, since 'what I look at is never what I wish to see', which is not to say that I am always looking at the wrong thing, only that what I see *is not in itself* what I intend to look at, which latter is what my gaze tricks me into thinking must lie behind it. What is less often quoted from

Pliny is the immediately following passage, in which Zeuxis' attempt to sharpen his own mimetic talent only reveals again his own inadequacy to himself:

> *After this we learn that Zeuxis painted a boy carrying grapes, and when the birds flew down to settle on them, he was vexed with his own work, and came forward saying, with like frankness, 'I have painted the grapes better than the boy, for had I been perfectly successful with the latter, the birds must have been afraid'.*[43]

In the case of the boy, what the artist cannot produce is the effect of the boy's gaze on the birds, which, although they lack their own consciousness, nonetheless perceive the human gaze in all its monstrous unfathomability. 'Philosophy exists in order to redeem what you see in the look of an animal,'[44] Adorno remarks in conversation with Max Horkheimer, meaning that what you see is the look of mute incomprehension at humanity. If animals don't understand human cruelty or its opposite, apparently random kindness, human beings in the age of the culture industry come to look at the productions of art with the same blocked perception, the difference being that the human observer knows that he doesn't know what it means, whereas the birds swooping to feast on the painted grapes simply don't know. 'The mark of authenticity of a thought,' Adorno goes on, 'is that it negates the immediate presence of one's own interests. True thought is thought that has no wish to insist on being in the right.'[45] That naive unmediated responsiveness to painting that leads people to say they can almost smell the pungent sweetness of the water-lilies, or feel the texture of the expensive brocade in which the Venetian lady is attired, is at least properly disinterested in this sense, that it knows not to look beyond what it immediately sees to be the case, at the historical dimensions, the complex allegorical significations, the possible political undertow beneath what there is on the surface, but this precisely is symptomatic of the arrested subjectivity that the culture industry has inculcated in them. If all art is deception, as Nabokov insisted, the gigantic machine of mass-produced culture is what Adorno and Horkheimer diagnosed in the 1940s as the final stage of western cultural development, the Enlightenment reconceived as 'mass deception.'[46]

Art is the factitious heightening of reality, by means of aesthetic technique, for the purposes of altering its spectator's experience of reality. Its own relation to reality reveals an antinomy: the events and situations and characters that it depicts are not real, but the artwork itself is a piece of concrete reality. As it emerges from the music-drama of antiquity, it is the attempt to impose a subjective engagement on the individual's apprehension of reality, instead of his merely being a passive recipient of it or unthinking participant in it. The catharsis-theory expounded in the *Politics* of Aristotle establishes the threefold functions of purgation, education and relaxation: the rhythms and melodies that accompany the terrible actions produce a voiding of the negative emotions by calling them forth and promoting their expenditure, leaving the soul 'lightened and delighted', and thereby training the spectators in an emotional vocabulary by musical evocation of 'anger and gentleness ... courage and temperance' and much else, and also serving the function of pleasant *divertissement*, 'recreation after exertion'. As the acoustic effects resound through the amphitheatre, 'our souls undergo a change'. Because music speaks the language of emotion, and the innate human affinity for it can be trained to a sophisticated pitch, aesthetic response is held to be capable of producing moral tuition.

It must have such an influence if characters are affected by it. And that they are so affected is proved in many ways, and not least by the power which the songs of Olympus exercise;

> *for beyond question they inspire enthusiasm, and enthusiasm is an emotion of the ethical part of the soul. Besides, when men hear imitations, even apart from the rhythms and tunes themselves, their feelings move in sympathy. Since then music is a pleasure, and virtue consists in rejoicing and loving and hating aright, there is clearly nothing which we are so much concerned to acquire and to cultivate as the power of forming right judgments, and of taking delight in good dispositions and noble actions.*[47]

It is music primarily, and therefore the auditory faculty, through which moral education is mediated, but the visual arts, Aristotle allows, have a weaker cognate function, especially where they directly express 'moral ideas', as in heroic sculpture and painting, while the other senses, such as tasting and touching, have no moral connotations whatsoever. By the time of the *Poetics*, by contrast, the dramatic re-enactment of emotion is downgraded in favour of *dianoia,* thinking things through, learning by rationalising. Not for nothing does Athene, goddess of scientific knowledge as of art, throw away the flute she comes across. It can teach nothing. Purgation is gone from art, in a late realignment with Platonic austerity; all that is left are its educative and recreative aspects. But it was too late for aesthetic theory to evict from it the notion of spiritual conjuration, which had taken up permanent residence like a troublesome tenant. When cinema and television drama took over performative narrative from the naturalistic theatre, they poured the emotional semiotics of music back into the dry cup, and feeling was again a matter of the viscera as much as the mind. If art from earliest times potentiated the subjective engagement of its spectator, what became of the subjective engagement he already had, which was exactly what constituted him as a subject? He became defined through his responses to sensory, primarily visual, stimuli, which he was taught to feel as innately as he felt his instinctual responses to nature. Acquiring culture would eventually become one of the components of the alleged civilising process, but it simultaneously had a disastrously objectifying effect. It made him able to contemplate crimes against humanity as another aspect of that Burkean 'delightful horror' that was the obverse of the beautiful, positioning bestial cruelty in the same relation to selfless charity as the heaving storm-beaten sea stood to the sun-splashed summer meadow. In human affairs, a generation after the theory of the sublime and the beautiful was constructed, the circle linking them was closed by the Jacobin Terror, and the wager that enough destruction now might buy at a premium the reconciliation to come, whether virtuously willed or not. By the time of the Irish Easter Rising and the executions that followed, the principles are linked inextricably in the Yeatsian 'terrible beauty', which precisely does not pre-exist the events, but is born from them in their elevation to didactic spectacle for history's onlookers. What they look at is never what they wish to see.

The first complaint of Lacan's observer, it will be recalled, was 'You never look at me from the place from which I see you', which seems to call forth the age-old humanitarian dream of seeing things as others see them. 'Could a greater miracle take place,' asks Thoreau in *Walden*, among a chorus of countless others, 'than for us to look through each other's eyes for an instant?'[48] The ecumenical wish troubles itself by the certain realisation that, were one indeed to see through the other's eyes, one would only be substituting their own one-sided vision for one's own. Where a collective subjectivity is postulated, it is only efficiently functional at the level of mute common purpose, as Simmel observed. Communities are best united when they only passively see but do not speak to one another, as in the attentive cohorts of factory workers, of students in the lecture-hall, of soldiers at drill, of crowds drinking in the ringing imperatives of the demagogue. What is more devoutly to be wished is a transcendent subjectivity, the substance-become-subject of Hegel's absolute knowing, a human consciousness made in the image of the God of whom it had conceived. Only so, as the Preface to the *Phenomenology* has it, might philosophy cease to be the mere love of knowledge its etymology boasts of, and instead become knowledge itself. For such a meta-evolutionary turn to come about, subjectivity would have to abolish itself as such, allowing itself to be absorbed by osmosis into a greater objective consciousness, which would then be consciousness only of whatever remained, including its own voided subjective being. 'Take a bone from a dog: what remains?' the Red Queen demands in Alice's oral examination.

> *Alice considered. 'The bone wouldn't remain, of course,*
> *if I took it – and the dog wouldn't remain; it would come*
> *to bite me – and I'm sure I shouldn't remain!'*
> *'Then you think nothing would remain?' said the Red Queen.*
> *'I think that's the answer.'*
> *'Wrong, as usual,' said the Red Queen: 'the dog's temper*
> *would remain.'*
> *'But I don't see how – '*
> *'Why, look here!' the Red Queen cried. 'The dog*
> *would lose its temper, wouldn't it?'*
> *'Perhaps it would,' Alice replied cautiously.*
> *'Then if the dog went away, its temper would remain!'*
> *the Queen exclaimed triumphantly.*
> *Alice said, as gravely as she could, 'They might go different ways.'*[49]

The pity of it is that of greatest interest to the disembodied consciousness was always what it itself looked like to others, for all that the ability 'to see ourselves as others see us' in Burns' address to the louse might only be counted a 'small gift', as small as the louse that disports itself on the lady's bonnet in church, of which she remains entirely oblivious. Such projected vision might free the subject from fallacious and idiotic thinking, from the urge to dress herself up and walk with assumed poise, and even from 'devotion' itself, the pointless longing after another, perhaps also even the very devotion being enacted in church. If subjectivity were able to give itself the slip in this way, in what sense would the I on whom it was now casting its backward glance still be I? Not all the withering visual acuity in the world could penetrate it, because it would no longer be I. Her viewpoint would have become that of another, to which she remained as impervious as when she was still herself. The thought is founded on an implied temporal sequence, in which the projection takes place for a limited time that is long enough to register everything about the self that needs changing, before the return to the original body allows one to make the necessary adjustments, but the consciousness one returns to is exactly the consciousness that has a distorted idea of what she looks like to the outside world in the first place. The critical objectification, best approximated in those split-second moments when one catches one's reflection in a mirror before being conscious of directly looking into it, only lasts as long as she isn't herself, and its predication as *negative* consciousness – it's somehow never the handsomely achieving hero one sees, only the self-deluding buffoon – is what sharpens the intended humility of the experiment into the sting of astringent shock.

A thinking that truly overcame the differences between cultures, or between male and female, would first have to divest itself of the cultural construction of the differences themselves. Perception would have to be usurped from its load-bearing role as the keystone of identity. The gender politics of the 1970s sought to render mythical the heterogeneity of perception between men and women, so that there was no reason that either of the sexes shouldn't be able to experience the forms of perception traditionally attributed to the other. If the husband noticed the make and age of the next-door neighbour's new car, his wife was aware only of its lurid colour, but also that his eldest daughter was looking ill, and these habits of seeing were held to be reifying because of their essentialist nature. Since then, gender politics has been more reconciled to the essences, and more keen on subverting the binary logic that sees one perceptual mode as more dispassionately truthful than the other, objective reason given precedence over the emotive response. The next stage would be to acknowledge the differences, but prevent them from being the structuring principle of perception, so that they became something as incidental to individual identity as the colour of one's irises, as contingently specific rather than definitively generic. All but impossible to visualise in current circumstances, it would involve treating what presently seems to be the other's blind ideology as an accidental quirk of his present state of consciousness, rather than something heteronomously driven into his nature by a set of beliefs from which our own set of beliefs recoil. Postmodernism's version of such a thought-form amounted to nothing other than flabby cultural relativism, the auto-suggestive fallacy that the other's acceptance of female genital mutilation was no stranger or more reprehensible than one's own predilection for the music of Meat Loaf, whereas an ethics advanced to the stage of fulfilling its own concept would see the latter as an agreeable irrelevance and the former as another of the eternally propagating peculiarities by which historical human suffering has been extended.

However futile the attempt may seem, the mutual social transformation of the perception of others would be an improvement on the solution offered to the ecumenical wish by the culture industry, which has only sought to abolish differential vision through the homogenising of perception, not by encouraging everybody to see as others see, but by making everybody see the same things in the same way. The mass production of perception by ubiquitously imposed fashion trends, the menus of multinational fast-food outlets, viral video-clips, online polling, league-table list-pieces in print or broadcast media that eternally confirm and reconfirm what everybody knew to be the case anyway, attempt to bridge the gaps by offering the cultural equivalent of the single party on the ballot-papers of the former eastern bloc, which at least offered the possibility of registering a hypothetical No to the sole prescribed option, along with the implicit 'Woe betide'.

Insight

Heightened vision of one sort or another has been privileged since antiquity. Clear sight notionally is unillusioned sight, often the paradoxical prerogative of the unsighted – the blind seer Teiresias, the poet Homer – who see into the depths precisely by virtue of not being distracted by the mundane. More than any other sense, vision has an inner efficacy. Deprived of sight by blindness or darkness, the perceptive can still see inwardly, while the ideas of tasting or smelling inwardly mean more or less nothing. Exceptional vision meant being able to distinguish things at great distance, which could by extension be taken to mean temporal distance. Teiresias sees to the heart of the present matter, that Oedipus himself is the cause of the plague, and he also sees what will happen. To be so gifted, however, is construed as a curse, as is indicated by his first words in Sophocles: 'How terrible – to see the truth / when the truth is only pain to him who sees!'[50] The Greek original refers more generally to the profitlessness of wisdom: *pheu pheu, phronein hôs deinon entha mê telê / luêi phronounti* (ll 316-317). 'Alas, to know (through thinking, understanding, wisdom, sagacity, prudence) is dire, because there is no fulfilment in knowing.' Clear sight then is a profoundly ambiguous gift. It distinguishes the seer, confers authority on him, but leaves him unpopular, an accursed figure, because he cannot but be the bearer of the bad news that nobody wants to hear. The wager on precognition is the utopian element in thinking. It wishes to be told that things will not always be as they are, and on hearing the *toujours la même chose*, it turns on the prophet, as Oedipus does, for telling the shabby truth. Disaster may take various forms, but that there will be disaster is non-negotiable. The wisdom of Teiresias could only be profitable if he were able to point to the sunlit uplands, but they are the region that nobody would need warning about, whereas the treacherous gorge that yawns ahead is worth preparing for. Prognosis remains more conformable with the negative mode down to the present day, when the homespun apocalypses of freelance religion jostle for attention in the marketplace with political jeremiads against terrorism and scientific predictions of ecological doom, exhaustion of resources, extinction, natural catastrophe on a scale beyond the reparations of human ingenuity. Fortune-telling lives in fear of the old bit of folk wisdom that says that if you knew everything that was going to happen on a particular day, you wouldn't get out of bed, not noticing that this is the exact condition in which billions already live, but clouding its predictions anyway in a fog of vacuous incertitude to insure against their turning out to be rubbish. The prudential advantages that might accrue from knowing what will happen, where something is after all going to happen, disappears behind what psychoanalysis knows as the superego, already a more powerful heteronomous agent in preventing the subject from doing what he wants. In the interest of pathetic hope, the medium or fortune-teller becomes the agent of an external authority that points as ineluctably to his doom as the administered world indicates his social fate, where fate, the primitive compulsion that millennia of enlightenment had tried to sweep away, keeps breaking back in like a stubborn infestation. No matter how special the sight of the medium claims to be, it can do nothing to remove the blindfold of a fate that careers grimly on its way, and to which all are subject. At the Delphic oracle, the evanescent mountain air was mixed headily with gas escapes from an ethylene seam in the rock fissure, to produce a state of entranced possession in which the world of tomorrow might be conceived as the piece of the other-worldly that it properly ought to be. A psychotropic state lifted the officiant and her clients out of the quotidian of a day that was already here, and into one that might be, which gained concretion from its suggestion of the transformative. It took a transformed consciousness to see a transformed future reality. The monotheistic religions imported the mood of projection from such practices, investing the canonical prophecies with retroactive force, but allowing them to dissolve for later generations into arcane mystical symbolism and glossolalia, as though the future was too disturbing to be looked at directly. Astrology and crystal-gazing would have liked to take up some of the slack, but remain hidebound by their own antinomical orientation to the concrete. 'I see a man in a blue car; he wants you to know he loves you.' Where aversive advice is dispensed and followed, either in the eldritch warning of the medium or in the computational random response-generation of the I Ching, the client will never know whether the course she was warned against would have brought calamity. Only bravely disregarding the warnings feels like the mastery of fate the consultation itself promised, while anything inevitable, rather like the future aetiologies indicated by the scrutiny of her genetic coding, only embroils her all the more in its clutches. While occultism is seen as the abandonment of reason by its critics and by many of its subscribers alike, its functioning effectively grants instrumental reason that triumph over the subject that her trust in its intuitive wisdoms sought to escape. The future can only exist in pure thought, so any attempt to allow prognostication to influence the present moment is a triumph of rationalism over the sensuous immediacy of present conditions. Even if every last tap of the seance table, or effulgent emanation of the departed – nearly all of which take place in the dark, to signalise the sleep of reason where reason remains all too obviously wide awake – were true, they would tell their witnesses nothing about present reality, other than that it was as delimited to its respective realm as were the departed themselves. 'The unreality of [children's] games gives notice that reality is not yet real,' Adorno writes.[51] Communicating with the spirit world makes the same announcement about the lives of adults, with the difference that reality's realness is not a matter for them of not-yet but of no-longer.

Infuriated that contemporary opinion had discerned the traces of Spinoza's pantheistic rationalism in his own *Critique of Pure Reason*, Kant went tearing through the tenets of the intuitive grounding of reason. God must be the supreme entity that understanding can conceive without recourse to sensible phenomena, whereas for Spinoza, he becomes a thought that thinks itself, an incidental conception that shapes up into a substance on no grounds whatsoever:

> *Spinozism alleges that it has insight into the impossibility of a being the idea of which consists solely of pure concepts of the understanding, which has been separated from all the conditions of sensibility, and in which a contradiction can never be met with; and yet it has nothing at all by means of which to support this presumption, which transgresses all boundaries.*[52]

It is for this reason, he alleges, that Spinozism leads directly to fanaticism. A reason conceiving itself as autonomous, refusing subjection to the limiting laws of logic, for example, doesn't lead to illumination but to superstition, since it has no immanent terms to which it may appeal: 'if reason will not subject itself to the laws it gives itself, it has to bow under the yoke of laws given by another; for without any law, nothing – not even nonsense – can play its game for long.'[53] The only way to avoid the relapse of deistic thinking into mere fancy is to subject the metaphysical concepts, which would include the future as much as they would the existence of God, first to the operations of reason. If rational faith, to which Kant brought all his own faith in rationality, is to be overturned by intuitive procedures, what emerges in opposition to it is 'another faith which everyone can make up for himself as he likes.'[54] That this is what has happened in the proliferations of latter-day New Age spirituality is undeniable enough, but what rational faith cannot in turn free itself of is less the fetters of deductive reasoning, but the motivation by self-interest that seeks to prove its propositions true. The charge against belief that scientistic atheism keeps primed above all others, that is precisely belief and not a cognisance of available fact, is handed out to it for free by the credal structure of Christianity in particular, which sought a watertight means of overcoming doubt in establishing its oath of allegiance at Nicaea. Thenceforth, ecclesial authority would not rest content with faith as mere obedience to divine precept and the exercise of goodwill to others, but would insist on a juridically fideist version, in which a weekly statement of what one actually literally believes is required of its participants. Thus did it hand the enlightenment, and its current crop of scientivist apostles, the gift of an evidentiary case against itself. Meanwhile, the appeal to fact itself collapses into superstition, for scientism as much as for Spinozist freethinking, in that fact is exactly what is impervious to reason: 'what results is the complete subjection of reason to facts, i.e. superstition, because this at least has the *form of law* and so allows tranquillity to be restored.'[55] Nothing else drives astrology's attempt to divine the drive of objective reason in the disposition of the constellations at each person's birth. If the moon can pull the tides back and forth according to some invisible force, why shouldn't all the heavenly bodies, rationally perused, turn out to influence what goes on in the sublunary world? The pathos of such belief, underpinned by pseudo-scientific consultation of astronomical charts, lies in its confusion of concomitance and causation, the unshakable certainty that no two dynamic forces could ever coexist without somehow influencing one another, so that everything in human history takes place in a world that is after all camped out under the stars.

Watching

If looking is the more focused version of seeing, watching is the strongest sight of all. Its potency is mobilised both ways. The film critic David Thomson suggests that anyone who doubts the power of moving images only needs to look at the mesmerised passivity in the faces of people watching television. Meanwhile, in the surveillance society, everybody is being scrutinised intently to see what they are going to do. Where the post-war welfare states thought to cast a paternalistic eye over the whole of society in order that each individual should be protected and nurtured, the surveillance society beadily follows their every movement in case they do something wrong. The origins of the panoptic tendency in which none may escape the attentions of the state derive from the requirements of medieval tax systems, the attribution of hereditary surnames to everybody, replacing patronymic nomenclature and physiognomic nicknames from the eleventh century on, being nothing other than a bureaucratic measure. Voyeurism and spying of all kinds turn what might be the comforting aspect of being noticed into a form of visual assault, and it has taken barely more than a generation for people to cease noticing the security-cameras that are trained on them day and night. It helps that the cameras are as prone to malfunction as any other kind of technology, but what has undoubtedly also helped is the development of a widespread ambivalence about being watched. Nobody likes to be stared at, and yet many people want everybody else to look at them. Even more than money and material opportunity, what drives the ravenous desire for fame is the chance of being admired, worshipped, gazed enviously on, by others. Warhol's famous dictum about fame in the future becoming a matter of spending a mere fifteen minutes in the spotlight expressed not just the increasing transience of the condition in a culture that would become less and less patient with looking at the same thing for very long, and not just the more benevolent idea that fame would become democratised, giving everybody a chance, whether they had any claim to talent or not. It spoke of the parcelling out of fame in strictly limited portions, foreseeing its transmutation from a status that accidentally came upon the great and lived on after their deaths into the banality of everybody having a turn at the wheel before their time was called. No nineteenth century operatic celebrity or popular novelist imagined that renown could be turned on and off like a tap, but the winners of today's pop talent-shows are solemnly warned by the entrepreneurs that the business is famous for its fickleness, and today's ubiquity will be next year's relapse into obscurity. The reduction of individuals to fungible anonymity brought about by the administered society find its hopeless yearning in the idea that one doesn't matter enough to be noticed, just at the very moment in human history when there are more cameras, media tools and databases trained on them than ever before. Fame is like a cathected version of that tendency, but one in which the aspirant celebrity fools himself beforehand into thinking that he will be in control. It then turns out that the gaping masses are not simply gaping after all, but very often actively loathing what appears before them. Communications culture has ended not by entrancing its clients into a spellbound state of awe after all, but by enabling hysterical articulations of hatred, which are only in themselves a more toxic and vociferous variant of entrancement. Celebrity is at once enviable and contemptible, dazzling and ridiculous, more dialectically interesting indeed than the days when parents might send a birthday card addressed to their child's idol with a note asking her to sign it and send it back, only to have the request as loftily disregarded as if it were a humble petition to the Vatican, but more rapacious in its commoditisation than the commodities of mature capitalism that Marx invested with the character of primitive fetishes. Where relations between people congealed into relations among things under the capitalist mode of production, relations among things have since taken on the character of relations between people, the exchange and circulation of commodities more dynamically interactive than contact between humans in their isolation. Fame itself is another such commodity, and if its emblematic signifier is now the sobbing teenager on the talent-show, that only serves to lend it the spurious imprint of the human that its objectification otherwise ruthlessly denies. Celebrity is no longer something one becomes but something one possesses, however transiently, as slippery as a greased eel, but all the more valuable for that, while those who don't yet possess it or, even more poignantly, have now lost it, look on despite themselves in envious distemper. The conveyor-belt nature of its production tarnishes what was once its innocent allure as the mark of gifted individuality, while the mechanised process has robbed it of the excitement of chance by brutally conforming it to the methods of industrial manufacture.

Ban on Images

To look forward to a future conceived in concrete images, materialising the immaterial by conceptualising it, was avoided by dialectical philosophy precisely because it seemed to turn a blind eye to the exigencies of the present. At the same time, the preservation of the utopian element in critical thought means the present can only continue to dream of its own redemption somehow, where the 'somehow' scarcely matters. An ethical vision would be one that neither dismissed what it could see now as the blasted ruins of a fallen world, nor simply looked to its more emollient features for soothing distraction, but saw everything for what it had really become under the transformation of vision by heteronomy. Marooned in the blinding spectacle of commodity culture, consciousness helplessly seeks out evidence of a reality that was once properly part of what philosophers have always called the external world, rather than the one he has been forced to internalise down to the last corpuscle, and finds that moments of authentic spontaneous feeling have either been as carefully formulated as the plots of soap-opera, or are swiftly co-opted by the reigning spectacle and assimilated to its regular procedures. And yet only such fleeting moments might provide liberation from what Benjamin described as 'homogeneous empty time'. The rest is a mere staring off into the distance, that lofty attitude of looking over the heads of the jostling mob in order not to be subsumed into it.

> *A certain optical conceit would indeed seem from beginning to end to mark the ideology of 'life' as that which prolongs by dissimulating the mortified condition of a fallen nature. Every gaze into the 'blue distance' – from the Romantic Fernsicht to the schauendes Bewusstsein [seeing consciousness] of a Jung or a Klages – would placate the viewer with the consolation of unattainable ideals all the more enticing for being 'eternal' and thus present in their very absence.*[56]

In the age of the necrology of consciousness, thought is nothing more than merely aware of what it sees, and of the response expected of it. Awareness of its awareness has deserted it, because it can no longer withstand the violent recoil that a fully objectifying consciousness risks delivering to it like electric shock therapy. Theorists of the Paris *évènements* hoped that just such a consciousness had been ignited in the demonstrators, shocking the producers of society's wealth into seeing the facticity of the cultural superstructure as well as the humanly constructed nature of its economic base, but the slogans were always more obviously romanticist in their libertarian yearnings – *'Sous les pavés, la plage!' 'Il est interdit d'interdire!'* After the failure of the uprising, Foucault for one had a go at relocating the utopian wish away from a theory now condemned as complicit in the rigidification of hope and in the direction of a sensuous bodily practice, in which congealed present conditions might liquefy under the entrancements of psychotropic drugs and sex, the future figured not through thought but through the adventurous solipsism of inner experience. Nothing could have pleased the authorities more than to hear, after the paving-stones had been relaid, that the revolutionary transformation of society was now to be sought through a mixture of dope drivel and sexual incontinence.

The confounding paradox of utopian thought is that envisioning a wholly transformed future leaves the present conditions intact, as though ending misery were nothing to do with its present causes, which could just be wished away by imaginative fiat, whereas fastidiously refusing the imaging of a redeemed world appears to leave people with nothing else but present circumstances, contributing to the disastrously unambitious gamble that a little tinkering with the battered engine might get society a few more miles along the road. Neither the pneumatic abstractions by which a written revolutionary constitution might try to guarantee society's freedom, nor the concrete ameliorative reforms of social-democratic manifestos, offers a way out of humanity's entrapment within administered society itself, while to either side of these compass-points, only fascism or a puerile inner-directed anarchism hover. Following the Incarnation, Christianity revoked the ban on graven images because it saw that even a fractional visualising of transcendence was better than no vision at all, and encouraged those who had no capacity for metaphysical conceptualisation to glimpse the infinite. Even while the scripture insisted that eye had not seen, nor ear heard, nor the imagination figured, what God had prepared for those who loved him, evasively hinting at it in such a way conjured some kind of involuntary mental picture, to which the iconology of the Orthodox churches and the efflorescence of Renaissance art made due acknowledgement. Heaven probably doesn't look like a fairground all lit up on a summer night, but without the image of even an artificial happiness, there may well be none of the real kind. The challenge posed to thought by a better future that stubbornly doesn't come forth from the shadows is how to imagine it without borrowing the shabby raiment of the present, but also without dressing the present in the grotesque motley of a mythological future. Only a transfigured consciousness that doesn't simply surrender to the perception of what there is, but sees it in the redemptive light of how it might one day look to a world that had superseded it, stands a fleeting chance of doing it, and doing itself, justice.

The icon paintings of the Orthodox are hyperbolic stylisations intended to emphasise the divine element in Christ that is mingled with the human, where western art offered only the increasingly beautiful naturalistic form of the fleshly individual. Caravaggio's Christs, such as the twisted balletic figure in his loincloth in the Naples *Flagellation* (1607-10), in which the condemned man's muscular body is spot-lit against the tenebrous flanking figures of his ugly tormentors, is a study in eximious masculinity assailed by its inferiors, the dropped head refusing to meet either their or the viewer's gaze. By contrast, Orthodox icons of Christ Pantocrator stare boldly out of the flat picture-plane, commanding the onlooker's reverence with wide eyes, heavy brows, long ears, a nimbus of luxuriant hair, an exquisite beard, a small mouth that requires nothing of the sustenance of this world, and a nose sufficiently stenotic to inhale only the vapours of Paradise, the mask-like visage derived from the commanding features of the departed in Egyptian funerary memoria. Even the crucified Christ of the icons eschews visible human suffering in favour of a pacifically resigned acceptance of his divine function. If he doesn't look back at the viewer now, his mind is literally dwelling on higher things. 'Through the icon,'

Anthony Coniaris states, in confirmation of the medieval sensual hierarchy, 'the Orthodox Church appeals to the eye which ... is the pope of the senses. We remember much more easily what we see than what we hear.'[57] The individual standing amid the icons that crowd the walls of the church is not alone, but enveloped in the community of Christ and the saints. He observes and is observed. His God watches him, assesses him, expects of him, loves him with a purer, more singular love than the fragile human kind, draws him on invitingly to his reward. The bullied Christ of western iconography, weeping, suffering, bleeding, crying out, even standing off from the viewer at a remove to preach or judge or alleviate the suffering of humanity, is himself still human, all too human. Dalí's *Christ of St John of the Cross* (1951) in Glasgow, while removing the nails, the blood, the wounds and the crown of thorns, and hiding the face, offers the suspended body from an aerial view, the spread-eagled arms and contracted trapezial muscle bearing the full weight of the physical suffering. The two ideas are unconformable. If one pictorial style represented the humanity and the other the divinity, they would be obverse sides of the same representational coin, but one tries to show the imbrication of the human and the divine within one image, while the other solicits sympathetic identification through the catastrophe of human presencing alone.

The notion of looking as in some way incipiently dialogic, in the tradition that extends back to Socrates suggests a responsive world that changes under the human gaze and, in becoming what it is, in turn affects the viewer's self-perception. In *Beyond Good and Evil*, Nietzsche warns against getting too close, spending too long in the presence of the utterly alien: 'Whoever fights monsters should see to it that in the process he does not himself become a monster. When you look long into an abyss, the abyss also looks back into you.'[58] Not at you, but into you. Just as the importuning eyes of the Orthodox icons make demands of the faithful, the abyss of evil calls to certain propensities in his soul too. For Benjamin, there is a salvific, empathic quality to this dialogue, as when the aura of the authentic work of art, horrifyingly absent for Baudelaire in the new technology of daguerreotypy, which would become photography, returns the gaze turned on it: 'Experience of the aura ... arises from the fact that a response characteristic of human relationships is transposed to the relationship between humans and inanimate or natural objects. The person we look at, or who feels he is being looked at, looks at us in turn. To experience the aura of an object we look at means to invest it with the ability to look back at us.'[59] What has gone wrong with this model by the time of Sartrean existentialism is that the world has become a mere two-dimensional tableau, flimsy but nonetheless impenetrable, provoking not empathy but only the famous nausea in its affectless blankness. The dung heaps and empty rooms that Beckett's characters inhabit stubbornly offer no response, either to their factitious flights of rapture or to their despair. Consciousness of the world around has atrophied to a state of blunt estrangement, in which nothing, not even the light in the eyes of those who say they love him, truly looks like the reflection of his own gaze, but instead insists on its own radical alterity, admitting of neither appeal nor dialogue. 'The spectacle,' says Debord, 'presents itself as something enormously positive, indisputable and inaccessible. It says nothing more than "that which appears is good, that which is good appears." The attitude that it demands in principle is passive acceptance which in fact it already obtained by its manner of appearing without reply, by its monopoly of appearance.'[60] If no dialogic relation to the world is available, it is largely because the refusal of response that commodity culture reserves to itself, precisely by imitatively parodying the sensitivity that auratic mutuality once set in motion, has in turn changed the subject to the depths of his being, and made him unrecognisable to himself. Every time the culture industry tries to make itself sound as though it speaks the language of its clients, it estranges them from another little piece of their own subjectivity, which, appearing projected before them, feels as though it must always have been as ersatz as it now sounds. 'The externality of the spectacle in relation to the active man appears in the fact that his own gestures are no longer his but those of another who represents them to him.'[61] A favoured trope of advertising now is for the companies to appear to alienate themselves from their own products, the better seemingly to inhabit the consciousness of their consumers. The bacon when fried exudes less of that 'white stuff' that appears to be as much of a mystery to the producer who pumps it with saline solution as it does to the purchaser. By appropriating his own response, the producer has neutralised it, even while offering no explanation for what the consumer sees for himself, thus causing him to doubt the veracity of his own doubt. The schoolboy's reaction to something that failed to live up to its billing – 'what a swizz!' – reflects not just the fact that it isn't what it says it will be, but also that it has thereby done him out of something, but what he doesn't yet suspect is that what he will chiefly be done out of in his maturity will be the legitimate feeling of having been done out of something. Disappointment is not an option. If entrepreneurial capitalism at the onset of its hegemony depended on disguising the shoddiness of its goods from consumers, in its late phase it relies on the greater complexity of the consumer pretending not to notice the shoddiness. The function that it used to reserve for the small print to fulfil, that of taking back what the large print offered, has now been inveigled into the very structure of the transaction, so that the experience of dissatisfaction must be something to do with the consumer's own carping attitude, rather than the immanent incommensurability between the product and the claims made for it. One's own apprehension of the gap between the entrancement on the children's faces in the advertising and the shabby actuality of the *soi-disant* magic of the kingdom is all that risks its demythologisation. The magic depends crucially on pretending for their sake that the enchanted palaces and spooky mansions are something more than a swizz.

Authority of Vision

All accounts of vision that accord it primacy among the senses rest on the unquestioned assumption that visuality is itself unquestionable. It furnishes sensory consciousness with what it knows about the world, and which consciousness then metabolises into the form of objective knowledge, founded on conceptuality. This was classical philosophy's way of eliding the problem raised by the apparent relation between essence and appearance, in which the mirages of appearance hovered between the subject and the Platonic Forms, the spiritual being-in-itself, which lay behind them. The era of ideology-critique reversed this polarity, so that rather than the world's façade concealing the kernels of truth, it was essence itself that was what generated the deceptive nature of the appearances, requiring them as the more or less substantial fig-leaves that hid the grisly truth from view. Recalibrating the categories for negative-dialectical thinking, Adorno insists that 'essence passes into that which lies concealed beneath the façade of immediacy, of the supposed facts, and which makes the facts what they are.'[62] The role of the visible facts is precisely to deny the nature of the invisible essence, on behalf of which they raise an ideological truth-claim. Objective consciousness of the world in terms of the concepts of epistemology, the scientific knowledge that understanding has bled from it, has the character of visual apprehension. Mental concepts take on the aspect of visual objects, lending a physiognomic phenomenality to their noumenal essences, so that what is perceived of the world is what there is. 'That mental objectivity,' Adorno writes, 'corresponds to the moment of direct vision. Pre-shaped in itself, it can be viewed like things of the senses. Only, this view is no more absolute and irrefutable than our view of sensory things.'[63] If such cognition had insight into the nature of the thing itself – the sense in which it is never quite what it claims to be – it would represent true insight, but where it has frozen into a scientifically posited piece of immediate knowledge it takes on mythic form, becomes an aspect of that allegorisation of the world that employs the surface phenomena to mask the way things really are, even as the concepts, *qua* symbols, claim to be representing it. Sensual hierarchies that placed vision at the top, which is to say – until the twentieth century – all of them, turned a blind eye to the evident possibility that sight can be deceived, not just by the obviously transparent trickery of optical illusions and *trompe l'oeil*, but by the gilding of lilies and whiting of sepulchres, and by the fraudulent insistence that something that glisters is bound to be gold. Vision knows it can be fooled, and has often been trained to enjoy the show, but when it lent its foundationalism to the objects of consciousness via conceptuality, it took on the willed gullibility of spiritualism's clients, solemnly declaring its illusions to be as indicative of fundamental truth as the rattling of tables was evidence of the restless spirits of the departed. Precipitated by consciousness into pre-formed images that exactly match the objects around it, the stubborn objects come to have as little to say for themselves as do the dead ancestors one has laboriously summoned back.

The ouija-board, whose name derives doubly from European words for the affirmative, only developed its ring of alphabetic characters as a technological refinement of the original, where the sole response was 'yes'. When the spirits were asked a question that required more than just a positive confirmation, the entire alphabet had to be recited for each character of the response until the appropriate letter was alighted on. Thus the riveting intelligence that one was recognised by the late Uncle Albert took many minutes of trial and error to be enunciated. It at least intuited the truth that all that was wanted of the spirit world was that it simply affirm our own in an eternally reiterated 'yes'. Just so does the intellect, with what Kant termed its synthetic *a priori* judgments, constitute the phenomenal world as an affirmation of its own cognitive processes. It conceptualises what is presented to perception, what it can see of what there apparently is, and then conforms the objects to its mental representations of them. Recall Schopenhauer: 'The world is my representation.' That is what it irreducibly *is*. If all conceptual thinking had borne the character of what one could hear, as certain strands in radical musicology are now beginning to claim, it would have possessed a more obviously temporal and evanescent character, instead of laying claim to the timeless factual concretion of what one can see. What one can see changes too, but each perception of it is the work of an instant, not a time-lapse sequence. In this sense, hearing sub-serves the interests of memory rather than of static perception, at least according to Simmel, who holds that deception can be more easily contrived through auditory means than visual, because – *pace* the Orthodox theologian – hearing is more readily imprinted on memory than seeing. Hearing somebody speak involves a temporal access to the consciousness of another, whereas their appearance presents the solidified, fully formed pastness of their being. What one hears of a person reveals their transiently shifting mental states, while what is seen is the more permanent record of who they are, but Simmel retains a belief that the whole picture is necessarily built up from the variant, but simultaneously available, sources of information. The eye sees the standing stone, while the ear hears the water rushing past it. By contrast, religion is founded on the unifying effect of what we can all see – the blazing sun, the sheltering sky, the scintillating stars, the looming mountains and plunging chasms – regardless of individual viewpoint. 'This fact must foster, on the one hand, that transcendence from the narrowness and particularity of the human subject which every religion contains and, on the other, support or favour the element of a union of the faithful, which every religion likewise contains.'[64] An ideological critique of the thought might contrarily point out that the elimination of differential angles of perception is precisely what reduces perception to a falsely homogenised universality, the function that global capitalism readily stepped in to take over from the antique religions in the era of their decline, erecting on the cleared site of the universal confederacy of humankind a many-mansioned pleasure-palace, founded on the palpable untruth of an *à chacun son goût*. Everybody has a different view, to which he is as entitled as all the others, when what would serve his interests best of all would be a vision that penetrated to the untruth in all things, which has deceived nearly all people. A democratic diffusion of consciousness only serves the status quo, by playing along with the myth of infinite diversity, whereas hope resides in the ability of those who have survived the reification of thought to point out, like Andersen's small boy, the socially engulfing tyranny of the lie that has blinded the rest.

Valéry's dictum at the head of this chapter, to the effect that seeing represents a forgetting of the nomenclature that informs conceptualisation, could provide the key to a renewed seeing, the seeing-through that spellbound postmodern consciousness urgently requires. For one thing, it could liberate the ahistoricality of much of today's critical discourse, particularly with regard to an accounting of the senses and the body in modern experience, from its superstitious fear of the pastness of the past. There can evidently be as much dangerous rage in demythologisation as there is in ideology, as the history of iconoclasm of all kinds attests. The destruction of historic artefacts in Cultural Revolution China, a pathetic attempt to ratify the unmooring of the present from the corruptions of the past, only established the futility of blinding oneself to the deep-rootedness of any putative state of liberation in the antecedent circumstances of imprisonment, the organic movement by which a redeemed present would use the best of the past to furnish itself with what human development had attained, in the process transforming the elements of an exploitative past in themselves, much as a *quattrocento* portrait can now be released, as a pure aesthetic object, from the conditions of patronage and philistinism in which it was originally made. To explode the truth from the phenomenality of the material present requires a deeper level of demystified vision than can be reached simply by destroying it. The rioters who smash the windows of fast-food chains don't appear to be able to smash the power of fast food, only symbolically, impotently hit out against it, reinforcing its already overdetermined economic potency. If the mass of consumers could see it for what it is, how it is produced, what ecological degradation it demands, in what abusive circumstances its retailing is organised, it would no longer have one unequivocal meaning for them, and its demise might be brought about by the only means finally practical, rendering it economically worthless. Seeing is the constant sense. The objects of the other senses, even lingering smells and persistent noises, have more obviously intermittent temporality, but what one sees is continuously there before vision, whether actively noticed or not. This is what comports the simultaneously semantic and non-semantic nature of the visible, as a recent work on Romantic sensibility puts it: 'sensation's mere resemblance to meaning does not simply block access to language or meaning ... Instead, this resemblance has its own particular, vertiginous power. Unintelligible physical sensation abuts against this other power, intelligible as the sensation of intelligence; sensory meaninglessness intractably and hauntingly exists alongside the sensation of meaning.'[65] There is a way of looking at the fallen world that doesn't just see what there is as it wishes to be seen, but sees its elements as no more and no less than the things that they have long since forgotten they are, in their over-determination with functional meaning. In restoring their thing-like quality to them, a restored human consciousness would find the feeling returning to its own anaesthetised sensibilities, and its own petrifaction into a thing would be revoked. Instead of seeing only the furious image of a godlike tyranny in the idol he wants to shatter, the iconoclast could glimpse himself in the image of God returning his gaze.

Chapter Two

Hearing

All my constituents have the same right to act for themselves as I have. I wish them to take the same pains to be informed & then to act according to their own minds without being duped, or cajoled by a noise & rattle of words, or overborn by the frightful authority of numbers, or majorities.
David Howell, delegate to the US Congress, 1782

Ears that have preserved their sensitivity cannot help hearing that someone is trying to talk them into something.
Theodor Adorno

Nothing is more permanent than the temporary.
Panorama Sightseeing bus commentary, Helsinki

Hearing and the Immaterial

Sound was primordial humanity's first access to the immaterial. What they saw was there; what they heard came from somewhere else. Even when sound is produced by objects in front of it, the animal is baffled by noise, especially accidental noise, as an extraneous element of what it can see. Sound is not *pneuma*. It is not the inner soul or spirit of an object being released, as its scent may be conceived. It is the potentiality for an entity's action. It is something produced by something it might do. When sound emanates from who knows where – as did the crashing of thunder and blasting of wind at the dawn of historical time – it exercises supreme noumenal power over the world of the physical. The noumenal world may itself be conceived as silent, the realm of pure ideas liberated from their material attributes, but sound is so often its emissary.

Sounds, divorced from the visual, need interpreting. Who's there? What was that click in the adjacent empty room, the snap of the twig, the bump in the night? The auditory nerve, alert even in sleep and in the final oblivion of the dying body, long after the contact of touch has ceased to register, survives the atrophy of consciousness, and is the channel by which fear most subtly inveigles itself into the waking organism. 'What we learn in the middle of the night,' warns Michel Serres, 'is that the world makes us flinch, and that we would do anything not to hear it, to keep it far from us.'[1] The sounds of menace may be culturally variant, but the sounds emitted by the menaced body are universal – quavering high-pitched uncontrolled wailing, whimpering, the chattering of teeth, the stuttering of breath. Nineteenth century science would become obsessed with precisely calibrating the gap between perception and consciousness, how many sub-second intervals elapsed from the moment of the organism registering an external phenomenon and the brain becoming aware of it, the caesura between sensing and knowing. What emerged was what now seems obvious: the ear registers quickest, then the eye, then the skin.

Where the eye assimilates, the ear negotiates. What is audible insists on the distance of objectification. Sound itself being invisible, the nature of its incorporation by the thinking subject bypasses the appropriative action of vision. Its very immateriality is what guarantees its objectivity, as something other to consciousness. If the objects of sight exist apart in external reality, they nonetheless appear to offer no resistance to the surveying gaze, whereas sounds demand the hermeneutic action that makes them intelligible. The medieval sense hierarchies that invariably placed vision at the top of sensory experience, for all that postmodernity, suspicious of hierarchy as such, wishes to scatter them, did so at least as much for its evident functional simplicity as for its alleged nobility compared to the organic bestialities of sniffing and guzzling and groping. Hearing, like sight, is a distantial sense, but it is more distantial still. Even when it is precisely evident where a noise is coming from, and what is causing it, it remains unlocatable in its essence, as surely for its inhabiting its own temporal zone as for its invisibility. Even persistent sounds eventually die away, leaving no trace of themselves, no concrete history, at least until the advent of recording technology, which strips them more ruthlessly of their aura in Benjamin's sense than the technological reproducibility of the visual arts that stole their souls from classical paintings. Precisely its perishability, however, suits sound to be the transistor of the emotions. It fills in the emotional texture of reality that cold seeing often lacks. For this reason, Serres, comparing the two primary senses, suggests that vision and hearing correspond at the intellectual level to understanding and intuition respectively – what German idealism knew as *Verstehen* and *Anschauung*. Stripped of the audible, visual signs turn mute, which is why deaf sign-languages generally rely on facial performativity by the signer for their full semantic effect. Sound vouchsafes to the subject something of objective reality that remains unassimilable to it, thereby altering its relation to the empirical. It has always already given the slip to Kant's transcendental apperception, not by harking back to the naive realism that preceded the 'I think' which accompanies all subjective representations, but just because it tasks the 'I think' with more conceptual labour than was allowed for in the transcendental model. If it was always a stretch to picture transcendental apperception on a Königsberg street corner, placidly applying its cognitive proboscis to the great world while wooden carriage-wheels clattered past on the cobblestones all around it, it remains just as challenging to imagine it cataloguing the auditory in the same intellectual filing-system in which it deposited its concepts of the visual images. Even the Hegelian turn, which gave the dialectical twist to Kantian perception by including the subject itself in the frame of reference, but with the proviso that subjectivity becomes itself the very gap that separates individual consciousness from reality, still allows for the consolidation of the sensory world as an incorporated bit of externality. The stage reached in romanticism according to Hegel, in which the beauty of the forms that classical art had created as an external manifestation of spirit, is reincorporated into the inner life of spirit itself, so that what it is reconciled to is its own subjective being, which retains the residues of external beauty to illuminate the subterranean dark of its inner chamber, is less disposed even than classicism was to grant the external its status as external. Subjectivity promotes itself to the objective rank for which it previously had to rely on sensuous existence to recommend it. Immersion in corporeality can no longer help it, but only tie it to a heteronomous and frangible ideal, a more assayable version of which it is henceforth better off generating for itself. Writing its own rules, setting its own standards, it satisfies itself with the only criterion for reconciliation that matters, its own, so that what it perceives and knows most certainly is itself. With the ascent of human spirit to the Absolute, the anthropomorphic principle, by which external reality was conformed to the human in classical times by furnishing it with semblances of the human, attains its consummation by the scarcely radical step of ignoring externality altogether and establishing its own inner standard with which to reconcile itself.

Nothing about the hermetic nature of spirit expounded by romanticism saved it from incursion by the din of a rapidly industrialising world, not even when it angrily closed its windows in order to concentrate. Precisely because it is the most external of the sense-impressions, sound is the least ignorable. Everything about it, up to its most supremely organised form in music, calls attention to itself by its second-order nature, the characteristic that is practically the first thing Aristotle notices about it. 'For sound in actuality is always of something or against something or in something.'[2] In other words, it is never *in itself* something, like a visible object. It is the effect of a cause, the actualisation of a potential. It is for this reason, thinks Kant in the late anthropology, that language, along with music – the most richly signifying sound-system in the human world–, is most appositely suited to the abstraction of conceptual thought. Victorian aesthetics agreed: the complexity of linguistic representation suits language to be the superior form of artistic expression. 'Poetry ... has this superiority over all the other arts, that its medium, language, is the least imitative, and is in the most complex relation with what it expresses.'[3] Whatever phonic correspondence language may primordially have had with physical phenomena has long since disappeared into the confusion of tongues, so that the names of things, as Saussurean linguistics confirmed, are mere random signifiers of their referents, but precisely that leaves them free for the construction of conceptual thought:

> *The shape of the object is not given through hearing, and the sounds of language do not lead immediately to the idea of it, but just because of this, and because they are nothing in themselves or at least not objects, but at most signify only inner feelings, they are the best means of designating concepts.*[4]

Talk of 'inner feelings' sells the pass. If concepts germinate out of the internal significations of linguistics, how can one Kantian anthropologist be entirely sure that he understands what the other one intends by his concepts? The one grand narrative of western philosophy on which all are agreed is that it has been, since the Cartesian cogito and Leibniz's windowless monad, a consistent progress in the atomising individualism of consciousness. Subjectivity's emergence in the heroic generation that produced the first rationalising individual in the philosophy of Descartes, not long after the theatre had given birth to his elder brother in Hamlet, prepared an intellectual legacy that tied all speculative consciousness to the individual, triumphantly or tragically as taste determined. The one attempt to propagate a transformative collective praxis from the socially produced nature of consciousness having misfired, philosophy turned back to linguistics on something like the late-Kantian model, and then back further still to the sceptical Cartesian in deconstruction. Every consciousness in conceptual thought is a Robinson Crusoe, washed up in the middle of nowhere, struggling to make sense of its environment and listening intently for any other sign of life. The audible world turns out to be no more unifying than the sense of taste, which standing conceptually for subjectivity par excellence, leaves two men unable to agree on whether meat tastes better with seasoning or without. Indeed, sound is just as productive of stratification as any other aesthetic medium, as was suggested by Adorno and Horkheimer's anachronising reading of the myth of Odysseus and the Sirens in *Dialectic of Enlightenment* (1947), in which the hero, lashed to the mast to prevent his being seduced by the singing into redirecting the ship, is as able to enjoy the recital nonetheless as is the bourgeois gentleman in the concert-hall, while his crew, their ears plugged with wax so that they keep rowing on oblivious, are the insensate proletariat for whom the Sirens could just as well be caterwauling harpies. Where language isn't for modernist consciousness a lure, it is more conventionally a prison, falsely incarcerating the 'things of the world', according to Serres. Having left the task of establishing communication between humans unfinished, it moved on to the creation of learning, generating the sciences and the racket of knowledge, its deep structures of syntactic rationality producing the metaphysical where it didn't consider itself to be adapting to it. For Kant, language is the principal object of hearing, the instrument that bodies forth the thoughts of others, but by the era of Wittgenstein's *Tractatus*, the instrument is playing the man. Language is a series of games with its own rules, by means of which it is taught to infants and animates the circulation of functional communication between isolate adults. It would lose even this level of concretion in deconstructive thought, where linguistic terms are only very loosely bound to their referents, and empty signifiers float by like cumulus clouds, covering the whole earth for a moment with their passing shadows. '[S]ound is, as it were, the least incorporated matter,' compared to the other sense-objects, according to Jean-Luc Nancy. 'After having been heard, it still remains somewhere out there,'[5] a fatuity modern experience put to flight on the western front, eighty years before it was uttered.

Only when sound became the immaterial background to irrationality turned lethal, in the relentless explosions and gunfire of the Great War, did it finally manage to unite men by smashing their nervous sensibilities to bits. The war did not quite inaugurate the technique of dismantling humans to their bare components – the neurological condition that would come to be known as shell-shock was recorded during the Boer War of 1899-1902 – but the mass production of subjective destitution it undertook produced around twenty million casualties among the survivors who never recovered from the alternation of relentless bombardment by shells, grenades and machine-gun fire, the screams of wounded and dying men, the shrieking of mutilated horses, with intervals in which a condition of hyper-tensile aural vigilance was all that might lie between death and survival. The last war of European imperialism was the first in history in which men habitually couldn't see the enemy, leaving combatants entirely dependent on the sense of hearing that the daily racket of battle did so much to destroy. Those who returned typically spoke of the din as being the hardest thing, next to the squalor and insanity of the slaughter itself, to endure. Field hospitals carried out what running repairs they could on the shattered, before their commanders returned them to the front.

Two-thirds of war invalids on all sides ended up being sent back into action. What they saw would haunt the survivors to the end of their days; what they were forced to hear, over and over through the tumultuous chaos of a static conflict that wouldn't quite grind to a halt, sent them home disjointed, prey to sudden terrors, brittle with hyper-acusis, their dreams haunted by oneiric detonations real enough to wrench them awake. Posted to France in November 1915, a private in the City of Liverpool King's Regiment approached the guns for the first time:

> *[O]n the night of the 29th, we actually started for the front line. Where we had been lying in bivouac the noise of the guns had been an incessant thunder. We had found time to pity the poor devils who were already in the thick of it. Now we found ourselves approaching the monster. Gradually, as we moved, we were enwrapped in that almost homogeneous sea of sound, and shells burst nearer and nearer. A young soldier of my own section was hit by a shell fragment square between the eyes. His cries haunt me now. 'Mother of God! Mother of God!' he shrieked time and time again. We left him behind where he lay, whimpering 'Mother of God! Good God! I'm blind!' It got in my ears. 'Mother of God!' I reiterated, scarcely knowing what I was saying. Forward we stumbled into a mist that seemed to grow ever thicker. So great was the noise that the order to keep touch with one another was passed only by means of shouting our hardest, and our voices sounded like flutes in a vast orchestra of fiends. All at once I became conscious of another sound. A noise like the crisp crackle of twigs and branches, burning in a bonfire just beyond my vision in the mist, made me think I must be approaching some*

> *burning building. I realised, when my neighbour on the right dropped with a bullet in the abdomen, that the noise was machine-gun and rifle fire...*[6]

Although those the Great War damaged irreparably found it impossible to reconnect the sonic landscape they had endured with a post-bellum world roaring and hooting and clanking peaceably on its way, advanced art had already begun to incorporate the textural noise of everyday life into its practices. Luigi Russolo, house composer of Italian Futurism, had written a manifesto in 1913 that bade an unsentimental farewell to what had become the tired timbres and formal delicacies of the expired classical mode. 'For many years Beethoven and Wagner shook our nerves and hearts,' he wrote. 'Now we are satiated and we find far more enjoyment in the combination of the noises of trams, backfiring motors, carriages and bawling crowds than in rehearsing, for example, the *Eroica* or the *Pastoral*.'[7] The *intonarumori* (noise-makers) that Russolo built, each emitting through an amplifying horn a different species of one of the six noise families that the manifesto outlined, howled and shrieked in cacophonic recitals in Milan and Genoa, Paris and London, mostly accompanied by the rioting with which audiences of the early-twentieth century greeted every fresh aesthetic outrage. Rumours of the recent war did nothing to shame the Art of Noises into respectful silence. Silence was the abode of the long-dead past, the solace of the moribund, and in any case, the father of Futurism, Filippo Marinetti, had seen action on the eastern front in Turkey, and had written a sputtering ecstatic account of it in a letter home to Russolo. In the 1920s, noise-music entered an embattled truce with traditional sonority at concerts that combined formulaic orchestral work – serenades and chorales – written by Russolo's brother Antonio with the accompaniment of an *intonarumori* ensemble. Under the banal progressions of the orchestral melodies, the noise-makers crepitate and gurgle, wail and bleat in a tortured *obbligato*, sounding to later ears nothing like the urban landscape as intended, but more like the effects used in early sound-films to suggest the emergence of spectral apparitions. The surviving recorded fragments of *Risveglio di una Città* (*Awakening of a City*) evoke instead the awakening of zombies, the kinds of zombies that the war eventually delivered back to societies that had no further use for them. While its younger sibling Dada reviled the world war, Futurism revelled in it, but although their purposes were diametrically at odds, they used strikingly similar artistic tactics in furtherance of them – remorseless noise, gibbering phonetic meta-languages, calculated assaults on sensibility. The metaphysical dignity of the avant-garde in the 1910s is that it refused the consoling note that might have been expected of it, whether in the interests of naively reflecting or of belligerently confronting the mechanised world, whose incessantly stridulating gears not even death escaped.

To the shell-shocked, only quiet helped, and then only partly, and then only with the corollary that quietness all the more threw into relief sudden incursions of monstrous sound – the clink of a spoon in a teacup, a door-handle turning, the telephone ringing – which their ragged nerves could not withstand. The shattering din of the trenches, alternating with tensed periods of waiting, during which one would hear the gathering premonitory sounds of the next assault, rendered the auditory dimension primeval once again, but with the added torment that, compared to their paleolithic ancestors, men now understood its significations all too well. Across the Channel in Kent, the distantly audible crashing of explosives from Flanders and northern France was like a daily rumour of war. In *Shell Shock and Its Lessons* (1917), a pair of Manchester medics, G Elliot Smith and TH Pear, wrote that 'before this epoch of trench warfare very few people have been called upon to suppress fear continually for a very long time ... [S]uppression of emotion is a very exhausting process. As Bacon says, "We know diseases of stoppings and suffocations are the most dangerous in the body; and it is not much otherwise in the mind".'[8] Steeling themselves against fear as best they could, the victims of shellshock were preparing their entire surrender to it when the danger was over. Nearly ten million combatants had been consumed in the clash of empires, but the world, pausing to memorialise them with an un-ironic silence every November, largely preferred not to dwell on what had happened, racketing on regardless, whistling through the dark like the approaching shells that had once lit up the faces of the terrified.

Politics of Sound

All processes of human cause and effect beget politics. Somebody who does something that has an impact on others should sooner or later have to answer for it. This is what politics ideally is, and since universal suffrage in conditions of parliamentary representation, it has taken upon itself the duty of giving voice either to the proletarian voiceless or to the bourgeois silent majority. Noise became politics at the midpoint of the nineteenth century when the bedlam of the industrial world grew so deafening that aestheticians couldn't hear themselves think through it. Thomas Carlyle had a sound-proofed room built for him in the 1850s at the top of his house in Chelsea, which, although it efficiently muffled the duller sounds, still allowed the sharper to penetrate. The air about had gradually filled up with cockerels crowing with clockwork regularity, in competition with the screeching of a neighbour's macaw, the piercing blart of steam-whistles from the railway, boys rattling sticks along the railings, boys yelling the headline news, the shrill pneumatic piping of hand-cranked street-organs churning the same melody over and over while their operators bellowed for money and boys sang tunelessly along. Not just Carlyle and his wife Jane, but the inventor of the difference engine too, had been reduced by the heedless racket of the modern world to purgatorial phono-phobia, helplessly soliciting the insolent defiance of those who produced it:

> *As [Charles] Babbage lay dying in 1871, his son Henry, who shared a suspicion of beggars from years of military service at outposts of the East India Company, found 'a man inciting boys to make a row with an old tin pail' while organ-grinders converged on Dorset Street day and night to triumph in his father's passing.*[9]

Campaigns for noise abatement flourished throughout the latter part of the nineteenth century and the early years of the twentieth – hardly any was more tireless in its social-psychological researches and its lobbying than Julia and Isaac Rice's Society for the Suppression of Unnecessary Noise, launched in New York in 1906 in response to the incessant nocturnal hooting of horns by tugboats on the Hudson – but they found themselves everywhere confronted with accusations that they wished to return the modern world to a long-vanished bucolic somnolence, or that their imagined right to peace and quiet outbid the right of others to go about their business. If city-dwellers wanted the privilege of living in advanced urban civilisations, they had to accept the way privilege sounded. Factories blew their steam-whistles, corn-vendors and newsboys yelled along the sidewalks, dogs barked, cats yowled, the newly fashionable domestic parrots squawked and prattled, barrel-organs extruded Strauss waltzes like yards of Bockwurst being hand-turned from the machine, and horse-drawn carriages clattered in concert over the cobblestones, at least until they began to be replaced by privately owned motor-vehicles with their backfiring engines, spluttering starters, merrily hallooing drivers and honking horns. Tranquillity was for the agrarian hinterland. Abatement campaigners achieved significant partial victories around the world, mainly over the barrel-organs and the night-time intonations of horns and sirens, but about the roar and bustle of commerce and traffic, they could do nothing. If practical politics is very largely the art of organising people to prevent other people from doing things to them, its besetting weakness is that it only begins, by definition, when the problem it has identified is already well advanced. Pressure-groups especially can only wish that more people had seen it coming at an earlier stage, or ideally before it all started, or that those who did had been heeded. That they hardly ever do is what handicaps all campaigns with the air of hopelessly trying to turn back the tide, which is not to say they are never successful, only that the tide has always already had a head-start. Nor was there much general agreement about what constituted an acceptable level of noise in the urban environment.

In an article for the *Fortnightly Review* in November 1878, 'Civilisation and Noise', the British psychologist James Sully argued that modern ears had been overtaken by a 'whole Iliad of afflictions', resulting in a 'jerky or jarring excitation of some of the nervous fibres.'[10] The great cities were hotbeds of neurasthenia, breeding unstable and damaged individuals whose finer sensibilities were being shredded in the interests of careering commerce, or in no interest at all. Modern noise was an anthropological development of unprecedented magnitude, tending to the etiolation of the senses in general, and ultimately to the depletion of moral responsibility. Barely was the cry of protest raised than it was shouted down by a *Spectator* editorial that poured scorn on Sully's sense of priorities: 'We cannot be at the same time both manly and superfine. If we are to elevate questions of minute sensibility into questions of morality, we shall soon pass over questions of morality, as of relatively even less importance than questions of minute sensibility.'[11] Sully had complained of the barking of dogs, the cackling of hens and the screaming of babies, all perfectly natural sounds about which nobody could do anything, unless they were to stoop to the recourse alleged against Goethe, that he had once poisoned a neighbour's dog to be free of its interminable yapping. The Dr

Sullys of the contemporary city were on the losing side of the argument, according to the editorialist: 'the superfine must either go into retirement, or adapt themselves to the average habits of their fellow-creatures'. They should either make sure they live well away from noisy neighbourhoods or, where they cannot, they should learn to disregard the surrounding noise, or just exercise a little patience, and 'if none of these remedies be adequate ... try a little cotton-wool'. It was the thin end of a dangerous wedge. If you acceded to the demand for peace and quiet, you would soon have to accede to demands for the removal of eyesores and other offensive sights, or of objectionable smells, such as the pungently distracting musk worn by some people at the theatre, or the fume of a lady's scented notepaper. Those who suffered offence to their 'auditory sensibilities', the writer contended, enclosing the words in ironic scare-quotes each time, were wishing on the whole of civil society, not just themselves, a wholly paradoxical reclusion. For Sully, what aggravated the nuisance of noise itself was the evident complacency towards the feelings of others of those who caused it – manual labourers, pet-owners, nursing mothers, boys setting off jumping-jacks in the street, and many another insensitive brute.

> *The man with a finely set, musical ear has practically to live with barbarians who actually take pleasure in harsh and unlovely sounds, and with many more semi-civilised who are quite indifferent to such noises. Not only children but adults love to tease and excite their dogs, and this seems to show that they positively enjoy the sensations of loud sound which they thus evoke. The fondness of a certain class of people for screaming birds points to the same primitive conditions of sensibility.*[12]

For the better part of the next half-century, campaigns against noise would be accented with the tones of class disdain, even where the vociferous had the welfare of working people, who both generated the noise of labour and had to endure it more than others, conscientiously at heart. In the present era, anger over the noise made by others is frequently accompanied by caricatures of the intellectual level of the 'morons' or 'brain-dead' who produce it. This tone is the tactical recourse of those left defenceless by the invasiveness of noise, now widely characterised as a form of pollution, and almost as insoluble. It is the exquisite angst of those who object to being kept awake at night by thudding techno, or the voices of troubled couples screaming at each other, that they don't want to be banished to the silent limbo of uninhabited regions, only to live without sonic excess. Where the people next door have long since stopped hearing each other enough, their neighbours are likely to hear them too much.

The socially divisive view of noise hardly chimes harmoniously with the philosophical conception of the auditory sense as in some way archaically unifying. Adorno and Hanns Eisler, pondering the regressive tendencies of contemporary film music in the 1940s, suggest that 'to react with the ear, which is fundamentally a passive organ in contrast to the swift, actively selective eye, is in a sense not in keeping with the present advanced industrial age and its cultural anthropology.' Technical progress in auditory media has hardly kept pace with developments in ocular technology. 'For this reason acoustical perception preserves comparably more traits of long bygone, pre-individualistic collectivities than optical perception.'[13] Not all unification is socially beneficent of course, which is why a fascist demagogue instinctively resorted to sound media to weave his society into a close-grained uniform fabric. At a time when motion pictures were still silent, the radio was an obvious propaganda tool. Those of the enlightened who used the medium to counteract the hypnotising effects of mass society, such as Walter Benjamin, who gave regular talks for youngsters and their elders on German radio in the late 1920s and early 1930s, worried diligently about the distantiating nature of the medium even as they did so. The technical marvel of early radio was soon subject to the congestion of increasing numbers of stations interrupting each other across ever narrower margins of wavelength, which led in the last days of Weimar Germany to the establishment of ten large regional radio stations that would ostensibly guarantee unimpeded reception, but only exacerbated the problem by constructing their own packed schedules. In any case, there was always more likely to be sinister intent, as Benjamin noted: 'Long-range propaganda instruments are desired in case of war.'[14] And indeed by the time of the Nazi takeover in January 1933, one day after Benjamin had given what would be his final broadcast, a ready-made state network of radio stations lay at Hitler's disposal. The technological fascination of radio during its early years had scarcely weakened by the turn of the 1930s. Developing out of wireless telegraphy from Hertz and Marconi onwards, it stood at the forefront of the great leaps in communications technology by which the last century transmuted scientific breakthroughs into forms that were both miraculous and alienating. The allure of an invention that could relay voices from the ether out of what were apparently the crudest types of apparatus – literally often nothing more than a metal box on the table – was altogether bewitching. It held its first generation of home users spellbound, and did nothing to conceal the apparent link to the spirit-world that its very immateriality seemed to promise. During and after the gargantuan slaughter of the Great War, there were many who fancied they heard the voices of their lost ones, embodied in their very disembodiment, crackling over the airwaves through the radio cabinet, in hopeless compensation for their actual bodies having been blown to irretrievable pieces. Benjamin adopted the language of the séance to greet the audience of one of his adult talks – 'Dear invisible ones!' Even while he used the medium to educate and contend, he remained deeply suspicious of its inherent contradictions. A cultural institution that doesn't engage the receptive expertise that all previous cultural forms inculcated in their audiences, from the Greek tragic theatre to Victorian pulpit oratory, suggests that it will treat them as nothing more than passive consumers. What reduces people to the philistine idiocy of switching it off in protest is not the content, but the voice in which it talks to them. 'And why is it that no one tells the voice what is expected of it, what will be appreciated, what will not be forgiven?'[15] – Benjamin demands. The answer to those questions would prove to lie in the very medium that provoked them. Regression to the indolence of political defeat, reinforced by the ideological narrow-mindedness of those in control of the entertainment media, are the story the Frankfurt School would tell of twentieth century culture. A voice booming through the speaker telling Germany to awake conceived its audience in much the same way as would its successor, peddling the soothing balm of 'easy listening' after the ensuing cataclysm – as a malleable mass it hardly needed to see.

Historical forces acting on the human ear began to effect profound anthropological changes in the first era of domestic radio. Not only did the broadcasts have a heteronomous quality that one didn't experience when playing phonograph records of one's own choosing but, overriding the chatter of local stations, the medium quickly assumed a nationwide remit in each of its territories. It brought with it a new kind of social homogeneity, one that did not involve participating in large gatherings or sitting in audiences in the concert halls and theatres, but could be enjoyed comfortably and comfortingly in one's own home. Although the structure of transmission was from a distant centralised source to the private domestic setting, everybody knew that everybody else was listening to the same concerts and plays and news bulletins, the first Royal Christmas message broadcast throughout the British Empire by George V in 1932, the inaugural year of the BBC's World Service, or in the United States, between 1933 and 1944, the 'fireside chats' of President Roosevelt. An imagined cultural community became entirely real. Even Goebbels' propaganda ministry, having at first commandeered the airwaves for the broadcast of Hitler's speeches, the harangues of party rallies and military marches, quickly realised that there was something that brushed against the grain of the medium in using it exclusively for these purposes. In due course, the Grossdeutscher Rundfunk would broadcast much the same mixed programme of variety shows, classical concerts and dance-music as was being beamed at British and American audiences, only with the lingering minatory proviso in the Third Reich that tuning in to a foreign radio station was a punishable offence. If the malevolent intentions of demagogues, blasting in sonic tirades from the ubiquitous loudspeakers mounted on lamp-posts in the Germany of the 1930s, tended to create inner resistance in their hearers, to the form of address if not its content, the subtler tones of friendlier voices were considerably more ingratiating, but perhaps for that reason all the more unsettling in their potential.

> *When a million or more people hear the same*
> *subject matter, the same argument and appeals,*
> *the same music and humour, when their attention*
> *is held in the same way and at the same time to the*
> *same stimuli, it is psychologically inevitable that they*
> *should acquire in some degree common interests,*
> *common tastes, and common attitudes. In short, it*
> *seems to be the nature of radio to encourage people*
> *to think and feel alike.*[16]

This at least was the conclusion of researchers at Harvard University in the same period. Their laboratory experiments established that subjects given a piece of contentious text to read would be inclined to be critical of its assumptions, but a parallel study group who heard it as a radio broadcast through loudspeakers were more inclined to accept it unquestioningly. The voice, the broadcast voice pre-eminently, was mightier than the pen. The suspicions of emigré intellectuals in the New School for Social Research in the United States were being objectively borne out. Trained in passive listening by the mass entertainment media, people had been softened up for the dictatorships that had already broken upon Europe in the form of totalitarianism, but doubtless also for the cultural hegemony that in all countries would outlast their defeat. In an expansive history of sound that included a programme about radio history, broadcast on BBC radio, David Hendy claimed that

> *This, then, was radio's great triumph: even though the words it broadcast were disembodied, came from hundreds of miles away and were addressed to an anonymous mass audience, they somehow still felt to the listener at home as if they were addressed personally to him or her – and by a real person, someone who was there in the same room.*[17]

The extrapolation missing from this account is that precisely this character is what suited it perfectly to be the bearer of the exogamous consciousness that people mistake for their own, the effect of which depends crucially on its employing the most refined means of deception at its disposal to inculcate its messages. Consumed every day, the mass media of radio and its successor, television, soon enough pardoned their recipients from the duty of remembering that their apparently cohesive effect was only a simulacrum of political and cultural community, relying for its efficacy on the stealth operation encapsulated in Hendy's 'somehow'. 'This might sound as if the dictators and salesmen won in the end,' he adds. 'But they have always had to meet listeners largely on the listeners' own terms. The broadcasters' voices reach us in *our* territory, not in theirs. And if they try to seduce us, we are always free to remain blithely unmoved.'[18] As to the idea of the listeners dictating the terms of the engagement, Benjamin had already noted in the early 1930s that 'no one tells the voice what is expected of it', and if they have been allowed to become more vocal since, it is only to demand more of what is being prepared anyway. It is just because the broadcast media are consumed at home rather than in the purpose-built arenas of other forms of entertainment that they achieve the illusory effect of consensus. Everybody turning on the radio or the rolling TV news channels in the morning is convinced that they are choosing to receive it. The alternative, what Hendy calls remaining blithely unmoved, is the stance of impotent denial, illustrated by the example he promptly gives of the Welsh family observed by the BBC in 1938. Amid a hubbub of domestic noise, arguments, neighbours calling in to chat, the radio is on, broadcasting a concert conducted by Toscanini. Only one person in the room is trying to listen, and even though the effect is entirely ruined by everybody else's philistinism, he doesn't turn it off. 'And I suspect that if he ever did,' Hendy interjects from the next century, 'everyone else in the room would very quickly shout at him to turn it back on again.' But why? This is his paradigm of being blithely unmoved, remember. 'Even if they are not listening with their full attention, they are still listening. Even in the background, radio's burble is still more than a meaningless noise. And if it weren't there, they would miss it like hell.'[19] It would be difficult to imagine a more elegantly concise explanation of the operations of ideology. Almost nobody is aware of actively listening to it, and yet all are conscious of it. What seems to be nugatory 'burble', and therefore entirely harmless and ignorable, is anything but meaningless. The cognitive discomfiture promised by the torment of its being turned off signals that it has become a kind of life-support system, indispensable for creating and sustaining the illusions by which the subjects of a purely functional collective are reconciled to its monotony. If this dependent state can be construed as being 'blithely unmoved', it is only in the sense that what would brutally move the consumers is being deprived of it, an unthinkable condition in which, thrown back on their own resources in a private space with no external voice, they would miss it like hell, exactly because its function is to disguise hell.

Passivity of Hearing

If the eye categorises, apprehends, analyses and conceptualises its objects, turning material things at the same time into phenomena that can be acted on as well as ideational propositions that comprise the objective world, the ear typically only receives its sense-objects passively. True, it must often interpret what it hears when the cause isn't immediately apparent, but its functioning is otherwise one of tensed receptivity rather than active instrumentality. Looking at the unwieldy pile of books on the desk, the eye is the means by which intentionality functions to tidy them back on to the shelves. Intentionality is not characteristic of audition. The sound of the dripping tap may prompt one to fix it tomorrow, but the general disposition of the ear is one of idleness. Adorno and Eisler argue that the function of hearing in advanced industrial society, and its accompanying entertainment industry, is both archaic and modern, the former in the sense that it harks back to pre-conceptual levels of consciousness, the instinctual life of primitive collectivities, the latter because the rationalised society, in which human activity is as ergonomically programmed as are the routines of factory and office workers, has seized on the very pre-conceptual character of sound – music especially – to reconcile its members to prevailing social conditions. 'The greater the drabness of this existence, the sweeter the melody.'[20] The lack of practical application in hearing, which serious music attempted to overcome, is precisely why it is prized as a sense by commercial culture. That phenomenon familiar from the earliest days of television, when the volume seems to turn itself up as the advertising breaks intervene, is not imaginary. The intention is to pin the viewer's ears back, because he cannot pin them back for himself. It has led to the widespread habit of pressing the 'mute' button during ad-breaks, so that their peremptory babble can be denied, even though the viewer still stares untroubled at the soundless images. Sound is political partly because it so easily lends itself to manipulation for these ideological ends, but also because it is the very image of externality acting on passivity, from the neighbours' inconsiderate din to the hubbub of imperative voices that hermetically encapsulate the individual in their web of intentionality and lies. Hurry now while stocks last! Your last chance to enter! If you don't play, you can't win! Lines will be closing in sixty seconds!

Use your vote to make your voice heard! The mendacity of representational politics, in which voters trust a member or members of a centralised parliament to carry out their wishes, or at the very least act in the best interests of the country as a collective, is founded on the metaphor of hearing, a stance that it only feels itself obliged to perform parodically at election time, when the members must once more solicit the popular vote. Once re-elected, the class of political functionaries continues to please itself, in covert or open defiance of the popular will. The gradual emergence of universal suffrage in the western world and then beyond, convinced its clients that patronage and privilege were a thing of the past. Voters were the masters, hiring and firing governments at will every four or five years. Any government that failed to listen to the people was as doomed as the self-perpetuating bureaucratic oligarchies of the *soi-disant* people's democracies eventually were. As the systematic fraud of electoralism has sunk in, voter participation has begun dropping away in the democratic countries, and indeed, in the early years of the twenty-first century, abstention – often wrongly construed as apathy – appears to be the only kind of popular disaffection that genuinely worries the parliamentary class. Participation in elections to the European Parliament is often minimal, and not just in those countries, pre-eminently the UK, that are temperamentally unreconciled to its corrupt and flaccid institutions. What has replaced cooperation at the ballot-box and, in the more affluent countries at least, organised dissent in the streets has been the growing popularity of online petitions, which have the advantage of not necessitating voter registration and of being the most indolent form of declaring an opinion, which may well have changed by the following week anyway. To give the impression that such exercises count, governments have become minimally adept at looking concerned about them, and might even act in accordance with the wishes of an occasional sufficiently well-subscribed one. These instruments are, however, no more effective in turning the citizen into an engaged political agent than is stepping into the voting-booth and arming oneself with a pencil. Nobody in their right minds could have imagined any government responding to a mass petition not to bail out the criminal banks following the financial disaster of 2008, the global policy that made those ruined by the banks pay for those who had ruined them to carry on regardless, but a petition to stop a rancorous controversialist from entering the country might succeed. He was probably going to be banned anyway, but it suits the executive to pretend that it is responding to the wishes of the populace. Town meetings may rowdily preserve something of the flavour of people assuming responsibility for what happens to them and their communities, but they can only be fully effective where everybody is in full possession of the facts, a potential catastrophe that is generally the concern of local authorities to preclude. Meanwhile, if the argument against Wikileaks was that if nobody in a position of power is ever able to say anything private, the affairs of the world would never be subject to amelioration, it was also true that much of what is said is depressing either for its cynical manipulativeness or its cretinous *naïveté,* and the same state authorities who watch over every last movement of their citizens through an industrialised surveillance apparatus go to inordinate lengths to avoid any return scrutiny. Where hope persists in triumphing over experience in electoral politics, people will from time to time be sufficiently enthused to vote for a candidate or party that appears to be ready to take a transformative, or even just more honest, approach, with the proviso that as the *status quo ante* then rolls on unchecked, the enthusiasm is easily transmuted into the cynical wisdom of saying that they probably really wanted to change things, but the mechanisms of the state won't permit it, as though anybody standing for election within those mechanisms wasn't already eager to help run them. In a telling aside as early as 1985 in his chapter on hearing, Michel Serres speaks of 'these times when politics has been reduced to publicising the State'.[21] Once conceived as the activity by which official structures were challenged, politics is now only the means of perpetuating them. Everybody is free to endorse the incumbent government's programme, or else to opt for an alternative party's programme, but the technicised procedures by which the programmes are arrived at, which are entrusted to a variety of agents, from economists with axes to grind to public relations consultants for whom the political process is much as a saleable commodity as are digital entertainment consoles, together with the purely administrative nature of political programmes themselves, are taken as given. What online petitions bring about, by contrast, is the idea that merely hearing its own voice is enough to persuade the atomised collective of its own political efficacy, but listening to its own voice was never the problem. What it needed was to make executive power stop prating and listen to it but, as Serres also contends, '[t]he collective only believes in its own noise'.[22]

Of all the technological means of disembodying sound – the

human voice in particular – from its origins, the telephone has been the most deeply entangled with the experience of everyday life. Even in the era of micro-electronics, and despite the development of online telephony with visual access between callers, its essential function remains unchanged. The act of holding an apparatus to the side of one's head so as to hear the voice of somebody distant, as though listening for the sound of the sea in a conch, which looked ripe for being superseded even before the cradle telephone began in the 1920s to replace the candlestick model with its separate mouthpiece, continues to be the most widespread form of direct distance communication in the world. Premised on seventeenth century experiments by Robert Hooke into the acoustic phenomenon of vibratory sound conduction between two cups connected by a string or wire, the electrically modulated device that had as many inventors two hundred years later as there were entrepreneurs who saw its commercial potential, but which was famously patented by Alexander Bell in the United States in 1876, the telephone was conceived as a vocal adjunct to the electric telegraph, an apparatus that could transmit human speech rather than just the dots and dashes that stood in for it. The breakthrough moment for Bell came when his assistant Thomas Watson in the adjacent room of a noisy office, its windows open to the racket of the street on a hot June day, twanged a clock-spring that was connected to a similar device on Bell's desk by a wire. Amid the general clamour, the tiny sound was clearly audible. The telephone might be a means of privately conveying intimate sound within a general ambience of noise, but its domestic and business dissemination soon made it the harbinger of noise, both in the ways in which it was used, with early subscribers shouting into the receiver in acknowledgement of the distance being covered, but also because of the background array of inexplicable noises transmitted along the line.

> *Watson hung about in the lab well into the night 'listening to the many strange noises in the telephone and speculating as to their cause'. Was s snap, followed by a grating sound, the aftermath of an explosion on the surface of the sun? Was something like the chirping of a bird a signal from a far planet? What occult forces were just-noticeably at work in the recesses of telephonic sound?*[23]

Telephones combined this eerie aspect with the more prosaic peremptoriness of their functioning: the insistent ringing of a machine next door when there was nobody there to answer; the shrill whine they were designed to emit in the case of malfunction; the shouting of many voices at once in an office. Hearing one-half of somebody else's conversation being yelled into the transmitter, a phenomenon that still aggravates people in the context of the widespread use of mobile phones on public transport, led Bell himself to forgo having a telephone anywhere near his own office once the thing was in general use. Then too, there were the circumstances in which it might ring at an unexpected hour or in a discommoding social context – 'Pardon me, Mr Walton, you are wanted on the telephone' – and which could only presage the communication of some news that was too dire to await other means of conveyance. No sound is more instantly evocative of the crash of doom than a phone ringing during the night. In the business context, what was divulged over the phone required an instant response, the more so since the cogitative silence that might elapse during a face-to-face meeting is anathema to the structure of telephone communication. Silences were and are a breach of etiquette, or at best indicated that you had probably, at a crucial moment, been cut off. Early domestic systems were constructed as party-lines that might be open to six or more separate subscribers, with the result that your shouted confidence might innocently be eavesdropped by another caller on the line. This is the animating plot set-up of Anatole Litvak's film noir classic, *Sorry Wrong Number* (1948), in which a wealthy bedridden heiress (Barbara Stanwyck) inadvertently listens in on a plot to kill a wealthy heiress, who turns out to be herself. Stanwyck's panic-stricken demeanour, one hand clutching the side of her face while the other holds against the opposite ear the monstrous black apparatus from which she cannot tear herself away, is compounded by the restless eyes whose focus alternates between a point directly ahead of and a little below her gaze, or else to a notional window in the left middle distance, beyond which the nefarious plot is being implicitly concocted somewhere. Where does one look when speaking on the phone? When the transmitter was mounted on a stand, you looked into that. Once it was built into the same part of the apparatus as the receiver, the telephone user accustomed herself to looking without seeing at a fixed spot. If what her eyes take in becomes for a moment consciously distracting, she stops hearing what is being said to her on the phone. Equally, however, when the phone is delivering threat, one readily constitutes the caller as a visible presence inside the receiver, as a way of nullifying the sinister nature of an unembodied voice. The victim in the slasher movie harassed on the phone by the psychopath screams her defiance back at it without holding the receiver to the ear, as does Jamie Lee Curtis in *Halloween* (1978). Somebody who has been subjected to the indignity of being hung up on conventionally stares quizzically into the mouthpiece before following suit. The phone could hardly been better fitted for the purposes of general menace and sexual harassment, preserving as it does a safe distance between offender and victim. It lent itself ideally to abuse by blackmailers, bullies, sexually infatuated stalkers. Only a generation ago, it wasn't possible to tell what number was calling before one decided whether or not to answer, or identify the number of a nuisance caller subsequently without asking the telephone exchange, once the line was free again, to trace the call, which as often as not would turn out to be a usefully anonymous public call-box.

Mendacity was built into the function of the technology from the very beginning. The play-acting of incorporeal voices at eighteenth century phantasmagorias and at the séances of the Victorian era now came within the ambit of everybody who could afford a telephone. A wife calling the office after hours to see whether her husband was working late, as he had said he was, could put on a different voice to disguise herself. Pranksters only needed the sound of a clattering typewriter in the background to convince a victim they were calling from a tax office or police station. Anybody being faced with an accusation they didn't want to confront could suddenly pretend that the line was bad, as it frequently was, and that they couldn't hear, a bad line often resulting in being abruptly cut off. In the present day, crank-calling has become an entertainment medium, while the telecom systems are now permanently polluted by cold-calling and telemarketing seven days a week, so that nobody any longer wants to answer a ringing phone, although surprisingly few people will yet admit they don't. Answering-machines and call-blockers are the evidence of an entire parallel technology, which has developed in concert with abuse of the network by commercial computer-dialling, in order to negate the purposes of telephony itself. In the era of wireless broadband, landlines are becoming functionally irrelevant, and even the mobile phone, which stands by in case of emergencies, lends itself to hundreds of other uses. If the telemarketers could be driven off the line, it might be possible to imagine leisurely telephone conversation coming back into fashion for nostalgic reasons, two people sharing vocal intimacies with each other over an apparatus whose rudimentary form, two tin-cans connected with string, was once known colloquially as a 'lovers' telephone'. The advantage of incorporeal contact is that one hears the inflections of doubt or of devotion, panic or misery, that one doesn't hear when the face is present to over-perform them visibly. Everybody can recall an instance of suddenly hearing, the first time they speak to somebody on the phone, the strength of his regional accent, which they hadn't remarked in face-to-face conversation. The polygraph, which assesses the veracity or otherwise of what somebody is saying by measuring the frequencies of their vocal tones, is a fallible but more reliable indicator of dishonesty than visible gestural clues, and the telephone, before it was subordinated to the exigencies of purely functional communication, could be just as revealing, which explains why psychological ingenuity was determined from the very first to outwit it.

Spacelessness of Sound

Even where the source of sound is concretely known, sound alone possesses a spacelessness that lends itself to other kinds of mutability than the obvious material one of its delimited temporality. In an influential essay of 1930, 'Spooks in Radio', Günther Anders analysed the transient lack of a sense of place by which even the broadcast of a live performance was characterised.[24] The effect was doubled into even greater eeriness by the experience of one who leaves his apartment, only to hear, a few doors along the street, the same broadcast emerging from another house. Where precisely is this music coming from? The phenomenon is structurally analogous to that which Benjamin analyses in his famous essay, 'The Work of Art in the Era of Its Technological Reproducibility' (1936), in which the aura of the original work, in large part deriving from the spatial context – the mountaintop temple, the municipal art gallery – in which the original was experienced, vanishes ethereally from mechanically reproduced works.[25] The entertainment media of the early-twentieth century, the cinema pre-eminently, acknowledges the loss of aura by adapting its technical means and mode of expression to the culture of non-auratic reiterability. The film seen in a movie theatre in Cincinnati at the same time as it is showing in San Francisco is the same undifferentiated cultural artefact. Just as there is no distinction between them, no particular print or screening of the film earns itself the title of original – at least not in aesthetic terms. Sound stands in an ambivalent relation to the optical realm. It wants at the same time to be connected to its concrete source, where it has one, and to be granted ontological status in its own right. Neuroscientist Michael O'Shea claims that 'we tend to want to look at what we are listening to,'[26] as the eyes readily turn to any sudden source of sound that the brain's auditory response system has accurately located, just as they turn towards anything significant that might appear in the peripheral visual field, but whatever rapid autonomic response may occur, consciousness isn't subsequently as insistent on looking at sound-sources as that first perception demands. In many cases, there is nothing to look at anyway. Machines in the office emitting a low electronic hum while they function make no visual appeal, but nor do the voices of others coming through the telephone, or over the music-system. Secure in their lack of physical presence, they become material in themselves, rather than simply being acoustic properties of material objects. The continuities emphasised between the spirit-world and the disincorporated media of radio, phonographs and telephones are functionally dependent on the autonomy of the human voice as a substance in itself. In one of her simple early ghost stories, 'Wireless', written in the period when radio had come under intense cultural scrutiny for whatever spiritual significance it might possess, Agatha Christie has an elderly widow, Mrs Harter, hearing the voice of her departed husband coming to her over the radio, announcing that he will be returning soon to bear her off with him. The salient detail of the plot is that she has never owned a radio before, but has been talked into having one by her nephew as a distraction from her ill health, and is therefore only too capable of believing that the same apparatus that plays a concert of ballads from somewhere in the 'ether' may well also be capable of transmitting the voices of the dead from much the same place, both phenomena emerging from an aural bath of ambient electrical sound: 'in the middle of "Annie Laurie" a strange thing happened. There was a sudden break, the music ceased for a moment, the buzzing, clicking noise continued and then that too died away. There was dead silence, and then very faintly a low buzzing sound was heard.' It presages the voice of her late husband, Patrick. 'Mrs Harter got the impression that the machine was tuned in to somewhere very far away.' A couple of days later, during an 'orchestral selection', the same event recurs: 'Again, there was silence, the sense of distance, and finally Patrick's voice, not as it had been in life – but a voice rarefied, far away, with a strange unearthly quality.' The radio's phonic access to an immaterial realm beyond comprehension is not least evidenced by the repertoire of unfathomable noises that is its innate mechanical language. It belongs to the dawn of modern communication technology when, practically for the first time, people who used the new devices with which electrical science was furnishing the home hadn't the faintest idea how they worked, or in most cases the faintest inclination to know. The miraculous had become tangible, but in the most intangible of ways. It mustn't come as any surprise if occasionally it revealed aptitudes that hadn't previously been expected of it, veering off at its own disquieting tangents in its own sonic medium. 'Then click, buzz, and the orchestral selection was in full swing again.'[27]

These disembodyings of the voice should not, after all, be entirely unfamiliar. Something similar happens in everyday conversation when, as has been experimentally validated, the speaker in a face-to-face exchange looks at the addressee in a more sustained and focused way while speaking than the addressee looks at him. During the moments that the listener is not looking at the person speaking to her, the averted gaze is what enables her to concentrate on what is being said. Very often, particularly where some important information, or an argument at variance with their own, is being conveyed, people choose some neutral spot in the immediate environs, perhaps the patch of floor at their feet, to deaden their sight while they focus on the voice, so that as little optical distraction as possible enters their visual field, the speaking face with its mobile features and performative expressions frequently being the greatest distraction of all. For the same reason, people often demonstrate that they remember in greater detail what is said to them on the phone than what is said by somebody standing in front of them. The voice and its medium, human language, connotes the highest semantic value of sound outside the religious and aesthetic contexts. When Aristotle terms it 'a kind of sound *with meaning*', he invokes not just its intentionality, but its polysemic richness also. It aims to transmute passive audition into the alertness of active comprehension. Constructing an active engagement out of the passive sense of hearing is what led to the transformation of public attentiveness out of the oblivious or rowdily vociferous spectators of the opera-houses and theatres of the seventeenth and eighteenth centuries, into an attitude of orderly contemplativeness in which they earned the name of audiences. When theatre-goers entered and left as they pleased, chatted among themselves in full voice, transacted sexual and other commercial liaisons, and expressed their approval or derision at the performances as they saw fit, the dramatic presentations and music recitals knew their place as mere background. The arts of virtuoso performance grew out of the determination to capture and hold the attention of the crowd, or at least a section of it. It was the Romantic era that finally began to encourage people to shut up and concentrate, praising them in reviews in the public prints when they did, and initiating the process of enforcing auditorium etiquette on the masses. Eventually, it was only the social elites who still felt at liberty to talk and clink their wineglasses during performances, and even they were sometimes shamed into silence by shushing from the stalls below their boxes. 'The listening revolution represented a triumph not of aristocratic but of middle-class codes of conduct.'[28] What the invention of cultured listening also produced, however, was the incidental effect that those incapable of sitting still in self-restraint for so long betrayed themselves as the uncultivated rabble by their very incontinence. The measure of educated taste would henceforth consist in being able to remain statuesquely composed throughout every movement and every scene, to be able to stare transfixed at the pictures in the gallery, to be able to read in concentrated silence. Attentiveness enjoyed only a relatively short anthropological span, from roughly the dawn of the nineteenth century to the advent of the motion-picture, and has given way once more to the fidgety restlessness of cinema crowds, the renewed habit among classical audiences of applauding between movements and even during bravura solo passages, and outbreaks of mobile phone use even in the theatre. When the house-lights at Bayreuth were innovatively dimmed just before the start of performances from the 1870s onwards, Richard and Cosima Wagner were under the impression that they had returned total art to its origins in the mystical, in which the proper attitude on the part of communicants was an intense respectful quiet. In the case of music especially, the worshipful demeanour required cut across the very transports of feeling that the medium had sought to invoke ever since the storms of passion in the late Beethoven. While the filigree technicalities of Bach's toccatas, which would have repaid the studious attention fashionable by the following century, were heard where at all amid a natural public brouhaha, the riptides of the soul unleashed by romanticism were expected to be received in politely motionless vigilance. The effective class division by audience etiquette in the performing arts led to the abandonment of classical music to highbrows and the socially pretentious, while working people escaped instead to nightclubs, music-halls, café orchestras and dinner-dances, where it wasn't considered unruly to want to speak to the people with whom you were ostensibly socialising, instead of sitting in serried silent rows on a night out, all ignoring each other.

The idea that attentive listening is undermined by visuality is what led to the revival during Victorian aestheticism of the cultural trope of blindness as acute perception. Precisely because the unsighted had to fix their concentration on what they could hear, which led to the durable belief, partially validated by the brain sciences only relatively recently, that they hear more acutely than sighted people, they were also thought to perceive more deeply because their cognitive faculties were not seduced by the optical, as though cognition were not equally susceptible of aural blandishments. Blindness was capable of being parsed into privileged insight in Victorian sensibility, much as other forms of disadvantage, such as poverty and backwardness, could be ideologically construed as unsullied purity. 'In 1860 ... an article in the *National Review* wrote admiringly of the ancient philosophers who put out their eyes in order to concentrate their attention on the deepest meaning of things.'[29] Closing them might do just as well, as did the attendees of séances adjured to listen intently for the voices or rappings of the dear departed, the better that they might not see the spirit medium knocking on the table herself, or busily preparing the soap-and-egg white gloop that would be classified as ectoplasm when the credulous at last opened their eyes again. There may be meaning in human sound, but the Aristotelian interpretation may not have taken into account that meaning can be produced for all sorts of reasons, not least to the advancement of deception.

Whereas most of what is in the visual and tactile fields around human beings will outlive them, sound is imprisoned in temporality as humans themselves are. Concentrated listening is at least partly predicated on the idea that you might as well pay attention because you may not hear this again. The sense-objects of audition are as finite and as perishable as those of smelling and tasting, arguably more so still. This imbues aurality with the pathos of a fragility those covering their ears amid the din of the industrial cities would have been hard put to it to recall, except where they wanted the overlay of urban clamjaffery to cease so that they could listen to what remained of the emollient utterances of the natural world. 'Sound is always disappearing,' commented the composer David Toop on a radio broadcast about the links between sound and fear. 'That connects it with a sense of loss. Sound is always intimately connected to death.'[30] It was always easier for spiritualism's clients to imagine that the chasm between this world and the next had been bridged through auditory means than through the optical or the haptic. Ghosts are notorious for not keeping their visual appointments with the hopeful, and still less can they be relied on to brush one's hair lightly in the night or fasten throttling hands around one's neck, but any sound, the better if only momentary, can be elucidated as the incoherent signalling of those marooned in the spiritual hinterland. Recordings of their voices, known in the pseudo-science as EVPs (electronic voice phenomena), are remarkable for their strangulated fragmentary nature, as though they barely had anything to say, and for the fact that their receivers have blithely, or wilfully, forgotten how unfiltered radio signals behave. An audio-recording of the voice of the deceased ought to be more cheering to surviving relatives than the guttural phonemes belched out on magnetic tape for the enlightenment of paranormal researchers, but an EVP is taken for evidence that they are still alive somewhere in another dimension, not the abode of the blessed perhaps, but a place where they are apparently kept in a state of marginally articulate befuddlement. Rather than a loquacious afterlife, the death to which Toop feels sounds are tending is their own, their extinction committing them instantly to internal auditory memory until they can be heard again a second or a minute later, or a lifetime, or never.

Disquisitions on the predatory nature of the modern soundscape, which reached a peak in the 1930s after the formulation in 1929 of the decibel scale for recording intensities of noise, might be wishing fondly to hearken to the gentle sounds of the natural environment – the squawking roosters and howling dogs, the chirring of crickets, the moaning wind and rattling rain and booming thunder – but they also implicitly tended in the direction of an ideology of silence, as though the most comforting sound in the world was no sound. Where no-sound had ever existed wasn't certain. Not in the womb certainly, where the banging of Mother's heartbeat, the roaring circulation of her blood and the gurgles of her digestive system, made the microcosmic world an enveloping commotion. Nor in the trackless wastes of the cosmos, the constant expansion of which had in 1931 been extrapolated in logical retrospect back to a single infinitesimally small point of space and time by the Belgian physicist and Roman Catholic priest Georges Lemaître. Creation hadn't after all involved the design of a zoological garden in the Near East, posited Fr Lemaître, but more a divine breathing on the spark of the one bit of stuff that existed, igniting a material proto-apocalypse that would be semi-sardonically described by British astronomer Fred Hoyle on BBC radio in 1949 as the 'Big Bang'. Calculating the impact of sound waves up to 200,000 light years long against what the primordial air pressure can be assumed to have been, in accordance with the decibel logarithm, produces an estimate that the Big Bang probably peaked at a little under 120 dB, making it only a biggish bang in terms of how loud it would have sounded to anybody equipped with the auditory apparatus to hear its extremely low frequencies. The output of the sound-system in a large nightclub is typically around 130 dB. The atomic bombs dropped on Hiroshima and Nagasaki in 1945 each generated a shockwave of about 248 dB, the final eruption of

Krakatoa in 1883 probably more than 300 dB (a barometric reading equivalent to 172 dB was recorded at the gasworks in Batavia, one hundred miles from the blast-source). An expanding universe that was nothing more than the continuous aftermath of an explosion is only counter-intuitively conceived as naturally silent, but the exponentially expanding din of an industrial world of rapid population growth, increasingly given to wars fought with ever more titanic arsenals of munitions, seemed to be screaming out to return to, or at least explore, the blissful silence that was either its original element or *terra incognita*, depending on how different interpreters looked at it. Whether the yearning for silence was a nostalgia for the primeval – the depthless forests, the fathomless oceans, the wide empty plains across which transhumant paleolithic peoples tramped in search of survival – or whether it had a radical utopian dimension in its dream of an as yet unrealised state, contemporaneous with the communist imaginary driving the construction of the Soviet workers' state by show-trial and error, it could do no more than insist, in defiance of its own principle, on competing for public attention amid the bountiful sources of noise. Having finally desisted from the racket of building his shack at Walden Pond, Thoreau settled back to drink in the magnificent silence, only to find it was a relative luxury that gained scarcity value once it had suffered the steam-whistles of passing freight-trains to screech their worst. There was true silence in Antarctica, as Captain Robert Scott discovered on the Terra Nova expedition to the South Pole in 1910-12. It was captured on silent film by a documentary film-maker who accompanied Scott's party, Herbert Ponting, and released some years after under the title *The Great White Silence* (1924). The restoration of the print released in 2011 was accompanied by a bespoke musical soundtrack, but such audiences as there were – and they were not plentiful – in the 1920s listened only to the haunting silence of a frozen uninhabited continent. There was nothing Edenic about either the landscape or the desolate peace: 'The Antarctic Continent,' begins Ponting's first intertitle of the film, 'is an ice-clad wilderness of dazzling whiteness and appalling silence'. Nothing can rescue the idea of complete unbreachable silence from its status as life's negation.

Silence is not a case of not hearing anything, but of actively hearing nothing. With no other sense is there quite the wish that it be freed from its own sense-objects. The impulse can be a reflexive response to the habitual daily noise, but also to the anatomical fact that the ears never rest, not even in extremis, not even in coma. They are the body's alarm-system when the brain is taking a break from consciousness, but by the same token, they seem to let in too much of external reality when cognitive intensity is required. Ancient wisdom already knew the idea that wisdom itself needs to be fenced off from noise if it is to flourish. The voicelessness of silent monastic orders is not silence, only a liberation from all other voices but the internal, and the one that reads from the scriptures in the refectory. Officially imposed silences, as in the reading room at the library or in the silent carriage on the train, are straining towards their own fragmentation, as when people begin whispering or tapping at keyboards. Total silence, which is less elusive even in the modern metropolis than the popular conception would have it, is not a neutral medium like a vacuum, but is in itself something to listen to. Experiments with creating noiseless working environments have often foundered on the discomfiture that workers feel when there is virtually nothing going on in the aural ambience. Students writing essays frequently feel they work better in a chattery café, with the coffee-machine regularly adding its raucous spurt to the surrounding babble of conversation, than they do alone in the house. Silence, where it doesn't feel simply characterless and bland, a zone of dead neutrality that denotes stasis, is often felt to be threatening in some way. It is often used strategically as a cinematic device to suggest the imminence of menace. The only thing more frightening than the ticking of a time-bomb is the moment it stops. To a troubled sensibility, dead silence is in itself troubling; even when peaceful, it seems to portend something. Concentrated listening in silence is one of the indelible images of terror, because the sound of no-sound is the medium in which something frightful might be heard all the more clearly. What is unsettling about waking during the night is less the darkness than the apprehension of what one might hear. At such moments, consciousness, recently released from its suspension, is at its least reconciled with the external. It is as though the full functioning of the senses, of sight and hearing particularly, are what beguile subjective awareness to the existent, whereas their relative inoperativity forces them back upon their own resources, which are nothing but the distorted residue of what it gleaned in the broad daylight.

Silence during waking hours unsettles those whom it does primarily because it is the sound of nothing happening. If sound in its evanescence is always a token of the past, of what has been and gone, silence ought to figure a realm of atemporality, where nothing is perishable but everything endures. Ears disposed to a minimal level of background chuffle and mutter hear only that nothing can perish because nothing has come to be. If silence easily seems premonitory in many cases, whether menacingly or promisingly so, to people who don't like it, it represents the deadening of all possibility, a thick opacity through which nothing can be glimpsed. The trepidation they feel may be related to the isolating nature of silence, its lack of any evidence of other human activity, except that they often feel the same anxiety in silence even when somebody else is with them, particularly then because quiet can so often be misinterpreted as cold indifference. Those odd moments of silence that sometimes descend over two people conversing are electrified with anxiety by both parties frantically searching in their heads for something to say. Silence in such moments is rashly experienced as the defeat of intimacy, as though any prattle will suffice to cover a natural pause. In the realist British theatre of the early 1960s, the famous silences were routinely interpreted as all-too-eloquent chasms into which reified communication kept falling, but they could equally obviously just have been the natural rests that occur when neither party to a conversation is given to monologic effusion. Not so the entrenched hostilities of aphasia that George Steiner heard between competing sectors of society amid the incessant racket of the counter-culture:

> *The mumble of the dropout, the 'fuck-off' of the beatnik, the silence of the teenager in the enemy house of his parents are meant to destroy. Cordelia's asceticism, her refusal of the mendacities of speech, proves murderous ... We empty of their humanity those to whom we deny speech. We make them naked and absurd ... Break off speech to others and the Medusa turns inward.*[31]

Where the world falls silent, which is to say when the bedlam of pop music fills all the spaces that were once consecrated to civil converse, one of the load-bearing pillars of human community has been left structurally unsound. So it seemed to Steiner at the outset of the 1970s, composing an elegy for cultural decrepitude at Yale while music-systems in the rooms all around him pounded at the physical and sensible walls. The new 'literacies' of electric guitars and repetitive beat may make contestable claims for themselves, but their savagery has devoured the traditional linguistic aptitudes on which a predominantly literary culture was built. Language, according to Steiner, even the demotic, is a gamble against death. The verb-forms of the Indo-European language families are performative expressions of the hope for survival, through the very means of active agency. As long as we are doing something, we aren't dying. The point holds in both temporal directions: 'What the poet terms "glory" is a direct function of the felt reality of the future tense. The ordered density of remembrance hinges on the prodigal exactitudes of Indo-European preterites.'[32] There was once an unbreakable link, now broken, between the being-towards-death, as Heidegger formulates it, of all temporality and the conceptualities of linguistic tense-systems, the was, is and will-be that structure the expressive articulations of the 'fabric of life'. The insolent muteness that Steiner had begun to detect high and low at this period threatened nothing less than the apocalypse of a culture founded on spiritual loquacity, a culture not imprisoned in language in Wittgenstein's conception, but constructed from its versatile materials. 'Diminish that role, subvert that eminence, and you will have begun to demolish the hierarchies and transcendence-values of a classic civilisation. Even death can be made mute.'[33] Nothing in this analysis takes cognisance of the degree to which a linguistic culture has connived at its own diminution and subversion, by lending itself so readily to those very hierarchies, such as the political, juridical and ecclesiastical, that have so often not scrupled to crush whatever human detritus appeared in their way. The transcendence-values, sublime enough in the mind of Burke, were quite as adept at granting power the licence to destroy humanity for their own survival as they were at impressing on it the beauty of the lilies. Lyric poetry is notoriously helpless against institutionalised cruelty. And perhaps death, after all, having made numberless multitudes mute over the entirety of history, itself now deserves to be silenced.

The timelessness in silence, if timelessness there be, must struggle to overcome the desolation that a lack of both memory and futurity appear to threaten. If there is no tomorrow, there is no hope, which rests on the possibility of what might yet be. Hope is the troubled conscience of the not-yet, the evidence that things are anything but right in the present. Unreconciled life can only hear in silence an eternal present, which would be its redemption rather than its doom if it had arrived at fulfilment.

Origin of Language in Music

In the interstitial darkness where myth and evolutionary history meet, there are accounts of the emergence of language from music, narratives of a primordial separation that prepared one of the central fissures inherent to humanity's development as a self-knowing, but irreparably sundered, species. The first vocal communications were groans and hums, snarls and bellows, signifiers of instinctual emotion that eventually acquired rhythm and differentiated timbre, and were accompanied by drumming, blowing through hollow bones and shells, and the collective movement of bodies, becoming a collaborative representational practice. By some indecipherable process, sounds became denotative as well as connotative. Rather than being merely immanent expressions of the unreflected self, vocal tones could also refer apodictically to things, differentiating one from another, alluding to things that were not immediately present or things that had been and were no more. A temporal and conceptual structure of utterance produced reason, the syntactic order of postulation and declaration, the first languages in which claims of ownership could be articulated and aggressive intent be furnished with its logical armature. Music, now bereft of its referential force, migrated to the purely symbolic, or the purely performative. 'Myth, language and art,' as Ernst Cassirer puts it, 'begin as a concrete, undivided unity, which is only gradually resolved into a triad of independent modes of spiritual creativity.'[34] Eventually, the process of music begetting speech might be subjected to a reverse flow, as antique Chinese aesthetics conceived it, accounting in the second century BC for the emergence of poetry and music not from the mimetic impulse favoured in western theory, but from the linguistic sources of subjective intentionality:

> *Poetry is where one's intent goes. In the mind, it is intent, and coming out in words, it becomes poetry. Emotions are stirred within and are manifested in the form of words. When words alone are not enough, one heaves a sigh. When sighing is not enough, one sings out. When singing out is not enough, without knowing it, one waves one's hands and stamps one's feet in dancing.*[35]

Music gives birth to language, which in turn reconceives music. The continuity between eastern and western theories, however, lies in the acknowledgement of the separation of these modes of expressiveness. To the writer in Han Dynasty China, there may be a causative flow from the one to the other, but in that flow a transmutation nonetheless takes place. Musical and linguistic expression are not the same language. The roots of linguistics in musical utterance are thought in conventional aesthetic theory to be the reason for music's being the best bearer of the emotions among the arts. If it is widely conceded that it remains difficult to account for exactly how and why certain music directly mesmerises the emotional registers of the listener, it is less generally admitted that what the summoned emotions in themselves are is just as unclear. Language has no means of adequation by which it might account for the affectivity of music, but nor can it account for that affectivity itself. There is a confusion of tongues between the two systems that is structurally analogous to the disaster of Babel.

The deeply hidden historicity of music, and the entwinement of its origins in religious ritual and mythology, is no licence for taking its expressive function for an accidentally inherent quality of it. 'The odd thing about music is that we understand and respond to it without actually having to learn it,' thinks Diane Ackerman. 'Each word in a verbal phrase tells something all by itself; it has a history and nuances. But musical tones mean something only in relation to one another, when they're teamed up. You needn't understand the tones to be moved.'[36] The interrelations of musical tones do not vacuum the historicity out of music; indeed, music history just is the aesthetic development, with all its socio-political implications, of those relations. The concert-goer grimacing at the prospect of having to endure the Schönberg Five Pieces for Orchestra while waiting for Mahler's Fourth is hardly under the impression that musical meaning is unclouded by historical sediment, while the notion that the words in a sentence are, unlike the notes and chords of music, distinctively possessed of nuances has overlooked the tendency of its own argument, the recognition that music is arguably all nuances, precisely because its verbal articulability has never been assured. Music has been pressed into the service of social anthropology in western milieux since, at various points in the late Renaissance, its ambient ubiquity in the lives of common people was forced to surrender to the territorialisations of art. It was 'not that sixteenth century peasants failed to recognise the difference between the bagpipe and the bleating of their sheep, but that music, like bleating, was simply in the air'.[37] From this point on, music was theorisable into high and low, with a middling category eventually interposing itself, and in its higher variants, it could be tied, emblematically but explicitly, to forms of social identity and early formulations of the aspirations of taste. Castiglione distinguished in 1528 between the respective music of labourers in the fields and the nobility who needed neither to labour nor to mingle with the general multitude. Later in the same century, Pierre de Ronsard gratified the cultural expectations of his sixteen year-old king, François II, by reassuring him in a work of 1560 that elevated courtly music 'has always been the sign and the mark of those who have shown themselves virtuous, magnanimous, and truly born to feel nothing vulgar,'[38] and so was just the kind, happily enough, to suit the Valois court, even if François himself was only imperfectly able to hear it owing to the abscess in his middle ear that had killed him by the end of that year. Music not only defined status in hierarchical societies, but it did so by encouraging self-identifications in it in the manner Ronsard offers the young monarch. To this day, music for which one has no taste is experienced as alien to one's sense of self-definition in more immanent ways than tastes in the visual or literary arts allow, while treasured songs and masterpieces become interior to one's own life-experience. These affinities and antipathies are not only intercultural but intracultural too. If the apparently undifferentiated shrieking of singers in the Chinese opera means nothing at all to most western ears, nor for many do the formulaic reiterations of global dance music, as extruded round the clock by MTV, or did the thundering of heavy rock through Steiner's study walls in Connecticut in 1970. The emotions that music can evoke include rage at its idiocy, especially when everybody else thinks it the summit of refinement.

Music in its ubiquity has returned to something like the permanent aural element that Leppert and others identified with the lives of the medieval poor, but its precise functional value is no more easily explained in the MP3 era than it was then. What is its purpose? Reproductions of famous paintings might hang on the living-room walls as a constant backdrop, but music is more actively consumed than that, and yet at the same time, is just as unattended to in its innermost workings. A hint at its social function has always been suggested by the proposition that it is a healing medium, an agent of reconciliation that can't compensate for faulty life, but can at least talk its listeners out of the rage of thwarted desire, its charms famously soothing a savage breast, according to the Restoration dramatist William Congreve. 'I've read,' claims the speaker, Almeria, 'that things inanimate have mov'd / And, as with living souls, have been inform'd, / By magic numbers and persuasive sound.'[39] Even inert objects can be 'informed' – that is to say, given form – in themselves by music, by analogical extension from its axiomatic power similarly to construct 'living souls'. There is a property in music by which self-formation is enabled, a formation implicitly unavailable from other cultural means, but which has linked it, since antiquity, to the spiritual precipitations of religious practice. By the eighteenth century, music wasn't just an emollient, it was an active curative agent, one of the indispensable commodities that an enlightened society kept among its *materia medica*. The tarantella was a much theorised musical genre specifically formulated to accompany the southern Italian dance ritual that, by promoting the sweating out of toxin, helped those bitten by poisonous spiders to recover. There were sympathetic resonances between the music, which was generally frenzied and relentless, and the return to bodily composure of the poisoned, an 'intimate correlation between vibrating strings and the nerves of the victims'.[40] It would appear to be a late survival of cathartic Dionysiac rituals, in which music helped drive celebrants on to the purgation of their innermost beings. If music were only curative, however, it would have no greater power in human life than returning the troubled soul to the status quo ante. As was abundantly apparent by the eighteenth century, it could also provoke reflection on a troubled world by disturbing consciousness, ruffling its surfaces until the depths stirred. By this stage, music – opera in particular – was beginning to occupy the same terrain that the classical theatre once had, piercing awakening sensibilities to the quick with depictions of heroic ruin, and evocations of tempestuous mood achieved by dissonances and suspended resolutions. Music was as much emotionally deconstructive as it was morally restorative, perhaps in the age of sensitivity more so. As Veit Erlmann puts it,

> *The new craving for sweet terror, even at its most aestheticised and ethically inconsequential, was an essential ingredient in the struggle for the individual.*

> *In a way, it was through the cultivation of a specifically aural type of frisson that enlightened audiences came to experience themselves as subjects in the first place.*[41]

True, there was ultimate reconciliation in the lyrical tragic operas of Rameau, but the tensile cohesion of the audience's emotional receptors was tested to snapping-point along the way. Tension and terror were the antitheses of the centre of spiritual gravity in music expounded by Plato, in which musical harmony reflects the Pythagorean harmony of the spheres, encouraging everything in being to resound in accord with the same divine order manifested by the seven planets in their orbits. There is a tonal geometry in music that connects it, along with actual geometry, to the fixed dispositions of the heavens. The idea that music might profoundly disturb the inner peace of its auditors would have seemed a crude perversion to Platonism, only another instance of the degree to which aesthetics, if let off the leash, will confound the mathematically aligned perfection to which Being otherwise tends. But even within the precincts of divine harmony, was there not space for that eidetic variant of harmony by which mimetic *poiesis*, including the aural *poiesis* of music, reflects what is elemental in a world that knows all too easily how to dwarf human apperception of it? The vertiginous effect of octave runs up and down the scale to suggest the babbling and rushing of water in brooks and falls, an acutely hackneyed technique by the 1770s, had a disorienting, even nauseating effect on audiences, and yet 'a wild music evenly welling up and down,' thought the philosopher-musicologist Christian Friedrich Michaelis in 1801, 'pull[s] at our imagination with such force that it is unable to grasp it all, calling upon reason to furnish the idea of eternity,'[42] the same idea of eternity there was in the foaming cararact that inspired it. Michaelis already knew to give such perceptual effects the name of the 'sublime', but they were hardly new. Even the harmonising Plato acknowledged that music had more insidious ways of loosening the close-knit moral fibres of the virtuous male citizen. It was the emotional affect in music that had the tendency to make a man surrender to his softer nature. A judicious education in the melancholic sweetness of music 'tempers the spirited element in him, as steel is tempered, and makes it useful', but as always there is a golden mean, and too much soothing of his natural savagery, *pace* Congreve, results in dissolution to flaccidity of the hard edge of his will, 'till he pours out his spirit in a stream, cuts as it were the sinews of his soul, and makes it "a feeble warrior".'[43] Music may unsettle the soul as much as the body and its limbs and, in both operations, it reminds its listener that things are not right with him: 'no matter what it might "say" to our minds, it cannot disguise what it says to our bodies: that most exist in some state of unwilling bondage, which music reminds us of by inviting us to move'.[44] The exhilaration in music is its objectivising of the internal, as though something in an external reality that is otherwise anything but compliant with the inclinations of fettered subjectivity knows how it feels, and both reflects it back and animates it to recognition of itself, without subjectively having had to project itself consciously outwards as it might do with the visual arts. Whether this makes it a force for good or a socially destabilising phenomenon depends on who is making and hearing the music, and why.

Music and the Diabolic

The brain interprets musical sound by contextualising it. Each new tone or harmony is heard in relation to what has preceded it. Broadly speaking, music is heard vertically – that is, in its chords and harmonic relations – in the auditory cortex of the right brain, and horizontally – sounds in succession, the sequence of notes one after the other, and their rhythmic relations – in the left-brain cortex. These also correspond to the way we process linguistic utterance, the sounds of words, such as the variances of vowels, in the right brain, and the sequences, word order and grammatical structures, in the left. One of the primary tasks of the brain is to organise and classify the sense-impressions that reach it, which is why the simple melodies of traditional folk tunes, or of classical works for that matter, lodge themselves so readily in memory. The simplest tunes to memorise are those that have the smallest intervals between notes in the melody's progression.

Music is, like all the arts, historically rooted in the perceptual and emotional habits of the individual cultures from which it variously springs, and which have stubbornly endured through successive attempts to refashion them. Despite the assiduous iconoclasm of the modernist movements of the early-twentieth century, certain tropes within music – dissonant chords, uncomfortable intervals, irregular rhythms, particular frequencies – continue to sound obstinately wrong to unreconciled consciousness, with a wrongness that extends its roots deep into society's moral and ethical soil. The belief that music can have demonic effects is of ancient provenance. In the Judaeo-Christian tradition, it dates at least partly from the peripheral theological belief that Satan, before his fall from grace, was Heaven's musical director. From a highly tangential reading of passages in Ezekiel, he was construed in this tradition to be God's consummate musician, particularly skilled at the tabret (a primitive tambourine) and pipes. The same legend has it, however, that when he was cast out, he didn't take music with him to the infernal regions, where the only sounds are the shrieks of the tormented, but had to leave it behind. In Hildegard of Bingen's musical morality-play of the mid-twelfth century, *Ordo Virtutum* (*Order of the Virtues*), the Devil speaks or screams his lines, because he comes from a musicless abode. When the devout Hebrew youths Shadrach, Meshach and Abednego are commanded to worship the monstrous golden idol erected in Babylon by King Nebuchadnezzar, on pain of being burned alive, the cue for the bowing down expected of them is the striking up of a cacophonous orchestra (Daniel 3). The entire combined resources of Babylonian polyphony – cornet, flute, harp, trigon (a triangular stringed instrument), psaltery, dulcimer and 'all kinds of music' – are deployed as introit to the solemn business of falling flat on their faces before a ninety-foot gilded statue. It requires in them nothing less than the adamantine strength of the divine to remain impermeable to both pagan music and the flames of the furnace into which they are cast for their punishment.

In what senses, though, can music itself be diabolic? Can it summon up malevolent spirits, or persuade its hearers to acts of destruction? Currents of opinion within American Evangelicalism remain convinced that there is a devil's music as well as the purer sort, but they have often fallen rather literally for the infantile satanist posturings of heavy-metal outfits like Slayer. Prior to any obvious representational aspect, though, the question remains as to whether music harbours within itself the technical means of transmitting a malign force. In the medieval era, at the very dawn of the western harmonic tradition, a particular interval in the chromatic scale, known as the tritone, was invested with just such capability. Exactly three whole tones apart in the twelve-note spectrum, it is known in the diatonic scale as the augmented fourth or diminished fifth. In the key of C-major, it is the interval between the tonic C and F#, or between F and B. Played together, the two notes aren't quite as obviously dissonant as the semitone interval between C and C#, or the seventh interval between C and B, but it sounds jarringly misaligned, nagging, awkward, as though it is awaiting resolution. It can indeed be resolved by drawing the interval inwards from the tritone into the conventional major third, from, say, B/F into C/E. To modern ears, this sounds perfectly logical, but the tritone interval was found so unmalleable to composers of medieval devotional music that it was hardly ever used. In the

Micrologus, an eleventh century musical treatise by a monastic vocal tutor, Guido of Arezzo, the tritone is explicitly rejected as an unsuitable interval for vocal music. At some point, possibly contemporaneously with Guido, it acquired its Latin nickname of *diabolus in musica* (the Devil in music). By the early years of the eighteenth century, its diabolic reputation was held to have been firmly established long before – Telemann in 1733 notes that, to the Renaissance, it was 'Satan in music' – although by the time of the Baroque era, the medieval prohibition on it had been effectively revoked. To later composers of the classical age, it is useful as one of the accepted means of creating a sense of tension and then relief, but Renaissance church music wasn't constructed of such textures.

By the Romantic period, the tritone was being openly used to suggest infernal themes. It is deployed by Liszt in his rendering of Hell in the *Dante Sonata*, and it proliferates in his aggressively unconventional piano work *Bagatelle sans tonalité* of 1885. It will go on to suggest tension and conflict throughout the twentieth century, from the orchestral storms of Charles Ives to the drunken *Singspiel* of Kurt Weill. Since the 1960s, it has served the interests of nefarious music-making very durably, appearing in Black Sabbath's eponymous early track, Jimi Hendrix's 'Purple Haze', and on the soundtracks of many horror films. The whole symbolic complex receives thorough-going treatment in the American composer George Crumb's 1970 work for electric string quartet, *Black Angels: Thirteen Images from the Dark Land*, in which quotations from Schubert's *Death and the Maiden* and the *Devil's Trill* violin sonata of Giuseppe Tartini are interlarded with references to the *danse macabre* tradition, squealing clouds of nocturnal insects, and much plangent insistence on the tritone interval.

There may have been no music in Hell, but that didn't stop its technical apparatus from having infernal resonances. To a certain visual tradition, there is something reminiscent of implements of torture in musical instruments, particularly those that feature strings stretched over a frame. The bottom right panel of Hieronymus Bosch's great triptych, *The Garden of Earthly Delights* (1490-1510), features a passage in which the damned are tormented on giant instruments. A naked figure is bound to the neck of a lute, another is crucified on the strings of a monstrous harp, while a third disappears down the end of a shawm. A dog-like demon batters gleefully on a bass drum, a hole in its casing revealing the distressed gape of the man imprisoned inside it. In the central panel of the same artist's *Last Judgment* triptych in Vienna (c1482), musical instruments are shown as the proper preserve of those languishing in Purgatory. Here, they parodically mimic the efforts of human musicians: a simian demon plays a lute balanced on top of its head while, behind it, a standing bird like an infernal penguin fashions an obscene wind instrument from its own elongated beak. Bosch was working at the end of a musical tradition in which sacred music was exclusively vocal, the measured intoning of male voices in Gregorian chant. Instrumental accompaniment belonged to the profane world of sensuous earthly pleasure, of drunken dancing and singing, and was therefore an apposite medium for the chastisement of the damned. The stretched strings simulate the yowling of animals, while the parping of woodwinds is no more than a kind of sublimated flatulence, parodied as such by those Boschian demons that stick the mouthpieces of wind instruments into their rectal passages.

The disparagement of music in medieval theology acknowledges its unfathomable power to conjure the emotions. Repetitive figures played at brisk tempos invite the human body to dance, and dancing, in its corporeal ostentation and display, is the origin of concupiscence and licentiousness. While the plainsong heard during Mass confines itself to unaccompanied stately declamation of sacred texts, the people's music was too easily the setting for unbridled revels. It also figures incriminatingly in variations on the Faust legend, in which those who have signed treaties with the Devil are rewarded for their sacrifice by having virtuosic gifts, typically musical gifts, bestowed on them. A demonic mythology, unsubtly cultivated by the maestro himself, clung about the violin prodigy Niccolò Paganini, not hindered at all by the suggestive evidence of his name, 'the little pagan'. He lost his lower teeth early, which gave him the vampiric appearance that fitted his emaciated pallor, an effect he consciously enjoyed by dressing all in black. His recitals were electrifying exercises in frenzy, customarily ending with one or two strings snapped and his finger-ends dribbling blood. It was popularly believed that, when he played, Satan himself stood invisibly at his side, admiring his own handiwork. As always, however, there was a Faustian price to pay for such a pact. Alongside the dazzling technical gifts that prompted Paganini to compose violin works that only he could play, he was a martyr to ill-health, suffering successively from syphilis and tuberculosis in his later years, having been born with probable Marfan syndrome, which gave him the long slender fingers essential to his talent. Refusing the last rites in what was to be his terminal illness in 1840, he died of laryngeal cancer without having received extreme unction. For this omission, the church refused him a Catholic burial, and his remains hovered in an indeterminate state as they travelled from Nice to Genoa, until they were finally permitted a sanctified interment at Parma, thirty-six years after his demise.

Tall tales of pacts with the Devil retained an irresistible attraction during the development of popular music throughout the twentieth century. It was believed by many that the delta blues legend Robert Johnson had sold his soul to Satan at a crossroads outside Rosedale, Mississippi, now officially commemorated at the intersection of Highways 49 and 61. A crossroads outside the city walls is the *locus classicus* of catastrophic events in Greek mythology, and is notoriously the site of the doomed

Oedipus' unwitting act of parricide. In return for his own carfaxual compact, Johnson supposedly learned his unearthly guitar technique, typically a freeform mix of chromatically slippery triplets over driving bass strumming, with odd hiatuses between the lines. 'Hellhound On My Trail' (1937), replete with whining tritones under an alternately humming and wailing vocal, captures his jagged genius most poignantly. While he never explicitly claimed it as his own, Johnson did nothing to dissuade people from the satanic legend, and his death – he was almost certainly murdered with the aid of strychnine-laced whiskey – reinforced the myth that those on whom the Devil has conferred his blessing will discharge the debt with an untimely and gruesome end.

If music can speak of the Devil, however, its maledictory power can also be harnessed to the expulsion of unclean elements and scapegoats. Traditional ceremonies of excommunication from the Catholic Church used to feature a bell alongside the Bible and candle, for the pronouncement of anathema on those accused of heresy, blasphemy, or particularly heinous sins. It recalled the tolling of the funeral knell, signalling that the soul of the accused was bound for the nether world. Something of this survived in secular folk tradition in the form of 'ran-tanning', in which rural communities would drive a gossiping or backbiting neighbour from their midst by means of a cacophonic performance of bells, rattles, drums, and the hammering of kitchen utensils. Also known as 'rough music', it would be kept up on successive nights for as long as it took to persuade the disfavoured villager to pack up and leave. Its last vestiges survived into the twentieth century. A newly posted Lincolnshire constable, Thomas Jukes, was astonished to come across the case of a crowd of thirty or forty people attempting to ran-tan a woman out of the village of Quadring Fen in February 1928, for the resonantly biblical alleged offence of bearing false witness against her neighbour. When the practice continued on a second night, a force of five constabulary descended and arrested most of the perpetrators. They were charged with disorderly conduct, and mounted an optimistic defence on the contention that this was the last remnant of traditional mob law to survive in England. The argument cut no ice with the court, which fined most of them, and succeeded in ending a centuries-long form of popular justice. It continues as a piece of folk ritual in the Northamptonshire village of Broughton, where a midnight racket known as the Tin Can Band is struck up on the third Sunday of every December, in defiance of occasional attempts by Kettering borough council to force the villagers to desist. It probably originated as a means of scaring off any evil spirits in the period before Christmas.

The punitive use of music was infamously practised in recent years by US forces on Muslim detainees at Guantánamo Bay, where American values were dinned into the prisoners through hyper-amplified repeat plays of tracks by Eminem, Meat Loaf, Aerosmith and Bruce Springsteen, whose ironic anthem 'Born In The USA' was repeatedly co-opted, against the wishes of its composer, to serve the cause of bellowing nationalism. Although now officially discontinued, the practice of music torture, while it reigned, cast American rock in a state of interesting ambiguity. The music at once defiantly stood as the sound of unbridled cultural freedom, while simultaneously intended to be horrible enough to act as punishment. If it didn't brainwash its victims into compliance, it could at least, in its blaring repetition, drive them mad.

Music and Functionality

Music that has nil effect on beings for whom its social function has become its primary purpose – all forms of background music, shopping-mall and elevator music, the car radio tuned to the classics station, the industrialised produce of the Muzak corporation – is an affront to aesthetics. It has been reduced to one of the species of environmental sound that prevents people from having to attend to the silence of interiority, or of the tomb. Its opposite is a music that breaks through the inner ear and into the enigmatic circuits of the associative self, triggering bursts of synaptic response, setting emotional springs in flux. It is for this quality that it lends itself so readily to the fomenting of collective purpose, in military marches, the songs of sports supporters, national anthems and the anthems of allegiance that cemented loyalty to the mass political movements of the modern era. In these manifestations, music has become directly instrumentalised, its signifying language an unmediated outgrowth of its communal functionality. At its simplest, it elides the signification process altogether, and stands for its referent in its absolute essentiality, as though liberated from the mendacities and the imperfect conceptualities of verbal speech. This is so even where its means include emotive lyrics. For something like this reason, Nietzsche notoriously came to prefer *Carmen* over *Parsifal*, the gleeful imitation of Bizet's street-urchins at the changing of the guard in Seville more stirring in its depiction of being stirred than all the heroism of self-renunciation in Wagner's Grail Knights. Songs of political affiliation sweep the masses up, the *Internationale* in the gathering embrace of a net flung wide, the *Horst-Wessel-Lied* in a motoric march that hammers its imperatives into bodies destined for war. 'Tomorrow Belongs To Me', John Kander and Fred Ebb's pastiche Nazi anthem for the musical *Cabaret* (1966), is a pitch-perfect rendering of the genre, its oompah crescendo clambering doggedly to the summit of gloating triumph. The melody of Alexandrov's (originally Soviet) Russian national anthem opens on a counter-intuitive, methodically descending figure that no sooner reaches its bottom rung than it begins a reascent, taking the people with it, the lyrical trajectory beginning in simple comradeship, which then produces social happiness, and finally national glory. Militancy's drumbeat is heard in the *Marseillaise*, and in more obviously operatic mode in Michele Novaro's *Canto degli Italiani*, precipitating into popular consciousness during the liberal revolutions of 1848. The same pure instrumentality is to be heard in all forms of dance music, especially trance and techno, in which the insistence of a functional beat is underscored by often non-musical electronic timbres, and offset with the fluctuant dynamics and temporal breaks of classical music, most typically gathering crescendos often accompanied by a snare-drum effect that doubles in tempo towards the climactic moment, which is prepared by a sudden anticipatory pause, before the riotous plunge back into the principal figure. Nothing about these uses of music leaves their consumers in any doubt about what is expected of them.

Between meaningless music and functionalised music, the category of music that signifies without expressly stating what, which does not necessarily exclude every kind of programme music or lyric settings, represents the semantic hinterland that stretches beyond the purely linguistic. If metaphysics perishes in thought as soon as thought turns metaphysical, because thought cannot help imaging the metaphysical as one of its objects, musical meaning more obviously connotes the metaphysical as such, that which cannot be expressed or summarised. The reason that most critical writing about classical music is such empty gush is that it cannot accede to the status of the meanings that music carries within itself. While popular scorn doubts that the characteristics of great wine can be formulated verbally, it is considerably more tolerant of the encomiastic descants on Beethoven and Verdi, which are hardly more than the equivalent in musicological terms of the plot summaries of novels in elementary literary critique. The meanings in music resist such summary, or there would be no need of music. Even when one helplessly particularises the urgent *espressivo* of the strings into one's own recent experience of loss or love or fury, an unrepresentable remainder eludes capture. What music does to people is a function of its having taken on the duty of precisely such expressivity from the visual and literary arts. Jean-Luc Nancy specifies a historical moment for this movement in the Romantic era:

> *The passage from a plastic and poetic paradigm*
> *to a musical paradigm corresponds to this: the order*
> *of significations articulated according to the translation*
> *of an easily identifiable and (re)constructible reality*
> *gives way to the expressive order of an essentially*
> *ineffable intimacy (Schopenhauer called it 'will';*
> *the 'will-to-live', that is to say, being as desire rather*
> *than being as reason).*[45]

What romanticism achieved was the foregrounding of an expressive language as the voice of a composer throwing his whole subjectivity into his works, as distinct from the mathematically patterned style of the classical era, but nothing in that narrative accounts for the resonances of musical expression itself, which were already apparent in the theatre at Epidaurus, in the early Christian basilicas, and in the impoverished villages of the peasantry. It may be that the corruption of listening derives, at least in part, from the reversal of music's innate affectivity into the deliberate production of affectivity through music in totalitarianism and the modern nightclub. Functional music is not just music composed for a specific function, but can also be originally free music pressed into extraneous service, as in advertising, which is all the more reason to press the 'mute' button when the ad-breaks come on. Whether music is at its purest when not composed with the direct intention of producing an obvious psychological effect is an undecided question. Nancy suggests that the directive tendency in such music confers on it 'a finality that music itself does not have,' so that the crime of functional music is that it collapses the indispensable distance between sound and sense, 'a distance without which sonority would cease to be what it is.'[46] If music is neither linguistic nor immediately semantic, neither is it even conformable to a conventional 'language of affects', the pathetic fallacy that unfailingly attributes a sense of melancholy to the minor keys, or of wistfulness to the oboe. By refusing the yoke that would attach it securely to expoundable meaning, music retains the means for a restitution of that part of experience that must make do without expression. It isn't in itself the substitute for some other kind of expression, but rather fulfils itself by acting as both repository and reagent for what perpetually goes unsaid. It is the sound of the unsayable not being said.

If music doesn't conform, however, to propositional or deterministic utterance, how is the ear to know it isn't being deceived? There is an abiding tradition that insists on sound's greater propensity for deception as compared to vision, which Simmel attributed to the paradoxical effect that people remember what they have heard longer than what they have seen, perhaps because memory works harder to imprint what is necessarily evanescent, as distinct from what appears in the relatively stable visual field. '[I]t is much easier to lie to the ear of a person than it is to their eye, and it is obvious that the entire nature of human intercourse is supported by this structure of our senses and their objects.'[47] For Debord, the primary senses, foremost that of sight, have been conjured into vehicles for the spectacle of consumer society to present itself, non-dialogically, to the masses. Sight may be 'the most abstract, the most mystifiable' of the sensory faculties, and thus most readily conformable to the generalised abstraction of exchange society, but just because it mesmerises its clients through their senses, the same senses cannot also be mobilised to see (or hear) through it: 'the spectacle is not identifiable with mere gazing, even combined with hearing'.[48] Far more than a mere ideological *son-et-lumière* staged by late-capitalist media culture for its participants' entertainment, what it is constituted of is nothing less than reified social relations themselves projected into the form of tyrannous images or, to rephrase the stone-dead T-shirt slogan cliché, this is what reification looks like.

According to romantic aesthetics, which had never heard of reification, for all that its daffodils were the uncorrupted emblem of it, music ought to be able to penetrate the general mesmerism, piercing even as far as the benighted subterranean thickness of a cretin's sensibilities as mordantly as do the shafts of conscience with which the superego torments the troubled mind. So observes Wordsworth in the seventh stanza of one of his most profoundly meditative odes, 'On the Power of Sound' (1828):

As Conscience, to the centre
Of Being, smites with irresistible pain,
So shall a solemn cadence, if it enter
The mouldy vaults of the dull Idiot's brain,
Transmute him to a wretch from quiet hurled –
Convulsed as by a jarring din;
And then aghast, as at the world
Of reason partially let in
By concords winding with a sway
Terrible for sense and soul!
Or, awed he weeps, struggling to quell dismay.
Point not these mysteries to an Art
Lodged above the starry pole;
Pure modulations flowing from the heart
Of divine Love, where Wisdom, Beauty, Truth,
With Order dwell, in endless youth?

Despite what is traditionally predicated of music's pre-rational powers, what it lets into the untutored mind here is, precisely, reason, the unsettling potency of rationality in a mind unhabituated to it, bringing discursive inner articulacy where there was previously only the sepulchral 'quiet' of idiocy's 'mouldy vaults'. The effect of harmonious music in such conditions is, paradoxically, discordant in that it disturbs the somnolence, lacerating its way through the dullness like the 'jarring din' that it isn't, or else, even more disquietingly, it dissolves the hearer to the tears that his uncomprehending mind can only conceive as 'dismay'. If dismay itself there be, it lies in the idiot's unformed realisation that the rest of his existence is so far apart from the sublime realm in which dwell the spiritual graces of Wisdom, Beauty, Truth and Order, eternally juvenescent, emitting a music that is ceaselessly renewable in its efficacy like divine love itself. The eighth stanza throws the light of long retrospect on the dawn of melody, when the lyre of Orpheus charmed the beasts to enraptured attention, and Music graciously deigned to inveigle the 'grosser sphere' of mortal nature, but in a guise that enabled it to outdo nature, a bold admission for romantic pantheism, in pricking forth a tear 'softer' even than those nature itself inspires. The complexity of its effect derives not from the simple intentionality of art itself, the fallen state to which Nancy alludes with his reversal of incidental affectivity into its engineered production, but from the fact that, thus stirred in some inchoate way, consciousness then provides the vehicle, 'an urgent equipage / Of rapt imagination', with which to speed music's power on its way. As with the senses themselves, the aptitude followed the development of the capability for it. Rather than music having invented the affective life, its art was the product of anterior responsive sensibility, 'daring because souls could feel'. While all Hell bends in acknowledgement of its force, Heaven turns jubilant that humanity has forged itself a means of scattering the now 'wan disasters' that would afflict it. And not just humanity. In the myth evoked in the ninth stanza, the Corinthian dithyrambist Arion, granted a final chant on his lyre by his piratical captors on the high seas, summons a rescue brigade from the deeps: 'the dulcet sound / Steals from the deck o'er willing waves, / And listening Dolphins gather round'. He hurls himself on to the back of one, which bears him, still strumming, to the safety of a friendly shore. There he is in the engraving by Dürer of 1514, nude, self-entranced, his harp under one arm while his other clings to the giant head of a squamous sea-creature, an even more discrepant rendering than the same artist's celebrated rhinoceros. The dolphin's polychrome prehensile fins, huge staring eyes and perpendicular tusks, *retroussé* jaw, catfish's barbels and thrashing shaggy flukes are a masterpiece of teratology, but that's the point. If Arion can enchant something like this, he – and music itself – can enchant anything. Back on dry land, the effect can only be enhanced by wine, whose tutelary deity, surrounded by fauns and satyrs beating time with their hooves on the ground, is found rollicking in *ekstasis* in the centre of stanza ten, where 'Silenus swang / This way and that, with wild-flowers crowned', that obsolete preterite having only gained in drunken apposition in the centuries succeeding Wordsworth. If only the music would never stop, wan disasters might become a thing of the past.

The industrialisation of music that radio and the recording industry made possible has removed both the directly communicative element that roused people to group solidarities of all stripes, but also the intimately expressive moment. It pours out of car-radios, supermarket muzak systems, the personalised and eternally repeatable selections on MP3 players, and from the soundtracks of advertising, occasionally catching the hearer unawares with a familiar hook that he had forgotten how much he liked. Such flashes of truth as there are in commercial song-lyrics are often buried amid a fog of idiotic banality, but can once in a while rise to the level of a poignantly accomplished whole work, such as Brittany Jean Carlson's 'If I Were A Boy', recorded by Beyoncé Knowles in 2008, which is eloquent on the distribution of emotional power in heterosexual relations. A girl paying close attention to the words hears a summation of everything there is that makes boys' lives easier, but also joins the singer in conceiving, through subjective projection, a way that a boy could be towards girls, while still being a boy, that would make him 'a better man'. A boy hears his privileges enumerated, but is (or ought to be) touched in his conscience by the girl's attempt to understand, from his point of view, how he could have saved the failed relationship. And then, as though the dialectical complexity of the whole structure is too great, it collapses under its internal contradictions and turns to formulaic rejection, the very idea that men and women could understand each other reduced to a utopian conceit again. *Il n'y a pas de rapport sexuel.* But for a moment, in the aftermath of this latest demonstration of Lacan's eternal verity, there imaginatively was. At the other end of the sexual encounter, at the excited outset, there are depths of unillusioned truth in Springsteen's 'Tougher Than The Rest' (1987), a drink-emboldened seduction scene that pierces its own cynical wisdom to the extent of talking up a last-chance offer that sounds genuinely irresistible, and in the Pet Shop Boys' 'Young Offender' (1993), in which the arch knowingness of gay middle-age, confronted with boisterous teenage enthusiasm, assumes the ingenu romantic tone and finds itself believing it.

The problem with constructing music's expressive dynamism in terms of emotional affect is that the emotions are transitory states. They are not intended by consciousness to survive their immediate occasions, even in memory, where the emotions reawakened by recalling them are recollections in tranquillity, rather than being the raw atemporal responsiveness they originally were. If all music does is strive towards that affectivity, it loses its dialogic character, with which it was able to express other things than sadness or anger or the trance-state of love, however technically proficient it may have grown since romanticism in those fields. Concentrated listening to music uncovers the structural principles that underpin these moments, but also prepares for them diligently by suggestion and anticipation, much as a conversation may work around eventually to what its participants want to say to each other. The ramifications that music, and aural culture more generally, have undergone in the past century are of a wholly different order to the more widely acknowledged pervasiveness of the visual. It has been a limitlessly absorptive process, one that has liquefied the boundaries between high and low, ancient and recent, sacred and profane, pacific and aggressive, partly because of the greater capacity for beguilement, noted by Simmel and others, to which the ears lend themselves, partly because there are few or no theoretical constraints on what people might hear, compared to what they are expected to look at. The cacophonous music of Charles Ives, the marching-songs of authoritarianism, the auditory assaults of thrash metal or the obscenities of militant rap, may not be everybody's cup of tea, but there is very little to stop them from working their way through, even if only vicariously, to everybody's eardrums. Nancy notes that this process has hardly begun to be accounted for:

> *A becoming-music [devenir-musique] of sensibility and a becoming-global [devenir-mondial] of musicality have occurred, whose historiality remains to be thought about, all the more so since it is contemporaneous with an expansion of the image whose extent does not correspond to equivalent transformations in the perceptible realm.*[49]

Traditional aesthetics might have attributed these divergent developments to the relative affinities between the sensorial and perceptual functions at work in the respective art-forms. Simplistically put, music in its concrete immateriality conjures a subjective response, while painting and the other visual arts train the eye to an objectifying contemplative relation, but in practice, the two functions have long been imbricated with each other, tightly so in the era of Victorian well-rounded sensibility and the *Gesamtkunstwerk*, more loosely, but all the more ineluctably, so in the age of formal dissolution in the arts. The subjectivity that music at once constitutes and could throw into question may have equipped it to extend its sway across the range of social experience, but that this has taken place just at the moment that social experience itself has become so finely woven and thinly spread as hardly to deserve the name of experience is not accidental. Music's ubiquity is not the antidote to the ubiquity of industrial clamour, but is as much part and parcel of it as it threatened to be when barrel-organs incessantly cranked out the 'Wiener Praterleben' on the streets, 'Adeste Fideles' at Christmas. The visual arts, on the contrary, have for the most part worked assiduously at throwing off the yoke of the objective, encouraging consumers into visceral pre-linguistic responses that only sound academically pretentious when aesthetic theory belatedly tries to put them into words. What accounts for the morphological and functional evolution of music that Nancy gestures towards is the aspect of its subjective nature that is left when affectless subjectivity itself has departed from it, which is just the fact that music must be subjective because it cannot be an object. It exists only temporally, unbounded in physical space, and has surprised itself by the porosity with which its own technical procedures, once securely differentiated into various contexts, purposes and styles, have been capable of intermarrying. Nobody, from Wordsworth's idiot to the girl in the cinema cramming her sleeve-ends into her eyes as James Horner's theme-tune wells again at the end of *Titanic* (1997), doubts the potential of music to engage sensibility in representing it, but the historicity of sensibility as such is hardly noticed. A homogeneous music blended of heterodox elements pervades the known world, and has become the synonym for a sensibility ossified into second nature, which only needs music to tell it what to feel, and where feeling is not required to provide a background for talking over, and where talking is not required to supply an auditory fuel for stuffing directly into one's ears. In a world antagonised by noise but horrified by silence, music has oozed into the interstices between them until it has filled them up everywhere like water, the acceptable evidence that life hasn't quite yet, despite what everyone feels in their bones, dried up.

Listening for the Inaudible

If the consumption of processed music offers the paradigm case of society hearing what it wants to hear in the culture furnished for it, the greatest exercise in paradoxical listening – of listening for what, officially at least, it doesn't want to hear – is constituted by the continuing investigations of the Search for Extra-Terrestrial Intelligence (SETI). Generously funded by the United States government, SETI aims to find concrete evidence, if evidence there be, for independent alien life out in the universe, even while any and all claims from members of the public, police forces, the armed services and so forth, are officially variously disavowed as misidentified natural phenomena, optical illusions, intoxicant-induced hallucinations, even observations of the testing of (now no longer) secret weapons technology. The Brussels incident of March 1990, in which a pair of F16 fighter planes were scrambled to intercept and challenge a large unidentified object in the nocturnal sky over the Belgian capital, began with a sighting by a police officer, confirmed by colleagues and members of the public. Whatever the object was, it showed up on the pilots' radar. Each time radar lock was achieved, the object took nimble evasive action, swerving in the sky, rapidly descending and re-ascending, until it eventually disappeared without any form of signal communication having been effected. The Belgian defence minister issued an official statement on the incident, acknowledging that the government and the air force were unable to explain what the object was. No conclusive explanation has been offered in the quarter-century since.[50] This incident is significant for its being the first time that an unidentified object sighted from the ground was subsequently brought within radar contact by military aircraft. There have now been something in the region of 120,000 reports of UFO sightings globally, mostly highly contestable compared to the Brussels incident, in the post-war period, although flurries of sightings are interspersed with periods of relative global indifference. It is estimated that about three-quarters of the reports can be accorded everyday explanations, but the rest remain in an unfathomable shadow zone of official denial, indifference, and popular occultism, nourishing conspiracy theories of every degree of infantility and paranoia.

While reported sightings ebb and flow like the tides of fashion, governments continue to build ever larger and more powerful radio telescopes, so that even though public sightings are discounted as imaginary or deluded, official belief persists that there will probably one day be concrete evidence of other life-forms somewhere in the probably expanding universe. As the giant ears of radio receivers endlessly sweep the skies, and devices are periodically launched into space containing capsules summarising the pinnacles of human achievement, with artistic peaks tellingly represented by music, Bach to Chuck Berry, rather than anything in the visual arts, the whole of humanity is represented as listening out for what would be the greatest otherness ever to enter its history. Even the gods are conceived as having generated the earth and the human race in various ways, so that humanity is somehow partly, imperfectly, reflected back into the divine as its legitimate issue, but nothing in traditional cosmology precludes the possibility of another race, which would doubtless have its own myths of origin, travelling here across unimaginably vast distances of space and time. The Buddhist and Hindu philosophical systems have since ancient times conceived of the existence of multiple worlds, as has the Talmud, which divulges that 'God flies through 18,000 worlds'

(Avoda Zara 3b), though whether these are exogamous physical worlds or levels of the spiritual is not clear. The same might be said of the ambiguous acclamation of the Psalmist: 'Your kingdom is a kingdom of all worlds' (Psalm 145:13). Italian Renaissance science, shot through by its conflict with ecclesiastical authority, did not discount, unlike official Christian theology, the notion that one solitary inhabited world was an inherent improbability, as had been the argument of the ancients such as Epicurus and Lucretius. Giordano Bruno, writing in 1584, allowed for a firmament replete with 'all those worlds that contain animals and inhabitants no less than can our own earth, since those worlds have no less virtue nor a nature different from that of our earth.'[51] In the *Nouveaux Essais* (1765), Leibniz accepted that extra-terrestrial life existed, but that humans would be very unlikely ever to find it, and anyway, such other creatures would be likely to be species 'intermediate between man and beast', so only half-worth getting to know if we did happen upon them. The youthful Kant, in one of the most extraordinary speculative works rational philosophy ever produced, *Universal Natural History and Theory of the Heavens* (1755), only translated into English in 1900, proposed that all the planets in the solar system were inhabited by progressively more sentient beings the further they lay from the sun:

> *Kant's Mercurians and Venusians are consequently dullards, whereas his earthlings occupy 'exactly the middle rung ... on the ladder of beings', and his Jovians and Saturnians are greatly superior beings. 'From one side we saw thinking creatures for whom a man from Greenland or a Hottentot would be a Newton, and on the other side some others would admire him as [if he were] an ape.*[52]

The aliens were subject to a suggestively red-faced excision in a later edition of the book, and yet by the time of the first *Critique,* the anti-speculative Kant was still prepared to bet the house on the conviction that the earth was not the only inhabited place in the universe: 'I have not merely the opinion, but the strong belief, on the correctness of which I would stake even many of the advantages of life, that there are inhabitants in other worlds.'[53] Hegel would have none of it. The *Encyclopedia of the Philosophical Sciences* (1817) pours rationalist scorn on the entire time-wasting notion. Life has appeared on earth because earth is uniquely equipped to support it; to posit that organic life could analogously appear on other heterogeneous worlds is a failure of logic. Contrary to the permanently awestruck nature of contemporary and subsequent astronomy, the stars are nothing: 'Matter, in filling space, erupts into an infinite plurality of masses ... This eruption of light is as little worthy of wonderment as an eruption on the skin or a swarm of flies.'[54] All there is in space is pure externality. The otherness that the voyages of discovery uncovered in indigenous populations, which prepared the way for the worldwide colonialist enterprise, has long been partially absorbed into First World conceptions of global social totality, only belatedly recognising, as Lévi-Strauss was to point out, that all races tend to see themselves as the foundational people in humanity's history. By the post-war era of decolonisation, a new wholesale concept of alterity at the species level was required in order to save the human species from the trauma of its fractured self-identity. Heidegger's conception of the late anthropological development of the human race into *Homo technologicus,* in which, no longer the object of divinity's gaze, humanity itself rises to overcome its habitat through advanced instrumental means, overseeing the whole of creation, exalts it to a position of empty sovereignty, its technological apparatuses becoming the prosthetic extension of its dominion. If aliens there be, they must surely, as Schopenhauer maintained, be ready to submit to the overlordship of humankind as the pinnacle of organic being.

This implicitly imperialist reading has not survived in the age of alien abductions, howsoever construed, where the chasm of the mutually uncomprehending bears more the character of the objectifying gaze diagnosed in a post-war existentialism at the topping-point of paranoia: 'the alien gaze sometimes deprives people of their subjectivity, so that no reciprocal social recognition is possible between human and alien. Readers unwilling to accept the possibility that aliens involve genuine "otherness" of one kind or another, may hypothesize that abductions are very intense nightmares that reflect an individual's feeling of powerlessness in social relationships.'[55] At the heart of much of the yearning to glimpse suggestive evidence for extra-terrestrial life is an irreducible inclination not to be able to understand it. While it remains a mystery, its otherness is pure and unblemished, and its regard of fallen humanity may imaginatively be one of either terror at its aggressive subsumptive instinct, or else pitying astonishment at its self-negation.

The necessary objectifying distance that puts the postulate of extra-terrestrial life beyond everyday comprehension, and guards its alterity as a precious elixir that could one day guarantee the preservation of humanity, is reflected in the fact that, as with much other paranormal phenomena, the great majority who have never had such moments of personal experience, rely on the reports of others in the mass media and on the internet to supply them. The improbability people secretly feel at the prospect of aliens from another world observing the earth is made good by the apparent conviction of those who do claim to have seen what may be evidence of it, but what this mechanism enacts is the derationalisation of the arcane. Rationalism once allowed for a gnostic residuum in which speculative fantastical theories were permitted space to explain what science had not yet accounted for. Indeed, one of the names for this residuum was philosophy. In the post-industrial age, when science exercises a more presumptive right of veto over its own mysteries, advocacy of the fantastical acknowledges its own defeat in the face of triumphant rationality, which always only needs a little more time to solve the mystery of the lights in the sky. Rationality indeed would be what rendered the aliens prosaically material. They can only either be wholly unrecognisable as life-forms, or else by the law of convergence written on the cosmic scale will resemble humankind. If they do, they may well be looking to invade and conquer, as the science-fiction films of the 1950s worried, or else they will have arrived here in utter desperation, having largely laid waste to their own world, and having stolen a march on humanity in developing the technology by which they could reach out for extra-terrestrial salvation. In such hopeless circumstances, the cold satisfaction to be had from being contacted would at least lie in the mutual reflexivity by which we too could experience ourselves as exotic aliens, a vicarious frisson cognate with the agreeable sense of self-objectification to be had from reading a guidebook to one's own culture written for foreign visitors to it. Even this transcendent version of otherness has the living warmth drained from it by the dialectical implication in each other of the opposing principles, as Benjamin observed in the 1939 French revision of his essay, 'Paris, Capital of the Nineteenth Century':

> *Saturn's ring becomes a cast-iron balcony on which the inhabitants of the planet take the air in the evening. In the same manner a cast-iron balcony would become ... the ring of Saturn and those who traversed it would see themselves caught up in a phantasmagoria wherein they would be transformed into inhabitants of Saturn.*[56]

The solitary individual who saw not just lights but an entire fully formed alien craft hovering in the sky outside his bedroom window one evening, while transfixed with the thrill of fear, wanted with all his heart for it to be true. A world in which nothing else obliges human yearning, or acts in human interests, can only gain from contact with what is entirely external to it, or so it is hoped. Science fiction, which constructs its fables as a secularised visionary theology, positive or negative, has always known this. It defies the ban on images, and in so doing, often reminds the reader of the reason for the ban in the first place. Kant warned in the *Anthropology* against attempts to envisage the extra-terrestrial beings in which he believed, precisely for the reason that their depiction immediately makes them as unbelievable as Dürer's dolphin, for which reason the three-dimensional worlds of science fiction are no more amenable to adult credulity than Hogwarts, and somewhat less so than the paralogical, metamorphically human domain to which Alice descends. Solemn accounts of alien abductions, or of little space-creatures scurrying around in the desert aircraft hangar after the UFO crash at Roswell in 1947, reduce their narratives to mythology, whereas the rhomboid pattern of lights that flees the reconnaissance plane's radar lock, and is never seen again, is ufology's grin without a cat, an inconceivable phenomenon in which all may believe, since it respects the conceivability of logic.

A popular poster shows an old-fashioned frisbee-style flying saucer in the sky above the motto, 'I want to believe'. More accurately, what it means to say is that 'I believe that I want to believe'. Only the full subjective assumption of the desire as a matter of belief in itself is capable of giving this belief its proper resonance, just as Kant declares his 'opinion' that there are extra-terrestrial beings to be potent enough to constitute itself as a belief. Wanting to believe is the classic position of agnosticism, and is itself a disavowed belief. If one allows the possibility that there might be a God, there is one. Only if God is consigned to the irrelevance of true oblivion can one be sure that he doesn't exist. Anything that remains as a factor in the equation, whether hypothetical or not, has independent objective existence. The next step, which properly introduces the apocryphal element in the status of a given, is fully to appropriate the desire to believe by believing it to be a real desire, and not just the otiose cynical reflex of a sceptical intelligence that secretly believes there is nothing it doesn't believe. The fallacious version of this conceptual structure is wanting to believe you believe, the act by which belief is infinitely deferred to some ulterior state, while one continues meanwhile to enjoy the luxury of not appearing gullible. Believing you want to believe is the attitude of those who mean it. They know that they don't yet believe something, but in all sincerity believe in their desire to assume the belief. It may well be that making contact with such extra-terrestrial life as there is depends less on its having developed the technology to intercept and interpret the radio-signals that the earth has only been emitting for just over a century, and return to it comparable signals of its own, and more on knowing that whatever primary species inhabits the earth ultimately believes that it wants to believe in them. If the fate of the exoplanetary life that humanity is constantly listening for, even while it pretends to be doing no such thing, is to prove scepticism wrong, then the only role it will have played in human affairs is that of the white whale. Punching through its appearance to the reality beyond will have sufficed to terminate that quest to pierce the web of illusion on which humanity has been intermittently engaged since Aristotle gave his *Physics* precedent place over the *Metaphysics*. On the contrary, if the life out there is what might rescue human error from itself, by becoming for it the fully objectified externality that it has never been able to conceive without the means of transcendental apperception, the phenomenological subject, the postulate of a creative principle that must have conceived it in its own image, since both it and the creative principle itself were so transcendently pleased with themselves, and a thousand other such wild surmises, then humanity might be liberated at last to live up to its own principle. The mortifying impulse running through all history has led humans either to fear what they don't understand, or to destroy it with the aid of any means from imperialist annexation to the reifying structure of conceptuality. Chimeras, innocently comforting or leering with threat as culture has dictated, have been conjured into imaginative life to serve as decoys from the unknowable, but the role of the unknowable would be to grant humanity the freedom from having to imagine what it can't know. All listening to the skies is the attempt to find what would provide the respite from listening, just as thinking tries to liberate itself from the need in it that thinking cannot apprehend, thereby sustaining that need as what is heterogeneous to it. If the earth were to be visited by an extra-terrestrial civilisation, or even merely to receive a reply to one of its perpetual helpless signals, it would release earth's inhabitants from their obligation of hegemony, not least hegemony over themselves. Humanity would then become something more than what its own evolutionary consciousness, the consciousness precisely of its own evolution, has paradoxically condemned it to being, a largely dysfunctional biological specimen in a teeming but isolated biological world. The fact that the chances of it appear infinitesimally small is just what makes it a going concern. Whatever can be thought of it has the structure not of another human conquest of *terra incognita,* but of humanity's attempt to break out of its own immanent self-imprisonment. Nothing else indeed animates the sensory faculty of hearing as such. Hearing, actively listening, is the subject's petition to the beyond for reassurance that it isn't alone.

Chapter Three

Smell

'We have a machine down there,' the Sergeant continued, 'that splits up any smell into its sub- and inter-smells the way you can split up a beam of light with a glass instrument. It is very interesting and edifying, you would not believe the dirty smells that are inside the perfume of a lovely lily-of-the-mountain.'
Flann O'Brien, *The Third Policeman*

What will never happen, what can never be, has a fragrance of its own, scents the air.
Paul Valéry, *Analects*

Smell as Essence

The full complement of the senses being five, an odd number, the necessity of mathematical symmetry demands that they must have a middle unit, notes Aristotle (*De Sensu et Sensibilibus*, 5). Smell occupies this median position to perfection, because it bridges the gap between the higher distantial senses of sight and hearing, and those that rely on physical contact, tasting and touching, for their operation. The action of smell is not the intellective apprehension of concrete phenomena like the three-dimensional objects of vision, nor quite the haptic appropriation of objects that can be grasped, chewed and swallowed. Aromas are emitted by concrete objects, but they are subject to the transformative intervention of the medium by which they are transmitted, namely air. If smell was correctly perceived in the earliest inquiries as being inextricably linked in its actualisation to the sense of taste, in that blocked nasal passages inactivate the taste buds, and if smell is, also correctly, acknowledged to be the sense that has most atrophied in humans, compared to the olfactory sensitivities of most of the quadrupeds and even marine creatures, who are thought to be able to scent their prey through water, which neutralises scent to the human nose, there is another, less obviously remarked sensual homology between smelling and hearing. Odours are as bereft of concrete being as are sounds, and must like sounds inveigle their way into the organism, rather than being immediately, concretely present to it. Smell is ethereal, its traces invisible like those of audition, but with less solid substance still. Where sound penetrates by wave-force, scent inveigles, invades and occupies certainly, but more intangibly, more insidiously perhaps, as Kant suggests: 'smell is contrary to freedom and less sociable than taste, where among many dishes or bottles a guest can choose one according to his liking, without others being forced to share the pleasure of it ... For taking something in through smell (in the lungs) is even more intimate than taking something in through the absorptive vessels of the mouth or throat.'[1]

The ancient writers don't subject smell to anything other than a simple biological analysis; it has no culturally symbolic aura, as do vision and hearing. It supports no aesthetic practice, has only limited applicability to the survival of the organism, and might not be missed at all if it were to fall into disuse, other than that its absence would impair the enjoyment of food and wine. Nonetheless, there is something properly haunting about it, and where one does pay attention to its messages, it doesn't fail to be replete with meaning. Before Aristotle wrote, Plato had already proposed that smell was indicative of the changing state of organic matter – its ripening, putrefaction, combustion, fermentation, the blooming and withering of flora, the denaturing of culinary materials by heat, the stench of filth's accretion, the physical exuding of secretions through warmth, anxiety, laceration, menstrual flow. Aquinas's commentary on Aristotle teases out the ontological differentiation of the sensory functions of sight and smell by their comparative action on their medium of transmission, usually air.[2] Whereas the objects of sight take on the mode of being of the incorruptible, inasmuch as they are laid before the eyes in their formal actuality, objects of smell cannot, for the reason that what reaches the nostrils must be a 'spiritual' essence of the odorous article, by virtue of what modern science knows as its aerobic volatilisation. It is a mediated property of an object rather than being the thing itself, as with visible objects, but it is also, despite its mediated status, more the undisguised product of its action on the receptive sense. If a visible object looks, in the concrete actuality of its apprehension, as though it possesses a perduring solidity, its smell cannot so deceive, because it is in itself the evidence of its own evanescent perishability. These distinctions continue to mark the history of smell through the late antique and medieval eras. It is seen as at once a crude sense, in that the entry of odours through the nostrils appears to afford them direct access to the brain, but at the same time an utterly sublimated one, in that scents are implicitly the spiritual emanation of their objects, capable of carrying an even more pungent emotional charge than sounds when encountered again later. In the sensorium of modernity, smell is a primitive sense, the one that the human species has most extensively discarded in its transition to an upright posture, and yet it still functions as a precisely calibrated indicator of the cleanliness, social status and pretensions of others.

Despite its relative marginalisation in Aristotle and the later tradition, smell is still held to have discriminatory power. In the *De Anima* (II:9), it can be easily deceived, in that something foul-tasting can smell tempting, while delicacies may conversely smell bitter or rotten, but in Heraclitus, olfaction has the forensic potential of qualitative discernment that characterises humankind. In the words of the seventh fragment, to which Aristotle refers in the *De Sensu*, 'If all things were turned to smoke, the nostrils would distinguish them.'[3] If everything were to be vaporised into a visually homogeneous fumid emanation, humans would still classify, taxonomise, tell things apart, sorting one from another even amid the fug. The fragment is widely interpreted to say that, even where there is apparent unity, men nonetheless insist on sensing diversity, but this is to misread the smoke in the metaphor as being a purely homogenising image for the Many as One. What the smoke does is in fact to conceal differences by obscuring them, in which conditions men must rely on their noses to uncover the underlying differentiation of which the One is composed. However, compared to the senses of sight and hearing, which are as preferred by Heraclitus as sources of knowledge (fr. 55) as they will be by Aristotle, the sense of smell is still only approximative in its power of distinction. Indeed, it is possible to read the fragment on smoke as being entirely about concealment rather than heuristic revelation: 'Smell least of all is capable of embracing the distinct contours of things in such a way that they become manifest as they are. In utmost contrast to sight, the sense of smell lets things remain submerged in indistinctness, sunk in concealment ... What the fragment poses as correlative to the concealment (of smoke) is human comportment to concealment.'[4] Such a reading depends on a parallax shift in the understanding of the metaphor itself. Smoke can't be thought of in the Heraclitean hypothesis as concealing everything, since everything itself has become smoke, so there is nothing for it to conceal. Rather, it is itself the ontological essence of concealment: 'as itself impenetrable to sight, it is peculiarly self-concealing. For all things to become smoke would mean that they become concealed from sight, not by something else that would come to stand in front of them, but rather by themselves, by their own self-concealing withdrawal from sight.'[5] But in what sense is smoke 'impenetrable to sight'? The eyes cannot see through it, but they can see it. It doesn't conceal itself, not even 'peculiarly'. If everything has turned to smoke, to be sure, it has concealed itself as itself, but thereby revealed itself in the guise of smoke. There is temporality at work in the metaphor, a change of state –

what *was* the multifarious everything *is now* the engulfing medium of smoke – and the olfactory, as the later tradition has it, is the indication of the change. It is left to the nostrils to sense what the eyes and ears previously knew. Knowledge does not dissolve in its reduction to a homogeneous essence; it merely has to rely on a less certain sense for its divination. The alternative reading, unabashed by sublime tautology, says no more than that when things are subjected to the principle of concealment, they are recognised in a concealed way.

'Souls smell things in Hades,' says the ninety-eighth fragment.[6] They use their sense of smell because nothing else is left to them in the underworld, where the sunlight cannot penetrate and all is quiet and mournful. Hades is the great absence, the great negation, whose tutelary deity connotes darkness and death against the creative and festive principles of Zeus and Dionysos. If olfaction is the operative sense, it can only be inferior to the others, and yet there is still something to smell, something to discern, a way to be found through the murk. The condemned souls are not entirely insentient, even if they are thrown back on the most vestigial of resources. In some translations of the fragment, indeed, the mephitic exhalations of Hades are sustenance to the damned. Lacking for other nourishment, they feed on them. Thus are they degraded to an actualised state of the perverse metaphorical conception Goethe's Mephistopheles has of humanity in its earthly existence, in which reason, elevating it above the bestial, produces a hell on earth that returns its victims to an entomic bestiality:

he seems to me
Like any long-legged grasshopper to be,
Which ever flies, and flying springs,
And in the grass its ancient ditty sings.
Would he but always in the grass repose!
In every heap of dung he thrusts his nose.[7]

Thrusting his nose inquisitively into each dung-heap of course prevents him from seeing the essential, and once removed from the light of God, he will have nothing but his questing proboscis to guide him through the infernal realms. Olfaction is the sense-faculty of extremity, desperate near-resourcelessness, the marker of a multivalent lack, but better than nothing. 'And how could Shakespeare not have intuited Heraclitus on the damned smelling their way in hell when tortured Gloucester is tauntingly bidden smell his blind way to Dover?'[8] The expropriation of his eyes reduces him to the animal whose keenest sense was always his nose: 'Go thrust him out at gates, and let him smell / His way to Dover' (*King Lear*, III:vii).

A century before Heraclitus, Sappho's lyrics are drenched in perfumes. Wreaths of incense steal around the altar in the apple-grove, spring blossoms waft on the breeze. Her lovely maidens are draped in garlands, their bewitching scent agreeable to the Graces. Shoots of dill, trampled hyacinth, bushels of violets, crocuses, honey clover and parsley aromatise her poetry, and nothing is headier than the crowns of roses that adorn the heads of the Muses, eternally outlasting those that fade with summer. The cruel tone of fr. 68, apparently addressed to an uneducated woman who cares nothing for poetry, deprives her of the fragrant coronation of the lyrical gift, and consigns her to the dimness of the infernal. In Henry Wharton's Victorian paraphrase (1885): 'But thou shalt ever lie dead, nor shall there be any remembrance of thee then or thereafter, for thou hast not of the roses of Pieria; but thou shalt wander obscure even in the house of Hades, flitting among the shadowy dead.'[9] No light or warmth awaits the forgotten, and no fragrant memory survives them. All they can do is flit about like bats in the gloom. Only those touched by the Muses live on in the light of posterity, like the deathless blooms of the Pierian spring, the waters of which are the nourishing source of all arts and knowledge in the myth.

Smell and the Mystical

What perfumes the air in antiquity more piercingly than floral adornments is the odour of sacrifice. Ritual immolations indicate that the gods are susceptible to the blandishments of smell, which can appease and delight them like nothing else mortals do. So persistent are its wisps and trails, despite the proverbial evanescence of fragrance, which the important ritual function of aroma in pagan sacrifice passed into the monotheistic faiths. The aroma of torrefaction is propitiatory, expiatory, socially unifying, cleansing, festal, an ecstatic marker of gratitude. In the antecedent myth of the Flood that appears on tablet XI of the Mesopotamian Epic of Gilgamesh, Utnapishtim celebrates safe landfall by building a sacrificial pyre on a ziggurat, where he kills and roasts a sheep, lights incense, and throws cedar and myrtle wood on the fire. The gods are beguiled and come to the sacrificial party, all except the unwelcome Enlil, whose handiwork the flood was. More than a millennium later, the exact lineaments of the story recur in the scriptural Noah, who gives thanks to the Lord for the landing on Ararat by offering the ritually permissible creatures in sacrifice: 'And the Lord smelled a sweet savour; and the Lord said in his heart, I will not again curse the ground any more for man's sake' (Genesis 8:21). The scent of roasting meat restores and renders henceforth inviolable the natural order of seedtime and harvest, cold and heat, summer and winter, day and night. The undertaking lasts only as long as the outbreak of celestial fury in Leviticus: 'I will make your cities waste, and bring your sanctuaries unto desolation, and I will not smell the savour of your sweet odours' (Lev. 26:31). This last is the self-denying ordinance of a God whose predilection for the deliciousness of meat cookery informs the precisely detailed methodology outlined in the first three chapters of the book. An unblemished bullock is to be offered for atonement, Aaron the priest placing one hand on its head while it is accepted, before killing it with a blade. His sons are to gather the escaping blood and sprinkle it about the altar, while their father skins and joints the carcass. The sons pile up a fire from the requisite aromatic woods, before adding the various cuts, the head and the fat to the sacred barbecue, although the organs and legs, being ritually impure, are to be washed before they too can go on the fire. Sheep and goats, perfect male specimens only, may be treated in the same way. For fowl such as turtle-doves or pigeons, the procedure will be to wring the bird's head off its neck and burn it on the altar while the carcass is drained of its blood. During plucking, the crop – the distendable pouch in the avian oesophagus – is removed and discarded amid the ashes, and the bird is spatch-cocked before being placed in the fire. Non-carnivorous offerings are acceptable too: 'unleavened cakes of fine flour mingled with oil, or unleavened wafers anointed with oil ... green ears of corn dried by the fire, even corn beaten out of full ears. And thou shalt put oil upon it, and lay frankincense thereon' (Lev. 2: 4, 14-15). Leaven, the symbol of mutability and malice, is unwanted, as is honey, which connotes the excess of sensual pleasure, the surfeit of sweetness when what is required is holy smoke, savoury, empyreumatic, purifying and properly nourishing.

Not just meat itself, but the fragrance of incense and oil, with which the altar, the sacrificial animals and the processional route to the tabernacle were anointed, contributed to the olfactory beguilement of the Almighty. Terpenous arboreal and floral gum resins such as balsam and myrrh, bdellium, galbanum (the musky bitter exudate of *Ferula gummosa*) and onycha (probably the sweetly spicy resin of the wild rockrose, *Cistus ladaniferus*), as well as the widely prized frankincense, produced by bleeding and hardening the resin of *Boswellia sacra*, enriched the air and aura of the sacrifice, and were alike pleasing to God. The ascending smoke of incense was material evidence of the aroma rising to his nostrils. It created a two-way route of transmission, by which he might come down to the human scene to offer his protection, and via which his people might reach up to him, their prayers carried up in the swirling billows. The intensity and concentration of so much aroma was insurance against its fading too quickly, the sacrificial site retaining the fragrant imprint of its purposes, to both the faithful in whose hair and clothing it lingered, and the unbelieving heathen who might come among them, smell being as much as a materially didactic and educative sense as an ethereally symbolic one. Oil for anointing, according to the recipe in Exodus (30: 22-33), is to be composed of myrrh, cinnamon, sweet calamus, cassia and olive oil. Everything on the altar and in the tabernacle is to be daubed in it, including the high priest Aaron and his sons, though not the common people, and any imitation of it will bring about ostracism from the community. Scent is the intangible, invisible emblem of institutional power, its formulation at once apothecarial and unutterably sacred, its airborne trails both cleansing and qualifying the priest to perform the holy office. The smell of dirt is an abomination, so an essential item of the tabernacle furniture is the laver, the freestanding bronze water bowl, itself anointed, by means of which all who entered washed their hands and feet of the day's grime. Small spigots in the sides allowed controlled outflow, since cleansing was always to be performed under running water, so as not to leave floating residues of incriminating muck behind.

It is possible that the origins of the perfume industry in antiquity lay in the gradual abandonment of slaughter in sacrifice. Already by the sixth century BC, Pythagoreans worried about the ritual killing of animals, which were as ensouled as human beings were, their souls subject to transmigration after death. This was a version of the Orphic belief system that had made its way from the barbarous north-eastern fringes of Hellas into the greater Greek colonies of coastal southern Italy, perhaps with Pythagoras himself. Although it was eventually driven from the polis of Kroton (present-day Crotone in Calabria), where Pythagoras had founded his sect in around 530 BC, its central tenets remained influential down to the Platonic Academy. It contributed to the expulsion of the slaughter of animals from the sacrificial rituals, leaving only the sweeter scents of burning incense and the oils with which the celebrants were anointed, and promoted an ideology of comparative cultural sophistication. 'In this respect the "refinement of perfume" was used to distinguish advanced society from a more degraded one associated with the sickening odour of burnt flesh.'[10] On this premise, much of the recent cultural history of smell has focused on perfume through the ages, without much noticing that, at least until the late-nineteenth century, this is exclusively an elite history. The controlled isolation of smells from the natural world, their transformation from contingent appurtenances of the natural into vehicles for the expression of social demarcation, nonetheless traces a sequence of complex symbolic reconfigurations in which the natural, the very condition in which the lower orders were most obviously enmeshed, became significative of higher social status. Culture's efflorescence, everywhere else predicated on the construction of the aesthetic by the sole class that had the leisure-time to cultivate it, is thrown into relief by the appropriation of scent, to which theoretically everybody might have access. It is no coincidence then that, from the very beginning, the perfume trade was commissioned to supply the rarest, most distantly gathered, and therefore most commercially valuable, fragrances to its clients. Anybody could have violets. Court perfumers blended bespoke scents for the mighty. The ritualistic religions reserved particular compounds to themselves, on scriptural authority. Undisguised personal odour became indicative of innate moral disposition, the homiletic temper in which godliness requires the contiguity of cleanliness. While the poor were encouraged to wash off the evidence of their mortality, the upper strata had the option of disguising theirs. Roman women of the elite habitually did not bathe, since washing was the professional obligation of whores, those who needed to smell fresh again for each new client. In the Egyptian Middle Kingdom, members of the highest circles added dye to their perfumes, to emphasise the cloud of fragrance that trailed them about with the visible evidence on their clothing of how much of it they could afford to use. It was commonly believed by the fragrant of many eras that those who stank had no sense of smell, or they wouldn't be able to endure each other. The theory of miasmas held that the noxious odours that attended the plague were themselves the carriers of the pestilence. Bad smells were the exhalation of Hell itself, the stench of the burning and morally putrefying damned, and the filth in which they blithely wallowed, so that in an olfactory version of physiognomic theory, bad people gave themselves away by their emissions. Satan, for Freud, is the personification of repressed anal eroticism, a haunted faecal memory of a scent half-lost in the transition to a higher mammalian state, the evidence of which humanity can never wholly cleanse itself of, not least because, in the apocryphal Brecht line cited by Adorno, what it smells of is the shit used in building the palace of culture.[11]

Bewitching scent, on the other hand, is what brings celebrants closer to the divine in the rituals. If the God of the Levitican prescriptions can enjoy the scent of roasting flesh and combusting perfumed woods, why should not his worshippers also? The immediacy of scent brings him closer through the pleasing aromas they share with him. Eventually, the Protestant tradition, particularly its Lutheran and Puritan offshoots, would come to worry that sensory triggers in the context of worship – the ornately decorated altars, the ravishing architectural flights, the hypnotic music, the spellbinding smoke of incense – had become enjoyments in their own right, substituting sensual satisfactions where there ought only to be direct contact with the divine, facilitated by sensory austerity. Many in the Catholic tradition had wondered about the matter too, and there were consequently few voices prepared to speak up in favour of the senses as channels through which godliness and grace could be attained. Already in Paul, scent has become metaphoric. The incense burned on wayside altars to celebrate Roman triumphs on approaches to the Capitol has become the pervasive aroma of the disseminated gospel: 'thanks be to God, who in Christ always leads us in triumph, and through us spreads the fragrance of the knowledge of him everywhere' (2 Corinthians 2:14). Cosmetic perfume is an invitation to concupiscence but also, more subtly, to speculation as to what it might be hiding. What seems fragrant on the surface may be fetid and corrupt within, but even if it weren't, the revelling in scent that accompanies the gourmandising and gorging on sex of the Roman elite spoke its own indictment. In the Domus Aurea at Rome, erected by Nero on ground cleared by the great fire of AD 64, guests were captivated by an image of the nocturnal heavens painted on a rotating ceiling beneath the dome, its mechanism turned by the unseen hands of slaves, while perfume was sprayed through the hall and the company was showered with rose-petals. More penetrating than these fleeting pleasures, however, is the 'sweet smelling savour' (Ephesians 5:2) of the sacrifice of Christ, while the gifts of charity between comrades, such as that between Epaphroditus and Paul commended at the close of the letter to the Philippians are also likened to 'a fragrant offering, an acceptable sacrifice, pleasing to God' (4:18). Nothing about this metaphoric shift helps the early Christian writers out of their ambivalence in sensual matters. Sensory delight is a gift of God, but also the gateway to temptation. The same Gregory of Nyssa who excoriates sensual indulgence in his meditations on the Lord's Prayer – 'the loveliness of sight or smell or taste presents the senses with very transitory delight; except for the palate, there is no difference in the foods consumed, for nature changes all things equally into an evil smell'[12] – elsewhere values the sensory faculties for the access they offer to the glory of the creation. '[W]e are in touch with those things which affect our life in many ways by means of our senses,' he writes in *On the Making of Man*, 'for there is one faculty, the implanted mind itself, which passes through each of the organs of sense and grasps the things beyond.'[13] The senses supply the information the mind requires to make sense of the world, but enjoying them for their own sake leads to purblind excess. You might like to be surrounded by lovely things at home, but one lovely thing leads to another, until you are up to your eyebrows in 'silver couches, soft divans, and transparent, gold-embroidered veils, magnificent chairs and tripods, washing vessels, mixing bowls, drinking horns, wine coolers and pitchers; water stoups, candlesticks, censers and similar things.'[14] The crashing irony, as Susan Harvey points out, is that 'variations of all the mentioned objects were, by the time Gregory preached this sermon, becoming standard utensils and ornaments for liturgical celebration.'[15] Only with fittingly opulent paraphernalia could the earthly eucharist proximately gesture towards its celestial counterpart and model. The view of late antiquity, that the senses are the traducible but nonetheless precious faculties by which knowledge is transmitted to the soul or mind survived into the medieval era. Robert Grosseteste, bishop of Lincoln, commenting on Aristotle in the early-thirteenth century, sees the senses as appendages to the incomplete soul in its aspiration to wisdom:

> *Because the purity of the eye of the soul is obscured*
> *and weighed down by the corrupt body, all the powers*
> *of this rational soul born in man are laid hold of by the mass*
> *of the body and cannot act and so in a way are asleep.*
> *Accordingly, when in the process of time the senses act*
> *through many interactions of sense with sensible things,*
> *the reasoning is awakened mixed with these very sensible*
> *things and is borne along in the senses to the sensible things*

> *as in a ship... The experimental universal is acquired by us, whose mind's eye is not purely spiritual, only through the help of the senses... And from this perception repeated again and again and stored in memory, and from the sensory knowledge from which the perception is built up, the functioning of the reasoning begins. The functioning reason therefore begins to wonder and to consider whether things really are as the sensible recollection says, and these two lead the reason to experiment...*[16]

It is as though, to the early Christian commentators, the life of the senses is deplorable until one imagines what existence would be without them. The mind into which they pour their impressions is initially a nearly empty warehouse, each new arrival of goods from the world outside being gratefully seized on to replenish the diminishing store from the last consignment. If the world is brimming with traces of the divine, they are to be snapped up for what they can tell the inquiring mind about the nature of God. Aristotle already noted that the animals have keener senses than men do, but they are limited to the immediate concrete knowledge supplied thereby, whereas it is given to humanity to subject that knowledge to forms of analytical and emotional intelligence, which in turn compensate the human species for having inferior sensory aptitudes to animals. Thus does rationality leave the senses behind, until it comes to believe it can survive without them. Gregory of Nyssa believed that, even without the senses, the soul could still be filled with a divinely inspired wisdom imparted directly to it by the deity without need of sensory mediation, but the greater part of humanity required the physical faculties with which God had specifically furnished it for that purpose, so engagement of the senses was by no means irrelevant or inimical to the aims of liturgical veneration. The church billowed with the smoke of burning incense and the volatile fumes of aromatic oils because these fragrances were a reconcretion of divine knowledge from the Pauline metaphor. If Paul had turned the scent of burning sacrifice into the figure of the spreading gospel as a sweet-smelling savour, ecclesial practice converted the sanctified analogue back into the literal fragrance of ritual censing.

The risk that deployment of sensory receptivity in the liturgy carried was that it allegedly became an end in itself, the gorgeous elements of the Corpus Christi procession, the settings of Bach and Beethoven, the veils of camphorial smoke comprising a kind of ecclesial *Gesamtkunstwerk* that reduced its participants to enchanted viewers, listeners and smellers. Theologians in the trans-denominational Radical Orthodox movement have recently rethought these convergences of aesthetics and devotion in the context of the antique dialectic of the senses and the intellect. In the caricatural version of Christianity, which Protestant austerity to a large extent sustained, the physical senses and their passions are the enemy to be vanquished, perpetually destabilising the higher calling of the spirit by permitting the ingress of temptation. The alternative early tradition of Augustine and Aquinas taught that the body was an integral part of humanity's relationship with divinity, which had been rebalanced by the incarnation of God in human form. If the exemplary corporeality of Jesus is inseparable from his return to the Godhead, the bodies of human beings themselves are thereby rendered more conductive of divine grace. There is, to be sure, still a balance to be struck, but as Catherine Pickstock has argued, it lies not in the dreary negation of the carnal with which all branches of Christianity have at different stages been stricken, but with a renegotiation of the value of bodily sensibility to the intellect, which was primally subverted by the surrender to greed and power-lust dramatised in the Eden myth:

> *The body, the senses, and the passions, like our mother Eve, are relatively innocent; they have simply been given undue weight.*

> *The mind, like Adam, is guilty of a far more positive perversity. So the senses must now be deployed, liturgically, to reinstruct the mind... As the Eastern Orthodox tradition has emphasised, matter – and particularly the human body – is now more porous to the passage of the divine light. The play of the liturgy is therefore a play of the newly transformed and heightened senses, beckoning the intellect to follow them back into the true divine ludic economy.*[17]

Although moralism has always insisted that people are enslaved by their physical inclinations, the greater damage has been caused by the too complete victory that rationality, including the rationalisation of sensuality, achieved over them. Only the corporeal senses can lead the intellect back towards a reconciled apprehension of the world, in which objective reality will cease to be either the wilderness of reification into which the economic relations of society have led it, or indeed the manifestation of radical evil that the various heresies – Manichean, Cathar, Gnostic, and so on – saw in it. For Pickstock and others, the liturgy is precisely the means by which the created are eternally reintegrated into the creation. Those who would accuse the religious of merely enjoying a concert when the B Minor Mass is sung have invested sensory response with the status of a thing-in-itself, which is exactly what they think the devout have unwittingly done, as though there were ever any context in which sensory response functioned autonomously, free of any association, through memory and the emotions, with other times and places. When a waft of Givenchy instantly brings back the presence of a long-absent other, and the period of one's life that was lived with her, nobody would be so tragically prosaic as to claim that all one was doing was appreciating the scent of it for its own sake. Nor do the engagements of all five of the senses comported in the liturgy need to be seen as isolated from their referents in the spiritual, in what lifts the intellect above what it merely abstracts from, judges and comprehends, and into a realm in which astonishment might be restored to it.

For the Radical Orthodox, beginning with their true progenitor GK Chesterton, Christians should be more, not less, attentive to their bodily senses, both to fulfil and rise beyond them, to sublate them perhaps, in some Hegelian dialectical fashion. The secular version of such a procedure would involve a thinking through the senses, not just a rigorous thinking-through *of* them, but a thinking *via* the sensual body, in which rationality doesn't insist on its ancient right to abrogate what the senses seem to be telling it, but nor does it simply surrender its own capacity for objectifying reflection in some Sadean or Crowleyite imprisonment in the fatuity of mere indulgence. Both tendencies have resulted in untold suffering. The suspicion of pleasure has darkened the greater part of human history for all but the elites. 'If it feels good, do it,' countered a piece of 1960s ideology, blurting out a rapist's pretext in its retarded innocence.

Smell and Truth

The sceptical Hume's nervous breakdown of 1730 cured him of the notion that sense-impressions were at all separate from the processes of intellection. Much as the senses informed the mind, so prolonged immersion in melancholy thought could comprehensively sicken the physical being of a young man of nineteen. What preoccupies Hume, though, in the *Treatise on Human Nature* (1739-40), is the process whereby the transient impressions of reality offered by the senses turn into fixed, stable ideas about relations between and among them. Despite the possibility that the senses can be deceived under certain conditions, the information that perception conveys is always of the immediate, and never of anything beyond itself. That is the task of intellection: 'When the mind looks farther than what immediately appears to it, its conclusions can never be put to the account of the senses; and it certainly looks farther, when from a single perception it infers a double existence, and supposes the relations of resemblance and causation betwixt them.'[18] The true nature of the objective world cannot be found in simply observing it, because perception itself transmits different orders of knowledge and sensation about reality. Objects possess primary attributes (shape, size, density) and secondary (colour, sound, smell, temperature), as well as the tertiary consideration of whether the sense-impressions they convey are subjectively pleasant or unpleasant. All this is compacted and elaborated by the mind, until it takes its leave of the actuality, which is as often as not subject to substantial change when it is absent to consciousness. The solid ideas on which philosophical thinking rests must derive their character nonetheless from innate correspondences between certain of the sense-impressions and the imaginative and speculative faculties, but it is a mistake to attribute these solely to those impressions that appear most forceful or involuntary: 'For it is evident our pains and pleasures, our passions and affections, which we never suppose to have any existence beyond our perception, operate with greater violence, and are equally involuntary, as the impressions of figure and extension, colour and sound, which we suppose to be permanent beings. The heat of a fire, when moderate, is supposed to exist in the fire; but the pain, which it causes upon a near approach, is not taken to have any being, except in the perception.'[19] The essence of reasoning lies not in the 'force and vivacity', 'coherence and constancy', of external sense-impressions, but in the force and coherence of the mental conception itself. Long after the mountains and the sea, or for that matter the pealing of the church bells or the aroma of the sizzling meat, have been removed from immediate perception, a strong conceptualisation remains to internal consciousness, a conceptual scheme that is then thrown into doubt when confronted anew with the discontinuity of the external objective world. Hume's acknowledgement of this disjuncture constitutes one of the earliest critiques of identitarian thinking: 'there being here an opposition betwixt the notion of the identity of resembling perceptions, and the interruption of their appearance, the mind must be uneasy in that situation, and will naturally seek relief from the uneasiness. Since the uneasiness arises from the opposition of two contrary principles, it must look for relief by sacrificing the one to the other. But as the smooth passage of our thought along our resembling perceptions makes us ascribe to them an identity, we can never without reluctance yield up that opinion.'[20] What undermines the fallacy of identity thinking is reality itself, which constantly either subverts the settled conceptuality of metaphysical thought, or at least offers a form of vacation from it, as is easily seen by the fact that philosophers are as little immune to its access as are the vulgar, 'by which means we can humour our reason for a moment, when it becomes troublesome and solicitous; and yet upon its least negligence or inattention, can easily return to our vulgar and natural notions. Accordingly we find, that philosophers neglect not this advantage; but immediately upon leaving their closets, mingle with the rest of mankind in those exploded opinions, that our perceptions are our only objects, and continue identically and uninterruptedly the same in all their interrupted appearances.'[21] The very stability that metaphysics in its sophistication denies to the objects of contingent reality, it nonetheless arrogates to its own concepts of that reality, which it takes at some foundational level to be cognate with them. There is no inherent continuity between the objects and the sense-impressions they convey, as may be seen by the multitudinous evidence of differential sense-perception of the same objects from one person to the next. The scent of a primrose, while it may be an inherent property of the flower, is not in any way equivalent to the object itself, but is no more than a contingent attribute of it, only reason has fallen into the trap of seeing the two things as ontologically coterminous. 'Thus there is a direct and total opposition betwixt our reason and our senses; or more properly speaking, betwixt those conclusions we form from cause and effect, and those that persuade us of the continued and independent existence of body. When we reason from cause and effect, we conclude, that neither colour, sound, taste, nor smell have a continued and independent existence. When we exclude these sensible qualities there remains nothing in the universe, which has such an existence.'[22] What is called for, on the threshold of the European idealist tradition, is an escape from idealism, a thinking that would neither content itself with the delusion of sensual immediacy, nor substitute for the object of cognition a body of ideas, conceptual images, that would then stand in for it, and which would subsequently become known as ideology.

If the concretising senses of vision and touch can be deceptive, how much more so, Hume's argument seems to imply, might be the more evanescent evidence of the olfactory sense, traditionally conceived as utterly immaterial? And yet scent, just because it isn't susceptible to material imaging like the objects of sight, might in some way be thought of as issuing from the concealed innermost workings of the object. Many of the classical thinkers erroneously believe that odour is never deceptive, and that a noxious object always smells bad, deterring the unwary from picking it up or tasting it, and the credo that its natural perfume reveals the true essence of a thing has endured. By the same token, cosmetic perfume is always a kind of camouflage, at best an exercise in self-flattery, at worst a desperate recourse to disguise. The ambivalence about scent reflects the indeterminacy of its functioning: it is at once the most fleeting of the sense-impressions, and yet apparently capable of long perdurance and transmission over great distances. The physiologist Haller reported in the eighteenth century that papers that had lain untouched in a drawer for over forty years were still strongly redolent of the single grain of amber that had been enclosed with them. Sailors on trading vessels could detect the aroma of cinnamon on the sea breezes when their ship was still twenty-five miles off the coast of Ceylon. Despite its paradoxical potency and versatility, however, smell was held to be obdurately resistant to attempts to classify it. Thomas Jefferson's English physician Robley Dunglison, writing in the early-nineteenth century, swiftly dismissed one such doomed venture by Linnaeus, on the Kantian grounds that smells are too implicated in subjectivity to be objectively taxonomised. Asafoetida, the unmistakable waft of paradise in cuisines from the eastern Mediterranean to central Asia, was once known as 'devil's dung' in the west. Garlic, an indispensable element of the northern European medieval kitchen, came to be reviled as the stink of southerners in the twentieth century, but had come full circle again by the century's close. Theories that aromas can be medicinal or poisonous in themselves are discounted by Dunglison. It isn't the smell itself of a substance that is toxic or hypnotic, but the volatilisation of its essential alkaloids by aeration that causes the effect. It was implicitly believed once that the smell of food could be fractionally but adequately nutritive. Plutarch tells of a people in India who subsisted only on pleasant smells. Democritus apocryphally survived for the last three days of his century-long life on nothing but the aroma of baking bread. Francis Bacon cites the case of a man who lasted through a fast of several days by inhaling bouquets of alliaceous herbs. The evident credence such theories were granted was already coming unstuck by the seventeenth century:

> *[Thomas] Fuller ... affords an amusing instance of litigation, arising from this supposed nourishing character of odours. A poor man being very hungry, staid so long in a cook's shop who was dishing up the meat, that his stomach was satisfied with only the smell thereof. The choleric cook demanded of him to pay for his breakfast; the poor man denied having had any; and the controversy was referred to the decision of*

> *the next man that should pass by, who chanced to be the most notorious idiot in the whole city; he, on the relation of the matter, determined that the poor man's money should be put betwixt two empty dishes, and that the cook should be recompensed with the jingling of the money, as he was satisfied with the smell of the cook's meat.*[23]

In the eighteenth century, a consuming obsession with smells, their social effects and their cultural influence, reigned. The quality and content of the air determined the quality not just of urban life, but of the reasoning intellect that dwelt in it. Air itself, at the moment of its physical description in Newton's 'ether', had become as much a material element as water, and the smells it carried could sicken the individual, pollute society, render art and thought decadent. Once miasma theory had been superseded, however, smell had become for the scientific mentality a purely incidental property of things in nature, and fascination with it became the preserve of Romantic sensualism, just as ideas that it could be instrumentally beneficial to the ailing or famished human frame were discounted as obscurantist flimflam.

Recent historians of smell have been understandably preoccupied with the history of the perfume industry, which secretes within itself the histories of social differentiation and stratification, as well as apparently creating, at least since the widespread use of perfume from the late-nineteenth century on, a whole aesthetic category where previously none had existed. All today's *eaux de toilette* and *parfums* are descendants of the original Eau de Cologne, used medicinally in the eighteenth century as a specific against residual outbreaks of plague and lesser ailments. That was derived in turn from an original formulation, Eau de la Reine, made by a Florentine perfumer for the young Catherine de Medici, which subsequently went into commercial production in the city after which it came to be named. It was an infusion of rosemary and essences of citrus fruits in neutral grape spirit. From being a medicinal application for ladies, it had gradually become by the nineteenth century a purely cosmetic addendum to the male toilette. Female fragrances returned to the scents of flora for their inspiration, although rosewater was thought a suitably manly adornment in Victorian times to be an ingredient in variations on cologne. By the turn of the twentieth century, French *maître-parfumiers* came to be as highly regarded as *couturiers*, and the two trades have been industrially linked ever since. Aimé Guerlain's Jicky, launched in the year of the Paris Exposition Universelle in 1889, is the oldest perfume still in continuous production. Although details of the formula have diverged somewhat since its inception, its essential structure remains unaltered: its scent is a culinary blast of vanilla and steam-distilled lavender, boosted by lemon, herbs and civet – that last originally the anal gland secretion of the African civet cat, the faecal pungency of which lifted floral scents attractively once it had been house-trained by dilution. Jicky was originally worn by both sexes, although its florality would eventually make it a women's fragrance. The point of commercial fragrance was at first about smelling clean, before it was about smelling appealing in culturally loaded and gendered ways, and the entire industry is now predicated on scent as an expression and extension of personality. A perfume has to fit its wearer, but also say something about who he or she wants to be, how they ought to be viewed by others, in a context that doesn't just define their social status, where the deep roots of cosmetic fragrance have reached since Egyptian antiquity, but their emotional being as well. The different components of perfume, their blending into what the industry calls an 'accord', are tied to different personality types, much as are the signs of the zodiac. A scent of mossy wood such as sandalwood and cedar connotes the manly outdoor type. The more obviously aromatic herbs – thyme, rosemary, sage – suggest a thoughtful, intellectual demeanour, while patchouli, amber, musk, vetiver, and oriental resins announce the bohemian non-conformist. Most floral scents are associated with a virtually feudal conception of delicate femininity, just as leathery fragrances, with their distant suggestions of male perspiration, are the preserve of the competitive, acquisitive *homme d'affaires*. The latest generation of perfumes, which are redolent of gastronomic ingredients such as sweet spices (nutmeg, ginger, vanilla), chocolate and honey, reflects the recent growth of interest in aspirational home cooking. Some perfumes are formulated more or less to disappear as soon as they are applied, leaving only the vestigial suggestion of some essential attribute behind. Others are intended to make an insistent, irresistible statement that lingers in the room long after the wearer has swept out to their next scene of triumph.

Analysis of the cultural meanings of scent has tended to stop at the superficial psychologism that forms its topmost stratum, not noticing that, in their impulse towards conditioning of the individual, perfumes are traces of the historical process. They mark the bourgeois individual's emergence from the undifferentiated feudal crowd, initially as one whose economic aspirations are supported by his hygienic credentials, someone who no longer has to mingle with the people he employs, but is elevated above the workshop floor and the transmission routes of viruses and bacteria, and then as someone whose cultivated taste is expressible not just by participation in metropolitan culture, but also in the distinctive personal adornment by which he turns himself into an ambulant work of art. The man-about-town of the mid-Georgian era and the Regency is one whose personal presence becomes the more conspicuous as his economic activity becomes opaque to the mass of society. If richly coloured clothing fabric and ostentatiously gilded carriages indicate to the drabs that they ought not merely to stand aside as he passes, but look on in mesmerised envy, the cloud of scent adds a bewitching note of the ethereal to the whole ensemble. Where it was once the privilege of the elites to smell of next to nothing, compared to the foetor of the labouring poor, a further social chasm was driven between them when the rich began to smell of the better things in nature. The scents of roses and violets, herbs and citrus fruits, expropriated from the natural context in which they might conceivably be available to all, and distilled into their essences, became luxury commodities, privately appropriable in their potency only by those with the means to acquire them. A violet-scented perfume smelled more hauntingly powerful than the wild flowers themselves, as though its essential nature had been isolated, domesticated but at the same time trained to a ferocity that warned off the lower orders, much as the family dog, once the symbol of fidelity and amity between the species, could be trained to snarl at beggars. The movement of capitalist economics, the dissolution of everything solid into air of which Marx and Engels' manifesto speaks, invested concrete commodities with spiritual essences, by which they would come to hypnotise relations between humans, and hardly anything indicates the tendency more piquantly than the appropriation of natural odours to the beautification of the fortunate. Perfume alienates its olfactorily recognisable components from their natural contexts, and its application to the person adds a spiritualised note to the alienation of the bourgeois from the realm of immediate need. Gorgeous apparel, however singular its impact at first viewing, can always be worn again, but scent comes and goes in an economy of gratuitous consumption. Even haute cuisine nourishes as it disappears into the system, but scent does nothing other than hover about the individual for a brief interval before fading off. Inasmuch as it performs an erotic function, beguiling those in the vicinity into more intimate contact with the other's body than social etiquette permits, it both invites and repels the sexual impulse of the potential lover. Its attractiveness bids him to get imaginatively closer to the wearer's body as a prolusion to seduction, a seduction that is already being practised on him, at the same time that its reference to the realm of nature, to the woodlands, meadows and orchards that supply its constituents, throws him off the scent of the purely carnal. The sexual secretions of the civet cat and musk-deer that appeared in bespoke perfumes from the earliest days, and which are still there in synthetic form in the mass-produced scents of today, represented the attempt to reconnect the flowers and herbs to the corporeal functionality of sex, no matter that it was a bestial form of corporeality they drew upon. Professional perfumers nowadays talk of the need to match a particular scent to one's underlying odour, in advancement of the theory that the same brand can smell very subtly different from one user to another, but the motivation for wearing it has always been to smell as little like oneself as possible, to smell more like a feral animal in heat if necessary, at any rate of bunches of lavender, precisely in order that one's admirers may be dazzled by an image that is not just idealised, but distilled into a potent singularity, of which he will be reminded every time he chances to catch this particular perfume. Although the perfume industry would like to persuade its clients that, by careful selection, this *eau de toilette* or that might become part of the buyer's personality, in reality the process is more about the buyer becoming the perfume, which is after all, despite its mendacious claim to exclusivity and its fabulous price, a mass-produced commodity. The point is demonstrated whenever somebody uses too much of an especially penetrating perfume, an inclination to which men in their general bafflement at the operations of female desire are more susceptible than women, whereupon it seems to bind and gag the wearer's identity, as much as its fumes belabour the nostrils of everybody he talks to.

For all the alleged sophistication of its formulas, applied scent returns relations between people to an archaic state, but with the intention of misleading. In primordial times, the way other creatures smelled betrayed their true nature, whatever techniques of camouflage and deliberate deception they may have resorted to in order to disguise it. Scent is a fundamental element in predation, both to the pursued and the pursuer. It both announces the approach of the predator, and gives away the prey, no matter how assiduously he has tried to blend in with the surrounding woodland. Remaining perfectly still so as not to give away his presence by any sound, he nonetheless cannot mask his scent, even when he consciously tried to do so, since the scent camouflage itself would then give him away. Those indigenous Peruvian people studied by Alexander von Humboldt, in a case cited by Dunglison and many others, who could distinguish between people of different ethnicity by their variant smells in the dark, are only as remarkable as they seem in the era of mass urbanisation, where olfactory cacophony is the norm, and alternative means of interpreting the identity of others must be found. The diverse scents of other tribes, other races, one's enemies notably, furnish the earliest means of distinguishing between subsets of one's own social group, and thereby constitute one of the earliest blueprints for stratification. Notwithstanding its apparent crudity, smell is an educable sense, but with the paradoxical proviso that the more it is subjected to refinement, the more likely it is to be dulled. Nineteenth century anthropologies note that the savage has more acute olfaction than the civilised, partly because the latter is subjected to a greater variety of smells, but also because he needs it less, being able to rely on other discursive and cultural indicators to inform him of the nature of something. Advancing to civilisation taught dwellers in the first settled centres of population ways of offsetting rank odours with sweeter ones, estranging them from the realm of the natural as it manifested itself in the smell of putrefaction, burning flesh, the stench of their own organic functions, finally setting culture on the path of domination of nature through denial of it. Their stink fenced off the indigent from the upper echelons more securely than any physical barrier, and helped to identify them as closer to unrefined nature. The notion that they didn't notice their own smell was a piece of self-serving ideology on the part of the privileged from the outset, persisting into modernity in the obstinate myth that the nose becomes progressively immunised to offensive odours with sustained proximity to them. What is often said of past epochs by imaginative historians – that the first thing anybody travelling back in time would notice would be the smell – is at once a fallacious observation and an accurate one. The past undoubtedly smelled horrible, but its other-worldly pungency obviously smells alien to modern nostrils that are not habitually in the vicinity of rotting fish, open sewers, untreated disease, and so forth, and in any case, any reaction to it would depend on who one was in the reimagined society. By the time it served social segregation in the great urban centres, though, olfactory discrimination was never as secure as the narrative of a straightforward battle between the foul and the fragrant suggests, any more than the smell of distilled rose-petals can really eliminate the smell of body odour, as distinct from just mingling with it. It is true that smell became a marker of racial difference in nineteenth century American and European society as the visible indicators of race began to be diluted with inter-breeding. If light skin tone could be deceptive, it was held, the underlying smell of minority races gave them away. A medical establishment actively colluding in the mechanics of segregation in the United States solemnly explained the reason that black people had a strong native odour was that their bodies void alimentary waste not primarily through urine, which black people allegedly produced in more meagre quantities than whites, but through sweat. Furthermore, the respiratory structure of black humanity was closer to that of lower mammals, and generated more heat than it did in white people. Such theories were given credence even by the opponents of slavery, such as Thomas Jefferson, writing in 1785: 'They secrete less by the kidneys, and more by the glands of the skin, which gives them a very strong and disagreeable odour. This greater degree of transpiration renders them more tolerant of heat, and less so of cold, than the whites.'[24] The greater proximity to nature indicated by their innate odour has equipped them with a less refined emotional repertoire: 'Their griefs are transient. Those numberless afflictions, which render it doubtful whether Heaven has given life to us in mercy or in wrath, are less felt, and sooner forgotten with them. In general, their existence seems to participate more of sensation than reflection.'[25] And so on. If there were to be a general liberation, it ought to take place within the securely policed precincts of the ideology of racial difference and its hierarchies, one infallible indicator of which was present to the nasal passages.

By persuading its clients that perfume confers on them the idiosyncratic personality that its manufacturers have spent many hours confecting in the laboratory, the scent industry plays its part in social mythology. A system that hardly scruples to distinguish between one and another of its participants, each of whom has a role to play that might however just as easily be assigned to the next in line, requires that each believes himself or herself uniquely valuable. Each has a vote to cast at election time, each can buy a ticket for the lottery, and for each there is a special scent that blends alchemically with their own special scent, and helps them add up to fully three-dimensional beings. The quasi-astrological garbage with which perfumers sell their wares, which like astrology itself is drawn from the repertoire of social psychology, confirms the purchasers in their would-be self-images. 'This elegant lady aspires to be swept away and acts on impulse,' she is told. 'She is authentic, open-minded, captivating, and she knows how to take advantage of the surprises life can offer!' The ideological undertow of this caricature gestures towards that of the free spirit, in a pre-chewed gobbet of Nietzsche that long predates the advent of the electronic age. The lady who wears this scent is at once the jetsam of circumstance, tossed along on the currents of surprises that life can offer, positively yearning to be helpless, at the mercy of unmediated impulse, and yet, for that reason, authentic in some belated Heideggerian sense. Demanding that life do with her as it wills is misinterpreted as open-mindedness, her very frailty providing the opportunity for 'taking advantage of' it, and certainly nothing that would in any way compromise her elegance, which is founded precisely on her limitlessly yielding cooperation. She will captivate men by her utter malleability, and doesn't resent life for its shocks. Indeed, she welcomes them, which may well explain the perfume's name, Merci. The psychological profiling of men's fragrances is relentlessly predicated on appeals to the gigantic ego that men are told they ought to have, the more any possibility of self-completion is stripped from them. 'It is addressed to self-confident men who want to be the centre of attention,' declares the blurb for one, as though wanting to be the centre of attention were not already the admission of a disastrous lack of confidence. Others appeal to men's capacity for convincing themselves they are athletes, on both the field of play and in the bedroom. There are ideological yearnings to be addressed for him as much as for her. If she is a manipulable dimwit, he only gets what he wants by fighting, bending the force of circumstance to his steely will in a risible myth of autonomy. 'This is a fragrance for a man who is his own master. He is a hero, a man who defends his ideas and goals' [Eros by Versace]. 'Made for the man who knows what he wants, this fragrance is a powerful mix of excitement, allure and sensuality' [Gucci Guilty Pour Homme]. 'This new fragrance is perfect for the man who knows what he wants and where he's going. It captures the sensuality and emotion of a man united as one with the pure unstoppable power of water' [BOSS Pure]. The discomfiting fascist subtext to these scenarios reminds the purchasers of the powerlessness they are paying to erase, but there are occasional forays into a subtler mode that is altogether more sinister for evoking an air of the surreptitiousness with which impotence persuades itself it has the edge: 'Its spicy oriental fragrance epitomises the modern hedonist who passes by unobserved with a knowing smile inside' [Dolce & Gabbana The One]. The brand-names speak of damaged aspirations: Guilty, Fracas, My Insolence, Unforgivable Woman. I Am King is 'a statement for all men who care about themselves, respect their own attitudes and believe in themselves', a stance that social relations have turned from a natural proclivity into something that has to be painstakingly acquired like a martial art.

Perfumes aim to create an aura of mystery about the wearer, but no cultural affectation can make people more mysterious to each other than they already are. Their reduction to functional components in a seamless mechanism that nobody individually understands has bestowed a reifying opacity on social relations, which smelling like jasmine or burning tangerine peel or the carpenter's bench does nothing to throw into relief. If anything, it only augments the inhuman character of their estrangement, by broadcasting to those who venture into their vicinity that people would rather remind their intimates of things in nature, which their extromission from the natural at the dawn of civilisation rinsed out of them, than anything inherent to themselves as constitutive of their own nature.

Smell and Hygiene

The need for everything to smell pleasant – not to smell cleanly of nothing in particular, but actively to smell of things that remind everyone of happier times in a pre-industrial Eden – addresses innermost yearnings by the only means with which people feel they can be expressed any longer, extra-linguistically. What the educated in previous generations looked for in lyric poetry has been requisitioned by advertising, both in its images and in the sententious language in which the most everyday commodities are sold. Even non-verbal languages such as music and the visual arts have become a universal sales tool, a means for persuading somebody that he ought to buy something quickly if his life is not to be contemptibly bereft compared to that of his fellows. Scent, which despite the appropriative urge in all sales talk, resists translation into verbal categories, other than by comparison to other smells and tastes in a self-reflexive tautology, still possesses the power to captivate the subject, leading him both onward to a world of promise, and back to remembered times, in which a vanished happiness seems to hint, pathetically enough, that he has a right to more. Smell is processed in the amygdala, the same region of the brain that generates emotional response, so entwining scents inextricably with yearnings, bittersweet melancholy and unalloyed delight. For this reason, smells are pressed into service by commodity culture, for all that they cannot in the present state of technology be incorporated directly into visual advertising. The deep cleansing of the early antiseptic era, which replaced fetid odours with the scent of Lysol before replacing that in turn with nothing, has been overlaid now with the aromas of fruits, flowers and spices. Getting ready for work in the morning involves applying the scent of chamomile and vanilla under the shower, washing hair with something that smells of green apples, and then spraying musk and sandalwood under the arms, before adding a final dab of rose-petal and lemon to the neck. The resulting cacophony, which draws indiscriminately on the natural world to make everybody presentable for the stresses of the coming day, offers a volatilised version of a nature to which everybody is ready to return in spirit, even while secretly being thankful for being a virtual million miles from the mud and dung and undergrowth of the actuality. Social reality has not been deodorized, as is sometimes thought, but extraneously re-odorized. In a kind of olfactory surrealism, the person in the next seat on the train smells for a moment – sometimes longer – of camphor, lemongrass and violet, the irrelevant scents of which disappear into the general ether that only smells of stress.

The olfactory nerves were trained in prehistory not to allow the primitive to enjoy the world idiotically, but to be suspicious of it. What is the scent carried on the breeze telling him? Danger gives off a smell that is more important to self-preservation in a vastly heteronomous environment than what the wild flowers smell like. In this lies the eternally compromised nature of smell as the sense – even more so than taste, which gave its name to subjectivity – that communicates primarily via the faculties for pleasure and displeasure. The notion that bad things smell bad survived longer than the doctrine of visual correspondences in nature that it probably helped generate. In the re-odorized world today, everything is designed to convince people of its benign intentions, pre-eminently those of other people, but the displacement of smells into contexts where their gratuitousness means precisely nothing, together with the externally imposed nature of the pleasantness that supposedly characterises every squirt of anti-perspirant, and which is the product of a lucrative meeting of chemical science and soft psychology, cannot help but admit the opposite, that nothing that has to be so assiduously counterfeited can really be benign. By turning the spontaneity of natural scent into something that can be sprayed on as needed, the delusion that the world can be made pleasanter to order is sold to isolated individuals who have been denuded of spontaneity by the late form of their social being. In a society that smells of synthetic violet and cedar wood, the incursion of the natural occurs only in the aggressive pungency of those who have not had time to wash. Thus does nature stand convicted as that which the human species, at whatever cost to its own disenchanted nature, has struggled to rise above. Nothing is to be gained by relapsing into it when the technology for imitating it, or at least its sweeter moments, lies to hand. The sentimental proverb, 'A rose by any other name would smell as sweet', which was ideology from the moment of its first utterance, has been better fulfilled in odorized modernity, when any of the other names of the rose dreamed up by the perfume industry renders its fragrance at least as sweet, if not sweeter, than the original.

Smell and Nostalgia

The brute instrumentality to which smells have been subjected has robbed them of their associations, and reduced them to an olfactorily illiterate indiscriminacy in the interest of putting everybody into a better mood. Not just perfumes and deodorants, but the fragrances used in street-cleaning and on the underground systems and commuter trains in Europe, initiated by an experiment in Paris in the 1990s in overcoming the stink of scorched rubber and urine with the scent of spring flowers, has led to aroma-fatigue. Being overpowered by orange, lemon and lavender on the way to work turned out to be more hindrance than help. Supermarkets are sprayed with the distilled aromas of baking bread, roasting coffee and frying chicken in order to tempt buyers, while the drink department might emit a fugitive waft of whisky, or of oak barrels at least. These aromas at least have some contextual mooring, for all that the bread is really baked in industrial ovens elsewhere, rather than here on these premises. Opulent perfumes are routinely sprayed in the lobbies of grand hotels, to give the impression that everybody who has passed through them smells as exquisite, and as exquisitely rich, as the surroundings. Ford Madox Ford's love-letter to a London on the brink of technological modernity speaks of the particular quiddities that a city, recollected fondly by one far distant from it, arouses in him:

> *Above all his London, his intimate London, will be the*
> *little bits of it that witnessed the great moments, the poignant*
> *moods of his life; it will be what happened to be the*
> *backgrounds of his more intense emotions.*
> *Certain corners of streets, certain angles of buildings,*

> *the spray of dishevelled plane-trees, certain cloud-forms, gusts of white smoke, odours, familiar sounds – these, in their remembrance, will wring his heart.*[26]

The sense-impressions that feed these home thoughts from abroad are often of the unloveliest aspects of an urban milieu that was nonetheless defiantly itself, not one that had been cosmetically an apology for itself.

> *I have known a man, dying a long way from London, sigh queerly for a sight of the gush of smoke that, on a platform of the Underground, one may see, escaping in great woolly clots up a circular opening, by a grimy, rusted iron shield, into the dim upper light. He wanted to see it again as others have wished to see once more the Bay of Naples, the olive groves of Catania.*[27]

And smell it too, no doubt.

The extraneous admixture of scent to everyday life, which hopes to find elements of sensitive response still in benumbed human beings, through bypassing the linguistic realm polluted by the language of commerce, is a gamble on irrationality. If it remains hard to talk people into an enforced reconciliation with everything ugly, from which a wholly functionalised society threatens to make them indistinguishable, perhaps they can be mollified by an appeal to their inarticulable capacity for responding to beauty, even if the spring flowers that might cheer the senses have been vaporised into the form of floral air-freshener. Instant sensory receptivity has after all been culture's preferred mode since impressionism. The trouble is that the direct appeal to feeling, which was intended to do away with the sterile discursive methodology of arguing a case one way and the other as in a court of law, does nothing to encourage reflection on, and therefore resistance to, the very conditions it is designed to circumvent. An honest enough desire to make cities smell more pleasant is now made dishonest in the form of aromatherapy, in which the various essences are promoted as having psychologically ameliorative effects. The subject lies submerged in water in a semi-darkness that reminds her of pre-partum uterine security, only with the piercing scents of Peruvian balsam, lemon balm and hyssop added. Virtually everything is described as 'soothing', although certain substances – such as the balsam of Peru – are paradoxically stimulating too, like cocaine. The actual efficacy of such practices is a permanently contested area, as the characteristic bet-hedging tone of the University of Maryland Medical Centre website indicates: 'Researchers are not entirely clear how aromatherapy may work. Some experts believe our sense of smell may play a role. The "smell" receptors in your nose communicate with parts of your brain (the amygdala and hippocampus) that serve as storehouses for emotions and memories. When you breathe in essential oil molecules, some researchers believe they stimulate these parts of your brain and influence physical, emotional, and mental health.'[28] And others wouldn't give you a tinker's damn for such claims. Where linguistic reasoning dare not enter, or only stutters non-committally in vague references to 'some researchers', the subject is thrown back on the full force of historical contingency, against which nothing in the smell of neroli can immunise her.

Scent of Attraction

A modern-day consciousness unable to trust the evidence of the distal senses of sight and hearing when it comes to the crucial matter of personal relations might fall back on what its olfactory receptors were telling it. If it were possible in the pre-socialised state to distinguish between genders and ethnic groups by smell alone, does not something of that primordial ability survive even in the reified circumstances of today? The theory of pheromones, corporeal scents given off by the individual in a state of sexual arousal, and which are subliminally registered by those desiring to become his or her mates, has generated not only an entire field of scientific investigation, but has added capital value to the perfume and aromatherapy industries too, thereby realising the old cynical wisdom uttered at the sight of the successful sexual predator that, if only you could bottle whatever it is he or she has, you would become rich overnight. Pheromones exist in insect species, but there is no objective evidence for them in humans, or even any of the other mammals. In any case, the human olfactory bulb either registers scents or it doesn't; the vomeronasal capacity that would be required to sense a scent that nobody can actually smell is not present in the human organism. This is not to say that there are not bodily scents to which others respond, only that the responses are conditioned by a host of other factors more present to consciousness than the subterranean operations of pheromones allegedly are. Richard Doty, whose investigations have failed to find the slightest evidence for human pheromones, articulates the case against them: 'In this group of vertebrates [mammals], chemically mediated social processes are rarely hardwired, and most chemicals involved in their social communication are idiosyncratic and comprised of multiple compounds, a number of which are affected by stress, diet, and other factors. Even when neuroendocrine responses are involved, the influences come from multiple chemicals and depend as much on the receiver as the sender, commonly being influenced by the receiver's prior experience and motivational state... [M]ost such influences cannot be divorced from higher-order cognitive processes and rarely differ fundamentally from similar influences of other sensory systems.'[29] And yet experiments supposedly show women unwittingly choosing to sit in particular areas of a dentist's waiting-room where a chair has been sprayed with so-called male pheromone, or preferring the scent of a sweat-soaked man's T-shirt when the pheromones in it indicate the existence of a contrasting immune system to her own, so promising a union of healthy offspring. Most of the research has focused on androstadienone, a derivative of progesterone found in male axillary sweat, saliva, urine and sperm. Release of this compound has been found to affect physiological arousal in heterosexual women and homosexual men, as well as general mood, and it has therefore been widely nominated as the best candidate for the human male pheromone, as though the responses it elicits were not in themselves primarily conditioned by context. What also tends to undermine the notion that androstadienone is attractive to potential partners is that it is specifically present in oxidised (or stale) male sweat, which enjoys a widespread reputation for being powerfully repulsive. The compound in freshly extromitted sweat, androstenol, rapidly decays. Hormonal scent has a very limited range of transmission, typically no more than about 18 inches even at high concentrations, so the experimental subjects in the dentist's waiting-room would already have to have decided which chair to sit in before they became aware of the scent. In a crowded room, nobody would be able to say which of those people around her was the one whose particular scent she was picking up on. And in any case, pheromone theory tends to insist that the scent of pheromones is only subconsciously registered, so the mechanism of attraction is thrown one stage back from the immediate scent itself.

The desire to believe that the attractiveness of others can be captured in their scent is the motive force of Patrick Süskind's allegorical fairy-tale, *Perfume: The Story of a Murderer* (1985). Apprenticed to an Italian master perfumer in the Paris of the mid-eighteenth century, the protagonist, Jean-Baptiste Grenouille, develops an ambition to formulate what would be the most captivating perfume in the world, founded on the natural scents of girls just entering puberty. In order to preserve the pure essence, Grenouille must kill the girls, and so becomes a mass murderer, clubbing two dozen victims to death and extracting the essential oils from their skin. The *nec plus ultra* is reached when he meets Laure Richis, the voluptuous red-headed daughter of a wealthy town notable in the Provençal town of Grasse, centre of the world perfume industry, and kills her too. Finally arrested and charged with serial murders, Grenouille is spared execution on the scaffold by the erotic frenzy into which the town is driven when the killer releases the scent of Laure, a concentrated essence that contains in its accord background notes of all the other girls he has killed. Returning to Paris, Grenouille signs his own death warrant when he douses himself in the perfume in the company of a group of street vagabonds and ruffians who, driven by a different kind of appetite, carve him to pieces with their knives and eat him. Their disgust at their own descent into cannibalism is offset, however, by the satisfying knowledge that, in a world that regards them as savages, they have acted out of unalloyed innocent enthusiasm, even love.

Perfume is a sceptical fable about pheromones, and the determinist theory of desire. It is no accident that its protagonist is a misanthrope, a man who cannot bear the proximity of other human beings, their stench and their moral squalor. But nor has the sterility of solitude proved agreeable to him either. Hell is other people, but so is being alone. The solution seems to lie in capturing the essence of the most desirable specimens of humanity, and surrounding oneself only with that, but its effect on the despised masses is typically incendiary. They are either driven to orgiastic incontinence or to cannibalistic gluttony. Grenouille, named after the ugly frog of the children's tales, dreams that his invention of the irresistible perfume will make him king of the world, which it momentarily does, but beauty turns out to be terroristic, in that it leads a whole community to overlook his murderousness, even to the extent of the murdered girl's father offering to take him into his family. If desire could be distilled into an essence that literally led people by their noses, the story suggests, the result would be a destructive anarchy and the dissolution of morality. Not being able to live with other people reduces the eremitical individual not to purity but to the severity of a coldness that may well turn to pathological hatred. The seven years Grenouille spends on the mountain in the Massif Central on his way to the emerald city of Grasse, bedded into the dirt and rock and eating moss, conjoin him with the great ascetics of devotional history – the Buddha starving himself to enlightenment under the fragrant bodhi tree, the forty days of famine endured by Jesus in the Judean desert, the stylites who, following the fifth century example of Saint Simeon, climbed to the tops of pillars and wasted away over the decades amid the pungent stink of putrefaction. These rituals of purification are designed to throw off entanglement in the material world and its temptations, but for Grenouille, they only renew his ardour for the scent of new sexual purity he had first smelled on a pubescent girl slicing plums in the Paris street. Mortification does not abolish carnality, but fans its flames, because it holds out before the ascetic the promise of relief from it, regarded austerely as temptation by the devout. The salient detail about Grenouille is that, despite the circumstances of his own birth to a mother who squats to deliver him on the ground, having gone into labour while gutting fish in a street market, cutting the umbilicus with her knife, he himself has no natural odour. He only notices his own uncanny olfactory neutrality after the purification on the mountain, during which he has conceived his desire to become a god. It is as though he must first divest himself of his own humanity before he can beguile the rest of humankind.

If a cynically instrumentalised desire can be turned on and off at will by the application of the most devastating *eau de toilette* ever created, the result, predictably enough, would be the reduction of the amorous to blind automata, like the legends of those credulous girls who were supposedly seduced by mesmerists in the nineteenth century while under hypnotic influence. Their descendants would be the date-rape victim of today, unsuspectingly drugged into incapacity, before regaining consciousness in a state in which lingering pain is the only evidence of what has been done to her. If the mechanics of attraction can be made so empirically certain, the tiresome business of seduction, which often seems no more than a sublimated version of drugging somebody senseless by overcoming their resistance, can be skipped. Emergent desire is as susceptible of commodification as anything else, and must take its own turn at surrendering to the economic laws of society, where the totem of success achieved by means of eliminating the competition could hardly be better suited to the machinations of the erotic marketplace. It was only a short step from the elaboration of pheromonal theory in pseudo-science to the appearance of bottled products that promise to make the user – typically the blundering male – irresistible to whoever is in his vicinity. If he can't have the one girl he has set his sights on, he can at least be spoiled for choice among the rest. The fantastical nature of such a product recalls the love-potions and philtres of medieval romance, the spells of sorcerers, the magical kiss that might turn a frog such as Grenouille into at least a ravishing prince, if not the puppet-master of all humankind. That it should work not through inducing visual hallucinations, as in the story of the frog-prince, but by bewitching the nostrils, seems to reveal that carnal desire partakes of the same appetitive immediacy as the hunger of the belly. Once desire is enraged, the object of its fury may just as well be a sizzling steak as a voluptuous body, and the fable closes with Grenouille's apotheosis as the most satisfying meal the vagrants have ever eaten, satisfying precisely in that it has transformed their hunger from mere famishment into elevated gourmandising. The innovation the perfume industry has lately made in turning to culinary aromas reinforces the point. Desire, which is in danger of becoming an all-too- human skill where it has to be negotiated with another, is returned to being an appetite that must be satiated at any cost, before being piqued again in an endless cycle. Subjecting the aleatoric lawlessness of the rules of attraction to the structure of a scientific formula can easily seem a kindness when there is something so obviously unfair about the way desire works. Although beauty lies proverbially in the eye of the subjective beholder, and does to the extent that nobody can ever see precisely what it is anybody else sees in their beloved, there do nonetheless seem to be invisible objective standards analogous to those that obtain in aesthetics, or indeed gastronomy, and yet, just as in those other categories, they resist formalisation, and are anyway eternally subject to the mutabilities of passing taste, when their transmogrification confers on them not the indeterminacy that might bring hope to the hopeless, but only another implicitly objective, but equally elusive, concrete status. The attempt to commodify desire, as Grenouille does, is founded on the fallacious assumption that a commodity acquires immutability in its concrete materiality, rather than being subject like all commodities to the anarchy of the market. What everybody absolutely must have today will be unsaleable trash tomorrow, and must make way with decent haste for a more up-to-date model. If the 'marriage market', as it is called with cheerful cynicism, is just that, its own structural laws – such as that of supply and demand – are likely to be as capable of abrogation by unforeseen runs, panics, hostile speculation and criminal rigging as the commodities markets are. Desire, like capitalist economics, would like everybody to believe it is circumscribed by smoothly operating mechanisms, but can only survive in reality by creating a constant aura of crisis around itself. A love-potion would be the means of escape from the riot of jostling bodies in the earthly bazaar, and into the heavenly serenity of the plutocrat, into whose lap everything and everybody falls because he is rich enough not to need to compete any longer, and so liberated from the vulgarity of pursuit. Aiming to carry home the prize of the best-looking girl or boy in the room, the competitors in desire's marketplace attempt to purloin from each other what real economic relations have already thieved from them in surplus value.

Depth psychology has its own, often alarming, theories as to how physical attraction is conceived. Freud famously suspects the enamoured of seeking belated substitutes for one or other parent, whose unconditional love he lost some time in late infancy. The theory isn't entirely inhospitable to the postulate of pheromonal attraction, which characteristically holds that scents not detectable to consciousness subliminally attract the individual to partners who are genetically similar, but have the complementary immune systems that would guarantee healthy babies. Faces that are perceived as average in construction, rather than peculiarly distinctive, symmetrical between the left and right halves, and conforming to a putative ideal ratio for the disposition of the features relative to each other, are consistently the most popular in psychological tests, although individual judgments as to what constitutes regularity show some variation. When it comes to auditory characteristics, those looking for men value a deep-toned, confident but not strident vocal tone, while what is valued in women is a high-pitched voice, since vocal pitch rises with the production of oestrogen during ovulation. The unshaven look that all men below the age of fifty have adopted for at least the past thirty years is regularly found more attractive than clean-shaven for the evidence of testosterone and maturity it conveys, not to mention its deceptive hint of a refusal to conform to the rules of grooming, although a full beard has the reassuring effect of making a man look a few years older, and therefore more settled, than he actually is. Strong physiques and deep complexions speak of a man unafraid to confront the great outdoors, while discreet scarring suggests he may well be prepared to defend you in a fight. In women, ideal waist-to-hip ratio (70%) is valued for its procreative promise, as is an empathic manner, while a moderate degree of neuroticism is held to be indicative of her likely diligence in caring for the children. Luxuriant hair hints at the prodigality of a life at least partly consecrated to sexual indulgence, but too much makeup suggests she may be a deceiver. When the psychology of attraction refers at all to what it vaguely calls 'cultural factors', they are the immutable elements popularly associated with particular ethnicities, and which are held to have been unchanged by time: French lubricity, Spanish hot-bloodedness, Italian elegance, German coldness, British stand-offishness, and so forth. Not a word is spoken about the sedimentation of social and historical tendencies in consciousness, in which objective conditions are internalised and transformed deceptively into free subjectivity, shaping desire for certain social types above all others. As well as having the potential to be good nurturers, young women are now expected to have similarly structured sexual appetites to men, and be as capable of uproarious rowdyism beforehand. Any tendency to emotional vulnerability is to be sternly resisted, other than where it makes her helplessly pliable to the man who wants her, and woe betide any woman who comes between him and his male friends. Men, meanwhile, are required to give evidence of limitless competitive instinct, be materially acquisitive to the last degree, and especially profligate in nourishing their partner's own avarice. While his sexuality is conceived as bestially uncontrollable, he earns points for giving the impression of nonetheless just managing to control it. The post-war revolution in sexual attitudes having been widely presumed to have gone too far in closing the gap between the sexes, the antique gender-roles have returned in postmodern guise, with both coquettishness and muscle-flexing having become post-ironic elements of the negotiation between sexual participants. The word 'partner', once an evasive term for the other halves in same-sex unions, has now been adopted by all except the most senior generations; it efficiently sanitises the relationship so labelled of any suggestion of the erotic, but also of the legalistic aridity of the marital terms, and turns it instead into an amicable arrangement, a joint business venture that can easily be dissolved when one or the other partner decides to jump ship, or else go it alone. Nothing is more dispiriting than the suggestion that a partnership might go on indefinitely. The security once characterised by long marriages feels like imprisonment in the era of shrunken attention-spans. In their early stages, relationships are cheerfully referred to as 'entanglements', with the implication that the trick is to learn how to cut the knot, not embroil oneself all the more inextricably. Ambition, raised to a life-principle by a culture that mercilessly thwarts it at every turn, pervades the sexual arena too, reminding the lover that whatever he is settling for now, he is thereby missing out on something better. Women are encouraged to think men have as much sex as they can because they are trying to hit on the one perfect mate, as opposed to complying with the social dictates of the insatiable male, in whom the ideology that any sex is better than none at all, dinned into him by equally inexperienced schoolmates in his adolescence, proves as jealously disinclined to wither as did the dictatorship of the party-state in the adolescence of communism. To popular pseudo-science, what people are really obeying are the dictates of each other's pheromones, transmitted through the vestigial vomeronasal organ that human evolution has left them with, the mesmerising, consciously indetectable scents of which rise above the acrid odour of history, and guide them into autonomic mating behaviour.

Smell as Social Indicator

Commentators on the history of social smell always feel obliged to insist that noticing the smells of others cannot be rid of its historic discriminatory force, expressed in the tendency of exclusionary social attitudes and movements, all the way to fascism, to define human alterity by its foreign smell. On this view, implicitly, the gradual decay of olfactory sensitivity in the human species was a healthy accompaniment to socialisation. Smell will not, however, be denied by ideological fiat in this way, and if it could, it would tend to the homogenising of humanity. Writers often take the politically correct view that the smell of others is more or less imaginary, as though diet, gender, hygiene standards, body temperature, clothing materials and working environments had no impact on their organic beings. Children being taught to distinguish between different odours in junior school are encouraged to notice the comparative scents of fruits and spices, but not of each other. This desensitisation in the name of sensitivity is once again bound up with the notion that all smells are either pleasant or unpleasant, the neutral ones counting as pleasant. The terror that not liking the smell of the person sitting next to you means that you will automatically not like them leads to the kind of repression that can only return in other sublimated forms, even though smell is sufficiently immaterial to count as sublimation in itself. Suddenly receiving a noseful of the labouring poor in close proximity is what led the fortunate classes of previous eras to tilt their heads back at the encounter, and so appear to be looking down their culturally refined noses, fixing olfactory differentiation as definitive of social hierarchy, at least until labourers' dwellings began to acquire bathrooms. A bad smell is the bad conscience of a society riven by privilege and its conjoined twin, deprivation. The sweat of toil is the primordial curse of the human race since Adam: 'In the sweat of thy face shalt thou eat bread, till thou return unto the ground' (Genesis 3:19). If you want to eat, you'll have to work for it – the same warning the Nazis issued to the German people, but from which the landed gentry and the industrial plutocrats were somehow silently exempted. The longing for a purified world free of the smell of others is an effort at denial of what it costs others to keep the whole machinery in operation.

When smell becomes offensive to others, there is often an

indeterminacy between the age-old conviction that the rank-smelling have no sense of smell of their own, and the more realistic postulate of the deodorised world that everybody should be able to smell their own unwashed bodies, or insufficiently frequently changed clothes, or rankly garlicky skin-pores, and be able to take hygienic action accordingly. Either way, what has failed is consideration for the nasal sensitivities of others. Unsightly jetsam in the overgrown back garden, banging techno music in the middle of the night, offend the senses in ways that even the offenders themselves can understand, though they appear to have chosen the path of defiance in the matter. That smells should be just as disturbing to the peace is a more contested question, and is also thrown into relief where it is acknowledged by the inaccurate assumption that everybody stops noticing smells after a while. A smell is held to be a natural emanation, and so to complain about it is like complaining that the sun is too bright, although of course it very often is. The neighbour in the apartment-block who smokes cannabis for a good part of every day, the over-ripely pungent smoke insinuating itself through open windows into the apartments of others, becomes a nuisance to them, but how to decide the disposition of ethical rights here? One individual's human right to use a natural intoxicant abrades against the rights of others to inhale air that is free of noxious odours. It is an exemplary case of the conflict between positive and negative freedoms, freedom to (smoke cannabis) versus freedom from (the smell of cannabis smoke). The advancement of human social relations depends first and foremost on securing the negative freedoms, such as freedom from political oppression, from hunger, from the threat of violent crime, from ignorance, from other people's smoke, before any articulation of what individuals with their specific predilections and affinities might then like to do – found an agricultural cooperative, join a political party, form a band, conduct pharmaceutical research, smoke dope. Debates generated by the widespread bans on public smoking across the western world have often become embroiled in the standoff over how far individuals ought to be able to go in affecting environments in such a way that makes them noxious to the rest of society. Smokers have reconstructed themselves ideologically as a beleaguered minority whose legal rights, as distinct from the cannabis-smokers, are being directly curtailed, which creates at least the potential – though seldom the actuality – for a serious dialogue about majoritarianism, the arithmetical principle by which bourgeois liberal democracy reveals its disavowed obscene underbelly of totalitarianism. Numbers alone must decide every question, with the unlucky minorities in each instance being crushed, whether it be in terms of parliamentary representation in winner-takes-all electoral systems, or in which of the aspirant singers should be voted off the talent-show this week. Representational democracy has found no better way of allowing the people – the *demos* – to rule than by recasting its founding principle as the rule of the majority, in defence of which its perennial adduction of Churchill's remark to the effect that democracy is the worst political system, apart from all the others that have been tried, hears only the argument for making the best of a bad job, and not the stinging criticism of its inadequacy. What is required from the smokers, who have in all jurisdictions largely obeyed the new regulations, when they could very easily have made them at least temporarily unworkable, is that they try to imagine the vileness of second-hand smoke for those who don't wish to smell it, and for those (asthmatics, bronchial cases, young children and babies) to whom it is more obviously immediately dangerous. The non-smokers, meanwhile, have to consider how much repression they are prepared to exercise in pursuit of removing the evidence of other people's vices from the public domain. Smoking has generally been banned in enclosed public places, but not yet in the street. Should governments insist eventually that the mere sight of smoking is intolerable, and drive it back into private residences only? And then what happens when, as in the case of the lone cannabis-user, the smoke drifts out through the windows? Might it be possible to create an apparatus like a sealed bell-jar that smokers would have to step into if they wished to smoke, and from which they would only be released when they had re-inhaled all their own exuded smoke? Electronic cigarettes, the smokelessness of which should have closed the debate once and for all, have now become the locus of incendiary debate in themselves, because they seem to prohibitionists in some way to be letting smokers get away all over again with the idea that smoking is acceptable, even though they don't generate smoke at all. It is as if what campaigners are objecting to now is not smoke itself, but the visually triggered memory of it. Smoke, already no more than the vaporising of a solid element, has now itself become vaporised, its invisible trails only present to olfaction at a conceptual remove, no longer smellable at all and yet capable of being evoked in thought for something like the same reason that smell inspires both memory and emotional response. The equation works both ways. Emotional response can ignite the memory of smell internally, disproving the supposition of the ancients that the sense of smell is the most fugitive of all senses, leaving no imprint of itself behind in sense-memory. In fact, it lingers on ideationally, to the precise degree of its seductive gorgeousness or its noisome acridity in the first place. The aftertaste of foods and wines may linger on the palate, but it is unlikely that the sense-memory of them several days later is as potent as the memory of how a freshly manured field, a vase of full-blown lilies, the roasting duck or the richly gamey burgundy smelled when they first hit the sense-faculties.

The socialisation of smell brings with it a whole bouquet of ethical difficulties. In the state of nature, there is nobody to whom any appeal could be mounted, but as soon as cooperative social systems come into being, a notional set of precepts arises, as Hegel argues in the section on ethical life in the *Philosophy of Right*. 'Against nature man can claim no right, but once society is established, poverty [or any other bad smell] takes the form of a wrong done to one class by another.'[30] The perception of a wrong calls out for redress, but filthy odours have proved as stubbornly unexpungeable as poverty, which even Jesus acknowledges will always be with us. And it is interestingly in the context of a prodigal expenditure of fragrance – the woman who empties a box of spikenard over his head during dinner at Simon the leper's house in Bethany – that poverty's intractability is declared. Rebuked for drenching the Messiah in voluptuous perfume, which could have been sold at its market value in aid of the poor, the woman is defended by the suddenly radiantly fragrant Christ: 'Let her alone; why do you trouble her?' (Mark 14:6). The poor will always be with us, so there will never lack opportunity to help them, but a well-meaning act should not on that account be castigated. In so saying, he surely recalls the wisdom of the Torah: 'You shall give to him freely, and your heart shall not be grudging when you give to him... For the poor will never cease out of the land' (Deuteronomy 15:10-11). The spikenard sloshed out in Bethany, which appears to have been worth the equivalent of a year's wages to the average agricultural labourer, was either imported Asian muskroot or primarily indigenous lavender. It doubly scents the paradisiacal garden in the Song of Songs: 'Your plants are an orchard of pomegranates with pleasant fruits, fragrant henna with spikenard, spikenard and saffron, calamus and cinnamon' (4: 13-14). The intoxication of its scent can't erase the stink of poverty, but precisely for that reason, poverty and the obligations it calls on humanity to fulfil are not scanted or trivialised by it.

The Dissociating Sense

The smell of other people penetrates more deeply into one's own inner sensory being than any other of their contingent external attributes. Short of sexual activity, there can be no more intimate experience of the other's physical being. Simmel's argument that the smell of others in close proximity may be what led to the decay of social collectivity in the cooler countries, where large-scale socialisation took place indoors, and where the more people there were, the more odorous a gathering was, is not entirely a fanciful one. As cultural refinement tended in the direction of avoiding unpleasant smells, so it produced a corresponding social tendency to avoid substantial gatherings. In countries where the climate is too hot for large meetings, assemblies and parties to be held inside, gregarious sociability, and perhaps political solidarity, endured because the open air carried off most of the mingled odour of people's bodies. This would be one of the ways in which the operations of ideology, which are classically conceived as being sublimates at the idealist level of material practices and experiences, in fact have their own material side. Smell is the perfect sensory vehicle for this paradox. It is at once so profoundly expressive and definitive of the identity of concrete phenomena, and yet is in itself nothing in particular, compared to the objects of the distantial senses. Simmel again:

> *Smell does not form an object on its own, as do sight and hearing, but remains, as it were, captive in the human subject, which is symbolised in the fact that there exist no independent, objectively characterising expressions for fine distinctions. If we say, 'it smells sour', then this only means that it smells the way something smells which tastes sour.*[31]

That is, it refers to something else, some other external comparator, and yet it is, in itself, irreducibly an attribute of the concrete object that emits it. With regard to the sociological application of this insight, if smell is, as Simmel holds, the 'dissociating sense', then the deodorised world that has come into being in the century since he wrote should have brought with it at least the potential for a general re-emergence from the principle of isolation of cultural refinement, and yet quite the opposite is the case. Social atomisation is more strictly autonomously established than ever, supported by screen technologies that maintain secure distances between subjects even where they have apparently elided the immense geographical distances between them, and which permit levels of intimacy that would be premature, very possibly abusive, were one to engage in them in physical contiguity. Much of the behaviour on dating websites consists in extended flirtations with people one has no intention of offering to meet, even where they might live two streets away. As long as they are contained by the screen, there is no danger of them overstaying, messing up the bedroom, or discharging their bodily fluids at you, or of your having to smell them. With cultural development, thought Simmel, the perceptual acuity of the senses fades away, but the subjective element rises. People see less, but know more confidently what they like and dislike. The sensitivity of vision and hearing is reduced to shorter distances, which is why smell, a short-distance sense in the social context, comes to play a crucial role in the social appraisal of the other. If sight and hearing aim asymptotically at an assessment of the world of strangers with which nearly everybody comes into contact most days, smell appears to provide an honest register of all one needs to know about them. The misanthropic Nietzsche, fulminating in Alpine isolation, can repeatedly think of no more mordant castigation of his distaste for certain social types by saying that they smell – the shudder of a sense-memory more materially present to immaterial consciousness than anything about their absurd appearances or the grating of their voices.

The sense of smell may have become devalued in deodorized mass society, but the benefit achieved thereby, with relation to others at least, is that humans are not so thrown back on their animal instincts as they were when the unreflexive rejection of the foul-smelling governed social relations, and made men the slaves of nature. In a telling passage, Marx outlines the condition of working people in socio-economic relations in which they have become estranged from the objects they produce, and the objective level of civilisation such production makes possible: 'As a result... man (the worker) only feels himself freely active in his animal functions – eating, drinking, procreating, or at most in his dwelling and in dressing up, etc.; and in his human functions he no longer feels himself to be anything but an animal.'[32] In the contemporary era, what could be the complexities of human emotional and psychological response to others, and the limitless combinatorial potential that love relationships might comprise, have been reduced to the putative animal function of pheromones, in which the objects of pursuit become, in Diane Ackerman's phrase, 'love-zombies', much as socialisation itself in the eighteenth and nineteenth centuries became subject to whether one could live with the smell of others. These are human functions being reduced to the animal level. Meanwhile, wallowing in scented mud at the luxury spa, ostensibly at the highest level of a culture of sensual sophistication, the refugee from life's stresses blissfully turns herself to a hippopotamus.

Chapter Four

Taste

Tastes do not remain irreducible givens; if one knows how to question them, they reveal to us the fundamental projects of the person.
Jean-Paul Sartre

Proletarian language is dictated by hunger. The poor chew words to fill their bellies. From the objective spirit of language they expect the sustenance refused them by society.
Theodor Adorno

Subjectivity of Taste

A discomfiting antinomy with which considerations of the sense of taste have been grappling since Graeco-Roman antiquity, but which became particularly acute in the seventeenth century, and has remained so down to the present day, is whether a refined palate is the indicator of aesthetic discernment carried to the degree of hedonistic estrangement, the *nec plus ultra* of the human perversion of nature's intentions, or whether, by contrast, it represents a relapse into pure animalistic self-indulgence. The discriminations of Lucullus turn out to be the obverse of the opportunistic greed of domestic animals. Compared to the operations of the other senses, the enjoyment of taste – even more than its eternal *confrère,* smell – embroils the user in the most corporeal kind of satisfaction, returning him to one of his most basic functions in sublimated form. The ideology of gourmandism insists that its practitioners are anything but guzzling hogs, in that hogs don't much care whether the plum is Rhodian or Sicilian in origin, whereas they can appreciate the respective qualities of each, but its critics see in it only the rationalisation of naked appetite, one of the ways in which humanity has made an aesthetic virtue out of the biological necessity of survival. Consumption is the only one of the body's immanent functions to have become fully aestheticised in this way. Nothing similar has been made of respiration or excretion; even the sexual instinct, engine of the refulgent culture of romantic longing, has not quite attained to precisely the level of evaluative discernment as have eating and drinking, notwithstanding the pseudo-culinary approach to sexual methodology in the ancient sutras and Taoist compendia. Aesthetic form in the context of everyday life has more usually been concentrated in the external physical requirements of clothing and shelter, rather than in the organic mechanisms of the body itself.

The relishing of food, conceived as the sensuous background for social interaction and thought in Greek antiquity, rather than being merely an end in itself, enacts the moment at which sensory delight calls forth the aesthetic instinct that would elevate it to permanence, or at least to permanent re-iterability. Paul Valéry expressed this process in his meditations on aesthetics:

> *If a man is hungry, his hunger will make him do*
> *whatever must be done to annul it as quickly as possible;*
> *but if he finds the food delectable, his delight will strive*
> *in him to endure, to perpetuate, or to be reborn. Hunger*
> *impels us to cut the sensation short; pleasure to*
> *develop another; and these two tendencies will become*
> *so independent of one another that the man soon learns*
> *to indulge in delicacies and to eat when he is not hungry.*[1]

All art is the prolongation of a momentary sensory felicitude into a technical procedure, something that can be produced with an effort of will, and aims at reproducing that transient delight in others. Not the least reason that the sense of taste has struggled to establish its own autonomous status within aesthetic theory is that its practical elaboration stands at the obscene biological interface between physical satiety and superfluity. In order to carry on scaling gastronomy's heights, one must after a certain point force-feed oneself, the likely consequences of which were mythologised in the twentieth century into the ancient institution of the vomitorium, the fictive idea – possibly an embroidering of a reference in Seneca to slave-boys mopping up the vomit of the inebriated – that Roman banqueters habitually withdrew to a separate room to puke their stomachs empty in preparation for continuing to eat. The repulsiveness of the myth has proved so attractive because it fits a general notion of what indulgence of the sense of taste leads to, the behaviour of beasts. Going to three art exhibitions in one afternoon might induce eventual glazed exasperation; the twelve-course tasting-menu seems to lure its consumers towards the indignity of regurgitation, an act of physiological penitence that carries a moral charge somewhere amid the gastric back-swill. Intemperance is the only one of the seven deadly sins that brings with it its own prompt chastisement.

Far from its being an imperfect paradigm, however, it is in the very movement of aesthetic pleasure becoming manifest from the primacy of a biological requirement that taste most instructively defines the aesthetic. The transformation of instinct into drive, of basic need into active desire, is the mechanism whereby the most subterranean strata of organic life give birth to subjectivity, the one peculiar feature above all that separates humanity from the rest of creation, and that furnishes it ultimately with culture(s). Culture's own guilt about its extraneous, even parasitic nature, which reproduces itself in public hand-wringing about whether it can be right to spend money subsidising theatre companies when there are homeless people on the streets outside the theatres, but also in culture's acutely sharpened sense of its own pretentiousness, of the bombastic nature of its claims to truth in the midst of the universal untruth of consumer society, are not degraded by the notion that what is hideously termed 'fine dining' might be an emblem of it. It is indeed the flawless emblem of culture's gratuitousness, of the fact that surfeit exists amid insufficiency, that nothing in the world is not subject to the evaluative classifications on which culture rests, in which each economic stratum receives its apparent due, from the very best that is reserved for the elite down to the garbage that is democratically available to everybody. As with eating, there is something obscene about over-indulging in culture, because it results in the lie that it makes everybody better, and yet the consequences of living without it are even more catastrophic. Nothing separates barbarism and anorexia. Not merely the gratuitousness that can be pursued *ad nauseam*, but the central question of 'taste' itself, in the guise of the aesthetic discriminations that comprise the mature, fully educated and cultivated individual, is expressed in the apparently trivial questions of eating preferences. Everybody has something, some people entire sweeping categories of foods, they don't like to eat. These antipathies are entirely immune to rational analysis, but they become formative, even constitutive, of personality. Again, there is a suggestive hesitancy about the ontological value of these inclinations in the construction of subjectivity. There is as little point in arguing about whether Mahler was greater than Debussy as there is in arguing about whether pasta is better than potatoes, and yet in another sense, nothing could be more important to the foundation of discriminative consciousness, as a defence against the homogenisation in which social conformity enmeshes its participants. The standardisation of taste for which the global food and drink industries stand arraigned has absolved their clients from the childishness of personal proclivities – virtually everybody likes burgers, pizza, fried chicken, ice-cream and cola – at the cost of infantilising them back to the vanished days of prescribed school dinners, when Monday always meant meatloaf, Tuesday fishcakes, and so forth. Against this background, to dislike the taste of cola is an unfathomable eccentricity, if a harmless one, on a par with not watching television. Everybody believes official culture's piety to the effect that all are entitled to their personal tastes, just as all are entitled to their political opinions, and that no one taste is more legitimate than any other, as though it were a matter of credal sanctity, reacting with fury against any evidence of the retarding influence of such a belief. Taste is at once the denial of reason, and the reason for denial. The principle of *De gustibus*, written into the contract of aesthetic judgment since Kant's third critique, as though in the interests of fairness, has been interpreted ever since as though it were a ban on judgment. In enshrining the sacred principle of subjectivity, it has been warped into the occlusion of objective consciousness, so that nothing matters other than how the work made you feel, whether you had sympathy with the principal characters, whether you wouldn't have minded having sex with one of them, whether you cried at the end, but in which the distancing critical stance that might wonder why such events reduce you to tears, or even whether the situation as portrayed was worthy of tears, is seen as spoiling the fun, missing the point, or – the cardinal sin – taking it all too seriously. In a nice distinction, Valéry, conceding that there is indeed no legislating for taste, adds, 'but there has to be arguing about tastes,'[2] in recognition that, at the very least, even if taste is nothing more than the minor frippery the culture industry would claim it to be, it is hardly a static category. Even the canons of the great works, the classics, are subject to the mutabilities and deformations of shifting taste, since taste is socio-historically produced. That is what mutability is. Taste is rendered a peripheral matter by being reduced to nothing other than preference, whether one thing is more pleasing, and therefore ultimately better, than another, but the first stage of the exercise of taste is being able to see the differences between them, and what accounts for the differences, which is just what nobody feels either able or obliged to decide any longer, largely because differences between commodities are precisely what the culture industry has so assiduously smoothed away.

To a greater degree than ever, in the mediatised and internet age, people construct themselves from their subjective tastes as though in hope of conferring on themselves the sharply defined identity that the mechanisation of social relations otherwise denies them. Judgments that brush against the grain, either positively or negatively, are particularly helpful in this regard: 'I can't *abide* Brahms'; 'Say what you like about her, but Beryl Cook was good at what she did.' Strongly voiced, in scorn for the expected demurral of others, these opinions become the indicator of who one is in a world that doesn't noticeably care. The fearless assertion of *parti pris* binds such statements inextricably to the general social definition of taste as the discernment brought about by education, followed by a three-dimensional encounter with what life has to offer. In the eighteenth century, the nobility sent its idle sons around Europe on the Grand Tour, with the intention of lending the character-building aspect of practical field research to their accumulation of cultural knowledge, adding an element of self-construction to the construction into which expensive schooling had wrestled a young gentleman. Not coincidentally, the same period saw the emergence of the European *Bildungsroman*, the novel of formation in which a hero, by hacking a progress for himself through the social jungle, according to the lights of his own restless urge to moral self-invention, achieves the identity that only rites of passage can furnish. Wilhelm Meister is the prototype of all the heuristically questing young heroes in the nineteenth century novel: Eugene Onegin, Julien Sorel, Lucien de Rubempré, even Jane Austen's Elizabeth Bennet and Emma Woodhouse, George Eliot's Dorothea Brooke, Felix Holt and Daniel Deronda. The goal was an active process of the acquisition of understanding, even if – as with the monuments and cultural artefacts on the Grand Tour – it too often comported the risk of conceptualising knowledge as something that could be bought on the open market at the going rate, like a commodity. Today, people make these acquisitions in the pre-digested form that the culture industry prepares for them, and no embarrassment is incurred by condemning what is culturally distant from them as boring. If they have heard of something to the extent of being able to answer a quiz question about it correctly, they know it.

Judgments of taste lose their dignity when they become cheapened into a mere stance, an attitude. In this context, to say that you find Shakespeare tedious becomes an interesting, edgy postulate, as opposed to the groan of idleness for which one's teachers would have recognised it. Ignorance transformed into an opinion is no less ignorance, and does nothing to disprove the countervailing prejudice that most strong opinion is driven by either blithe or knowing ignorance. Truly to understand something involves setting aside taste, and assessing it immanently, according to its own concept of itself, and in the light of its objective emergence from the historical process by which intellectual activity becomes culture, and thereby begets taste. Only in this way are the elements of cultural productions, along with their ideological contexts, set in motion and, in the case of poor or inconsistent artworks, induced to reveal the inadequacy of their own construction. Subjected to nothing other than mere predilection, the work remains unpermeated by anything outside it, insolently reposing on its plinth in the museum, protected from any but the most static of scrutiny. It has nothing to say to the observer because it is seen as having nothing to do with him, as though the whole of culture's efflorescence were a matter of untamed vegetal growth, to be sniffed appreciatively or hacked away as taste dictates. The freezing stare of non-objectivised culture forces the spectator instead into his or her own self-assessment in relation to it, which assessment culminates, where the laden branch hangs just beyond reach, into the defiant affirmation that, after all, one doesn't care for its fruit. Culture, which once, by aiming high, sought to reflect human development back to itself, by showing it that it could be more than it already was, like the rising chants that flowed back into the ears of those standing below the Renaissance domes, convicts its clients instead of their own failure to measure up to it. Unable to situate it in the feudal religious context in which it emerged, an incurious contemporary hearer can only say either that Gregorian chanting is a bit depressing, or else utterly gorgeous, it scarcely matters which.

Taste, as long as it cannot free itself from its physiological origins in the taste of food and drink, both pleasant and unpleasant, retains the wrong kind of materialist force, being the transitory moment of judgment that is always the prelude to consumption. If historic culture is finally as commodifiable as anything else in a socio-economic order founded on consumption, and it has turned out to be just that, it can be relieved of the insufferable obligation it once incurred to tell the truth about the conditions in which it was produced, which are no longer thought to have any sway over its consumers in the present, but whose own order more than ever needs something like culture to cut them free of their embroilment in consumption. The products of culture are material objects that have become spiritualised matter, but which gain nothing from their being metabolised back into the raw material that brought them into being. In this respect, the metaphor of aesthetic taste, and of social judgment in general, would be better served by its being connected, as in physiology, to the sense of smell. The paradoxical equilibrium between smelling and tasting is reflected in the compensating awareness that, if there are more bad smells than good, there are more good tastes than bad. Smell is the sense of suspicions being confirmed, taste of hopes sustained. Even physical taste, however, is a matter of more than just nice or nasty, as is indicated by the taste categories, which have been instinctual since the earliest struggle for survival, and which, for all their relative impoverishment in the western tradition as against the oriental systems, helped structure the ethical and psychological materiality of social life, providing ready metaphors for everyday life-experiences. There are sweet faces, puppies, sweethearts. A salty attitude is one with edge, nip, pungent knowingness, the opposite of unseasoned immaturity. Sourness speaks of pessimism and spite, vinegary sarcasm, tart ripostes; it is hardly ever positive, and yet its absence would leave everything very bland. Bitterness is the flavour of regret, disappointment, an unreconciled response to sadness rather than a resigned or stoical one, the mood-music of recrimination. Hot implies sexy, exciting, startling in a good way (or an ambiguously bad-good way), something dangerous but exhilarating. Chinese gastronomy also classifies pungency, piquancy, spiciness; there are elements specific to Sichuanese cuisine that can be roughly translated as 'tingling' or, suggestively, 'strange flavour'. Weary of sweetness, as of relentlessly over-determined hotness, in a potential lover, one might enjoy being dated by somebody who subtly tingled, or whose psychological flavour, against the background of robotic conformity, was at least a little strange.

The social dimension of taste conceived in the French Enlightenment aimed to strain away its subjective element through a fine filter, like sediment from old claret. If the refined judgment of the *homme de goût* could perceive niceties of distinction between one vintage and another, between one landscape painter and another, the very faculty for differentiation, above and beyond the localised matter to which it was applied, was what defined a cultured individual, a person of taste. Taste recognised the crucial boundary-lines in a society founded on the discipline of sorting the excellent from the tawdry, the mediocre and the vulgar, the borders marking off the acceptable from the infra dig being so finely drawn that only the practised eye could see them. Nor are multiple valences specific to the culture-area of Western Europe. The concept of *rasa* connotes the same array of significations in Indian aesthetics, and indeed is of considerably older provenance. *Rasa*, etymologically the juice or sap of a plant, refers at once to the particular qualities of a work of art, to the effect it produces in the beholder in both his experience and his judgment of the work, and the overall state of cultural development necessary to be able to make these judgments. It also designates the constitutive principle by which works of art achieve their effects, as Carolyn Korsmeyer explains: 'Indian aesthetics refers to both the *rasa* of an object – the qualities to be appreciated – and to the experience of *rasa*. The term also designates the expressive power of art; the capture of emotional states in works of art may be likened to the combination of spices and foods in fine cooking.'[3] The discriminating subject is constituted by his response to attributes in the work that are in themselves imbued with this quality, and also constructed so as to call forth that very response. If the Grecian urn of western art appears coldly indifferent to whether the beholder sees it as evidence of an elevated stage of cultural development, the object in Indian aesthetic theory appeals to the subject to discover precisely its own careful craftsmanship in himself. The theoretical elaborations of *rasa* may be more complex than those governing western taste, and yet it is as solidly founded on the hierarchisation of sensibility as is taste. Indeed, there would be no taste were it not for the existence of what is distasteful. What the Enlightenment ideal of cultivation ensured, even in the British context, where the effetely polished glaze of the imported French article was roughened by a cultural sensibility both suspicious of Gallic over-refinement as of Gallic political tyranny, and – the other side of the same coin – too enamoured of the disputatious and satirical tone that their preference for empiricism over ethereal abstraction had nurtured in them, was that subjective judgment was transposed from deciding whether one liked the particular qualities of something, however that may be, to being able to recognise which were the tasteful things and which were the dross. There was an objective standard to appeal to, not only in matters of art, but in what came to be known as the social graces, but only the truly refined were properly conversant with it. Taste had lost the subjective triviality of its origin in physiology, and had acquired, in the aesthetic and social contexts, a false objectivity, but one that retained the scandalous secret of its subjective moment in the exercise of judgment required by the individual in polite society. Subjectivity, disguised in the trappings of the objective, had become a skill. Mass consumer society has returned taste-responses back to the ambit of the merely subjective, on the understanding that subjectivity, everywhere an effective nullity, is officially constitutive of the dignity of each equally important individual, a condition in which the objective critical consciousness that would prise them from the clutches of the collective is howled down as the nay-saying of the misery-guts, where it is permitted at all. Pseudo-democratic wisdom tells the consumer that there are no right or wrong opinions, as there chillingly were in the old eastern-bloc countries, soothing her with the reassuring news that there is therefore no point in having opinions at all, even while market researchers pester her for them day after day.

Gastronomic Style

Culinary movements are one of the means by which the gastronomic world has sought to ally itself to high culture. Prior to the emergence of the nouvelle cuisine in France in the 1960s, public catering was divided between fast-food chains, small independently owned neighbourhood restaurants specialising in one or other of the national cuisines (Chinese, Indian and Italian pre-eminently), and the elite dining of the grandest metropolitan venues and hotel dining-rooms, where a more or less faithful rendition of the canons of French haute cuisine, distantly descended from Carême and Escoffier, was accompanied by an atmosphere of high ritual. Against this background, the innovation represented by the earliest proponents of nouvelle cuisine – Paul Bocuse, Jean and Pierre Troisgros, Michel Guérard, Alain Chapel and Roger Vergé, culinary descendants of the post-war drive for greater clarity, lightness and freshness in classical French cooking, itself sparked by Fernand Point, under whom many of them had studied – was initially little more than a parochial matter within France's culinary industry, extending no further than the stomachs of a privileged clientele who had previously lived on lobster thermidor and truffled guinea-fowl. Identified as a movement by restaurant-guide editor Henri Gault in 1969, '[*nouvelle*] *cuisine* was lauded as if it were a redemptive gesture'[4] in the French press, and subsequently throughout the developed world. It was provided by Gault and his associate Christian Millau with a set of formulary desiderata that bore all the hallmarks of one of the early-twentieth century's art manifestos. Dishes were simpler, founded on fresh ingredients that had not been denatured through long cooking, marinating, or subjection to the glutinous, farinaceous, fat-laden sauces of the classical repertoire. Cooking times were drastically reduced in the interests of preserving innate flavour, and there was a sudden, almost pastoral care for the health of the customer, whose digestive robustness was now rather to be spared than medievally tested, as the quantities in dishes were pared back to a spare minimum. Novel combinations of components stressed the need to think outside the traditional envelopes, and vividly colourful, geometrically considered presentations that borrowed from the ambit of abstract, or even pictorial, art replaced the haphazardly laden plates of a culinary *ancien régime*. The new cooking was not afraid to incorporate some of the overlooked gastronomic traditions of the French regions, and it soon cast its gaze in the direction of East Asian techniques and seasonings, notably Japanese, to demonstrate that it represented a fully realised liberation from the old nationalist parameters. Every tendency that has followed *nouvelle cuisine* since its final demise has thought of itself as a movement. Its increasingly intellectualised over-refinements in the forms of Guérard's *cuisine minceur*, and Anton Mosimann's *cuisine naturelle*, eventually produced a demotic backlash that led restaurant cooking back to some imperfectly conceived notion of its roots – in France, *cuisine bourgeoise* and *cuisine grande-mère*, the standard cookbook repertoire of the middle-class home, or the robustly seasoned cooking of peasant families. Hearty casseroles that had bubbled for hours suddenly replaced tiny slivers of steamed protein. Terrines constructed in solid layers like geological strata supplanted the ethereal *foie gras* parfait, and potatoes returned in the form of clouds of mash, followed by thickly crusted frangipane tarts to fill the spaces not satiable by sorbets. In the UK, where *nouvelle cuisine* had been grimly tolerated for an improbably long stretch, the equivalent was a return to the home cooking of which the British had been trained to feel sheepish since the late Victorian era: chunky soups, prawn cocktail, fishcakes, faggots, hotpot, chops in coagulant gravy, roast meats carved to order, steamed sponge puddings with custard, rice pudding, trifle. As in everything from architecture to pop music, a back-to-basics approach is refreshing for about five minutes, before elaboration begins inevitably to insinuate itself again, which it did firstly in the form of fusion cooking, a technique originating on the Pacific Rim of Australia and the west coast of the United States, which involved juxtaposing the ingredients and methodologies of diverse culinary cultures within the same menu, and then before long within the same dish. This was succeeded by the appropriative, highly technologised style known variously as molecular gastronomy, or simply under any of the national epithets that follow the qualifier 'modern': modern British, modern Belgian, modern Czech, and so forth. The latter has been in every sense a culinary esperanto of the early-twenty first century, encountered everywhere from its original heartlands in Catalonia and the US metropolitan centres to family-run rural enterprises in the Palatinate, Flanders and Bohemia, and resort hotels in the Caribbean, on the Cape, and in Greenland. Localism is a watchword, as is the trend for natural ingredients, hand-foraged in the wild from hedgerows, woodland, sea-cliffs and shorelines, but then subjected to the kinds of radical transformations that would leave them unrecognisable, had anybody been able to recognise them in the first place.

The present obsession with food and drink, which began with people spending more than they had in elevated restaurants, and has been sustained by a broadcasting and publishing industry that caters to the need to hear about it, to look at it and talk about it, while not necessarily going anywhere near any but the simplest recipes, has resulted in a false objectification of food. The productions of celebrity chefs, who after a period of pretending that anybody could reproduce restaurant cooking at home, undercutting their own exclusivity in the process, have now reverted to an utterly mystifying technologism, in which special laboratory equipment is needed for something as simple as cooking an egg, and in which processes that take many hours and days are needed to produce a dish that can be eaten in minutes. The dignity of classical haute cuisine, which lay in the evident discrepancy between the time it took to prepare a dish, from the interminable simmering and skimming of stocks to the reductions and multiple sievings that produced sauces that shone limpidly, lustrously, intensities of flavour that the synthetic enhancers in bulk-produced processed food could only hint at, and the time it took to eat it, has been reified into the ultra-technological means of science. Refined cooking in earlier eras explored the paradox that culinary skill could make ingredients taste even more of themselves than they initially did in the raw state, but it nailed its colours to the mast of gustatory honesty. Molecular gastronomy has brought the techniques of processed food into the ambit of postmodern haute cuisine, where nothing is expected to taste of itself, and radical denaturing has vaporised its concrete reality into the airs, foams and purées that are all that is left of the original ingredients. All that is solid has melted into air, in a process of ceaseless self-revolutionising, as though nothing about the way people ate twenty or even ten years ago retains a shred of dignity. As soon as certain dishes become part of the *lingua franca*, they are abandoned in the most briskly avant-garde of kitchens. A technique first formulated by a superstar chef migrates from the metropolitan restaurant elite out to the country houses and spa hotels, and from there to the town-centre brasseries and bistros, then to the dining pubs, and then to the supermarket shelf as a ready meal, its final incarnation being the home cook's own effort at it from a recipe-book written by the superstar chef. The mechanism of endless circulation mirrors that of fashion or micro-electronics, which also can only survive by pretending that what was sold as ground-breaking and new last year is now hopelessly outmoded junk, the recourse of the *déclassé* who cannot afford anything more contemporary. Just as one's parents' generation only ever caught up with pop movements as the latest thing by the time they were already stone-dead, so those outside the inner circle of culinary vanguardism still imagine that anything that looks pretentious must be *nouvelle cuisine*, a movement that was over in western Europe by the end of the 1980s. There is an element of *épater les bourgeois* in serving nearly raw little turnips with a barely set egg-yolk in murky clots of ash made from burning onions. Menus are no longer obligated by the need to sound as though they are constructed from recognisably edible components, but instead deal in oak moss, pollen and coal. In some venues, the menu as a document has been abolished altogether, as though it were a constraining relic of a bureaucratic approach to eating, predicated on the illusion of freedom of choice. A fetish is made of the alienation from all things to which a heteronomously imposed culture subjects its clients. To discover that they scarcely even know what they are eating, or whether it is even technically edible, is the last thrill offered them in their traumatic detachment from their organic selves. The morbid cliché offered by those who send reports to the restaurant guides, particularly of a luscious dessert, the course that tends to be most understandable in traditional terms, for all its appropriation of root vegetables, olive oil and pig blood, that it was 'to die for', resembles that shop-soiled decadence that popular culture skims off the surface of works of the 1920s, but also acknowledges the bemusing terror that highly crafted food is designed to achieve over its consumers. You would accept martyrdom as long as you could have the chocolate marquise once more. At its most ideological, postmodern cooking insists that it wishes to return the adult palate to the inquisitiveness of childhood, when one was tasting everything for the first time, obtusely forgetting that childhood is the least adventurous stage in the life of taste. This perhaps explains why the predominant flavour component of much technologised cooking is the least demanding of them all, simple sweetness.

Along with their spiritual homology to the modernist art movements, culinary theories are beset with the full paraphernalia of political contestation. At exactly the time the European avant-gardes were proclaiming radical millennial breaks with the sterility of aesthetic tradition, dietetics was getting off the ground as a science of the determinative nature of eating, not just as to personal health, but to racial and cultural well-being too. Replacing climatic theories of cultural determinism with nutritional alternatives, individual campaigners formulated eccentric dietary systems, often based on patent products, which they urged the rest of society to follow. For a brief moment in the early-twentieth century, fruit and vegetables were seen as dangerously unhealthy, the common scrabble of the immiserated who couldn't afford the sustaining fortification of plentiful meat. A wheat-based diet, in contrast to the diurnal rice of the Asiatic hordes, was promoted as the fuel of successful societies by the Mexican racial theorist Francisco Bulnes in a work of 1899.[5] In later generations, the Chinese were adjured to accept that the reason for the paucity of the nation's athletic achievements was the absence of lactose in the diet. Today, the global pabulum of burgers, fried chicken, pizza and chocolate, accompanied by carbonated drinks laden with sugar or aspartame to taste, is the cause of galloping rates of morbid obesity and diabetes in the developed world but, more than being simply a medical time-bomb, is also held responsible for the affectless moronism of societies reduced to gaping passivity. There is hardly anybody left alive who doesn't run on caffeine, but its potentially sharpening effect on the brain is more than offset by the ton-weight of carbohydrate stodge and trans-fats ingested along with it. The peaks and troughs in energy created by the state of perma-sugar in which people get through the day are crude parodies of the cycle of exertion and exhaustion of which all working lives were once comprised, and a bodily system that spends most days recovering from the metabolising of last night's quantum of alcohol, prior to metabolising tonight's, is not best placed to withstand all the other onslaughts. Everybody's health is now everybody else's concern, and if he can't be bothered burning off the thousands of calories he consumes every day, the modern glutton ought at least to be worried about the economic might of the multinational food industries, not to mention the plight of farmers in the global South whose produce, which he doesn't want to eat anyway, is extorted from them at cut-throat rates by high-street retailers, and which the environmental movement tells him he should be shunning in favour of locally grown turnips. The meat industry, with its requirement for extravagant pasturage for its livestock, monopolises land that could be used to alleviate malnutrition in the underdeveloped world, but to insist that the lives of the poor in Africa, Latin America and much of Asia should remain chained to a daily round of grinding, milling and baking, on which are based the nostalgic practices of independent artisan food producers in the advanced economies, is to offer them no escape from one of the defining characteristics of poverty.

The standard critique mounted by theorists of food politics, that the sub-normal junk diet of consumer societies has led to cultural atrophy, is precisely the wrong way round. Cultural atrophy itself has produced this diet as its appropriate accompaniment. The decline in analytical seeing encouraged by the montage technique that cinema made its own from its inception, intensified in the video age by rapid jump-cut editing and the imperative voice of advertising; the erosion of structured, discerning listening to music in favour of the reception of a permanent soundtrack that can literally be worn to accompany nearly every waking activity; the homogenising of the olfactory world into a deodorised space impinged on only by scents and soaps designed to make everybody smell broadly the same: all these form part of a sensory closed circuit, in which taste too is required only to operate within narrow unvarying parameters as the ironic hypostasis of plenty, since uniformity has falsely been conflated into the principle of the regularity of supply that put an end to periods of shortage in the global North after the last world war. The same antinomy that has pervaded the global viticultural industry, that just as there are more countries producing wine, and with a more heterogeneous palette of grape varieties to choose from, than ever before, a process of commercial standardisation has frozen consumer taste to a demand for the same few varietals produced to essentially the same formula, has been at work in the food context too. There is potentially more to tempt the adventurous eater than has ever been known in human history, and not just in ambitious restaurants, but in delicatessens, specialist retailers, on market-stalls, and even in the high-street multiples, and yet all the great majority wants to eat is fast food and chocolate, because those are the products appropriate to a wholly administered world, and advertising works ceaselessly to invent new ways of pretending that every next burger will be as much of a treat as the very first one was, when it came to liberate western taste from the ancestral monotony of boiled meat and veg. More than that, the fast-food industry doesn't shy away from self-renewal. It accepts that its own products need refreshing from time to time, hence the Mexican chilli burgers, Peking duck pizza, Thai-spiced fried chicken, which offer variant spins – occasionally commercially disastrous ones – on the same formula, which the domestic cooking of homes on limited budgets hardly ever could.

The famous scene in Luis Buñuel's film *The Phantom of Liberty* (1974), in which people sit on lavatories around a shared table at a polite social gathering, and a man excuses himself for a moment in order to go and sit in a small room and eat, expressed more than the obvious truth that surrealism was ready to become comedy. It raised the matter of whether commensality had become the disavowed scatological underside not just of bourgeois conviviality, but of domestic eating itself. Food writers speaking up for one or other of the ancestral gastronomic traditions, which were largely invented in the past two centuries, reliably bemoan the decline of familial eating. The shared dining-table, for those who were lucky enough to own one, was held to embody the kinship bonds that united the family, and trained the younger members in social cooperativeness, its rituals and etiquette forming the basis for an education in the gentility that undergirded social harmony in the wider world. A dedicated room for dining was urged on the American middle classes in the nineteenth century by architects, writers of household advice manuals and the editors of ladies' magazines, specifically as a space for the performance and consolidation of family values.

'They stressed the need to make this room attractive, comfortable, and above all to use it daily for the family rather than reserving it for guests. Indeed, the dining room became an important space for enacting the ideology of domesticity that was at the heart of the idealised Victorian family. This creed saw the middle-class home as an important space of family unity in the both the practical and spiritual sense.'[6] Dinner in particular was a time when everybody informed each other of what had happened to them that day. It allowed the airing of personal concerns in a measured way, and it schooled the juniors into a proper appreciation of food, what it ought to taste like, and how to eat it. The reality in many homes had already taken leave of this idyllic conception in the early years of the past century. Youngsters sat largely silent while their elders discussed tedious domestic business, or else argued about politics. If they tried to speak up, they were told not to interrupt, thus preparing them in unintended ways for an outdoor world that would coldly ignore their needs once they had finished their education. When they were addressed, it was more often than not with enquiries about how they were doing at school, the one topic the festive air ought by rights to have rendered taboo, while the rules of dining etiquette – such as not resting one's elbows on the table, or talking with one's mouth full – often applied only to the young, reinforcing the conformist notion that adulthood was a time when you could get away with not personally respecting the rules you prescribed for your inferiors. Genuine preoccupations were almost always better shared with one other family member than with a tableful, as was emphasised by the acuity of suddenly being shown up at the table, an embarrassment more lethal for its being produced in such strictly controlled circumstances. Very little about food was learned, other than which days were consecrated to which dishes, and the drama of conflict forced on the young by their being made to eat things they didn't like, hanging on for grim death or pudding, whichever came sooner, made the scene of eating a horror-show rather than a fairy-tale, a point reinforced by Father assuming the role of the ogre, when he warned that little boys who didn't eat up their runner-beans wouldn't get any apple pie. The most minatory aspect of the communal table, which Buñuel's defecating cohort perfectly captures, is that there is no escaping it until business is concluded. Everybody must continue sitting there until not just the eating and drinking, but the conversation too, are deemed to have reached a conclusion. Even the desk at school, which he at least had to himself, permitted a young man a certain amount of fidgeting, but he carried into adulthood a sense of the dinner-table as something to be excused from as soon as dinner itself was over. The food that people eat now hardly lends itself to sitting around a table laden with dishes and serving-spoons, everybody spreading napkins over their laps and awaiting their turn. Enforced table-dining *en famille* today would quickly descend to the level of the chimpanzees' tea-party, in homes where nobody knows the rules, children are no longer required to eat things they don't like the look of, and everybody has something else they would rather be doing. Commensality today only takes place in public, either in modern brasseries where sound ricochets off the hard surfaces, and everybody must shout while eating to make himself heard above the racket, or else in the seating-areas of fast-food outlets, where families still in their coats eat rapidly off trays with their fingers, and the table fulfils its vestigial function of allowing diners the momentary amenity of sitting down, for those who don't yet care to eat on foot in the street.

Not only the mixed blessing of eating together has withered away but, along with it, the tyranny of eating at fixed times. When the industrial revolution turned the world into a gigantic workshop, people ate one meal when they awoke, and another when they got home again at the end of the fourteen hour day. For the worker, life was starkly divided between eating, working and sleeping, with church attendance and charitable duties filling up Sundays. Lunch is a late phenomenon, barely predating the nineteenth century for the mass of people, although the British elite – those of them who happened to be at home at midday – had already begun to invest it with almost as much ceremonial solemnity as dinner in the early Georgian era. In due course, the ideal of three square meals a day was supplemented by further interventions, high tea becoming a staple of English society when the Countess of Bedford began to invite friends over to fill in the deadliest vacuum in any leisurely day, the late afternoon. An early dinner might be succeeded by a milky drink and snacks in mid-evening, an interval known as 'supper' in the north. Elevenses rescued those who had begun to flag before lunch hove into view, expanding to American brunch, the status of which had been transformed from a late breakfast into an extra intervening meal between breakfast and lunch. The tendency to subdivide the day into progressively smaller units of fasting has resulted in the present era in the logical outcome of more or less permanent eating. People eat throughout the day at their office desks to disguise the tedium of having to sit there. No sooner do they board any form of public transport than they expect to start eating, to while away the boredom of the journey. A long car trip is dangerously under-provisioned if it hasn't been equipped with a nosebag of snacks and sweets to sustain the travellers until they stop somewhere for lunch. People eat while standing in the ubiquitous queues. They eat while talking on the phone, while sitting in the cinema, while watching sports matches, while sitting in doctors' waiting-rooms. Eating in shops, which was once utterly forbidden, is now increasingly tolerated. Waiting in line at the supermarket checkout, they surreptitiously unwrap something that they haven't yet paid for, and begin nibbling at it until their turn at the automated till arrives. Even the misery of sex can be cheered up a bit by incorporating the eating of ice-cream, yoghurt, melted cheese, chocolate paste off each other's bodies, the copulative bed transformed into the site of a picnic. Allying the sexual and nutritive functions in one combined activity is another of the evolutionary advances that separates humankind from the animals.

Surfeit

Visions of the Land of Plenty in the European medieval tradition – Cockaigne, Luilekkerland, Schlaraffenland, Lubberland – always betray a dialectical tension. On one hand, they straightforwardly fantasise about a life free of want and struggle, where the bounty of the earth is effortlessly available to all, hanging within reach above the heads of peasants, clerks, artisans, soldiers, just as it does in the actual world of the privileged. But there is also an anti-utopian impulse in Cockaigne that appears to recognise that abolishing insufficiency would universalise greed. Peter Bruegel the Elder's *Het Luilekkerland* (1567) encapsulates this ambivalence in the prone bodies of its three principals, who lie like wallowing hogs on the ground, the paraphernalia of their professions – the soldier's lance, the farmer's flail, the administrator's notebook – abandoned about them. They are not eating, they are already replete. This is the dyspeptic aftermath of gluttony, as is evident from the fact that they have ceased to notice the uneaten foods still offering themselves in the vicinity, including the pig with the carving knife slotted into its flesh, the self-slaughtering fowl that has fallen obligingly straight on to its platter, and the cracked egg and teaspoon still scurrying about on its little legs. Luxury is being able to look a roast piglet in the mouth. Bruegel likely intended the work as a satire on the cringing impotence of the Flemish nobility who, only the year before he painted it, had petitioned the temporal power, Habsburg Spain, for greater tolerance towards Calvinists. The Spanish regent, Margaret of Parma, dismissed their request as the pleading of 'beggars', resulting in an initial wave of anti-Catholic iconoclasm which represented the first stirrings of nationalism in the Habsburg Netherlands. The serious polemical intent of this late work is all the more significant in that Bruegel is the great painter of ludic themes, of comic illustrations of Flemish proverbs, of children's games, peasant festivities, folk moralism, and the representation of Cockaigne can be viewed in the mingled light of social comedy and political acerbity. A world of surfeit signifies the withering of human aspiration, its defeat amid the conditions of material superfluity, as the different estates of society surrender alike to the bestial privilege of stuffing themselves, as though nothing else mattered but having more than you could possibly want. The banal democracy of Cockaigne is an equality of indigestion.

Cockaigne was a materialist version of the Greek Arcadia, a place of bucolic tranquillity and lush vegetation peopled by peaceable shepherds and refugees from the cultural decadence of the cities. It was the refuge of nature, conceived against the corruption of civilisation into which humanity had fallen, but not without its material attractions. Even the highly urbanised society of the Roman Empire did not dispense with the Virgilian eclogue and the Horatian ode, poetic instances of the counter-intuitive postulate that civility was a regression from the ideal state. The promise of pleasure in the Christian afterlife has traditionally been more austerely represented, as in the convocation of heavenly notables present at the adoration of the Lamb of God in the lower central panel of van Eyck's Ghent altarpiece of the 1430s. All that looks consumable here is the water of crystalline purity that flows from an octagonal fountain in the foreground. The Islamic paradise, Jannah (also a 'garden'), by contrast, was a more physically realised place of sensual allurements. Octagonally bounded by eight gateways, it has more of architectural interest, with golden palaces amid the shady river valleys where honey, milk and unintoxicating wine flow as freely as water, and the blessed will be exquisitely attired, drenched in beguiling scent, and miraculously endowed with the capacity to feast for up to forty years at a stretch without needing to pause, every dish and every fruit tasting different again from the last ones. For all that the Pauline vision of Christian living is prescriptively anti-materialist – 'For the kingdom of God is not food and drink but righteousness and peace and joy in the Holy Spirit' (Romans 14:17) – aspects of the material did begin to creep into it in medieval times. After all, if food and drink didn't matter at all, there would be no necessity to feed the malnourished. Notwithstanding that, the context of Paul's comment bears some examination. He is disavowing the *kashrut*, the old panoply of dietary laws that laid down what was and wasn't ritually clean enough to eat. There is henceforward nothing unclean; the Christian communities, the Roman in the immediate case, can eat and drink what they want. However, he adds that if they are eating with people who do still observe dietary strictures, it is as well to go along with their wishes rather than risk dissension. Furthermore, if the sight of you drinking wine might tempt the teetotal into doing the same, and then hating himself later for having stumbled, you have been the agent of his self-excoriation, and so again you are creating friction where there should be fraternity. Insisting that there is nothing wrong with eating pork, in demonstrative defiance of somebody who thinks there is, has the paradoxical effect of turning something that you know is unproblematic into something egregious. 'Therefore do not let what you know is good be spoken of as evil' (14:16), which it will be if you don't respect the other's ordinance, fracturing the relations of mutuality between you. This is what lies behind the ambivalent nature of Cockaigne, in the Bruegel depiction particularly: material surfeit has the effect of undermining human relations by reducing each individual to the gratification of his own appetites. The three gorgers who lie about on the ground in a state of satiety are separated from each other by the gulf of their respective self-indulgences. There may well be sexual liberties in certain of the paradisiacal visions, especially the Koranic, but the sexual partners have the same status as the food and drink, as objects of endlessly varying consumption. Sex is not a relation between people in the abode of the blessed; it is an act of sensual satisfaction alone. Hence the adjuration that the kingdom of God is not about eating and drinking, since consumption itself is not the issue – 'food does not bring us near to God; we are no worse if we do not eat, and no better if we do' (1 Corinthians 8:8). Human solidarity matters more. The critique of the land of plenty in Bruegel and others is not that it is a vision of obscene superfluity, but precisely that it isn't enough. A perfect life, only imperfectly achievable in the earthly kingdom of the community of believers, would have to be more than one vast blowout, in which everybody stuffs himself to his stomach's content. The grasp at utopia in the notion of universal excess misses the point. Universal sufficiency is what is liberating, and that can only be produced by those in surfeit understanding what deprivation means, not by everybody rising to gluttony, as is judiciously argued by the outcast Gloucester in *King Lear*:

> *Let the superfluous and lust-dieted man,*
> *That slaves your ordinance, that will not see*
> *Because he doth not feel, feel your power quickly.*
> *So distribution should undo excess*
> *And each man have enough.* (IV:i)

Not food itself, but the circumstances, the spirit, and the degree of mutual respect in which it is eaten, are the salient factors. In one sense at least, it may seem as though the critique of the land of plenty misses its mark. By insisting that gluttony is always a matter of selfish indulgence, it overlooks the common purpose that more often than not distinguishes episodes of Saturnalian banqueting and riotous drinking. They tend to take place in merry company, indeed are often the very definition of comradely conviviality. The lesson, rather, is that if the revellers are tempted to think that heaven on earth would consist in being able to live like this to the exclusion of all else, they have deluded themselves into the state of stupor of Bruegel's trio. In the ideal state thus pictured, eating to bursting-point is ostensibly free of moral valuation, since in a world of plenty, there is no more moral judgment about the inequitable distribution of resources. Exactly because there is no limit to how much one can eat, everybody is free to become an eating-machine, even though the figures in the painting are clearly suffering the after-effects, and even in the Koranic sura, the blessed are assured of a physiological transformation that will allow them the relief of simultaneous eructation and perspiring as they eat and drink without cease. Back in the real world, the intention of Luilekkerland is to cure its spectators of the *naïveté* of such dreams. When eating and drinking become the supreme ends of this life, they lose their essential rootedness in social kinship, and disappear into the solipsism of greed.

Against the higher counsels of the spirit whispers the still small voice of enjoyment, which only wants to grasp at happiness while it can, and dares the immutable principle of the higher life to point out how exactly it might be conformed to a reality that bids it go hang. Since the present life knows nothing of the reason by which it is officially ordered, it would be unreason itself not to insist on sensual fulfilment where it presents itself. The land of Cockaigne may be a place of flatulent excess of which one would soon weary, but it stands only as a caution against wishing in the midst of enjoyment that life would never be any different, rather in the manner that the famous passages of classical music, the majestic tunes for which even those who don't care for classical music turn to it, warn the listener that if there were nothing but the formulaic repetition of such passages, there would never be need of anything other than pop. The higher principle that preached spartan asceticism where the warmth of revealed religion ought to have glowed adopted, despite itself, the thoroughly worldly position of talking people out of their happiness, and then trying to console them for giving it up. More certain than eating and drinking, and the making merry of intoxication, is the death that follows, and which doesn't mind whether there was any merriment before it or not.

Hunger and Greed

Much joy in eating and drinking depends on its continually being made new, a transformation for which the cycle of daily mealtimes, with every return to the table a kind of homecoming, appears to be ill-fitted. No joy, assuredly, is greater than the joy of assuaging the empty stomach, as was expressed in the old folk proverb about hunger being the best condiment, and yet virtually nobody in the developed world is ever that hungry. Then, too, there are different kinds of hunger. Even those who habitually miss breakfast, and are therefore inclined to overeat at lunch, accept the feeling of insufficiency that begins to creep over them around mid-morning as an unremarkable feature of the circadian rhythm, if they notice it at all. The sort of hunger that results from having had to wait unexpectedly to be able to eat, and which is often accompanied by a resentment bordering on fury, has the structure of thwarted ambition. Its prolonged deferral taints the final prize, when it does arrive, with a meagre character, in that nothing could adequately answer the explosion of tormented appetite that it must now satisfy. When the woodcutter rested from his labours for a moment, and was surprised to find the whole morning had gone by already, so that he must have earned his bread and cheese, his hunger, which had stolen up on him, made a banquet of prosaic plainness. Next to that, the mindlessness of feeding one's face at the appointed hour works in the opposite direction. The peculiar discovery made in childhood, that the sense of taste is as capable of being numbed to autonomic neutrality as are the other senses, so that it was possible to find himself feeling he ought to have a second dish of ice-cream, because he wasn't thinking about the first one as he ate it, is the mode in which unappetitive eating is carried on everywhere now. What the taste buds, and by extension gustatory consciousness itself, yearn for is for eating to be unshackled from its enchainment in necessity without becoming the indiscriminate snaffling of dogs. Eating out serves this purpose to some extent, but is subject to the reification wrought upon it by global brands with their formula menus and industrial approach to customer-processing. Ernst Bloch wrote in an early work that 'For the child, the food at other people's houses tastes best,'[7] where it was eaten at unfamiliar times, at a different table set with different crockery, the sandwiches cut differently to the way they were at home, and in an atmosphere of lightly applied formality, in which he was treated as slightly closer to adulthood than he tended to be at home. Later, his first intimation of independence emerged in the realisation that, alone in town with a little change in his pocket, he could buy himself a fruit tart or a packet of caramels, instead of having to petition an elder for them. The senses tabulated as the aesthetic ones in the era of Voltaire, smell and taste, whose rootedness in subjectivity was ratified by Kant's anthropology, betray that impulse to be free of their basic biological functions that one would expect of aesthetic faculties, but appetite keeps returning them to biology. Necessity is the enemy of art, which is why the fine arts appeal to the eye and ear, because those sense-organs are not bound fast to simple self-preservation in the way that smelling and tasting are. Nonetheless, since the objects of smelling and tasting constantly solicit the individual to the aestheticising decision as to whether she likes them or not, where even the attribution of their being neither delectable nor noxious counts as a subjective judgment, appetite and its precursor, animal hunger, want them to be more than they are. 'Mmm, delicious,' says the dinner guest at the first mouthful of every dish, remembering his manners to the hostess, as well as his own hope for a renewed eating that would transcend mere feeding.

Taste as Preference

Tastes in food and drink are to a great extent already constituted before they are subjectively assumed. Exactly as with the other senses, taste has a prehistory, of everything that preceding generations have tasted and enjoyed or rejected. The child learns what tastes good from his parents and elders, much as he learns his habits of mind, forms of expression and attitudes, until the moment comes in pre-maturity to reject them as a means of self-formation, before incorporating elements of the new, what is encountered outside the home, into the *dispositif* of his own adult taste. Within the overall process, there is nonetheless room for the kinds of idiosyncrasies only explicable by individual depth psychology. One person recoils at the seed-laden pulp of tomatoes, another at whole shellfish with their insectile antennae. A list of foods that are widely disliked in western cultures easily suggests itself: Brussels sprouts, broccoli and cauliflower; wilted spinach; avocado; fresh coconut; leaf coriander; liquorice; raw oysters; canned anchovies; most offal; blood sausage; tofu; polenta; granulous, rough-textured, dark-crumbed bread; biscuits full of blackened dried fruits; the marzipan layer in traditional festive cake; very ripe or blue soft cheeses... The strongest factor governing food antipathies is texture. Sliminess, especially in fish or meat, evokes acute disgust, as to a lesser degree does toughness. Anything that requires a lot of chewing seems to turn the act of eating into something more inorganically mechanical. The blandness of the universal junk diet has produced a suspicion of strong flavour other than spicy hotness, which is more of a physical effect than a flavour. Pungency of any sort is abhorred for the haunting way it lingers on the palate, even while synthetic tastes that stay in the mouth for hours, such as the metallic twang of energy drinks and cola, have become indispensable as daily staples. Bitterness is considered unfriendly, recalling too insistently the signal that the raw ingredient emitted in the wild, that it didn't want to be eaten. The ocular aspect is important too. Food that visually resembles something unpleasant is doubly disgusting, precisely because one is expected to eat it, and especially where it seems to suggest the swallowing of one's own bodily secretions. Mucous green, glistening salivary silver, arterial red are all strongly dissuasive, although there is virtually nobody who hasn't overcome an aversion to the uniquely excremental look of chocolate. An Italian historian of the Spanish conquest of the New World, Girolamo Benzoni, reported from Mexico in 1565 that chocolate, in its traditional form as a hot drink, seemed more suited to pigs than to human beings. After living there for over a year, he had still refused to taste it. Virtually everything the indigenes ate was filth, including insects, arachnids, worms and human flesh, as was their predilection for the smoked intoxicant, tobacco. They guzzled their native wine to the point of jabbering stupefaction, and had also perfected, by means of lowering a stick into the oesophagus, the habit of voiding their stomach contents as a preliminary to religious ritual, to prove to the gods that they were purified both inside and out. To the contrary view of the European observer, they were thoroughly contaminated by these consumption practices. Nothing is quite as rebarbative to the fastidious palate as what other people eat. And yet, to Benzoni, their blithe omnivorousness could all too easily be interpreted as a discomfiting *reductio* of the increasingly decadent sophistication of the diet of European civility.

The enactment of personal antipathies is a performance *in nuce* of the larger cultural processes by which certain dietary regimes, with all their incorporative potential to be sure, were chosen above others. 'Eating choices were usually retrospectively constructed into a narrative unity, but that unity was a social event ... an act of self-fashioning that joined private action to public self-presentation,' writes EC Spary.[8] The meanings that food takes on in contemporary society, however, shift more in accordance with their political significance than with personal taste, which has for nearly everybody now the status of a settled dispute. 'In the modern West, eating is argument,'[9] Spary claims, but the point applies more acutely to the debate about dietary health and its legislative corollaries, to food politics in general, rather than to the postmodern category of 'self-fashioning' that she also appends to it. Joanne Finkelstein too, in a study of modern restaurants, repeatedly invokes self-fashioning, only to pull the rug from under it by reflecting that public dining, which once opened a space for cross-class subjectivities to emerge, is now much more about the enforcement of normativity:

> *The several hundred years over which the modern restaurant evolved cover a corresponding period of cultural history in which the contemporary emphasis on psychological reasoning and the presentation of the self can be seen to have developed through a wide net of interconnected social processes. The restaurant is an engineered space, irrespective of whether it is the self-servicing fast food outlet or the silver service of the Fête Spéciale, and as such it promotes conformity.*[10]

The self-fashioning of eating practices, at least in the public domain, is therefore only available to those who are prepared to fashion themselves in accordance with the laws of conformity. Eating is no more a matter of personal foible than is the question of which TV programmes to watch. Desire in the modern world has already been engineered before the indvidual has adopted it as a marker of identity. As so-called fine dining has evolved steadily in the direction of fixed tasting-menus, which resemble expanded versions of the old *table d'hôte* from which glamorous eating once offered an escape, the chain menus that are set in stone at least allow you to decide which toppings to add to the pizza, to preserve the precious illusion of individual partiality. Not liking this or that ingredient answers the requirement of abstemious dignity amid the general gluttony.

Taste in Memory

If a sudden smell can so instantly place the one who smells it somewhere else entirely, offering him the fleeting utopian hint that there is a somewhere else, albeit one that lurks irretrievably in the past, the sense of taste appears more rooted in simple immediacy. Because it concerns the satiating of appetite, or of greed as may be, it needs the sense of smell to accompany it as its boon companion, to which it is as spiritually bound as the two physical senses are interdependent. To one who can't smell, all food tastes of next to nothing, and reduced to its mere textural properties, it loses its status as food. The degenerative atrophy of the two faculties in later life is not the least reason that the elderly are so often disinclined to eat. Even where they may still have energy to expend, eating isn't eating if it doesn't taste of anything. More than just the titivation of the taste buds is at stake. When the body seems to have rebelled against its own motivation to nourish itself, the value of life itself is called into question. The withering of sexual desire at a time when one's reproductive cycle is over or, in men's case, when the quality of the seminal material may have deteriorated to uselessness, may be cause for satisfied retrospect rather than envious melancholy, but nothing reassuring can be gleaned from not being able to taste one's food any longer. At its darkest, it feels like the irrational evidence that one has already hung around too long. In this state, what would restore life's faded colours is the full restitution not just of the lost senses themselves, but of their symbiotic connection with the operations of the other senses, a mood that the nineteenth century, with far fewer sensory stimuli at the disposal of the sensitive, knew how to evoke with the simplest of means:

> *Ah! I think I taste that whey now – with a flavour*
> *so delicate that one can hardly distinguish it from an odour,*
> *and with that soft gliding warmth that fills one's imagination*
> *with a still, happy dreaminess. And the light music of*
> *the dropping whey is in my ears, mingling with the*
> *twittering of a bird outside the wire net-work window –*
> *the window overlooking the garden, and shaded by*
> *tall gueldre roses.*[11]

If taste can succumb to old age, it has a corresponding infancy, being the one sense that needs to grow up in the early years of life. The structural principle Lévi-Strauss established in the first volume of his investigations of mythology is that primal societies accord the differential status of raw and cooked foods the role of controlling metaphors for all organic life, from the agricultural cycles to the maturation of human beings themselves. Heat is the operative factor. The planted seed is cooked by the sun, so that it germinates into a plant, which is further ripened in the summer. Its fruits or leaves will eventually be gathered and then cooked to prepare them for eating. Once ingested, the stomach cooks them until the body excretes what it doesn't need as a waste product, which then returns to the soil. The Pomo native people of northern California traditionally used fire pits to assist the generative and developmental stages of life among their women and girls. Following a four-week post-partum seclusion in a separate hut, a new mother was 'cooked' on a fire pit to restore her to normal functioning. At the occasion of her first menstruation, an adolescent girl was, like her mother had been, removed from the community for a number of days and required to lie on a bed of tule suspended over a smouldering fire, so that she would be cooked *à point* from the raw to a perfect state of womanhood. The process represents a negotiation of the interface between raw nature and the cooked state of culture:

> *The conjunction of a member of the social group with nature must be mediated through the intervention of cooking fire, whose normal function is to mediate the conjunction of the raw product and the human consumer, and whose operation thus has the effect of making sure that a natural creature is at one and the same time cooked and socialised.*[12]

A striking feature of this mythology is that it was the responsibility of women to undertake a crossing of the boundary between nature and culture. Men remained in the state of nature, untamed and uncooked, and only had access to the processes of civil community through their contact with cooked and socialised women. 'In essence, men appear to have represented the wilderness, and remained aligned with it throughout their lives. Men were born of Nature, and remained there, whereas women, like the first Humans, emerged from the wilds ... to align themselves with Culture (thus the need for their initiation into adult status).'[13] To undergo an unusually rapid process of early development is still known in advanced societies as being precocious (literally 'pre-cooked'). There may be something unnerving about untimely maturation, but not nearly as discomfiting as the failure, given normal physical development, of hardly maturing at all. The predilection in western culture now for healthy adults to make an effort to regress to childhood states of consciousness, under the ideological rubric of retrieving an allegedly purer receptivity to a world that wants nothing more than to treat them as just such helpless ingenus, would have been unfathomable to ethnic groups that placed a premium on transition to more advanced states of being. 'I'm afraid I don't eat that,' announces the troublesome dinner guest, as soon as the first course appears. Nothing speaks more clearly of the return to childhood than being unembarrassed about having a puerile attitude to food.

In the higher stages of civilisation from east to west, it was of course men who were held to have crossed the boundary from a state of nature to the refinement of culture, while women lay at the mercy of their corporeal beings. The Greek sympotic tradition, which allied commensality to the advancement of erudition in post-prandial speech and debate, was reserved for men as the natural exponents of reason, even in the extremity of inebriation. What early Christianity, otherwise generally permeable to the metaphysical customs of the Hellenic world, saw in the symposium that was not to its taste was not just the multi-vocality of it, with competing theories washing around the tables, often in riotous adversariality, where the singular authoritative word of God ought to be. Nor was the regular drunkenness quite the compromising factor that the new religion, particularly in its later anti-materialist iterations, would hold it to be. What made them most uncomfortable was the hierarchical nature of the symposium. Both its exclusion of women and the structures of authority performed within it, with the principal speaker holding court until such time as he was ready to take his plaudits, which were the more effusive the more prominent a community figure he was, stood in stark contrast to the collaborative egalitarian practices of the Christians. '[T]he elitist associations of the symposium would have seemed at odds with early Christianity's stress on inclusiveness (including the tendency to allow the presence of women, in contrast with the Greek symposium tradition) and its appeal below the elite levels of society. Early Christian feasting consciously broke the mould of hierarchical feasting.'[14] Diet was already profoundly indicative of social stratification, the variant regimens of rich and poor long predating in all territories the development of national cuisines. What was minimally required of commensality is that it would overcome those divisions by offering everybody at the table the same food, so that reinforcing the divisions in other ways, through priorities of speaking, the order in which food was served and in what quantities, was only to blight the scene of sociality with the inequity of the world outside it. It would be nearly two thousand years before the cuisines of the aristocracy and of working people began to approach each other, fuse and coalesce into what then became identified as the national styles, although even here there would be limitless mutability created by the cultural negotiations effected by migration, regional taste and the redrafting of national boundaries. 'In 1820, national cuisines scarcely existed. The older pattern of imperial high cuisines for the elite and regional cuisines for the poor persisted. By 1920, diners tended to identify cuisines as national, not imperial.'[15] What Rachel Laudan calls a new 'middling cuisine', which has been bequeathed to postmodernity, had begun to crystallise. If diets drew severe lines of demarcation between peoples, they acted as potent unifiers within cultural zones, so much so that medieval legend might have persuaded a people that the choice of their diet had been ordained by a wise ruler. The twelfth century Primary Chronicle of the Slavic peoples has Grand Prince Vladimir of Kiev in AD 988 auditioning representatives of the major western faith cultures to see which, in light of their dietary systems, would be most suited to his people. Inhabitants of Kievan Rus' were not to be denied this meat or that, and certainly not drinking, which was the pleasure of every Rus, without which his existence would be worthless, and nor was he much impressed by the notion of regular fasting, so the Muslim, Jewish and Latin Christian spokesmen were shown the door. Byzantine Christianity, whose advocate had presumably kept quiet about the fasting, was the rationally decided choice. As much as they were defined by their religious observances, the legend declares, a people's eating habits were the indicators of their cultural identity, even within the strata of class society on the eve of its transition to middling cuisine, and especially so in times of peril and their aftermath:

While the [British] middling and upper classes derided

> *fish and chips as unpalatable, indigestible, and a waste of good money that should have gone for plain home cooking, the working class disagreed. Fish and chips warmed the insides, kept Father out of the pub and home with the family, and, many believed, helped win World War I and prevented a revolution. They may well have been right.*[16]

The connection, evident already to antiquity, between diet and the health of the organism resulted during the Age of Reason in theories that extravagantly proposed that food, and the scientific methods by which it was prepared, could be used to engineer intellectual and social advancement. Progressively throughout the eighteenth century, cooks laboured to concentrate the essences of ingredients and liberate them from the base solutions, the 'earthy juices', in which they were suspended in the natural state. For all its avowed rationalism, this approach was a late manifestation of the principles of alchemy – the isolation and concentration of a precious substance that would then hold the key, if not to eternal life, at least to a society of highly refined intellects. The jus and coulis with which the twentieth century manifestation of advanced cooking sauced its dishes had their origins here, in what was known already in the 1760s as *nouvelle cuisine*. A restaurant, before it was a place where public eating was institutionalised, was somewhere that sold *restaurants* (restoratives), thick concentrates of meat stock that were thought to infuse the blood with pure spirit, resulting in vigorous agile bodies, lively imaginations, broadly capacious intellectual genius, and fineness and delicacy of taste, or so said the Parisian culinary writer known only as Menon in his *The Head Chef's Science* (1768). Although the theory was much satirised at the time, in terms that often did little more than reiterate the self-professedly outlandish claims of materialist physicians about the organic interrelations between mind and body, further support was being given to the idea that the degree of civilisation of a people or a class was decided by the quality and refinement of what it consumed. The medical writer Antoine Le Camus noted sympathetically of those condemned to manual work that 'their souls are exhausted by the labours of their bodies', an exhaustion only compounded by the 'base vegetables' that perforce constituted their diet, whereas the cultured elite with their access to food that, in its ethereal concentration, was liberated from the earth are living evidence that 'reason and judgment, never obscured by the vapours of coarse and indigestible juices ... exhibit themselves in their full vigour & exercise all their rights.'[17] *Esprit*, understood as the complex of sense-impressions, mental acuity and moral demeanour, was nourished and nurtured by what one ate. 'While disagreeing over the precise relations between these phenomena, writers tended to agree that mental phenomena were enabled and characterised by the state of the body, and that *esprit* was altered and shaped by physiology and in particular by the composition of the animal spirits.'[18] Even Descartes, from whom many of the subsequent meditations on the relations between mind and body flowed, allowed that eating and its nutritive effect on the physical constitution appeared to be the rope-bridge thrown over the otherwise impassable chasm between the corporeal and mental realms, and the ramifications of that thought were energetically explored in the first physiological treatises on the mechanics of the sense of taste that followed. Carefully constructed *ragoûts*, in which long simmering captured the beneficent essences of their ingredients, in freeing them from their untreated coarseness would produce a kingdom of civility, its rarefied intellectual genius nurtured by elaborate cooking. The exactly contemporaneous refutation of this theory, stemming from the Edenic naturalism in Rousseau's *Emile* (1762), held that the healthiest state was that in which the body, like those of agricultural labourers, was least subject to the elaborations of technicised cuisine, but subsisted and flourished on simply boiled vegetables, fresh fruit and unspoiled milk. It was precisely the concentrated richness of grand cuisine that produced alimentary and social decadence. The point rapidly acquired the force of the international rivalry it would hold for the next two centuries. 'Ragouts, believed by critics to stimulate unnatural, out-of-control appetites, exemplified French cusine. French ragouts and bouillons brought on a "national sickness" or "homelessness", complained Russians [such as Prince Mikhail Shcherbatov in *On The Corruption of Morals in Russia*], a state that could be cured by cabbage soup.'[19] Not that the Romanov dynasty necessarily set the best example, but they were at least in a position to know. Reduction itself was a decadent principle, wasteful in the profligate quantities of ingredients it concentrated down. The abbé Pluquet computed in his *Philosophical and Political Treatise on Luxury* (1786) that the food of ten gourmands could originally have fed three hundred of the hungry, while Coleridge, simmering at the intoxicative indulgence to which he was himself no stranger, balked at the prospect of 'whole joints ... stewed down into essences'. Nothing impeded the passage of this countervailing argument into the culinary ideology of Francophobic Protestant England. In the paradisiacal Garden, Eliza Smith's *Compleat Housewife* noted as early as 1727, 'apples, nuts, and herbs, were both meat and sauce, and mankind stood in no need of additional sauces, ragoos, &c. to procure a good appetite', whereas the 'depraved palates' of the French would eventually see their owners blown away by revolutionary fury for their sins.[20]

The Swiss physician Samuel-Auguste Tissot, who was trained in the medical faculty at Montpellier, was the late-eighteenth century's prime proponent of the influence of diet on the vital forces. He argued for ascetic severity in the matter of eating, accustoming the stomach to thorough digestion and the cyclical re-emergence of hunger, to guard against greed and over-indulgence. For Tissot, soulless materialism must lead to excess, unless reason could be trained and trusted to predominate over the appetites. In a series of lectures to the Royal Scientific Society at Montpellier, he advocated the subjection of mechanical appetite to the tutelage of 'animist' reason, where reason allied itself to the soul against the corporeal machine of the body: '*My soul, you like tasty morsels but experience has taught you that these liqueurs and ragoûts destroy the health of your body, which is the greatest good of life; read a fine chapter of Seneca, you will see there that nature is content with bread and water, and that [Luigi] Cornaro succeeded in living for nearly a century on this diet although badly constituted.*' [21] The Venetian nobleman and erudite Cornaro had in fact allowed himself a little meat and egg, not to mention half a bottle of wine, every day, but the point was he had established the vital(ist) importance of dietetics on the bodily constitution as early as the sixteenth century, and had survived into a long senescence on it. Tissot's theory situated the origin of reason in the soul, the existence of which Enlightenment reason itself now discounted, and offered its audience the vision of a free will supreme over the appetites, instead of mechanistically succumbing to them. The soul, then, was explicitly an anti-naturalist concept, the means by which God had invested humanity with its special place in creation. If it was man's misfortune to have become alienated from his natural origins, then that was also the means of his salvation, in that reason could free him from their tyranny. It was all very well for Rousseau to picture the child sitting under the tree in a reimagined Eden, contentedly nibbling one of Mrs Smith's sinless apples, but nothing stood between the child – the child particularly – and complete surrender to Lubberlandish gluttony. There may be none of the spiritually perilous ragouts, to be sure, but food itself, even in the state of nature, was a temptation to surfeit, exactly because it satisfied. Therefore, it would not suffice simply to establish the optimal quantity for decent satiety. Under-nourishment was the key. Make the body wait until it was pleading with you to feed it. In this argument is contained all the dialectic of moderation and excess that would inform every such case, not just against food, but against drink and other intoxicants too, in the succeeding centuries:

> *The more we seek out agreeable sensations, the further we get from them. The more we pleasure them, the more choosy the organs become, [and] it is only by remaining in an appropriate simplicity that we can be sure of experiencing continued pleasure; the drinker of water will always find it exquisite, the man who wants spicy wines is always wanting new ones, and it is the same for foods.*[22]

No matter that nature itself was teeming with edible delicacies. Cookery was the route to perdition because it wasn't nature, it was artifice. And it was artifice that over-stimulated appetite, which only unpresumptuously required bread and water to be entirely happy. After all, was it not the case that the taste for rich foods was acquired, whereas the child's innate instinct for sustenance was satisfied with the simplest and blandest regimen? 'Let us preserve the child's primitive tastes as long as possible,' advised Rousseau, 'let his food be common and simple, his palate only become familiarised with mild flavours, and let him not develop exclusive tastes.'[23] The system only misses its own fatal flaw in failing to consider the reversal of its postulates. If materialism comported the risk of excess, where it found itself unable to enlist the spiritual reason in which it was reluctant to believe as a counter-force against the power of appetite, so appetite itself might prevail over the power of a reason in which it all too readily believed, and which it very often had cause to resent. Asceticism turns out to be gluttony's ally, because it is always yearning towards its own revocation. What makes Lenten fasting bearable is the prospect of Easter feasting.

If the sated appetite resulted in gross subordination to corporeality, according to Tissot, it was also implicated in the opposite problem, too much thinking. Where the two activities were carried on at the same time, disaster lurked. Reading while eating contaminated the normal operation of digestion, and the general link between intellection and dyspepsia could be framed in an epigram: 'The man who thinks the most is he who digests the worst.'[24] Men of letters were notoriously impervious to the counsels of their doctors, priding themselves on firmness of purpose where there was only foolish obstinacy, and their indisposition towards physical exercise only aggravated the problem. Indigestion, discomfiting as it was, was only the least of the bodily dysfunctions caused by eating richly: 'succulent foods, ragouts, and sauces' also provoked outbreaks of masturbation and nocturnal extro-mission. Indeed, Tissot wrote one of the eighteenth century's most exhaustive medical studies of auto-eroticism – *L'Onanisme* (1760) – only to see it banned in Paris. Despite its proscription, the book was influential in linking male self-pleasuring to a range of maladies, including loss of vital strength, memory and reason, defective eyesight, neurological disorder, gout, rheumatism, genital atrophy, the passing of blood in the urine, and persistent headache. In an ironically vicious circle, over-indulgence in delicious food led to the disorder of masturbation, which in turn weakened the appetite for even plain food. Even more than what came out of the mouth in wicked utterances, what went into it to sustain the body was the means of incrimination and spiritual pollution. It took Brillat-Savarin, in 1825, to turn the prescriptive logic of this morality of eating on its head. Good food produces happy people.

Dialectics of Moderation

Tastes in drink were even more the vehicles of moral contamination, because the appetite they pandered to was not to fill the stomach but to intoxicate the brain. Although the altering of consciousness with intoxicants had played a privileged role in the classical religions, and had always been viewed in the complacency of folk wisdom as one of life's benefits, the recompense of nature both for the ravages of fate and for its own ravages, drinking had its corrupting side. It would, however, prove stubbornly impervious to the kind of late-Puritan relative schemas to which Tissot and the other moral dieticians subjected eating. If the choice in diet was straightforwardly between the ragouts of the rich and the simple honest earthy fare of the peasantry, where could an analogous territorialisation be drawn with regard to intoxicating drink? To some extent, social stratification was reproduced in types of drink – ordinary country wine against cask-aged brandy, vintage port and champagne in the viticultural heartlands; working men's beer against the pretension of connoisseurial wine in the northern cultures; home-distilled liquor against licenced drink everywhere – but what they all had in common, albeit in varying degrees, was their alcoholic content. This would eventually lead the moral atmosphere of drinking in either of two directions. It could abjure drink altogether, as would be attempted in Prohibitionism, the greatest exercise in social engineering ever undertaken outside the communist world, or it could propose a scale, inevitably of the sliding variety, by which drinking would be judged according to how far along the spectrum from sobriety to inebriation the individual travelled on any given occasion. The question that all reflection on intoxication has since had to confront is that of what the official discourse calls moderation. There is a boundary point – whether physically, psychologically, morally, spiritually, philosophically, or biologically defined – past which it is at best inadvisable, at worst ruinous, to trespass. What this would mean is that an essential underpinning of mature intoxicant behaviour was to find this limit, and then stay within it. But how precisely was it to be located?

In a little-noticed passage of his *Phenomenology of Mind* (1807),

Hegel considers the paradox by means of which, although humanity has been provided by its creator with a universe of delight, there is evidently such a thing as too much. Man's nature is inherently good, but is also constituted such that 'the superfluity of delight does it harm'. He can destroy himself by overreaching himself.

> *To prevent this, he finds reason a useful means for duly restraining this self-transcendence, or rather for preserving himself when he does go beyond the determinate: for such is the force of consciousness... The principle of measure or proportion has, therefore, the determinate function of preventing pleasure in its variety and duration from being quite broken off: i.e. the function of 'measure' is immoderation.*[25]

This is the core contradiction of what Freud would come to define as the pleasure principle, that what most endangers the chances of a sensuously pleasurable life is not lack of opportunity, but over-indulgence. Pleasure is not first and foremost a matter of unfettered Dionysian hedonism, but of restraint. It is precisely by remaining within the limits of restraint that the pleasure-seeker can continue to guarantee the 'immoderation' of pleasure, not by celebrating it to excess, which only undermines it. How much is too much, then, doesn't have to be quantified as such. What matters is that he is aware, like it or not, that there is a 'too much', and that the structure of this 'too much' is such that it subverts and corrodes and cancels the pleasure that leads to it. He has pursued pleasure to the point where it evaporates and turns into its opposite. If he wants to insure pleasure, therefore, he needs paradoxically to stop short during it, and the means of this stopping short is rational calculation, what Hegel calls 'the force of consciousness'.

The philosophical trope of moderation is of ancient lineage. Despite the caricature that later ages made of it, the Epicurean school of Athens emphasised the principle of restraint as the better means of enjoying what pleasures life offered one. The lover in Shakespeare's Sonnet 52 compares himself to a rich man in possession of treasures that are kept securely locked up:

The which he will not every hour survey,
For blunting the fine point of seldom pleasure.
Therefore are feasts so solemn and so rare,
Since, seldom coming in the long year set,
Like stones of worth they thinly placèd are,
Or captain jewels in the carcanet.

Enjoyment of the treasure is ensured by its not being constantly contemplated. When the metaphor is unlocked at the close of the poem, the thought of the beloved's beauty is revealed as the treasure that the lover keeps soundly locked inside his own chest, so that the next meeting with him will be all the more exquisite. When you have him, you can feel triumphant; when you don't, you have the luxury of longing. Order your feelings thus, and you can't lose.

By the same token, Ulysses' encomium to degree from *Troilus and Cressida* (I:iii), famously declares that the removal of due degree, of everything being in its proper hierarchical place in an ordered universe, is what creates universal discord. The point equally well applies to the appetites that are unleashed when 'everything includes itself in power'. Power is driven by will, as Nietzsche will eventually confirm, will by appetite:

And appetite, an universal wolf,
So doubly seconded with will and power,
Must make perforce an universal prey,
And last eat up himself.

Unchecked appetite, whether for power or for consumables, is finally self-destructive. Restraint, degree, proportion, measure not only ensure a harmonious cosmos, they also underwrite the happiness of men's individual lives.

Two immediate problems with this analysis present themselves. One is the obvious one that the restraint of pleasure, when imposed on the individual by an outside agency, can quickly turn malevolent. The idea that somebody else should determine your limits for you gave impetus to the moral compulsions of the nineteenth century temperance movements, and indeed many another act of gratuitous institutional privation, through to the formulation of international drugs legislation in the 1970s. The principle of externally applied restriction, by which a life of miserable austerity is recommended to the already miserable by those who feel they themselves have no need of austerity, is the pleasure principle turned vengeful. If there is such a thing as too much pleasure, there is certainly also such a thing as too much restraint.

The second problem with the pleasure paradox is that it is reason as Tissot conceived it – or, in Freudian terms, the superego – that is accorded the task of superintending the individual's self-restraint, and yet in the case of intoxication, the pleasure derived is precisely about the subversion of everyday rationality. This is not to resurrect a 1960s archetype of intoxicants as the gateway to some form of privileged liberated consciousness, a very late Romantic myth, but only to acknowledge that the type of pleasure afforded by intoxication is of an anti-rational, as distinct from irrational, nature. Hegel at least acknowledges that moderation may well only be recognisable once the hedonist crashes through its barrier. Reason is what preserves man when he 'go[es] beyond the determinate'. In its Latin etymology, from the verb *moderare,* moderation is about reducing, abating, tracking back, toning down, returning to a sense of proportion that has always already been exceeded. When Hegel's contemporary William Blake announces that 'the road of excess leads to the palace of wisdom', he appears simultaneously to restate the Epicurean tenet that stopping short of excess is the way to sustain pleasure, since that is what wisdom would consist in, and also to contest the very notion, in that wisdom is *only* attained via the route of excess. Those who are forced, or have chosen, to live without excess don't know what true moderation is, because they haven't experienced it as a welcome return home, only as an obstruction on the journey out.

What exactly happens, though, to the subjective experience of intoxication when the drinker fails to respect its natural limits? How is intoxication itself altered by regularly exceeding its bounds? When he decides to finish what's left in the bottle, even amid the first indicators of the onset of dehydration, the hint of a headache, possible queasiness and so on, something like a short-circuiting of the appetite for intoxication takes place. What began as a stimulating anticipatory desire for both the taste of the wine and its effect has now turned into blind consumption. And what intoxication is precisely *not* about is blind consumption. Consuming is about the satisfaction of appetites, but the appetites themselves differ. The human organism needs to eat in some measure, but it doesn't physiologically need wine at all. The desire to drink is mobilised by different pleasure-centres in the brain, so that the decision to do so represents a distinct kind of instinctual behaviour from the kind that drives it to eat. For all that it is a basic appetite, it is more of a willed appetite than the need for solid sustenance. At the extremity of intoxicant consumption, then, at the moment where he knows more or less that he has now had enough, to carry on drinking anyway is to nullify the original impulse. It isn't that he hasn't had enough of the taste of this particular wine, or even that he wants to be a bit more inebriated still than he already is. It is that the act itself has now become a purely mechanical procedure, and that makes it wholly antithetical to the controlled anticipatory enjoyment with which he began. Moderation isn't simply a general moral purpose, a watchword for the living of a right life, in the same way that people might generally intend to be considerate of others. It only achieves its self-fulfilment as a notion if it is rigorously practically applied in every encounter with intoxicants. Intoxication has a processual character, in that it starts as one thing and becomes another. It proceeds by degrees, and therefore the act of applying a limit to it is one that must be judged anew each time. On that judgment crucially depends the distinction between optimally satisfying an appetite and negating it through superfluity.

Is it possible to classify the stages of intoxication, to outline what happens as the drinker proceeds on his way through an episode of drinking? Its faint initial onset in the first glass of wine is perhaps its most interesting, and for many its most satisfying manifestation, in that it is the very beginning of the displacement of the ordinary apprehension of reality. Alcohol's complex and only partially understood action on neurotransmitters in the brain appears to involve the simultaneous increase of inhibitory neurotransmission and the suppression of its excitatory counterpart. Whereas caffeine, theophylline (in tea) and theobromine (in chocolate) act as stimulants by suppressing the production of the neurotransmitter adenosine, for example, alcohol acts to increase it, in other words to magnify the sedating effects of adenosine.[26] Put simply, the first impact of drinking is to relax, to mollify, to reduce low-level anxiety, and thus promote the loosening of social inhibition. It shouldn't be hard to see why those effects might be desirable, even though there may be other, less obviously sociable routes to them. A wine journalist once said that she sometimes wished she could spend the whole of waking consciousness in the state of mind induced by exactly one glass of wine. However this state may subjectively be characterised, what it represents is a first practical intervention in the *a priori* consciousness in which the rest of waking life is spent. It may be that the sheer contingent flow of events may produce these alterations too, but events are unpredictable, while the effect of alcohol, at least initially, is almost wholly dependable.

If the first stage is a general relaxation, the next stage, in company at least, is generally some transformation of that relaxed state into something more overtly and actively stimulated. Polite conversation and warm interaction give way to hilarity, bravado, often an amplified sense of closeness to others. There is a feeling that the invisible barriers of politesse that gently separated people earlier are coming down, that their wavelengths are becoming attuned. They are used to saying afterwards that this was an illusory state induced by alcohol's turning them into somebody they were not ('it must have been the Limoncello talking'), which is what Hegel means by reason being a useful means of restraining self-transcendence. This subsequent verdict retroactively transforms the content of an intoxicant episode, but its jurisdiction precisely only applies in retrospect. It always turns out to be null and void once more when the next session takes place.

Beyond that stage lie the more properly disturbing outcomes of intoxication: major or complete lack of physical and mental coordination; memory loss; a sudden access of hysterical aggression; emotional breakdown; depression, sickness and hangover. Learning to avoid these consequences is a question of managing to push them beyond the boundaries of one's habitual encounter with intoxicants, so that if and when they do occur, they are recognised as mistakes and misjudgments rather than normal risks. Consumption of alcohol that ends in these outcomes has misfired because it has ended by destabilising or virtually cancelling the subject's due sense of self, when what intoxication calls him to in the first place is precisely a festive enactment of the self.

In what, however, does this enactment consist? Self-assertion may be one of the principal goals of the altered state, and it isn't difficult to see why intoxication has become such a universally favoured method, when most of the other means of achieving it – excelling at sports, beating a rival candidate to a promotion at work, taking part in a military victory, just looking good in the morning – tend to involve rather more in the way of effort. But what intoxication is also about is the modification of consciousness, of what ethnobotanist Giorgio Samorini has called 'depatterning', the controlled disruption of habitual perceptual and cognitive structures.[27] It may be that herein lies the evolutionary advantage of intoxicated states. The evolution of the human species – and other species too – has selected a preference for intoxicant use that has remained tenaciously constant throughout all eras and across virtually all cultures. Indeed, it was one of the primary routes in human history by which nature became culture. Choice of intoxicants, and hence of their psychotropic effects, has varied, to be sure, often depending on what indigenous plant species were to hand, but the drive to alter consciousness is so durable that Ronald Siegel has termed it 'the fourth drive', following on from the instincts to eat, drink water and reproduce.[28] People can do without it if they have to – they can do without having children if they have to – but there is clearly some evolutionary benefit conferred by intoxication, which has ensured that not only has it never died out, but that they will go to extraordinary lengths, risk their own health, court confrontation with judicial authorities, even under savage repression, in order to procure it.

Altered consciousness allows the brain to dis-embed itself from routine patterns of cognition. This is thought to be the primary function of dreaming, in which the lineaments of everyday waking perception are subjected to a kind of constructive scrambling, sometimes with results that illuminate the psyche in unexpected ways. In being disturbed and reassembled, the component parts of interior life are literally *re-cognised*. Use of intoxicants can be the willed version of such re-cognition in waking hours. The gigantic evolutionary advance effected by the antecedents of *Homo sapiens* was founded on the development, and minutely intricate elaboration, of the intellect. It led humans to become creatures of language, of social cooperation, of analytical, objectifying intelligence, but that achievement was bought at the cost of the traumatic alienation from their natural environment that is self-consciousness. It could well be that what intoxicated states provide is a holiday period from the rigidities of processing, classifying and prioritising to which a hyper-developed consciousness is otherwise subject. One should be careful, however, not to fall into the trap of seeing everyday consciousness and the partially intoxicated state as two entirely distinct zones, between which one passes in either direction with the aid of alcohol and its eventual metabolic incorporation into the system. Intoxicants don't simply put a bomb under traditional thought patterns; they enable the user constructively to reappraise the world by executing a parallax shift in relation to it. It is here that the position defined by Hegel as 'Absolute Knowing' applies, the standpoint from which individual consciousness manages to grasp not only the phenomenal world as it appears, but the limitations of its own position within it. The much misinterpreted notion of Absolute Knowing in Hegel is nothing to do with some ultimately transcendental position of quasi-divine omniscience, but constitutes rather the full extrapolation of humanity's evolution from consciousness to self-consciousness, when the gap between what the external world is in itself, and the way it appears, is finally mediated. 'What Hegel calls "Absolute Knowing" is the point at which the subject fully assumes this mediation, when he abandons the untenable project of taking up a position from which he might compare his subjective experience and the way things are independently of his experience – in other words, Absolute Knowing is a name for the acceptance of the absolute limitation of the circle of our subjectivity, of the impossibility of stepping outside of it.'[29]

The standard view of certain strands of libertarian thinking, whereby the intoxicated mind passes from seeing the world as it is 'for us' and starts to see it as it is 'in itself' (argued especially with regard to hallucinogenic materials such as LSD and MDMA), misses the point. It is rather that the intoxicated mind precisely loses any sense of the distinction between these two perceptions, because it senses itself as part of the very reality that it previously sought to apprehend from a distance. Intoxication breaks down the Kantian model of transcendental apperception, in which the subject stands sovereign over all it surveys, and instead reinserts the thinking consciousness into its surroundings. To put it simply, you might spend your working hours scheduling and supervising and making decisions in a way that holds reality at an objective distance, but when the evening's first glass of wine begins to make itself felt, the effect is to elide that painstakingly maintained distance and re-inscribe the self into its surrounding reality. This accounts for that indefinably unsettling feeling that sometimes accompanies going to bed on the evenings when one hasn't had anything at all to drink. The operation of one's rational consciousness is still on the tight leash on which it has been all day. This is surely what explains the advantage of intoxication in evolutionary development. Why after all does the brain possess the susceptibility or aptitude to enter an altered state at all? Why aren't sleeping and waking enough? We now know that there is a receptor in the brain for tetrahydrocannabinol (THC), the active component of cannabis. Why has that evolved if it were not for the fact that some key benefit is made available by it for those who choose to exercise it? Other substances act to stimulate the release of dopamine or serotonin, the neurotransmitters involved in mood elevation and social empathy.

The standard cynical wisdom about the human condition is that there is a life that people would ideally like to live and then there is the one that they are stuck with. The former has underwritten the grandest human projects: theological visions of heaven, political utopias, the yearning towards happiness of the great artworks, the efforts of science to reduce human suffering, the perfectibility they hope to find in love relationships. And the rest is literally history, the whole exasperating one-damn-thing-after-another that has constituted the bulk of actual human experience. To the indelible image of these two securely bounded zones, forever closed off from each other by a heavily guarded gate, should be opposed the notion that it is exactly in the gap between the ideal and the real that one's life is lived, indeed that one's life just *is* this gap itself, which is constitutive of it. The function of intoxicants is to bring the user back to a fully three-dimensional awareness of that gap. He is not stranded in the barren desert forever seeing mirages on the horizon. He is instead perpetually somewhere on a journey between the two.

The most forceful argument of all for a due sense of proportion in the use of intoxicants is to be made in the light of this evolutionary awareness. One should avoid traumatic excess, not for the usual moral reasons, but because, beyond a certain point, which of course remains difficult to determine, intoxication stops fulfilling its important cognitive function and becomes instead a means of disabling cognition altogether. To some disturbed individuals, that latter risk has become precisely the whole point. Better to blank out the circumstances of a ghastly life than continue to be subjugated by them, even though the ghastliness itself may have come to consist largely in dysfunctional use of intoxicants. Capably handled, which is a skill that the overwhelming mass of humanity has acquired through biological heredity, intoxication continues to offer human beings a material means of insight into their troubled condition, and thereby the hope of a redemption from it.

Taste and Emotion

What Adorno calls the 'unfree equality of compulsory

consumers'[30] has rendered all consumption compromising. Where consuming isn't necessary to the sustenance of the organism, but only serves to perpetuate those parts of the global economic mechanism that are unable to perpetuate themselves, consumption that is biologically indispensable – eating and drinking – comes to look like greed incarnate. The popular image of luxurious eating has hardly moved on since Cockaigne, its opulence derived more surely from the calculus of quantity than from quality. 'All you can eat!' the restaurant shouts to those on limited budgets, luring customers in with an appeal to their instinctual sense that the normal practice of public catering is to cheat them where it can, inviting them to stuff themselves silly prior to suing them for taking it at its word. Where eating has been subjugated to the collective principle that is the engine of the culture industry as a whole, the quality of what gets eaten is sacrificed to the imperative for more of the same. Repetition helps to solidify the myth of good food on which the global fast-food chains are built, in a two-dimensional linear logic: if it weren't any good, you wouldn't keep coming back for it, and the fact that you keep coming back proves its worth. Outside these gargantuan commercial structures, the enjoyment suddenly rendered by rediscovering the taste of something one hasn't eaten for many years, or by one of those all-too-rare moments when something home-made really does taste, as food writers axiomatically insist it does, better than the mass-produced article, or even an individual moment of serendipity when some piece of mass-produced garbage in some unfamiliar context unexpectedly tastes ambrosial, dissolves all the moral valence of eating in a trice. In such moments, even the question of objective quality turns into an extraneous elitist concept. The worry that traditional aesthetics harboured about the pleasure of eating, in the *Critique of Judgment* and elsewhere, that precisely because what was consumed was evanescent, ceasing to exist with the last fading of the aftertaste, it couldn't be accorded the structure of true aesthetic pleasure, which was properly conceived as eternal, missed the point that the circularity of the eternal is just what makes its enjoyment pall. The transience of gustatory pleasure, which destroys what it values in the act of valuing it, makes it momentarily better than art, as if it didn't already possess that virtue by nourishing a fragmentary life more reliably than do paintings. Nobody, in the twentieth century especially, needed polemical materialism to exclaim that bread is the prerequisite for morals, the guaranteeing of which art turned out to be wholly useless at.

The pathos that can be awakened by seeing somebody eating alone is an alloy of the image of isolation with a concomitant awareness that one is seeing him engaged in one of the biological functions that isn't performed privately. He is caught in a moment that, against the argument of restaurant historians that eating is always self-performative, reveals him in something of the vulnerability that animals feel when they are eating. The defensiveness of a feeding animal is not, as is often mistakenly thought, the reflex of selfish greed – a dog will share its food with you in extremis – but the vigilant recognition that while it is feeding, it is almost as prone to attack as when asleep. Not every act of solo public eating, after all, is driven by gluttony, as distinct from a bodily insistence that won't be denied. Even in the private realm, especially in it, eating is liberated from the stranglehold of indulgence, even when the moral law within indulges the eater with the luxury of accusing himself of indulgence. Bruised to tears by the carelessness of one who loved him, a hungry boy didn't desist from eating his stir-fried noodles even while he cried, surrendering to two kinds of subjective destitution at once, wholly oblivious of now cutting the other to the quick more deeply than all his angry words had managed.

Chapter Five

Touch

Touch nothing unclean.
Isaiah 52:11

I held him, and would not let him go.
Song of Songs 3:4

Touch has a memory.
John Keats

Pleasure and Pain

The facts of consciousness that the empirical world offers to the mind via subjective sense-impressions are not always, or even predominantly, a matter of neutral factuality. Much of consciousness is of comfort and dissatisfaction, pleasure and pain, and provokes the mind into the conviction that, in eliminating the latter, there would be more of the former. This is the chief engine of its quest for knowledge, even though the mind-body dualism insisted that the knowledge gained by the somatic element of the mind was only a weak imitation of the real knowledge of true intellection. Idealism didn't scorn the thought that there was a corporeal element in happiness, even to the exclusion of any other factor. Even Kant, in the *Critique of Judgment*, acknowledges that 'all pleasure is physical', as was taught in the school of Epicurus, but thereby maroons it in the aesthetic realm, as an effect that the great artworks contrive to produce, its truthfulness and its transience as intricately bound together as are pleasure itself and its negative polarity, terror, in access to the sublime. Where potential pleasure flaunts itself, there lurks desire, and the admixture of tension in not-quite-fulfilled desire, which for Freud may well constitute the whole of pleasure itself, imitates the commingling of beauty and terror in the majesty of nature or on the classical stage. Physical desire, though, is what idealism would like the mind to be cured of, but it purchases the knowledge that raises it above desire as cheaply as does the Grimms' poor peasant Crabb, who becomes Doctor Knowall by no subtler means than acquiring some rudimentary stock and changing his name. Nor does the appeal of erudition dawn on him until he sees how well the real doctor dines.

To a certain dominant strand of sensual theory, touch is the sensual antecedent of all sensing, for all that it may not enjoy first place in the hierarchy. It is the most basic of the senses for Aristotle (*De Anima*, II:2), where 'basic' is to be understood in the sense of 'necessary'. The point endures to the high-water mark of Enlightenment and beyond. Even the other primary senses, vision and hearing, are for Kant in some sort functionally subordinate to touch, which has the honorary duty of ratifying their perceptions in order to furnish empirical knowledge. 'In reality all five senses can be reduced to one,' states a Russian dictionary, 'the sense of touch.' The sensory stimuli have all to touch the respective sense-organs of the body in order to be registered: sound-waves on the eardrum, food on the tongue and palate, olfactory emanations in the nasal passages, rays of light on the optic nerve. However metaphorical this sounds, if touch is foundational to the senses, its vital force is rooted in its being so deeply and directly implicated in pleasure and pain. There are dazzling lights and jarring sounds, foul smells and rank tastes, but nothing produces the paradigm of unpleasantness as immediately as physical pain. By the same token, pleasurable touch is what touches off desire: 'if they [living things] have the perceptive faculty they have also that of desire,'[1] says Aristotle (II:3), the desire to nourish themselves in both subsistence and pleasure, and the desire to avoid pain. Touch is the only sense necessary to survival. It ensures the basic being of the organism, which wouldn't be able to nourish itself in the absence of touch, whereas the other senses only afford it well-being.

If the operations of the mind were truly separable from those of the body, they would suffer a distinctly greater impoverishment by the divorce than would the physical axis. The senses cannot function by themselves – they need the objects and stimuli of external phenomena – but no more can the mind function autonomously, whatever it might – in the refinement of its analytical and synthetic skills – have persuaded itself. Sense-perception on the classical model is the fulcrum that holds the balance between the worlds of potentiality and actuality, being not quite identifiable with either the one or the other. To perceive a sense-object is to begin to realise its potential for epistemology, even though knowledge itself is the end-product made possible by the mental processing of perception. A passage from the particular to the general is effected, or, as Aristotle expresses it, 'perception in activity is of particular things, knowledge of universals'[2] [II:5]. The most obvious proof of this for him is that intellection can be a matter of conscious intention, whereas the operation of the senses depends on there being external sense-objects in the body's vicinity. The brain can will itself to think, but not to perceive. It can only know the sense-objects as and when they have contingently presented themselves to it. To the Kant of the anthropological lectures, this is especially so in the case of touch, which is required to confirm the three-dimensional presence of an object, which the faculty of vision can only approximate.

If the sensations pour potential knowledge into the mind's empty cup, they do so for Aristotle by a curious process that involves qualitative alteration rather than simple transfer. In perceiving, the sense-faculties become like the objects they sense. They are changed by what they see and feel. Rather than submitting physical reality to a filtering or percolating process, subjective sensory perception submits itself to a heteronomisation by the objects it takes in, as though only its own impressionability is what allows the world around it sympathetic access to the procedures of understanding. Something of this survives into the Christian adjuration that only by becoming childlike in their receptivity to the world will adults achieve the understanding that is required to transcend it.

If touch is the most profound of the senses, it is because its affect begins at a pervasively deeper level of interiority than do those of the others. While the body possesses sense-organs that obviously correspond to their respective senses – the eyes, ears, nose and tongue – it isn't immediately clear to Aristotle that the skin, which modern physiology knows as an organ in itself, has the same status. Not the least reason for this is that touch is much less evidently the medium for one category of sensual experience than the other senses are: 'what is the single underlying thing which is to touch as sound is to hearing[?]'[3] [II:11]. If skin is only the medium through which somatic sensations activate an interior element ('something else within'), that latter would be the true sense-organ of touch. In this case, the body, including the other heterogeneous sense-organs it incorporates, is 'the ongrown medium of the touch-faculty,'[4] so that haptic sensations are perceived not on it but through it.

Nonetheless, what concerns Aristotle about the perception of touch is that it contains a functional inconsistency. It is a contact sense. In the cases of vision, hearing and smell, the body doesn't have to be in direct contact with the sensory objects – they are perceived at a distance – but in the case of touch it does. Indeed, this is the definition of *con-tact*. Touching, however, is also self-touching. The fingers that touch the keyboard can feel themselves touching it. The ears don't sense themselves hearing, they just hear, but the skin is aware of itself touching. This should mean that there is a reflexivity to the tangible faculty, and yet most of the time, unless the mind consciously addresses the matter, there is no such thing. Consciousness disregards the medium of touch, which establishes the proposition that the skin is only the medium of tactility and not the sense-organ itself, but it also makes it at once vulnerable to haptic extremes – scorching heat, freezing cold, lacerating sharpness, abrasive roughness – as well as propositionally formative for sensation in general. Touching is active rather than passive, involves doing rather than merely receiving, and yet in its functioning, it imitates the passivity of the indirect senses.

Touch is the irreducible emblem of what subjectivity might do by means of the senses, as opposed to what it merely objectively registers through them. It is for this reason among others that its virtualisation in the electronic world has proceeded far behind those of vision and hearing. Developments in reverse electro-vibration technology since the start of the century allow users remotely to experience the texture, weight and shape of objects by means of a weak electrical oscillation around the skin, something akin to the hypothetical membrane that Aristotle suggests could as easily stand in for the body's integument in its mediatory role before the inner sense-organ. Not only can one view the Tang Dynasty ceramic at a distance, obviating a long trip to the museum to see it *in concreto*, but haptic technology permits the viewer to break the real museum's most cardinal rule: Do Not Touch. The technology works in both directions. Just as users can find out what remote objects feel like on the skin, they can also, by exerting pressure on a tactile sensor, move them about, and even operate machinery at distance. In due course, surgical operations will routinely be carried out by medical staff in one hospital connected remotely by video link to another. If the eye enacts the distancing of sense par excellence, on the Cartesian model, the use of hands draws the sensate subject into the world, and yet haptic electronics brings distance into that category of sensory experience too. The technology is inevitably celebrated as collapsing distance, as in the famous first electronic handshake of 2002, and yet what it is more obviously doing is introducing distance into one of the only two senses, the other being taste, that couldn't previously function over distance. Will there eventually be gustatory electronics, allowing the user, by the insertion of some kind of oral contrivance, to taste the dishes depicted on a restaurant's website?

Advocates of the use of touch in psychotherapy settings, such as Joen Fagan and Alma Smith Silverthorn,[5] insist that touching decreases the felt sense of distance between bodies, restoring an intimation of proximity to subjects alienated from their own lives, but go on to draw the more unsettling conclusion that 'the world shrinks when we touch'. Reaching out to touch the body of another, albeit in clinically controlled circumstances, enacts something like a much-needed vacation, however momentary, from the dreary household of the self, from the autarchic subjectivity that is the source of the subject's alienation from itself in the first place. Gabriel Josipovici describes feeling the need to dip his hand into the Pacific on his first visit to Los Angeles, to establish for himself that he had been there by imprinting a sense-memory of it, but recording also his 'feeling of disappointment that the water did not seem in any sense distinctive.'[6] In this context, the need to touch appears to be an extension of the tourist's insatiable desire to photograph everything; the pictures are the evidence to others that you have been to Los Angeles, touching part of it confirms it for yourself. Josipovici suggests that touch has a dual aspect, in that touching an unfamiliar environment is as much a way as confirming one's own presence to somewhere new, as it is of establishing its presence to oneself. It may in this respect, he thinks, resemble early medieval pilgrimage, in that those who journeyed to visit, say, St Lawrence's tomb outside Rome were hoping that coming into its presence would help heal them or their loved ones. When it became forbidden to touch the tombs, a system of contact relics was substituted, by which the same degree of efficacy could be invested through touching a bit of cloth that had itself briefly touched the tomb. In a phenomenal world in which everything appears untouchable, the act of touching becomes invested with primitive magic. The desire to shrink the world through touching it thus recalls prehistoric terror, not merely at the world's dimensions but at its substantive otherness. If subjectivity could only apprehend it, take it in hand, its mythological power over humanity might be diminished, but in coming to believe in its own transcendence over the world, subjectivity only replaced such power with an even more spellbinding mythology. No amount of touching, either in therapy or on holiday, will break the spell as long as touching remains a matter of bestially marking one's territory.

The therapeutic investment in touching makes of this particular sense a parodic image of human relations as such. If there can be no mutual understanding without some form of communication between individuals, making contact with the other's embodied particularity seems to offer a shortcut route to the mingling of subjectivities. Mere speaking won't bridge the gap, not at least since it filtered through to popular consciousness from the positivism of the pre-war era that language is all a game, a matter of shuffling shape-shifting signifiers from one meaning-context to another, and that the currency of ethical essences such as love and trust and respect is not readily convertible across borders. Touching another person or, more to the point, being touched by them appears to bypass these potential misunderstandings, offering direct access to the other's heart, and yet there is no more uncomplicatedly obvious proximity in tactile exercises than there was in talking to each other. Precisely because it lacks any semantic cover, touching can be as easily interpretable as sinister or appropriative in its intent as it can mimic the tender caresses that are said to help nurture dangerously premature babies. More even than either looking or listening, touching demands an explanation for its use, at least when it concerns other people. If listening to what the other is saying, or even in some cases looking at another, can be interpretable as an incursion on their selfhood, reaching out to touch them shatters the social contract altogether. Touch is the preserve of established sexual partners or, at the minimum, of the deep familiarity of close friendship, but has its roots either way in the unquestionable pre-existent. To extend it, in the interests of binding the damaged psyche or of general social amelioration, to the interactions of those who don't already know each other is to act out a travesty of intimacy, one that recognises its own fraudulence by its having faked the prehistory that gives true mutual familiarity its bottomless comfort. The owner of the willing body, supine on the massage-table or dreaming under the hands of the practitioner of oriental healing, may persuade himself that he has surrendered his aching consciousness to the ministrations of another, but the very attitude of 'let's pretend' betrays the fantasy. If the eye can be deceived by optical illusions, even in full consciousness of the source of the illusion, and the ear can mistakenly transform an innocuous sound into something monitory, the skin is much harder put to it to allow itself to be duped. Even wishing with its every follicle can't make it turn the healer's hand into the healing embrace of somebody who loves him.

Therapeutic touching purloins the subjective intention from true affectionate touching, under which the pleasurable sensation produced by another's touch becomes the metonymic evidence of the benevolence it enacts. Touch is the para-linguistic communication of emotional solidarity between intimates. It connects individuals by virtue of the fact that touch feels itself touching. The lover's hand that strokes her arm also senses its own contact with the loved one through her arm, notwithstanding the fact that the hand is the *primum mobile* of touch, its principal active implement. When the hand meets another hand, their owners perform their allegiance in the most overt manner, which is why lovers hold hands, and why comradeship and amity are symbolised by the shaking of hands. Where emotional intentionality is subtracted from these equations, as on the massage-table, the pleasure of touch is partially deactivated. Even the most vigorously satisfying deep-tissue manipulation represents a professionalising of touch, and the same is true of the touching in controlled therapy.

If the pleasure involved in the caress is the physical evidence of love, in what sense might it fit into Kant's anthropology, in which pleasure only gains authenticity by its following pain? '*[P]ain must always precede every enjoyment;* pain is always first ... Pain is the incentive of activity, and in this, above all, we feel our life; without pain lifelessness would set in.'[7] The bourgeois notion that all pleasure must be bought with a down payment of pain, with regular minimum repayments required if your credit-worthiness is to remain sufficiently solid to grant access to further supplies of pleasure, condemns the life of the spirit to the prudent bookkeeping of debit and credit columns. The account must balance. A surfeit of pleasures, one after the other, with nothing nasty in between, would kill you, declares Kant, a warning that does nothing to quash the suspicion that, all things told, one might be prepared to risk it. Advances in the *materia medica* of physicians and apothecaries, available at least to the mercantile classes and above of the eighteenth century, had begun to drive back the recurrence and intensity of physical pain, leaving in its wake the ghastly prospect that a time might come when life was all pleasure. Supplying the lack that the neutralisation of pain left was boredom, an invention of the late-eighteenth and early-nineteenth centuries. Whoever said boredom was the ecstasy of the bourgeoisie was only half-right. As Kant states, it was first pain, or rather pain's substitute: 'even if no positive pain stimulates us to activity, if necessary a negative one, *boredom,* will often affect us in such a manner that we feel driven to do something harmful to ourselves rather than nothing at all. For boredom is perceived as a *void* of sensation by the human being who is used to an alternation of sensations in himself, and who is striving to fill up his instinct for life with something or other.'[8] Climbing tall trees, reckless use of intoxicants, self-harming are among the behaviours that might be fashioned into pleasure by boredom, which is thereby as much of a positive influence to the sensual life as is angina. Like the idiot banging his head on a brick wall in the paradigm, he discovers that it's bliss when he stops. If the Kantian model supplies the dialectical nicety in the relationship between agony and ecstasy, in its prescriptive insistence, it nonetheless speaks the language of the reformatory. There may be a world of torment now, but you'll be grateful for it in the end.

The professional work ethic decrees that the function of pain or boredom is to insure human development, which would languish without the lacerating spur of discomfort. At least this is so for 'cultivated human beings', according to Kant, as distinct from bone-idle Caribbeans, for example, who are content to loll for hours with their fishing-rods, barely noticing whether they catch anything or not. The first stirrings of the industrial revolution have already begun to drown what once seemed to the European imagination an unvarnished idyll of tranquillity in the clattering of mechanised production. As the bustle that will by the twenty-first century reduce the velocity of activity to micro-seconds begins to gather pace, it brings with it the imposition that everybody ought either to be doing something, or have a very good reason not. To the non-labouring classes, anything will do to fill the hours: 'As someone in Paris said of Lord Mordaunt, "The English hang themselves in order to pass the time".'[9] The oscillation between pleasure and pain, and the necessity to be active, are imbued with the acute sensation of temporality, every foray against pleasure being an attempt to escape the present moment and enter the next one. Time stretches ahead as long as it isn't filled and, when it is, appears to contract. The end of a long wretched life may seem irrationally to the dying labourer to have been too short, just because it wasn't filled with anything better. Passing the time becomes, in the English usage of Kant's era, a matter of 'beguiling' it, tricking it into shrinking, like dropping lemon juice on a live oyster. Eventually, even fooling it doesn't suffice, because Time is no more gullible than the restless layabout whom it stifles, and so, having become the enemy, it must be 'killed'. Nothing appears more surely likely to defeat empty time than somatic pleasure, in which some form of physical engagement delivers joy to the sensate body and relief to the overworked mind, but what too often has to stand in for physical satisfaction is the thin gruel of amusement.

In the fairground Ghost Train of childhood, furry tapes were suspended that brushed over the screaming occupants of the carriages as they stuttered through the dark. If the illuminated masks and painted skeletons looked no more than comical, the invisible strands made a subtler, and altogether more disturbing, assault on the senses. The bored consciousness that can't find anything to do hopes to be taken similarly unawares in resorting to amusements, but the amusements too often fail by dint of their own programmatic character. A walk in the park may pass the time without doing anything to address the underlying longing for the unexpected, which only the likes of video-games or gambling can fulfil – 'Good God, have I lost that much?' The alternative, for Kant, is a renunciation to which, with bourgeois fastidiousness, he refuses the name:

> *Young man! (I repeat) get fond of work; deny yourself enjoyments, not to renounce them, but rather to keep them always in perspective as far as possible! Do not dull your receptivity to enjoyments by savouring them prematurely! The maturity of age, which never lets us regret having done without a single physical enjoyment, will guarantee, even in this sacrifice, a capital of contentment*

which is independent of either chance or the laws of nature.[10]

Even in the eighteenth century, there were individuals, and not always the most deprived, who regretted in extremis not having enjoyed life more while they had the chance, but in an age when the alleged right to self-fulfilment is felt all the more keenly, the more its universal annulment exposes it as a swindle, the arrival of disintegrating old age may well bring with it nothing but regret. The utopian hope in Kant's formulation, that there could be a contentment safeguarded against the tyranny of fortune or, better yet, against inexorable biological decay, is only unrealistic in its postponement to the seventh age, when powers have dwindled, senses dulled, and what remains to be expected of life is deliverance from it.

Kant's insistence on the reciprocal nature of pleasure, that to be true pleasure it has to involve an active participatory element, and not merely the princely expectation of being passively entertained, acknowledges what the succeeding generation would call its dialectical complexity, for all that it sounds in his example like frank superciliousness: 'If, for example, someone entertains himself with fine arts instead of mere sensual pleasures, he has the added satisfaction that he (as a refined man) is capable of such pleasures.'[11] But the point applies equally to sensual pleasures, of which, notwithstanding the maundering of official morality, hardly any are capable. If all else fails, there is always the time-proven recourse to Schadenfreude: 'It is not exactly the nicest observation about human beings that their enjoyment increases through comparison with others' pain, while their own pain is diminished through comparison with similar or even greater sufferings of others.'[12] He is right to point out the ethical distinction between drawing reassurance from these eventualities as a matter of psychology, and the moral stain of actively wishing misfortunes on others in order to cheer oneself up, but he misses the moral failing in encouraging others to reflect complacently on their own circumstances by deliberately comparing them with those less fortunate. That the crowds who attended public executions afterwards felt 'a mild but nevertheless genuine feeling of relaxation, which makes their subsequent enjoyment of life all the more tangible'[13] was no excuse for the executions. At the bottom of the gulf into which such bland heartlessness plunges people is not a due sense of measure in their own self-awareness, but the foreboding solace of nihilism: 'The most thorough and easiest means of soothing all pains is the thought, which can well be expected of a reasonable human being, that life as such, with regard to our enjoyment of it, which depends on fortunate circumstances, has no intrinsic value of its own at all.'[14] The proposition, havering through dilatory subordinate clauses as it does, finally arrives at the truth it hardly dared at first blurt out. Life isn't worth a damn. The proof of that is that the only value it might possess is use-value, arising from 'the ends to which it is directed', the certain reassurance, which is none, that only a functionalised life could expiate its worthlessness, the other-directed condition to which society in our own era has already condemned it.

Where a wholly bureaucratised society has subjected the human spirit to the deformations required by its functioning, the external world has become as alien as the variously hostile environments into which hominids on the move from Africa first ventured. Civilisation was only ever guaranteeable by adaptation to those aspects of nature that proved stubbornly unmalleable, until humanity stands at a point where the impact and extent of the malleability has produced the need for an adaptation that may be beyond it. As the auratic quality of the better things has become tarnished, their estrangement to sight and hearing has resulted in the atrophy of the impulse to touch. Disgust at tactility arises, even earlier than the recoil from what looks unclean, in the apprehension at complete alterity. A horror at contact with the alien object produces both fetishes and phobias, the twin poles of contemporary sensual experience. There is more to see and touch than ever before, but hardly any of it looks enticing enough. The transformation of nature into one gigantic and depleting warehouse has accompanied the commodification of life in reified economic conditions. If Marx's world looked like an enormous wholesale bazaar, at least where one trained one's sights away from the bustling toil of the manufactories and mills, ours is the sprawling shopping-mall on the eve of Christmas, where, despite many of the shelves having been picked clean by bargain-hunters, the relentlessly teeming choice leaves the consumer numb, but where the sway of enforced joviality never wavers. Nothing appears to invite the investigation of touch, but only demands that the consumer already know whether he wants it or not. Even the trying on of clothes feels like an ordeal, a matter of seeing whether he can make himself look acceptable to the jacket, rather than allowing it to transform him. Where there were once books, there are now discs that offer nothing to look at before he buys, while the ripeness of the imported fruits, bred and selected for their unearthly perfection, is to be taken on gullible trust. The allegedly freshly made bakery items sit naked on their shelves, defenceless against airborne bacteria, but equipped with plastic tongs for picking them up, as though the buyer were expected not even to trust the hygienic integrity of his own grasp. Medieval visions of the Land of Cockaigne incorporated the notion of inexhaustible plenty in their cornucopias, in an era when regular scarcity was lethal, but their concrete realisation in the developed world since the 1950s has made a reality of the obscenity of surfeit, which was better left as a hypothetical postulate of moral philosophy, while resulting in widespread impoverishment of natural resources, and entrenching the material chasm between the developed and underdeveloped worlds.

Surfeit, which had in any case already been available since the palaeolithic eras in the form of intoxicants, produces its own *noli me tangere,* the body's metabolic biology adapting itself to the rhythm of immersion and disengagement that botanical drugs and their processing provided. By contrast, the production of consumer goods in surfeit, intended as reward to societies that worked hard to produce their own wealth, by whatever rationalised means could be made of the exploitation of resources and labour, is precisely not carried on in the interest of satiating appetite, but of unendingly stimulating it anew. Confronted with thousands of products to pick up and look at, one hardly picks up any, since the brute overwhelming fact of their multiplicity homogenises them at best and, at worst, bestows on them the pestilential air of one of the ten plagues of Egypt. There may have been more delight in coming across some rarely seen fruit during periods of rationing, and though nobody alive would wish to recreate the privations of war, the better to appreciate the taste of a banana, the nausea provoked by having one's gullet stuffed with them turned the end of privation into something tasteless.

When it comes to touching other human beings, the predilection in the Anglo-Saxon societies, and in most of East Asia for that matter, is a Bartlebyesque 'I'd prefer not to'. Tactility between individuals outside the context of relationships has followed an eccentric course in the modern epoch. Confined in the Victorian age to the affection lavished on children, much of which looks like the inchoate expression of sexuality that Freud was condemned for seeing in it, it acknowledged its own infantilism. Kisses and caresses were not the gestural language of grown-ups. For half of the following century, platonic physical contact was in danger of complete extinction, until the coming of sexual liberation in the mid-1960s made it a manifesto item of a generation torn between confronting bourgeois society head-on and blithely ignoring it. The explosion of sexually transmitted infection since the 1980s, compounded by the discovery that child sex abuse, rather than being a matter of isolated pathology, occurs at the institutional level, and the formulation of a politics of tactility founded on the presumption of malevolent intent, not just in the workplace but in society generally, has revoked the nostrums of the liberation era. Anybody who touches anybody else must know, and be prepared to explain, precisely what he means by it, and with obvious cause. Few things short of outright violation are more unsettling than unwarranted touch. If the formation of all subjective consciousness, premised as it is on our sense-impressions, is preformed by the social moulding of the individual, the passive experience of touch is more declaratively so than any other somatic phenomenon. The odour of exposed rotting garbage on a hot day is offensive, but the brushing of another's fingers along one's forearm in an otherwise formal context impresses on the recipient, with all the force paradoxically lacking in the subtlety of the caress, an oppressive need to account for the other's intentions. Indeed, the more subtle the caress, the more self-evidently insidious it appears. Women assaulted by their male partners often report that the apologetic stroking that frequently follows an episode of violence is almost as repulsive as the attack itself. In the entirety of our social experience, the impulse to recoil from any physical advance other than that of people whom one wholly, intimately trusts speaks of the atomisation to which a society supposedly founded on and driven by interconnectedness has reduced its members.

Connectedness, which existentialism and the theatre of the absurd once wrote off as a doomed project, has been resurrected as an electronic actuality, but it has been rendered literally intangible. The wireless telegraph and then the telephone brought remote communication to miraculous presence in the same age that spiritualism was seeking to put its own speculations on a concrete empirical basis. Psychical research did not just strain towards contact with the dead; it sought to demonstrate that such matters as telepathy and telekinesis were genuine phenomena. The contemporary age of screens has extended remote seeing – and remote talking, remote touching, remote sexual congress, and perhaps remote eating eventually – into the lives of almost all, with the incipient evolutionary effect that proximate contact is becoming unnecessary, unhygienic and disturbing. In the case of the smartphone app that could transfer music files from one phone to another by gently knocking them together, touch was outsourced to appliances. Slavoj Žižek suggests unironically that electrical sex-toys might, in the near future, be encouraged to mate with each other by their owners on a first date, to obviate the over-familiarity that actual sex always incurs. In this way, a courtesy lost to prospective partners who feel the obligation to get on with it sooner than they might have wished could be restored.

If people who want to touch you are clearly weird, though, what does that imply about your own insuppressible desire to touch them? There is a moment of properly liberating objectivity in the consciousness of some aspect of another's physique that one finds oneself wanting to touch, especially where it isn't one of the body parts particular to the opposite sex. It acquires its objectivised state through the very character that would seem to invest it with the greatest familiarity, its outward resemblance to the same part of one's own body. What Sartre called our 'being-for-others', the version of oneself that is constructed in the other's consciousness, over which one can exercise only the most superficial influence, while its underlying foundation remains peculiar to them, comes most evidently to fruition in these moments. One can no more see the somatic velleity of one's own hand in the perception of another than one can see it in the mirror, that duplicitous objectifier. It belongs strictly to the conceptualising glance of the other. In these instants of genuine connection, even where the chance for their enactment does not arise, the solitary subject yearns to close the circle that would let him know what it feels like to the other to imagine touching him. If what human beings feel on their skin has an effect on what they feel inside, what they feel inside longs for release in the sensation of being touched by somebody they could learn to love. Touch and its pathologisation in contemporary society have become expressive of a desire sublimated to the utmost subtlety, but which issues from the deepest levels of being: the desire to fulfil, and therefore cancel, one's own desire in the state of being desired.

Touch and the Essential

The ambiguity with which the status of touch is shot through in classical antiquity and medieval scholasticism alike derives from the dual nature of essentiality. Something that is foundational, prioristic, in any hierarchic structure is, by the same token, also the most basic, the most unramified, the bedrock on which the more exalted edifice is constructed, without which it would lack support, but which, in its very indispensability, has the nature of the bare elemental or of subterraneity (Constance Classen's work on touch is entitled *The Deepest Sense*). When Aristotle turns to the question of a common basis of sense-perception, touch appears momentarily – but only momentarily – to be the prime candidate to fulfil the unifying function of meta-sensuality. Sense is not purely a matter of the properties of each object being sensed by the respective faculties, but there is an overriding sense of sensing, by which the organism perceives and analyses its own sense-impressions as such. Tantalisingly close to a theory of Cartesian self-consciousness, he observes that, not only does the eye see the object as white and the tongue taste it as sweet, but there is some internal sense that perceives that whiteness and sweetness are not the same category of perception. The sensorium is not only ordered; it is aware of its own ordering. So what might be the unifying sense that organises all five of the senses? It must be a form of sensation in itself, but it cannot be touch, any more than it can be any single one of the others, because everything would then be a matter of touching, of how things felt on the skin, which it self-evidently isn't. '[F]lesh is not the ultimate sense-organ; to suppose that it is requires the supposition that on contact with the object the sense-organ itself discerns *what is doing the discerning*.'[15] Nor does Aquinas misread this point into what would clearly be a category error, as has often been inferred from his *lectio* on the passage. 'If this be true [ie. that there is a unifying sense-faculty], the most likely sense-faculty would seem to be touch, the first sense, the root and ground, as it were, of the other senses, the one which entitles a living thing to be called sensitive. But clearly, if this discrimination were a function of touch, then the fundamental organ of touch would not be flesh; if it were, then by the mere contact of flesh and a tangible object, this object would be discriminated from all other sense-objects.'[16] Touch does not and cannot inform the intellect about every sensible property of an object, only the properties specific to the sense of touch. While touch is foundational in the sense that no living being can survive the loss of it, in the way that it can survive the loss of any of the other senses, that still doesn't qualify touch to be the unifying organ of meta-perception, only lends it at best the status of a *primus inter pares*. As Aquinas continues, 'Now this discrimination cannot be attributed to touch precisely as a particular sense, but only as the common ground of the senses, as that which lies nearest to the root of them all, the "common sense" itself.'[17] In adopting the synecdochic role of emblem of all the senses, touch is forced to shed its specifically tactile, haptic character, the property that distinguishes it from the other senses in the first place, and become emptily metaphoric, displaced. Looked at from the opposite angle, Aquinas's assertion is that there is a common sense (*sensus communis, koine aísthesis)*, but while it may lie nearest to touch, it does not consist in touch itself. The relation is one of adjacency, contiguity, and in any case, as the *De Sensu* of Aristotle suggests, the *sensus communis* isn't to be read as synonymous with the overall functional unity of the senses, which latter remains the best explanation of how the senses are interactively aware of each other. Aquinas writes effectively against Augustine, who in the *Confessions* had made sight stand for all the senses, inasmuch as both concupiscence and the drive to knowledge are powered by what the eye sees or, by extension, what the other senses perceive by analogy with the workings of sight, but the multi-operativity of touch has nonetheless outrun this thesis in materialist thinking down to the present, so that Jean-Luc Nancy can declare *tout court* that 'Sense *is* touching. The "transcendental" of sense (or what is "ontological" in it) is touch: obscure, impure, untouchable touch.'[18]

The anthropological Kant's inheritance of the primacy of touch from the Aristotelian-Thomist tradition is subjected to the emergence of a monitory note. For all that touch is 'the most important and most reliably instructive' of the three senses in the first class of 'objective' senses, along with sight and hearing, it is also the 'coarsest' because it relies on its sense-object being solid enough to determine its shape.[19] In this, he is considerably behind Aristotle, for whom touch is about much more than the discernment of shape, but what throws doubt on this model at the outset is that touch is placed among the senses that are more objective than subjective, those which 'as empirical *intuitions* ... contribute more to the *cognition* of the external object than they stir up the consciousness of the affected organ', whereas the predominantly subjective senses of smell and taste are more productive of '*enjoyment*' or its opposite than of cognition.[20] Derrida's reading of the moral archaeology of touch strips the mask of preponderant objectivity from Kant's postulate, suggesting that precisely because touch is the organically indispensable sense, without which the organism cannot survive, it is important that there always simultaneously be a minimal functionality to touch but also, in that haptic excess in the form of pain, heat, cold and so on are potentially lethal to the body, a moderately proportioned and legalistic delimitation of it.

> *Couldn't one say that this measure, this moderation of touch, remains at the service of life to the sole extent, precisely, that some kind of reserve holds it on the brink of exaggeration? A certain tact, a 'thou shalt not touch too much,' 'thou shalt not let yourself be touched too much,' or even 'thou shalt not touch yourself too much,' would thus be inscribed a priori, like a first commandment, the law of originary prohibition, in the destiny of tactile experience ... In the beginning, there is abstinence. And without delay, unforgivingly, touching commits perjury.*[21]

The entire discourse of moderation, as it applies to the gustatory, intoxicological and carnal histories of humanity, may well have its roots in the circumscribing of the vital and pre-eminent sense of touch, and the need both to protect it and contain it. As such, long before ritual cults, schematic religion or contemporary neurosis had made of touch a ferociously policed area of human experience, the organism's own sense of its fragility had ordained it. If aesthetic enjoyment properly belongs to the senses, the relative absence of touch in the multifarious experience of art might help explain Kant's objectification of this sense. When the various arts in their differentiation from each other indicate the boundary-line between art and reality, by each claiming for itself a demarcating threshold at which it adjoins one or another of the other arts, even Nancy holds that 'there is properly speaking no art of touching (not even a "minor" art such as those for taste and smell), for touching is sense qua threshold.'[22] In fact, sculpture was conceived in the classical world as the tactile art, the human form in particular, refigured in stone or marble, inviting the exploratory touch of the viewer, just as it had emerged from the shaping hands of the sculptor and his chisel. The sensuous touch might just as easily be a superstitious contact, according to which one touched the foot of the statuesque hero to bring oneself luck in battle or in the debating chamber. By the time of Winckelmann,

Enlightenment art appreciation was entirely about allowing the visual sense, by its very objectifying distance, to produce the correct inner response, and touching was the bestial preserve of monkeys and the lower orders. What were the Willendorf Venuses of prehistory intended for if not weighing in the hand? Under Pygmalion's handling, the inflammatory anatomical precision of the body of Galatea metamorphoses from lifeless ivory to the warmth of actual flesh, the myth comporting that double transfer across the threshold between art and reality that is art's own version of the superstition it supplanted. 'Art appears,' notes Nancy, 'as soon as sense makes itself atheistic,'[23] as the sensate body's refusal to attribute everything outside itself to manifest theophany tempts it to contrive to add to what there is, daubing its own likenesses of experience on to the cave-walls, but it thereby initiates the reverse transfer under which art itself turns back into the reality of which it thought it was only emulative. If contemplative vision, the reverent gaze in the museum prescribed in conduct books, could revivify the congealed form of reality out of the figurative artwork, how much more must the haptic feel of solid forms have referred the toucher back to lived experience? Touching the foot of Achilles is a fetishistic practice that defetishises itself through the immediacy of its contact with the votive object, whereas staring rapt at his full magnificent form is the attitude proper to that worship that the medieval church, anticipating Enlightenment art's *noli me tangere,* eventually prescribed as the correct relation to the effigies. Long before the question of conservation arose in a culture where museum exhibits were intended to be stroked, the smaller items to be picked up and hefted in the grasp, the issue of touch had become a matter of febrile debate. While Herder held touch essential to aesthetic appreciation, Schiller, speaking for ocular posterity, condemned it as the mauling of savages. At best, it seemed a throwback to the murkiest habits of irrational veneration, even where freed from any expectation of the miraculous, as when Pepys celebrated his thirty-sixth birthday with a tour of Westminster Abbey, during which, in the presence of his wife, he was privileged to be allowed to fondle the intact corpse of Catherine of Valois, Henry V's queen, in its casket – 'I had the upper part of her body in my hands, and I did kiss her mouth.'[24] There was enough left of her to embrace, according to the Abbey historian John Dart, writing over half a century later, 'the bones being firmly united, and thinly clothed with flesh, like scrapings of tanned leather, a view fit to represent to us the end of beauty, greatness, and what else sublunary things we boast.'[25] By that era, during the onset of the Enlightenment, the handling of museum artefacts was more likely to produce the opposite effect to Pepys's tremulous reverence, the carelessness that led Handel inadvertently to soil a rare manuscript at Sir Hans Sloane's museum in 1740, to his host's fury, by putting down a buttered muffin on it.

Physicality of Happiness

Whether all happiness begins on the skin, whether it is possible to imagine, as the medieval ascetics did, that there could be a self-renewing joy sourced in the spirit alone, is of less immediate significance to human history than the notion that its obverse, spiritual discontent, finds its origin and its structure in material travail. Crudely caricatured, the materialist case resembles a reductive biologism, in which humanity is just helplessly in thrall to the Medusa-like glare that Schopenhauer saw in the universal predation of nature, but the dignity of such thinking, which is what impels knowledge, the drive to ameliorate the human condition by arriving at a practical understanding of how things might be cured, lies precisely in the fact that it doesn't permit the mind to disregard its link to the body. In extremis, thought Jung, this is exactly what the mind does. As long as the brain is still supplied with oxygen and blood, it allows itself to transcend the calamity to which the body has fallen victim, but long before the extremity that forced the mind to evict somatic consciousness from its precincts, it knew the somatic for what it was, the principal motive force for the accrual and animation of its own knowledge. A more perfect state of tranquillity would depend indispensably on the material amelioration that world governments could deliver if they wanted to. No society deserves being called a society if it isn't acutely aware of needless suffering, but awareness of it at the individual level is what absolves the mind from its embarkation on transcendence, launched in the Platonic academy, refloated in the rationalism of Descartes. It isn't simply a matter of ethical credentials, but of the epistemological underpinning of an enlightenment conceived literally, in which what would illuminate the intellect is what mitigates the intimation of utter senselessness when the empirical world is engulfed in catastrophe. A piece of cynical bourgeois British wisdom used to insist that if a youngster wasn't attracted to socialism, it was because he had no heart, whereas if he was still attracted to it in his maturity, he had no head. The case the epigram tried to make, before British politics did away with socialism, was less about the conditions of economic production than it was about the idea that rationality ought properly to induce itself, in the full bloom of its normal development, to put materiality away as one of the childish things. The deformation of consciousness that would be required to overlook it, and which would leave men and women unreconciled to their own natures amid the very empirical injustice over which they were being encouraged not to trouble themselves, far from drying up the wellspring of discontent, would only aggravate the spirit further. Social hope resides in the breaking upon them of those moments of reasoned incomprehension such as Montaigne reported among the Brazilian tribespeople who visited royalist Rouen in the sixteenth century. After being treated to displays of court ceremonial, an audience with the king and a tour of the city, they were asked what had most amazed them, and replied among other things that they couldn't help noticing that, whereas some of the people lived comfortably in conditions of surfeit, others, worn to emaciation with poverty, were begging at their doors. '[T]hey found it odd that those destitute ... should put up with such injustice and did not take the others by the throat or set fire to their houses.'[26] If unhappiness arises in the material world, only the material world can make restitution for it.

The contention that a happiness rooted in sensual fulfilment should ordinarily recede as one progresses from youth to adulthood leaves open the question of what its fate ought to be in old age. In one of the two traditional narratives, early life is spent bursting with youthful idealism, which is then subject to the bitter disillusionments of middle age, when fighting to secure one's position allows nothing of the luxury of principled commitment, against which it turns in chastisements of the rising generation's *naïveté*. Old age then delivers a quiescent calm, in the form of a conviction that after all none of it mattered – neither the cynical reordering of priorities, nor the impassioned hopefulness against which the reordering was aimed, although the elderly often betray a vestigial indulgence towards the young over their immediate elders. The entropic structure of that story is somehow belied by the widespread apathy that has overwhelmed the young today, and which invests even their sporadic episodes of social unrest with the clueless emptiness seen in the short-lived Occupy movement, or the prospect of rioting for the sake only of looting electronics stores, whereas the end of life is marked more and more by a concern that the best elements of social development have been thrown to the winds, while the worst are allowed to persist ineradicably. In the alternative traditional account, youth is the period of exploratory sensual self-indulgence, middle age of hard-headed rationalism, and old age a resigned surrender to the disengagements of mortality. The latter version crumbles before the evidence that the espousal of abstract principles is so often the preserve of youthful apathy, because apathy can't muster the wherewithal to look into concrete matters in any detail, while in later life the sensual solace of tender embraces and decent wine matter more than the abstractly unattainable, precisely for there being relatively less of life left in which to enjoy them.

The antagonistic relation of contentment and dissatisfaction is imprinted on intellection in another way. If it is true that critical thinking is set in motion by the awareness of material inadequacy, it must *a fortiori* be the case that in the realm of bliss, no thinking would be needed. Indeed, that would be the definition of happiness, a mindless sterility, which may be why in traditional cosmologies, the life of the heavenly host appears to rise to nothing more uplifting than interminable worship, the notion that Huxley translated into the secular in *Brave New World*. Some of this is uncomfortably registered in the apparent mindlessness of much gratification, the reiterative quality of which too often mimics just that cyclical structure that modern working routine appropriated, albeit in grossly accelerated form, from the cyclical seasonality of rural life. Every act of sex, thought Balzac, was another unwritten novel, a rueful pang that did nothing at all to reduce his boundless rapacity. The state of nirvana awaits to evaporate the Buddhist's individual consciousness to a droplet in the great ocean of undifferentiated Being, the nearest institutional religion has come to the final relief of non-existence. Sensuality, freed from reflection either on the world or on itself, dissolves to a contentless reactivity, the very torpor from which consciousness impatiently emerged on the African grasslands.

Proximity

In the Middle Ages, life was lived in a state of rackety proximity. Eating went on at long communal tables in the refectories and great halls, everybody helping himself or herself from shared bowls, mugs of ale and cider passed from hand to hand for gulping at by turns. On the rare occasions people bathed, they bathed together, and they slept together, whole families bundled intimately close for warmth. The constant contiguity of other people's bodies made for hardly anything resembling a private life, but did establish the bonds of social and interpersonal trust. Only the feudal lords and ladies ate separately, seated at their own raised table in ceremonial isolation, but in full view of the mass. At court occasions, the king would eat magnificently at his own table, unencumbered even by queen and family, his status reinforced by the emblem of a sanctified distance from his subjects. From about the fourteenth century, the dining of the elite began to be removed altogether to private quarters where they were insulated against the surveillance of the people in the hall: 'There the lorde ne the lady liketh nought to sitte. / Now hath uche riche a reule to eten bi hymselve / In a prive parloure for pore mennes sake,' observes Langland's *Piers Plowman* ('The lord and lady do not like to sit there. Each of the rich now observes the rule of eating by himself in a private parlour, to avoid the poor.')[27] Constance Classen notes the social divisiveness of the gradual spread of literacy in the medieval era, in that it created a mandarin class in whom expertise and therefore authority over the illiterate conjointly resided, but the development of separate eating heralded epistemological stratification by enacting the distinctiveness of social classes physically. *Ressentiment* begins with the spatial awareness of segregation. In the early years of the Soviet Union, communal workers' dining-halls were prescribed, as much for the democratic sharing of the periodic shortages as for whatever solidary effect might result from mass commensality. Contemporary restaurant designers have here and there brought back refectory-style bench eating in imitation of monastic communities, or to conjure atavistic memories of school dining, even though everybody still eats only what they have ordered, and nobody feels like getting to know the people sitting around them.

A deeper exclusivity to the sense of touch was conferred by

the move away from naked sleeping in common. Where people had no other choice, as on long journeys, they began to adopt nightwear. Not just the transmission of widespread skin diseases such as scabies was thereby mitigated, but the risk of sexual arousal among the unmarried. The compromise strategy was bundling, in which courting couples, youngsters especially, were allowed to spend the night together as long as each of them was done up in a sack tied at the neck, perhaps also separated by a wooden bundling-board. Hotels and taverns routinely made provision for pre-marital bundling, often charging more for a bed that was going to be shared in this way. Originating in Anglo-Saxon Europe, the practice migrated to colonial north America, where it persisted until late in the nineteenth century, sanctioned as an enlightened way of allowing young couples to anticipate their nuptial intimacy without falling into sin. Its unavowed function, which must have become tormentingly obvious to most of its participants, was precisely to kindle physical desire to an extremity by simultaneously provoking and prohibiting it. Instead of being simply forbidden, it was being physically acknowledged and forbidden. Hardly any more excruciated an image of the ambivalence of erotic touch could be imagined.

Disengagement from proximity is the marker of upward social mobility at all times. To be another step further away from life lived in common with others is another step up the ladder, as the English colloquial usage of 'common', to denote the manners of the unelevated, declares. The habitus of a successful life would describe a progression from the room in a shared house of student days to an apartment in a multi-occupancy building, and from there to a small terraced or semi-detached house, and then to one that had no adjoining neighbours. For those with the appetite, that might be followed by a flight from urban living to the isolation of the rural, by emigration to a country where there are more open spaces, or something like the final misanthropic escape of Orwell to an island equipped with barely more than what Robinson Crusoe had, where the discovery of Friday's footprint would cast a deepening shadow over the day. To the notion that socialisation is powered by sensory contiguity, Simmel retorted that it depends rather on the confidence that people can know each other more intimately and profoundly by intuition than through the intermittent evidence of what they look like, what they say, and how they feel. Social consciousness is a matter of joining up those dots through 'psychological hypotheses' until they form a coherent unity. If one had to construct the identity of another only from external signs as they presented themselves, it would take many lifetimes before anybody felt they knew anybody; 'we must supplement the existing fragments with conclusions, interpretations, and interpolations until a person emerges.'[28] By the same token, a readiness and ability in late-medieval and early-modern times to accede to the institutional authority of what was not immediately apparent, but might lie hundreds of miles off, such as the royal court or the Vatican, promoted the capacity for abstract thinking, 'the ability to feel beyond the sensorialy immediate.'[29] Relations at a distance are characterised by the higher degree of intellectual development facilitated by the coolness and aloofness of separation, whereas relations with immediate neighbours and families are subject to the extremes of emotion. Writing in 1903, Simmel acknowledges that what capsized this construction is the growth of the modern metropolis, in which higher cultural development produces a more sophisticated objectivity, undergirded anyway by the dulling of sensual and emotional response brought on by constant contact with others in the city crowd. If life was being lived considerably less in common by the outbreak of the industrial revolution than it had been in the Middle Ages, the skill that the urban workforce had to learn on abandoning the farmsteads and villages was translating the marginal level of social autonomy it had gained to an environment in which people were bustling all around them in greater profusion than they ever had in the halls of feudalism, but with whom all sympathetic engagement was unavailable other than, eventually, by political praxis. If it was the fate of state communism ultimately to fail, it may have been less because the twentieth century deformed its governments into violent repressive bureaucracies, than because the interlocking structures of solidarity it originally sought to discover among the metropolitan proletariat were ideational propositions heteronomously introduced to urban consciousness by the remote intellection of theory. And yet without theory, it wouldn't have arrived even at the halfway house in which it became immured.

The Healing Touch

All touch aspires to the condition of a laying-on of hands, the hope that contact itself may retain the magical properties so nearly transmitted to the first man by Michelangelo's God, himself enwrapped in the voluptuous embrace of an orgy of angels and cherubim. The touch of those invested with institutional or cultural authority continues to confer benediction on the touched – the priest's hand of blessing, the celebrity's momentary brushing of one's own proffered hand at the crush-barrier. A king's touch reputedly cured scrofulous wretches of their pestilence down to its last ever enactment by Charles X in Reims in 1825. The monarchy's restoration, an act of desperate political optimism following the iconoclasm of the revolutionary years, was sealed by the king's anointment with a few recovered shards of the *ampoule* that had once contained the holy chrism, and which had been ceremonially smashed in Year II on the empty plinth where Louis XV's toppled statue had stood. 'The King touches you,' Charles told each of the 120 sufferers on whose foreheads he traced the cross. Voices in the public prints on both sides of the Channel roared their derision. 'There was a time,' scoffed the anonymous writer in the *Royal Lady*, 'and that not very far distant, when it would have been deemed blasphemy to doubt this miracle; but how are the times changed! Any one would now be accounted an idiot that should believe it!'[30] After monarchs abandoned the royal touch, it passed into the hands of freelance faith-healers and charismatic preachers, whose faith in the miraculous power of the Holy Spirit to induce a heavenly blackout was sufficiently feeble that it couldn't dispense with strategically applied pressure on the carotid arteries of their clients. The relief that the suffering claim to feel from the touch of a healer may well be derived from the stronger impulses of a healthy body's electromagnetic field against the depleted resources of his own. Bioelectric theory still feels intricately entangled with energetic mysticism, the improvised pseudo-science of Rudolf Steiner's anthroposophy, the therapeutic dynamism of crystals, the part-digested emanations of *qi* adopted by contemporary orientalism. And yet the consoling hand of the other, signifier of empathic care since it was first laid uncomprehendingly on the source of one's own tormenting pain, as though by manually detecting it she might be able to rip it out, may well bear a greater curative potency than electromagnetism.

Pure touching, where it isn't the medium of some ulterior function, is more freighted with significance than its instrumental counterpart in handshakes, medical examination, massage, and so on. Such tactility leaves an emotional trace on the body, by virtue of its freedom from the empirical constraint of social symbolism. The clinical or sacerdotal touch intends the bestowal of institutional supervision, the conforming of the recipient into an encompassing framework of authority that dispenses professionalised benediction and care as a matter of procedure. Authority's touch is both the reassurance and the warning that the individual is not free, either from the exigencies of his own physical and spiritual health, or from the operations of the institutional machinery in which he is enmeshed. Just because he is the object of continual pastoral scrutiny, 'from the cradle to the grave,' as was said in the first era of socialised healthcare in post-war Britain, he will neither be abandoned, nor left to his own devices, in a medical culture increasingly bent on administrating his physical being through micrological interest in his consumption habits. If the professional touch is always the touch of authority, it is very often also for that reason the hand of restraint: the policeman's grip on the wrists, the doorman's forbidding hand on the chest, the slaps of parents and teachers up to the time of their prohibition. The touch that is offered for its own sake alone, where it has been freely accepted, reminds both parties that humans pre-existed the social mechanism, and that physical contact between them did not always refer their existence to something stronger than them. What is stronger would like them to forget the touch of institutional hegemony to the same degree that they have forgotten what sympathetic contact between each other might mean, and has largely succeeded not by persuading them that its touch is benign, but by anaesthetising them against what remains of natural sensitivity. The evidence of desensitised numbness is apparent in people's readiness to be stricken with sympathetic grief at carefully prescribed prompts. Romantic cinema's popular boast, that its melodramatic plots would ensure that there wasn't a dry eye in the house, and which it inherited from the emotion-wringing vicissitudes of the nineteenth century novel, already stamped emotions with the character of something to be extraneously provoked, rendering those that did spontaneously occur, at the death of loved ones and the fracture of relationships, an imprecise imitation of the perfectly scored and formulaically acted emotional triggers of mass entertainment. Today, the mere sight of somebody else crying, on which the cameras of reality-shows always swoop in for the close-up, is held to be enough in itself to coerce emotional response without the bother of narrative contrivance, and people who found themselves unable to allow their emotions free rein at the family funeral readily weep torrents in unison with the lachrymose boy who has been voted off the singing contest. And yet, even if tears can be prompted over what is strictly nothing to them, the enactment of sorrow is the disguised emblem of all the real sorrow it successfully displaces. When emotional response is thieved from them by commercial agencies, disinterested touch, which such agencies can't as yet control, is all that remains to convince them that a liberated life might still be possible. At the opposite end of the spectrum, nothing verbal, and not even freely flowing tears, communicates to the departing beloved the desolation he is leaving behind than the final embrace, which irradiates inner being from the outside in, and tells the abandoned one that the only hope now lies in freezing over.

Sexuality and its Discontents

The refusal of physical contact in everyday social intercourse has been accompanied by a concomitant rise in sexual abstention among certain sectors of society. This tendency has many varying motivations, from principled celibacy for archaic mythical reasons to the dread fear of sexual infection amid the development of more virulent, less treatable forms of the traditional venereal diseases, and in some quarters from a simple distaste that gives the lie to the hypostatised view of sex as the greatest of all experiences, the one that miraculously unites the contingency of physical sensibility with spiritual transcendence. What unites these heterogeneous tendencies is the subject's alienation from his own body, an alienation that it inherited as an integral constituent of his species-being with humanity's domination of nature. In many cases, the loss of sexual desire that is attributed to what medical science calls the 'ageing process', a terminology that already casts organic subjectivity in the mould of factory production, is itself another symptom of the body's irreconcilability to itself as something undesirable. Ageing is the external evidence that one is no longer fit to engage in sexual activity, whatever one feels inside, and where the 'whatever' is determined to triumph over the body's atrophy, it hopes to restore its fitness through skin-lotions and cosmetic surgical work, in the way that an older person undergoing a job interview hopes to convince the potential employer that his youthful vigour and openness to new challenges will speak more strongly than the accumulation of experience on his CV. Where the refusal of sex is not so overtly connected to the life-cycle, it is characterised as dysfunctional by a psychotherapy industry to which the concept of the sex-drive is an unexamined Mene Tekel: those who appear to do without it have been weighed in the scales and found wanting. In Freudian theory, desire is the manifestation in sublimated form of the basic drives, its roots in animal instinct concealed by socialisation. What the abstinent appear to have achieved is the sublation of the sexual drive into pure desire, in their case the pure desire not to. Buried even further below the positive drives are their negative counterparts – the imperatives to avoid what would harm the individual, physical danger and infection, compounded into the instinct for mere self-preservation – and sexual abstinence looks uncannily like the triumph of a determinate negation over that instinct, the reversal of the negative drive back on to itself as the refusal of procreative activity. Early psychoanalysis for this reason rescued homosexuality from moral opprobrium by convicting it of fundamental immaturity instead, as though it was a form of mimetic sex for people who didn't feel ready for the real thing, but mimetic sex was still sex, and whatever cognitive gap there is between different styles of sexual practice is as nothing to that which has now opened wide between those who want sex and those who don't.

The traditional critique of the saturation of representational images in which media culture has immersed society holds that their superfluity has produced desensitisation. On that theory, non-participation in sex might arise from the very ubiquity of its representation, just as nothing is more surely likely to kill off the sex in an individual relationship than one of the partners constantly demanding it, and yet the same desensitisation has happened to many others who, notwithstanding its intrusiveness, have found their urges undiminished. Those who have not managed to separate the sexual content of commodity culture from their own desire may in that sense really be the maladaptive ones, because they have allowed desire to be purloined from them by those very media – mass culture and advertising – that have most assiduously worked at provoking it in them. Sensory response is malleable at the surface level by moving images, and even by text. The discussion of a piece of music in writing provokes the strong inclination to hear it, and the same is true of ekphrastic representations of the visual arts. Gastronomic writing can stimulate the appetite for a particular dish, and erotic passages in literature, painting and film have a directly mechanistic effect on sexual response, in both its male and female forms. The murmurous impulse that deterred traditional aesthetics in its dignity from ever quite owning up to its intentionality in this regard is what Tolstoy, whose puritanical fury found even conjugal sex repellent, tried shouting from the rooftops: 'All art real and counterfeit, with very few exceptions, is devoted to describing, depicting, and inflaming, sexual love in every shape and form.'[31] Where social mores forced art to fall silent about sex, as in the decorum with which the nineteenth century English novel papered over the graphic lubricity of its Georgian predecessor, its sexual content bulges tumescently at the seams, much as is the case with sexual repression in individual psychology. The less it is allowed to show itself, the more its imperatives migrate to the imaginative and metaphoric levels, where it becomes apparent in virtually anything. It is the misfortune of the sexually abstinent that their aloofness is often precisely what engages the sexual attention of others. Where desire is present, nothing is sexier than a vow of celibacy, particularly among young men, whose sexuality has been culturally constructed as uncontainable, and the austerity of the discipline that he has imposed on himself hints at how authoritative he might be *in flagrante* if he allowed his impulses free expression. 'No rule is more repressive that one that is self-promulgated,'[32] says Adorno, nor more surely productive of the willed resistance to repression. Wedekind's Moritz in *Spring Awakening* (1891), of all the boys the one with the most finely developed intuition of the transgressiveness of bodily desire, is all the more prey to it than even the undiscriminating Hans, masturbating over an image of the Venus of Palma Vecchio one minute, kissing and talking love to his best friend Ernst the next. People who have lost interest in sex may have done so originally with the unacknowledged intention of strengthening its flame in the very act of blowing it out, only to find that it is all too extinguishable.

Sex and Sociality

Sexual activity would like to reassure itself that it is one of those aspects of human experience into which social reality cannot penetrate, the more so since that reality came imperiously to require access to all areas. Like intoxication, it seems to delineate a sacred precinct in which individuals are free from responsibility and labour. Secret love trysts, sexual attraction that defies institutional norms and laws, those of warring families, cenobitic rules, the expectations of fit conduct at court or in the bourgeois family, are the means by which narrative art has strengthened the claim of the erotic by according it the status of outsider. Love achieves its best results when it has something to defend itself against, the world most of all. The properly sanctioned course laid out for it – the choosing of an appropriate partner who is qualified by material means and prospects, a rationally structured courtship supported by the approval of both families, and then a publicly witnessed wedding – represents the institutional wisdom of society over the erratic nature of sexual attraction, which nonetheless knows the untruth of the procedure because it is itself the product of that untruth. In their most intimate moments, however, lovers come to believe that sex is where the pressure of social expectation can't get at them, but precisely here, where its warrant appears invalid, are they most subject to it. There may well be more freedom in getting drunk, even in the prescribed social contexts, than there can ever be in private behaviour whose every element has been negotiated in advance by what is socially acceptable. In a culture that has dishonestly appropriated what were formerly the honest enough techniques of pornography, sexual conduct has become a matter of universal public concern, with the result that it becomes difficult for its participants not to feel they are being in some way observed, as though the hidden cameras of reality TV, which miss nothing, might have been surreptitiously stationed in their own bedroom. The politics of sexual consent, with their finely detailed requirements of mutual agreement and permission, are silently acceded to between the partners, applying with particular sensitivity in the gender relations between men and women, and taking on the character of imperatives most of all where they are cautiously, symbolically breached in the interest of excitement. Sexual response in its evolution by gender has sedimented into amorous relations between men and women in ways that are at all times reflective of their relative social standings, so that the prudence of a woman's instinct to ensure healthy reproductive succession has been made to determine her responsibilities to run a successful domestic economy, and embody transparent sexual fidelity, while the male drive to cast his seed as widely as possible, to improve his chance of propagating the species, supports the construction of his social role as one of enterprisingly taking on the world in a condition of relative autonomy.

The ideological currents are in operation down to the level of physiology. The climactic structure of male sexual practice imitates that of individual fate; women's refers back to the cyclical model of pre-industrial time, and the openness to life that fate closed off. Meanwhile, sexual receptivity itself is held to be asocial, but where society works so sedulously to provoke it for its own ends, which may be psychic hygiene as much as simply selling things, it ends up as anything but. Sexuality is no more the escape into nature that the ardent couple yearns to find in it than are the images of summer meadows that connote the freshness of fabric conditioner, just because nature itself has been thoroughly socialised. The ideological character of a practice that should by rights be capable of laughing at all ideology derives from the assertion that sexuality occupies a privileged realm, the fragrant garden that Sufism for example, in its conception of the afterlife, filled with obliging houris. There is no ontological autarchy about sexuality that would fence it off from social antagonism as a sublime being-in-itself, for all that its pursuit of ecstasy cannot imagine any other setting for it. In any case, if one of its prime animating impulses is the forbidden, then it must refer to a social milieu in which such interdictions arise. The element of the forbidden has lost its potency in a culture that has become proficient at imitating the forbidden element, what makes it sexy, in order the better to incorporate it. It is a moot point whether the alleged sexual liberation promoted by the permissive society of the 1960s and after genuinely liberated sexuality from the mesh of taboos in which it had always been ensnarled, or whether it simply drove them to a deeper level of repression. 'In an unfree society,' Adorno pointed out, before permissiveness was quite in full swing, 'sexual freedom is hardly more conceivable than any other form of freedom.'[33] By the time permissiveness broke out, sexuality's constituted naturalness had become an index of its healthiness. If adolescents must engage with each other sexually, let them do so in a psychologically and physically hygienic fashion, free of the taint of guilt and without recourse to the harmful influences of pornography and prostitution. The newly liberated attitude promulgated in advice manuals such as *Boys and Sex* (1968) and *Girls and Sex* (1970) by Wardell Pomeroy, co-author of the Kinsey reports, taught a generation of youngsters that their desires were normal, but worth constraining within the bounds of sensible practice, and by dint of their segregation into separate volumes, like the boys' and girls' dorms in the hostel or holiday camp, accidentally reinforced much of the traditional gender mythology, such as that boys had no interest in foreplay, or that girls were not likely to be aroused by the sight of a boy's muscles or the bulge in his pants, the corpus of belief that young people's own experiences were telling them was false. The effect of the hygiene approach was to desexualise sexuality, by wilfully adopting and identifying with the constraints surrounding it instead of chafing at them: 'the hygienic ideal is more rigorous than the ascetic ideal, which never wanted to remain what it was.'[34] It also helped smudge the dividing line between desire and its fulfilment by conflating sexuality with sex itself, which thereby took on the aspect of a recreational activity, a tendency that the availability of oral contraception had already initiated. The natural environment into which sex then led its participants was less the wild wood where things have no names than the legally protected national park, somewhere they might have a picnic on a day out, as long as they were careful to clear up after themselves.

Sexuality yearns to break free of the ordered precincts of the healthy life, inasmuch as a prudential attitude to one's own welfare cautions against the exchange of bodily fluids in any other context. It demands the right to its own context, for all that its territory has always been vulnerable to invasion by the venereal infections, which often stood for the mark of a man's having earned his stripes, where they didn't turn lethal. The infections were interpreted by morality, and then by medical propaganda, as nature's revenge on humanity for surrendering too much to a state of nature it was otherwise bent on conquering. In contemporary society, sex bears the responsibility not just to be safe and clean, but also to deliver the sensual component of people's lives that technology has efficiently stripped out of them. Nothing in individual experience is equal to the immense power of technology, which stands in a mutually determining relation with the total system whose tool it is, and the combined force of which overwhelms the individual's capacity to grasp it, thereby reminding the body of its own nugatory status, even as it flicks the switch or pushes the button that activates it. No more than any other aspect of individual sensibility is sexual experience able to withstand its ensnarement in reified technological consciousness. Exactly this is what deprives it of its claim to autonomous experience as such, even that special category of 'experience' that sex always stood for to the newcomer. Sensuality is of necessity always a response to something, and while each one hopes that what he is responding to, purely and simply, is the exciting presence and attention of the other, the truth is that the other is no more liberated from the entanglements of a faulty reality than he is. Another body, which in the variance of its responses should negate the sterility of one's own self-pleasure, acquires its covetable status not just for its alterity, but because one falsely invests it with freedom from the constraints to which he himself is subject. For fear of expecting too little of sex, he falls into the grip of expecting too much, like the deranged General desperately seeking political asylum among William Gerhardie's polyglots: 'To this idea he clung with that ready hope of the faint-hearted who, because he dreads the possibility of despair – his sole alternative, clutches at each straw with the assurance of salvation.'[35] Every lover is seized upon as a bulwark against the solitude that all superstitiously fear, without realising that the new relationship that joyously seems to put a period to bitter loneliness too often does no more than provide it with a home. The culturally sanctioned refrain of lonely people, that they have so much love to give if only they can find the right person, gives the game away by admitting that love, far from beginning and developing when the right person happens along, pre-exists every relationship as a source of potential energy, and therefore cheats the subsequent liaison of its own specificity, even while claiming to be acknowledging it in the very idea of the 'right person'. In the love-affair conceived as a respite from life's exigencies, which were responsible for his loneliness in the first place, the exigencies are still solemnly granted their power. Adorno says the same of the withering of expression in Webern's music: 'The subject has become so lonely that it can no longer seriously hope of finding another who would understand it.'[36] Its error would be to continue to look for whoever might be the right person, whose impossible credentials grow more overdetermined with every failed attempt.

Sexuality and Power

The reluctance displayed by females of many species to tolerate the attentions of the male at mating time sedimented in human relations in the form of power. Nothing about sexuality is more subversive of the harmony of which copulation ought to be the supreme metaphor than power relations, which figured as the practical expression of the respective physiques of male and female, and became the underpinning of their economic positions in society and the gendered division of labour. The levelling of such relations during eras of sexual frankness, such as the later Roman empire or eighteenth century libertinism, is always followed by a retrenchment to the asymmetrical relations that are held to be more natural. Victorianism's cult of the sacrosanct feminine, which conferred on women the role of self-sacrificing propagators only, leaving the hedonic element of sex to the husband, had the not incidental effect of increasing his own sense of satisfaction that he was in some way forcing himself on her. A wife's enjoyment of sex would reduce her to the bestial, by reawakening in her the ancient mythology that women's sexuality, once unleashed, was a ferociously devouring primal force, the source of men's entanglement in sin by carnal distraction. Male sexuality was thus constructed in a productive ambivalence between innocent temptability on the one hand and limitless rapacity on the other. A notional female sexual incontinence was the alibi for that of the male. The modern era, in the nobility of its attempt to put paid to the idea that there was such a thing as too much sex, where both parties were willing, was nonetheless impotent to preclude the operations of power even in the most socially advanced circles. Men's sexual frailty is their addiction to the exercise of physical authority, which at best they must hope women have been trained to admire, and where they haven't, produces episodes of sublimated violation. That cruelty should be sexually thrilling – the atrocities of Gilles de Rais, the gymnastics of domination and submission in Sade, the images that now hint at the after-effects of sexual violence in music videos and fashion-shoots – has chained humanity, men mostly, to its primordial imperative of self-preservation, the instinct that rewarded his injuring and killing his rivals and enemies with a sense of satisfaction in the accomplishment. Without the objective significance lent it by the feeling of having been victorious in competition, over possible rivals but also over the natural modesty or even disinclination of his girlfriend, a man's experience of sex all too easily resembles the masturbation that it so often is. Not for nothing is every successfully completed act chalked up as a 'conquest'. A series of popular novels celebrates the emergence of consensual rape, the oxymoron's most elevated achievement to date, into mainstream sexual desire, written by a woman for women as apparent collusion in their own subjection, the sentiment being that boys will be boys, and if you can't change them, you may as well try to humour them, on the off-chance that you might just get something out of it yourself. Rather than examine what such a development might imply for the reification of female desire, the tendency is referred only to the bland phenomenology of sex that drives all libertarian movements. It just *is*, neither more nor less, and whatever practices it solicits or legitimates are not to be examined for their psychological substrata for fear of appearing puritanical. In the novels, the man is naively presented as a powerful company executive, his sexual demands being the concrete extension of his abstract authority in a corporate enterprise. For the domineering partner to have been a penniless struggler would have been not just inauthentic at the level of shallow bourgeois social analysis, but would have obtruded a considerably more painful truth into the social motivations of sex, which is that sadism is the revenge of the powerless, the self-dramatisation of the victim who, having been kicked once too often, has now turned bully himself. If there is anything sexually stimulating in being ordered about and physically restrained in the bedroom, almost always a ludicrous pantomime that imports the dull hierarchies of the workplace into the very realm that was once the refuge from them, it lies perhaps in the pathos with which a man whose inadequacy has been drilled into him by life does his best to look authoritative. Such too is the bedrock of the widespread male urge to be on the receiving end of rough treatment from women. These practices, in their insistence on the enactment of power relations, have the effect of impelling sexuality ever further away from the mechanics of simple penetrative coupling, which comes to look as unappetisingly mechanical as the blind impulses of dogs. All forms of play-acting, including group spectatorship of sex, hope to invest mammalian sexual behaviour with the symbolic practices of specifically human institutions, so that the hierarchical principle that is brutally evident everywhere in nature, having been sublimated historically into a social structure that has robbed individuals of their capacity for true experience, might have its blinding glare extinguished at the very moment that it lights up the sexual scene. Power is not mollified by being pantomimically enacted in sex, only reinforced. The ambivalent slogan of institutional critique beginning with Foucault – 'Power is everywhere' – intended to reveal that all human practices were subject to structures of authority, a notion that probably hadn't escaped most people's notice, but has been absorbed by modern sexual consciousness not as curse but as opportunity.

Male homosexuality in particular has been saturated by the immanence of power relations. Centuries of excoriation, especially vicious over the three hundred years preceding the dawn of the libertarian era, have invested it with the character not of one of the variants of human sexual orientation, but as the exception to the rule, a trait on which certain strands of activism have positively insisted as the myth of gay exceptionalism. Having been made a perduring example of by ecclesiastical and judicial institutions over the ages, it has internalised its own transgressiveness to a fault, with the result that dramas of punishment and retribution are played out within its confines with neurotic obsessiveness, which practices it represents back to itself as a liberation from the delimiting conventionalism of the straights. Even the incipient discovery in the early 1990s of the genetic origins of sexual preference, rather than being the moment at which homosexual desire might finally raise a biological claim to constitutional equality, has been interpreted in some quarters as another attempt by science to constrain the sexual minorities, by making them helpless products of their genetic coding, as though they were, uniquely among humanity, impervious to such influence. If genetic impulses, which mutated into forms of socialisation and cultural conditioning in humanity's infancy, can be reconceived as nothing more than an option and simply eluded, and one's sexual identity constructed as a *creatio ex nihilo,* by the sovereign will, the implication is that one has in some sense overcome their original disposition, their primally heterosexual nature having been defeated by those who have chosen to take a divergent path. The benevolent immaturity that reviles the idea that genetic material holds its creatures prisoner fails to see that, however malleable human history has shown it to be, it is nonetheless an indispensable element of them, with the result that what sounds like an argument against the reifying shadow of scientistic determinism fizzles into tautology: 'Both aggressively heterosexual and campaigning gay neuroscientists have tried to locate regions in the brain that would "explain" gayness. But these behaviours don't require exceptional explanation so much as fitting into a picture that encompasses the full range of permutations of biological sex, psychological sexuality and sexual preference.'[37] The postulate that the biology and psychology of sex exist in a zone entirely autonomous from what goes on in regions of the brain is a phenomenological superstition, which the first half of the proposition helplessly admits to in the stupidity of its insistence that explanations are something nefarious, or that any genetic understanding of what it calls gay behaviour would have to be an 'exceptional explanation', as opposed to an explanation. A need to believe that his sexuality has been freely selected by himself from a 'full range', like a shopper choosing from different brands of the same product in the supermarket, is the expression of an individual's faith in the mendacity of consumer choice down to the instinctual level. Indeed, his insistence on his own autarchic authority would like to grant it the power of abolishing heteronomous instinct altogether, for all that it would gleefully commute the sentence every time it surrendered to its own desire. That this desire is, despite itself, still convinced by social deformation of the illicit nature of its predilection is evidenced by the universal longing of gay men for heterosexuals, who always look more replete with incendiary masculinity, precisely where they are least obviously trying to be. The cult of aggressive maleness that has led gay men to build muscular bodies, shave their heads like conscripts and dress up in soldiers' camouflage gear, is a compensation strategy against the effeminate caricature. It turns out that the outer integuments of masculinity, its gestures, vocal tones and even its conventional attitudes, are not hard to imitate, as a being-for-itself construction of sexual identity that is only missing the being-in-itself of wanting sex with girls. In a society that had finally risen above the demarcations of erotic preference, which accepted desire to be a continuum rather than a Venn diagram, in which perceptible variance only lay at the extreme ends, sexual orientation could forgo the need of being conceived in contradistinction to its perceived opposite, and while most people would still doubtless display an overwhelming preference for one or the other gender, every human being would nonetheless be divested of the strait-jacket of sexual 'identity' and its attendant ideologies.

Pleasure and Illusion

The amorous touch has not always conferred the warmth of tenderness. Its reduction to a function in contemporary sexuality was prepared by the calculations of the flirtatious in literary figures such as Balzac's Duchesse de Langeais, all voluptuary promise one minute, stern imperviousness the next. A technique for provoking ardour by denying it, the better that it might gush forth when finally allowed release, which gains some substantiation from the manipulable physical structure of climax in both sexes, turned against itself when it transpired that, as in much other deferred gratification, a reward too lengthily awaited was not worth having, its ripeness having turned to rot during the eager abstinence. The element of calculation was in any case toxic to what was imagined, ideologically or otherwise, as the purity of reciprocal desire. How many bundled would-be lovers in medieval times had become honestly tired of each other by the time they were unloosed in the nuptial bed? There is something tasteless in a display of appetite that isn't shared, and the fiery singularity of purpose that finally won the chivalric suitor his maiden would now be stalking. On the other hand, willing refusal, by turning the praxis of love into a negotiating position, dresses the whole transaction up as just that, a business transaction. Its wager on erotic transcendence in so doing employs the right physical means for the wrong reasons. The out-of-body experience that popular culture promises in sex, which its practitioners remember fondly as a vanished aspiration, where they don't openly smirk at it with an 'As if!', looks to the uninitiated like the last frontier of adulthood, if only they could overcome their fears enough to conjure the chance into being. That many young people still have their first sexual experiences in a state of idiotic drunkenness speaks less of the sleep of reason produced by alcohol than of an unreasoning terror they would die before admitting. Over-investment in what the advice pages call 'great sex' cheapens its value by turning it to mythology, because whatever sex one has just had is nothing compared to the hyperbolic experience one could have had with a little more effort. Every sexual episode shadows the ideal, which is only unattainable to those who lack the imagination, or are not sufficiently in love. The ancient male fantasy of having a different woman every night, which may help him in his head at least endure the same one, expressed not the luxury of eternal variety, but more the hope that he would find somebody capable of giving him the orgasm he deserves. His woman, meanwhile, hasn't failed to notice that his mind is elsewhere. 'He doesn't kiss me any more when he's doing it,' one such complained online, all too evidently aware that the sadness of expired desire lies as much in the idea that sex is something that he 'does' while you let him get on with it as it does in the lack of kissing. What keeps them going is the perennially enchanting mythology of the 'gift of heaven, tender love, sweet desire' that led Voltaire, in an unillusioned epigram of 1756 often misattributed to Wilde, to observe that 'Illusion is the first of all pleasures'. In an over-sexualised culture that has diluted sexuality to a function, the reverse is even truer.

Eros and Evolution

The quest for an ultimate experience to stand in for the radical impoverishment of experience in technological civilisation places its bet on sex, for its apparent ability to unite the stimulation of all five physical senses in one activity, but touch is the leading card, as Havelock Ellis stated in the early-twentieth century in his sexualised account of the 'natural order' of the medieval sense hierarchy. It scarcely required the taxonomic discovery of the erogenous zones to establish that touch is pre-eminent, because it seems to offer direct unmediated contact between individuals to a greater degree than the other faculties. 'Eros desires contact because it strives to make the ego and the loved object one, to abolish all spatial barriers between them,' taught Freud.[38] Touching, once psychoanalysis had begun to encourage its clients to talk openly about their sex lives, became the emblem of sexuality itself, so that all tactility came to be founded on the hypostasis of sensuality, and sensuality itself a striving towards the union of what is divided, a late reverberation of the Platonic postulate that desire is a permanent quest to find the lost half from which every living soul has been sundered. Not for nothing, according to Freud, is touching the principal taboo in obsessional neurosis. No sooner had he posited the transcendent unifying effect of touch in sex, however, than he began to suspect it of ideology: 'Sometimes one seems to perceive that it is not only the pressure of civilisation but something in the nature of the function itself [ie. of sexuality] which denies us full satisfaction and urges us along other paths.'[39] If the failure of sex to satisfy according to its own principle cannot be blamed entirely on the impairment of human relations in rationalised society, there must be some biological explanation underlying it, adumbrations of which are sketched in the accompanying footnote. These are the occlusion of the anal-olfactory element in sexuality brought about by the transition to an upright posture among early hominids, the surmise that Freud is most drawn to; the theory of universal bisexuality, by which the longing for both sexes feels itself short-changed by having to make do with one, which is hardly adequate to the full range of its potential sexual capacity; and what he calls 'a degree of direct aggression ... so often associated with erotic relations,'[40] the assertion of power through which desire is partly constituted, and permanently subverted, by an antagonism that is as much an element of it as are tenderness and delight. Later still, in the 1937 essay, 'Analysis Terminable and Interminable', the argument has turned towards a conflation of the latter two hypotheses, in which bisexuality introduces the death-drive into sexual response, in the form of free direct aggression, not because it can't find full satisfaction with either male or female, but because it turns against itself in hostility to its own dual nature, neither side being able to tolerate the other but finding itself chained to it regardless. Sexuality is constructed on the same model as that which, in antiquity, Empedocles suggested governed the entirety of human affairs, a never-ending oscillation between periods of love and periods of strife. Not only does this appear to prohibit the establishment of closure in the analytic context, it marks all sexuality too with the character of something unfinished, at odds with itself, in which the spiritual intimation of something sour or stale, inappropriate or dissatisfying, seeps through the tangible joy.

It would be easy, in the light of this, to construct a vulgarFreudian model of sexuality in which, while the body does its best to enjoy the act, the mind is telling it that there is something inadequate about it, something by which it falls short of being true to itself. The latter component of the mechanism is not to be conceived as the censorial superego, but as the intrusion of rationality into the very arena from which it had tried securely to bar itself. The deep alienation that overcomes those new to sex either during or after their engagement in it seems to suggest that, whatever they thought they wanted from it, this isn't it. If the fully elaborated theory is correct, that feeling doesn't disappear with age, it only become more deeply buried. There it lurks as the potential negativity of erotic relations, sometimes sublimated into the play-acting of hostility for sexual purposes, sometimes transferred entirely on to externalised fetish-objects, which project the absurdity of sex into concretely specific form, but most widely present as an obscurely sensed disinclination, which seems ready to short-circuit the electrical field of desire by the desire-not-to-desire. Where fetish-objects are not used, the genitalia themselves take over their role as the synecdoche of desire. A sex-manual of the 1970s that advised both parties to treat the penis as though it were a welcome third-party interloper in the proceedings may have imagined it was doing the male a clandestine favour, not least by inflating the potential of his equipment to the efficiency of a sex-toy, but served the function despite itself of expressing the alienation from their own organs for which participants in the game would do well to prepare themselves. In those indviduals who no longer want sex, even where the physical aptitude for it hasn't in the least atrophied, it may be that this latter negative desire has won through. Rather than the mind merely acting as the unimpressed spectator, however, it seems more likely that, in alienated sexuality, the body is failing to live up to the mind's expectations of it, the disjunction deriving from what rationality has trained the mind to hope for in sensual experience, namely its own unfettering. When sensual experience itself turns out to be saturated through and through with the deformations of rationalised reality, rationality, which had been ready to abdicate, has its rule indefinitely renewed. Sexual consciousness is like the over-eager parent on the touchline urging its child on the field to feats of heroism, in a game the child is neither very good at, nor possibly much interested in.

The moral discourse about sex in all epochs has been driven by the charge that the wrong sort of sex, or the wrong attitude to it, reduces it to a purely animal or even mechanistic function, where the ideal is a sublime state consecrated to the sacred business of procreation, supported by the galvanic impetus of love. This too has failed sex in ways it didn't suspect, precisely by subjecting it to an emotional catechism that convicts it daily of its failings, as surely as the Christian catechism does the miserable sinner. Love, which has its origins in primordial empathy, the instinct for mutual solidarity that helped the group survive against the depredations of others and mourn the loss of its own, might well aspire to be the generative agent of sex, the ecstasy of which ought by rights to reflect the glare of its own intensity, but its fathomless heterogeneity helplessly overwhelms sex. No matter what transcendent heights an individual sexual episode might reach, it only represents a fractional imitation of the historic emotional complexes of which love is comprised. Sex, just because of its inescapable physicality, has more the structure of a reflexive primary emotion such as anger or surprise, perhaps the visceral throb of pity, than the multivalent intricacy of love. Its procedure of putting love to one side for the moment, while it grasps at a brutally simple happiness, to whose fragility love struggles to reconcile it, induces it to confess that it knows love isn't entirely about happiness. Love may in many cases originate in nothing more than what Evelyn Waugh, in an exquisite phrase, called 'the bat squeaks of sexuality', which, intensified into the auditory range by prolonged lack of opportunity, accrete into an emotional state, but just as not all sex is powered by love, neither is all love impelled by the genital echo produced by the touch of another body. The over-determination of sex in relationships, by which people feel the obligation to make it more than it is, as opposed to a general physical expression of what they might as easily do in other circumstances, does it no favours, and only contributes to the nullification of what desire is telling them it wants to be.

Disjecta Membra

The end of the affair

Like happiness itself, love knows itself most surely in retrospect. In a world replete with fake emotion, in which the actual emotions of the individual count for a little less than nothing, the entirety of experience takes on the character of life lived in the immediate aftermath of a long relationship that has sickened and died. It is incumbent on the abandoned one to do his suffering in silence, in a gesture of ironic magnanimity, by which he refrains from adding to the guilt of the one who has left him behind, thereby implicitly absolving the other, and granting his own desolation the dignity of a decent burial. At the very moment when his suit cries out to be heard, he stifles its urgency in decorum, and is thus complicit in that lethal parody of love's mutual respect in which love itself can only have expired. The talk of the therapy industry in such circumstances is of 'dealing with the pain' and then 'moving on', as though there were a precise formula, borrowed from the world of physiological medicine, by which the wound could be treated, rendered aseptic, and allowed sufficient time to heal. The treatment need not be hurried, to be sure, but who doesn't want to be up and out of the hospital bed at the earliest opportunity? At the death of love, the organism obeys no such schedule. It refuses it precisely because what has been damaged always considered itself outside earthly time, was not subject to the biological rhythms to which the organism was otherwise susceptible. In any case, moving on (towards what?) is the last thing he wants to do, not only because he doesn't want to erase the present memory of the beloved, but because he doesn't want to relinquish the desire itself. The land of Moving On is a featureless terrain of insipidly beckoning normality, the very country from which the defunct affair had originally promised respite. To return there is like returning from summer holidays, with only another dreary year at school in prospect.

A refusal to get over the loss of a lover feels to the loser like nothing less than the tribute the affair deserves. Since the other has cast it aside with sincere regret, sincerely mingled with relief, the duty of obsequy falls to the survivor, in whom the love itself has, pointlessly now, survived. The work of mourning must be private though, for fear that any show of vulnerability will cause embarrassment, and so that he doesn't presume too much on the readily forthcoming sympathies of friends. 'Nobody knows you when you're down and out': the blues singer's lament of the 1920s, as true during periods of emotional indigence as of the material kind, already does the sympathetic ones the courtesy of not putting the point more accurately. Nobody *wants* to know you when you're down and out. Down and Out is a state in both senses – a condition, and also a place, with entry and exit points, unfamiliar customs, a meagre diet, and a draconian judicial system. The others will, at least, await your return from here in hope, and with an uneven display of patience.

In the chilled solitude of the previously shared home, still full of the ephemeral mementoes of the lovers' former happiness, which has now worn the lustre off the bits of junk they gave each other, revealing them to be precisely junk, everything looks like a lie. The smiles in the photographs take on the clenched grimaces of people hoping something isn't going to last too long, while their backgrounds, which were the lush or romantically bleak settings for the amorous passages in the opera, now once more resemble the half-interesting tourist attractions they originally were. As a layer of dust accumulates over it all, it isn't clear which is the more morbid – brushing it away to renew a mendacious sheen of presentness to the mementoes, or letting it lie, so that the lover's obscured face properly looks back from some distant geological era. What sickens in the soul during such periods of bereftness is the recognition that life has returned once more to its default condition. If hopeless striving was its medium, it is now restored in the form of the yearning for a love irreparably departed. The disappointment of thwarted ambition, in major endeavours and minor, to which one had become gloomily almost reconciled, now finds its true image in the form of a successful union broken apart. It is a condition in which the deserted one faces the future in a state of impotent longing, knowing that the only reward that would suffice is as grimly unavailable as the less attractive compensations of money or fame. Thus does love turn out not to be the escape from unhappiness it promised to be. Except, of course, that it was.

Let's be friends!

The proposition that former lovers can still be friends, after the bond of passion that once united them has been sundered, is one in which nobody implicitly believes. Despite this, one obstinately tries to convince oneself that there may be compensations enough in the nobility of the attempt. If the relationship hasn't broken apart amid irreparable acrimony, and if the deserted one doesn't find the other's physical proximity a standing torment, the effort at maintaining friendly relations promises some kind of solace. It represents a mitigation of the anguish, the suspending of the sentence. That it never feels quite right is what exposes the true nature and function of this shadow-relation. It is, finally, only the means of transit by which one travels from the land of love to the distant shore of forgetting. If nobody quite believes it will last, neither does anybody have any emotional appetite for what is called the 'clean break'. To remove the safety-net of the other's presence at once adds a vertiginous sense of utter desolation to what should be the beginning of healing. So a civilised amity is attempted, in which talk of the recent scission is kept within decent bounds, and the prospect of still going out to eat together remains a possibility. Even the one who has cut the knot will suffer from an overly abrupt separation, and there thus seems no mutual need of it.

As the weeks and months progress, however, the artificial

character of the reconstituted friendship stands revealed. It bears no relation to one's other platonic friendships, because it is founded on loss. As the memory of the romance it replaced fades into history, and loses its caustic edge, the friendship takes on the semblance of a poorly acted play, in which neither actor has troubled to learn the script sufficiently well, and to which no audience is paying attention. There is an excess of formalised courtesy wholly absent from true friendships, as the participants try to learn to approach each other from a distance, and with a formality, that their previous relations had ecstatically abandoned. The friendship is less a retracing of steps to some earlier period than a merciless dilution of the intimacy once enjoyed. After the intoxicating distillate of love, it is a sip of watered wine. The ending of any dynamic period in life can't help but seem a return to a less elevated way of living, an ingress of dinginess where all had been rich and bright. At the close of love, it chafes more severely than virtually any other loss apart from death, the grief of which it nonetheless seems acutely to portend.

Going it alone

The solitary life to which the abandoned lover returns often transpires to be nothing like the featureless wilderness it threatened to be, the truth of which is apparent in the disinclination to embark on another affair – even where opportunity presents itself – in the immediate aftermath of an extinct one. Solitude provides the forsaken with the chance to reflect on what went wrong, but it also crucially determines a space for the reassertion of the self. The productive aspect of relationships in the wider world is that they constitute a primary cell of social solidarity within the general atomisation. They enable their participants mutually to throw their self-consciousness into relief in the presence of a countervailing self. If this establishes a model of constructive interdependency that, multiplied indefinitely, might throw a softer light on an over-rationalised social totality, its fracture surely plunges that totality into gloom once more. That at least seems the case to the inconsolable. But what the enforced solitude makes possible is the return of critical consciousness. Chafing at the unacceptability of his loss, he relearns the value of not accepting things. In the discourse of popular journalism, people in long-term relationships were not long ago characterised clumsily as 'the smug marrieds'. Their marital status, conceived initially in the conventional terms of romantic fiction, was now transformed, under the general law of reification, into a possession, something to which the solitary neighbour with his midnight habits can't lay claim. Gloating – 'we have something you don't' – always sounds more enjoyable than the miserable reality, however, and issues directly from the pages of Sade, where the life-blood of sensual enjoyment is a delighted apprehension of the privations of others. If the romantic pair are truly delighted in such scorn, they may already be deflecting it from each other. In the single state, at least for a while, the truth about relationships becomes apparent, as the consciousness of the bereft expands back into something like Hegelian 'absolute knowing', where absoluteness is not to be confused with omniscience, but denotes the intellect's awareness that it is itself part of the whole phenomenal world it would seek to encompass. As one half of a couple, it was borne along, happily and calamitously by turns, on the currents of whatever happened; released, against its will to be sure, from such involvement, it suddenly sees the whole picture, not transcendentally, but with itself as one of the elements. The injured consciousness that has had the faculty of objectification restored to it once more notes the careering progress of a faulty world, whose faults include the loss of his love.

Erratum

One of the most grievous of all errors, virtually unquestioned from Plato to Schopenhauer, Hegel to Freud, is that romantic love is essentially engendered by, animated by, and coextensive with the sexual instinct. We only love where physical desire arises. As a universal truth, this permits of so many exceptions that the belief in it often appears to contain more of wish-fulfilment than of explicatory force. At the limits of love, in its margins, at its heart, there are regions where the physical is not at home, where one's consciousness is the more securely joined to that of the other, just because the union isn't complicated by the protocols of bodily engagement. It is here that, gazing back along the sunlit path it has travelled, or looking up ahead to the mountain-top, love may find its freest expression: freedom from mere physicality, freedom to run.

Chapter Six

The Sixth Sense

Perception and the Beyond

A thinking that looked beyond what was immediately apparent to existing knowledge had the merit of wishfulness on its side. In hopeful independence of the diagnostics of scientific understanding, which appeared in demystifying the world to have made it smaller, at least until its focus on the sub-atomic threatened to unleash the biblical apocalypse, the supernatural betrayed its own principle by only positing an adjunct realm to the natural, instead of reconfiguring the natural itself. To the banal phenomenology of sight, it appended another-worldly second sight, and to the five physical senses enumerated by Aristotle, a sixth. Physiological science itself has since counted many more senses than five, though none of them involves foretelling the future or communing with the departed. A thinking through objective reality by dialectical cognition was wishful in the sense that it wanted to disrupt the frequencies by which static consciousness accepted the existent as inevitable; the wishfulness of occult thinking has no wish to look again at the present world, only to make contact with a posited realm beyond it, where it turns out, however, that things proceed much as they do here, where the souls of the dead reassure the living that they are contented and enjoying each other's company, while advising the living themselves to keep in touch with distant relatives. The special vision of clairvoyants extends to informing those consulting them that they were born in January, as much as it does forewarning them that some unspecified peril lies ahead on the forthcoming journey, or that somebody with the initial G will prove significant, as though its precognitive tricks, which are unverifiable until the forecast events either happen or don't, must be reinforced by demonstrating the seer's insight into what the client already knows, meaningless intelligence that is purchased all the more expensively where it turns out to be wrong.

Spiritualism represents the attempt to fit what pure reason labelled the intuitions with a non-systematic structure. The element in consciousness that subjects material perception to integrative understanding, by which it knows what it sees without having specifically to test it, is transformed by adepts of the paranormal into a bogus analytical process, something that happens, unlike intuition, at speeds visible to the naked eye. Interpretative comprehension, which promoted the survival of the species in primeval times, and was freely available to all, is subjected to an extraneous professionalisation, as being the special gift of privileged individuals who see what others cannot, and who, rather than offering their assistance altruistically to the blind, have managed to conjure a living out of it. Nothing is more satisfying to the clients than to be told they are looking at something wrongly, since the consultation then mimics the break-throughs that psychoanalysis only offers by first presuming its customers are ill. The prickly defensiveness that spirit-mediums and others invariably display when the fraudulence or banality of their claims is challenged is indignation not just at the threatened restraint of trade, but at an attack on their own self-perception as ministers to the troubled, notwithstanding the fact that they themselves don't scruple to tread delicately around genuine trouble when there is money to be made. Scorning the efforts of positive religion, they nonetheless take as their guiding principle the same commonplace with which the institutional churches have fallen to justifying themselves before professional doubt: namely that if it gives people comfort, where's the harm? The harm lies in the facticity of its authority, whereby the crystal-gazer assumes the prognosticating executive power over the fates of individuals that organised religion by and large ceded to it when, in the process of its own enlightenment to itself, it threw out the concept of fate. Early-modern predestination has been rescued by fortune-tellers, and proves no less grimly merciless than it was when it struck fear into people's souls with the news that God already knew they were doomed, the only difference being that where the evidence of damnation lay deep inside, its tyrannical power resides in occult belief in the external physical contingencies of turned-up cards, falling coins, and the hieroglyphics inscribed on the surface of the hand. Exponents of these beliefs are fond of pointing out that they reach back at least as far as, if not in many cases further than, those of the monotheistic faiths, as though their own primitivity ought to guarantee their efficacy where that of ecclesiastical tenets is counted as condemnation. All that stands between the prognostic insight of occultism and the concrete truth is that it dwells in the land of the irrational, a permanently twilit, sparsely populated zone in which it nevertheless feels perfectly at home.

The access to the future that clairvoyance offers expresses the age-old predicament into which the development of consciousness pitched human beings when it endowed them with the ability to look ahead. Their proficiency in being able to judge inevitable or likely outcomes, which presaged the birth of science out of the survival instinct, removed them from the animal world by turning the vague foreboding that haunts all sentient life into the means for hermeneutic understanding and rational planning. And yet nothing about the apprehension of causal structures vouchsafes to consciousness any knowledge about what is going to happen to it. People who turn to scryers and prophets want to glean the certainty of a little foreknowledge of their personal circumstances amid the overarching menace of the foreknowledge in which everybody lives anyway, that a society consecrated to exchange relations will rattle on oblivious to their own concerns, indefinitely maintaining them in the state of being, as the cynical wisdom has it, overworked and underpaid. The premonitory impulse is thereby belittled to the purview of whether the client can expect something pleasantly surprising, or have any luck with the person in whom they have placed their romantic hopes, in the process aiming to spoil the surprise whose unexpected nature precisely constitutes its pleasure, while yielding the specifically human capacity for imagining and shaping the future to forces that everywhere loom monstrously above humanity. Even love, which advice columnists insist can be practically engineered by rational alterations to one's appearance and behaviour, nostrums in which nobody practically believes, is grist to the forecasters' mill, exactly because mutual attraction appears to have no rules, and therefore is as much a part of contingent futurity as is having a bit of a win on the lottery. Even more pitiful is the evidently flourishing belief that clues to what is to come lie hidden in certain texts and dispositions of physical phenomena, such as the accidental crossing of teaspoons, which everybody might interpret if they were only sufficiently sensitive. Poring over the ancient texts in search of prediction traduces the original biblical sense of prophecy as an interpretation of the state of things predicated out of existing circumstances, a transference that, to be sure, the Judeo-Christian tradition itself inaugurated by insisting that everything that came to pass during the Incarnation had been foretold in the time of the prophets. The dignity of such an interpretation is that it was primarily the duty of the messianic present to fulfil what was expected of it in the past, and in turn prepare the way for a redeemed eschatological future. The imagistic Revelation can be such only where its seemingly hallucinogenic visionary repertoire lays itself open to symbolic interpretation. Anything else would be a flagrant contravention of the ban on images. In secular terms, the charge much repeated against Marx, that he offers no other concrete delineation of the redeemed society than that it will allow each one to fulfil his innate potential without exploiting the others, missed the point that any utopia that could be depicted in concrete terms, as indeed many of them were, from Plato to Thomas More and beyond, would already be saturated in the swill of present reality. Where the adumbration of reconciled life was dreamed only in inchoate images, it stood a chance of becoming true, but the direct prognostic tradition expected the inchoate images themselves to be the guide to future concrete events, which only had to be teased out of their encoding, as in Nostradamus. If the fortune-teller could truly see what will happen, what would be the need to wrap it in esoteric mumbling? If astrology knows what will become of each of its clients, why doesn't it just say so, instead of shrouding its sagacity in the conditional? Prophetic books such as the *I Ching* at least had the excuse that what was written couldn't be unwritten, but astrologists are free to speak specifically to the matter at hand. Despite their efforts at incoherent certainty, the future in the minutiae of its contingencies properly remains a closed book, whereas the entirety of existing socio-economic relations, which could be transformed by human beings for the reason that they themselves have produced them, is taken to be part of the natural world with which the supernatural disdains to engage. Not for nothing was fortune-telling for many years one of the attractions of travelling fairs and the entertainments on seaside piers, where it had retreated into closed booths and creepily lit grottoes to escape the hooting of the crowds.

The liminal region in which paranormal phenomena exist are vitally constitutive of them. They don't want to come in from the cold, because they would then become just another component of the normal, like the previously unsuspected creatures that keep being discovered in the deepest levels of the ocean. It is the first duty of poltergeists to evade the video-cameras assiduously set up to record them. Occultism, which once resented the intrusion of empirical verification in case its claims were exposed as hollow, now openly welcomes it, not only as a sign that it is being taken seriously by science, but in belated realisation that hypothecation, unlike history, doesn't proceed by its negative side. The cameras and electromagnetic monitors can only fail to record the unearthly manifestations, not prove that they don't exist. Where something is recorded and fails to convince, it can always be presented as a matter of interpretation. Claims such as telekinesis, which if it existed could easily be demonstrated on light entertainment TV, have given way to the more extraneous phenomena such as ghostly manifestations and disembodied voices, for which one must patiently wait in darkened cellars in the middle of the night. The impulse to credit the existence of such arcana is the simple longing for something interesting to happen, in a context where social experience has shrivelled to nearly nothing, but in which the paranormal is not the antidote to such emptiness, but is itself one of its more virulent symptoms. If there were truly a realm that lay apart from present reality, and scorned its physical laws, it would only have compromised itself by intervening in the reality that either openly laughs at it, or else tries painstakingly to subject it to its own rules of measurement. Despite its occasional ill-advised openness to mortal access, articulated these days in the form of near-death experiences, the afterlife as conceived in the established religions remained an unimaginably distant destination, albeit one at which everybody was sooner or later guaranteed to arrive. The hope in occultism, by contrast, is that intermittent momentary encounters with it might shed a transforming light on the material realm, switching the consciousness of sensitive individuals between the two poles like the alternating currents of an electrical circuit, so that the beyond is materialised in earthly experience, even as earthly experience is granted the privilege of a flashbulb peep into the beyond. In popular theological tradition, while the other saints were received into heaven entire at the moment of death, Mary Magdalene was tossed into eternity as from a springboard, overcome for a moment at the apex of her parabola by the divine, before falling back to the mortal realm below, from which she once again ascended in heavenly buoyancy, fully reconciled in the moment of celestial *transitus* to both elements. Electromagnetic radiation monitors are the secular survival of the hope that the border between the two realms might be as airily permeable as it was to the saint.

The supposed empirical investigation of the supernatural, where it is credited by aficionados with positive results, never proceeds beyond the first stage of marvelling at its sheer occurrence. No further attempt is made to ask what the purpose would be of inert objects apparently moving themselves about behind their owners' backs. Only the fact that it happens at all is deemed sufficient to confer meaning on it, in unwitting confirmation that it doesn't happen at all. It needs the scientific paraphernalia in order to establish precisely that it has defeated science, which must reverse away from it respectfully like a grand vizier who may not turn his back on the sultan. Because it is thus rooted at the most axiomatic and shallowest level of consciousness, it is taken for granted by those who profess it, in a childlike presumption that everybody else shares the delusion. Its homology with all conformist habits of thought is fatally exposed, as it is in many other ways, by that presumption, which has echoes in the political conservative's tendency to assume that everybody else is conservative. People of otherwise robust intellectual powers are quite capable of casually describing somebody else as 'typically Taurean', creating a moment of radical estrangement in the very act of presuming like-mindedness. It is then up to the other to decide whether to risk the boorishness of pointing out for the record that he doesn't believe in that stuff, or whether, by acquiescing, to make himself into somebody who might well be as gullible as his interlocutor secretly knows himself not to be. The atmosphere of scientific observation with which the paranormal gratefully surrounds itself is intended at least partly to ward off the impression that only unutterably stupid people would believe its claims. A conspiracy of illusory belief, however, is the mental disposition of participants in torchlight rallies and, in less murderous form, of the audiences of mass media, where every onlooker is made to feel personally invested in a process that cares nothing for them, other than that they keep looking on. At the séances too, the communicants hope the spirits are trying to tell them something important, and not merely poking fun at their preposterous credulity.

Beyond Extra Sensory Perception

If society responded rationally to the rational interests of its members, there would be little need for them to resort to the irrational. The dimension of the irrational has served social well-being as its antipode since the days of the Bacchae, when due obeisance to its demands ensured the prevalence of hierarchical harmony in the state, and was only withheld at the greatest peril. Theatrical catharsis intended the same. By the time of the ascendancy of the monotheistic religions, the irrational was codified into ritual practices that in themselves bore the stamp of supremely well-ordered rationality, notwithstanding occasional exceptions such as the licence to drunkenness at Purim. Purely irrational belief migrated into the domain of personal superstition, the dimension of existence that the religious institutions couldn't fully penetrate. Elements of primitive magic were still retained by the established faiths, not least in the form of petitionary prayer, or in the uttering of penances in incantatory repetition, but the structure of worship and celebration was anything but orgiastic. Self-control, including the maintenance of a tight, often throttling, rein on the senses was central. The physical senses are not only the *locus classicus* of temptation, which begins with the impulse to their gratification, but are also the possible means by which the immaterial, properly spiritual content of belief might be cast into doubt. Peering too closely at the manifestation of St Anthony might reveal him to be a slide-projection, while the healing of the lame by charismatic church leaders is easily tarnished when one sees them topple over without their crutches as soon as they are hustled off the stage. The gradual abandonment by positive religion of these appeals to sensory empiricism left the field open for their co-optation by commercialised superstition, an opportunity that the occult has eagerly seized on. An item of clothing might reveal everything about an absent person to the inward vision of the spiritualist, albeit not quite as much as it does to the police sniffer-dog. All the recording apparatus brought into service to capture the unexplained tappings and ghostly emanations of the nocturnal vigil represents an attempt to reconnect the irrational with its precarious basis in physical sensory reality, the very element denied in the utterance of the hieratic formula, 'The spirit of God is moving in this place'.

The exception in occultism is the supposed sixth sense itself, extra-sensory perception, the sense that doesn't rely on physiological sensing, but is nonetheless held to be more powerful than simple intuition. ESP in the form of telepathy attempted to establish its validity through the relatively trivial procedure of guessing the pattern on concealed cards, or by one subject reproducing a drawing that a hidden colleague had produced. The continued absence of any verification by consistent results for these claims doesn't trouble their exponents, who often point to the halting progress through trial and error that official science has undoubtedly made during its long empirical history. If there remains more error than trial for the time being, that is only all the more reason to continue the investigations. What would be more useful to the field of inquiry, prior to hapless attempts to show that a volunteer can be made to think of a duck by somebody sitting in another room, would be any general theory of how telepathic communications between brains would work. While it remains true that physical investigation generally proceeds on the basis of observation followed by explication, there is nothing to prevent, and indeed everything to encourage, adherents of telepathy from positing a practical theory of its operativity while the laboratory tests continue trying to provide it with statistical support. Telepathics also dispute the temporal relations that empirical knowledge assumes between past, present and future, insisting that the future can communicate with the present, just as the present turns to the past for its antecedent authority, and also to reassure itself it has moved on. The idealistic moment in such thought is the reasonable enough hope that, instead of always being subject to what had gone before, the mind-set of conformism, human affairs might be opened to some redemptive force from the not-yet, precisely the impulse that lends the major religions their eschatological thrust. In the very act of laying the present open to the future, however, the precognitive telepathic does no more than repeat the gesture of heteronomy by which she charges conventional science with its pedestrian logic. The immutable future is granted the same sway over the present as the present is granted over the past in sequential history. Nothing about it can be changed, because the liberating knowledge that its futurity lies precisely in the fact that it hasn't happened yet is sacrificed to a miserable predestinarian consciousness that hardly differs from Calvinism, except in that the force controlling human affairs is not some supreme being but the constellations, that is to say, just another fragment of the inert matter of which the universe is largely constituted, and which doesn't otherwise have noticeably much to say to sentient life.

The question arises from the postulation of telepathy as to what life would be like if, its aptitude having been honed by evolutionary development, everybody could read the thoughts of others. Inasmuch as the cognitive processes of each reflects the personal specificity of each man and woman, there would effectively be no others any longer, no alterity. More than that, there would no longer be any thought as such, since everybody would already know the contents of everybody else's interiority. Interiority itself would vanish, and with it the psychological integrity of individuals. An ecumenical vision that saw in such an outcome the possibility of an end to misunderstanding, and a solution to the alienation from each other occasioned by failures in communication, reaches too readily for the mechanistic model of communication to which a society constructed as one gigantic business enterprise has subjected it. Advertisers would be granted the holy grail of direct unfettered access to every consumer, as there would be nothing to prevent consciousness in the mass from being connected to any one of a number of major telepathic networks, much as telephone subscribers are connected now. Intentionality would wither under the pre-emptive scrutiny of those towards whom even one's most benign intentions were directed. Amatory relations, or any other bonding process that currently takes place by heuristic degrees, would be rendered obsolete, since everything there was to know about somebody else would be laid out before the others from the outset, leaving only the instrumental functionality of the sexual encounter itself, which would see the lifeblood drained from it in the general erosion of otherness. Use of the senses, no longer required for interpersonal understanding once it could pierce directly through to the mind, would be confined merely to the awareness of inert material objects and animals, which have no minds to read, only the live circuitry of their instincts. An immense labour of mental discipline would have to be learned, far greater than that required by the superego's custodial power over the id, for fear that the irruptions of the uncensored id in themselves, now on permanent view, would lead to the war of all against all. On the credit side, the invalid would at least be able to ask for a glass of water without moving his lips.

Telepathy is no more capable of overcoming the sensory moment in consciousness than thought itself is when it considers itself to be rid of the sensory objects. The pure conceptuality to which every sense-impression is turned by mind may not be the diamond that emerges from the rough once the sensual dross is polished away, but the mind nonetheless refuses to be parted from the idea that something in sensual reality urges it to assume the duty of making a tarnished reality shine. While the chatter of commerce barks out its imperatives to stricken consciousness to exploit its senses to the full, the better to avail itself of the splendour of commerce, the part of consciousness that won't forget what sensual experience once was, long before it understood it was to bow in tribute to the prevailing racket, clings to the intuition of its own survival as to a myth of origin. The racket has persuaded it that its memory of sensual abundance is pure regression, even while it depends on regression to promote the abundance of its own goods. A thinking regressed to adult infantility can't revive the immediacy of which sensual gratification perpetually reminds it, because the infant state didn't recognise gratification for itself. Only a conceptualising subjectivity released from its subjection to pure subjectivity can grasp through thought what the sensual world might make itself into in its honour. The model for the released subject would no longer be the imperious ego, striding forth into the great world in order to see what it had to offer, like the hero of the European *Bildungsroman*, but would know itself to be another phenomenon among the things themselves, albeit one endowed with the ability, recuperated from its regression to magic, to breathe life back into them with its gaze. Everything about sensualist ideology, its binary relations between self and world and its solipsism, would dissolve in the truth of sensuality itself, the universal kinship of all with all. Thus transfigured, the constricted spirit could burst its metaphysical ligatures and make metaphysical things happen in the material world: unwithering love, the end of suffering, the transformation of labour, the abolition of time.

Appendix A

Beyond the Five Senses

Not for a long time have five been enough. Robert Burton in *The Anatomy of Melancholy* (1621) held that the five outer senses are matched by three inward counterparts – the Aristotelian common sense, phantasy or imagination, and memory – the actions of which are dependent on whether the individual happens to be sleeping or awake. Even if these are properly mental operations, not structurally cognate with the functionality of the physical senses, there is clearly more to the latter in themselves than just their five essential actions. The physical senses are easily sub-dividable into many supplementary classes of perception: sight, for example, includes the cognition of motion, colour, form, brightness, texture, contrast and so forth.

Beyond these, modern science has expanded the number of the senses to fifteen or more. The others begin with the *exteroceptive* abilities – a sense of the body's movement in space, the speed at which it is moving and the direction of its travel, its distance from other bodies, the ambient temperature. A complementary class of sense perception is termed *proprioception,* the brain's ability to sense the body's own relation to itself, including the awareness of pain and pleasure, hunger and thirst, muscular tension, the disposition of the body itself in external space, and the mechanisms by which it maintains balance, or judges the amount of physical effort needed to perform an action. *Interoception* constitutes an awareness of the workings of the internal organs, a sense that could alert the mind to forthcoming medical crises, where it doesn't remain entangled in the self-delusions of hypochondria. In short, every operation of consciousness is definable as some sort of sense.

What the entire sensory complex enables is not just knowledge of the external world, but of the body itself, of the individual human being of whom it is constitutive, and of the communities to which he or she belongs. Techniques for heightening the senses can be used therapeutically to allow people to recover lost or impaired functions, and can be used by the healthy to deepen everyday experience. The challenge remains to free the exercise of the senses from the solipsism of self-pleasuring, and apply them to the re-humanising of a technological global society. Engagement of them for its own entertaining sake leaves every stone unturned. Their highest function, which enabled primordial survival of the species and might bring about a restitution of human potential from the present disaster, is to provide knowledge, of the self and of the world on which it has been cast adrift. Sensory knowledge, the foundation of all understanding, is the lifeline thrown to the shipwrecked present from the furthest reaches of a history that could still be redeemed.

Appendix B

When would you like to eat? – The hardest way to become a food critic

The development of taste in infancy begins with the baby's initial introduction to milk, for which its palate is already pre-natally primed. There is evidence that the mother's diet during pregnancy and breast-feeding, where practised, has an influence on her baby's taste buds. A prevalence of strong seasonings in the maternal diet, such as garlic, pepper and spices, can be transmitted to the developing child, so that he or she grows up with a natural affinity for those flavours. However, beyond these usually unintentional triggers, parents remain in the West more or less wholly neglectful of tutoring the taste sensibilities of their offspring. They are taught visual skills with pattern-games and building blocks, moving on to reading at the appropriate age. Their sense of touch is developed through making them comfortable, even playing them improving music, but very few parents set out to educate their children's palates. One possible result of this is that everybody emerges to consciousness of food with only a very random set of criteria for judging it. Where Baby has been fed exclusively after weaning on the carbohydrate-bulked, sweet processed products of the baby-food industry, his or her taste buds may well already have been steered unwittingly in the direction of a certain homogenised blandness, so that anything unusual arouses intense suspicion. At best, this has bred a whole post-war generation of incurious, unadventurous eaters with variously finicky antipathies to certain ingredients. I watched an erstwhile colleague once painstakingly excavating every last sultana from an American muffin as she ate it. Why not buy a different muffin? 'Because I like this one,' she replied, the desk in front of her a heap of carefully rejected dried fruit. More seriously, however, uneducated taste buds can result in childhood eating disturbances – or, worse still, an actual eating disorder – which are then chronically distressing to the parents, and can inhibit the child's social development.

When I was two years old, for reasons that remain unclear, I stopped eating. The black-and-white family Polaroids show that I was rather a tubby toddler, with a little more flesh than might be accounted for by puppy-fat, and a riotously happy, double-chinny little face. I ate normally, with a small boy's normal voracity, so much so that I could be held up as a model to a more reluctant infant cousin. And then one day I didn't. I have no personal recollection of this, but there came a moment when suddenly, faced with picking something up and putting it into my mouth, I had what show jumpers call a refusal.

As the days and weeks wore on, and it became clear that the loss of appetite wasn't the result of a passing malady, my increasingly distressed mother asked for medical advice. Perhaps the reason I now refused the bowl of jelly I would once have wolfed down with relish, suggested the nurse, was that I didn't like the texture of it in my mouth. But that hardly explained the fact that I appeared to have gone off everything. My father took the phlegmatic view that no child would willingly malnourish itself, but mothers aren't so easily bought off with bland logic, and I was duly brought before the family practitioner. An examination established that I wasn't ailing physically, but gentle questioning of a child as puzzled by the general enquiry as was everyone else achieved nothing.

After four months of breast-feeding, I had been weaned on to semi-solids by being fed largely on the same things that my parents were eating, smooshed into purée in the Baby Mouli. Although baby-food eventually entered the equation, it wasn't what I was first fed on. I had eaten amply and broad-mindedly for the first two years of my life, and now it was as though I was growing out of eating as some kind of infantile indulgence. 'Will he eat baked beans?' the doctor asked my mother and, hearing that I would, declared that a boy could probably live by Heinz alone. There must have been a moment when the consultation lapsed into the inconclusive silence that attends all medical mysteries, and a barely placated mother took her recalcitrant infant home again.

It wasn't an affliction that my baby sister was to suffer from. Indeed, once she had got to the age of being able to put food into her own mouth unaided, she would wait hawkishly to see how much of mine I was proposing to leave, and as soon as I had demurred, like a wasp-waisted tsarina falling faint at the fifteenth course, she would move in and vacuum up whatever remained. As a system designed to obviate waste, it could hardly have been improved on, but did nothing to alleviate my mother's anxiety. She remembers asking herself at the end of many a weirdly abstemious day exactly what she had managed to persuade me to eat during the course of it, the sum total often amounting to no more than a few mouthfuls. It was as though eating had become a dreary pastime to me, over-frequently cropping up in days that might have been filled with merrier pursuits. And yet, despite the outwardly morbid self-denial, I thrived and was well.

I was by now as thin as a praying mantis, but more robust than I looked, and even though my ribcage extruded itself when I breathed in deeply, there was one boy in my school-class who was even thinner than I was. When we all changed for gym, you could see David Buckley's ribcage even before he'd breathed in. We were the first generation to grow up after the end of post-war rationing, so under-nourishment was theoretically a thing of the past. It was for perhaps this reason that, following those early visits to the doctor, nobody took any professional interest in either my – or, as far as I know, David Buckley's – dietary health. Some boys are skinnier than others.

If there was a unifying theme to the few foods I would deign to eat as I progressed through childhood, it was that they tended to be items that didn't require much chewing. I would eat Ready-Brek (the commercial version of porridge oats), and even Weetabix as long as it was mashed up in hot milk. I would eat a soft-boiled egg. Those processed cream-cheese portions that came in triangular gold-foiled packs in different flavours were a particular delight, as was cheese generally. At places where we'd stopped to eat a full meal on a family outing, I would eat cheese on toast as a main course, with an order of cheese and biscuits to follow. Thin sausages were acceptable, but only the skinless variety, perhaps accompanied by thin-textured mash and a spoonful of baked beans, which last I ate by swallowing each mouthful of them whole. Oranges were not the only fruit I hated, being averse to nearly all of them, with the predictable exception of bananas. Apart perhaps from the cheese, what strikes me now is that this was effectively a baby diet, a theory that gains further credence with the recollection that I continued to eat one or two varieties of actual baby-food until well past infancy. There was something nebulously called 'Fruit Dessert', which was a gelatinous purée in baked-bean orange with faintly starchy white ricey bits in it. I loved that.

What appeared to be happening was that, after the earlier meat-and-two-veg maturity, I was regressing to a narrower range of foods that had obvious sweet, salty and umami appeal (all that cheese), but I had no receptiveness to the more grown-up flavours of sour and bitter. Nor had I evolved much in the direction of solid foods. There was barely anything in my diet that required teeth to eat it, although I had perfectly good childhood dentition, and once this semi-infant regimen was established, I absolutely refused to countenance eating anything I didn't recognise.

Reinforcing the decision not to touch anything else child gastronomy had to offer were the few moments of disciplinarianism that were tried on me. Pediatric advice these days is to avoid this approach like the plague. It can only be counter-productive, and may lead to an even more deeply conflicted relationship with food than already exists in the refusing child. Tried beyond endurance, my mother once refused to allow me to get down from the kitchen table until I'd eaten a plate of sandwiches spread with one of Sutherland's finest fish pastes, which served the British perfectly well until everybody learned the word *pâté*. They came in tiny jars, all looking more or less the same colour and, I suspect, were kept in the cupboard after opening rather than the fridge. My detention at the table, needless to say, was a battle of wills with only one winner. Indeed, I might have gone on sitting there through puberty, were it not for the fact that, at some point, my mother tried a bite of one of the sandwiches, and discovered that the paste had gone off.

If trying to threaten rancid fish paste into the mouths of babes might be counted an innocent mistake, far worse primal scenes were to arise in the school dinner-hall. In the 1960s, what was given to children under the guise of school dinners may have compared favourably in its nutritional value to today's fat-fuelled, salt-boosted sugar-rush, but did nothing to advertise the virtues of the ingredients themselves. Most days consisted of some take on the roast dinner, the thin slices of meat-effect protein accompanied by a wilted harvest-festival of veg that had been boiled all the way to hell and back. At a certain point, having scraped most of it into as compact a heap as possible, you could raise your hand and ask to be allowed to leave what remained. A woman in a red headscarf and thick pan-stick, who patrolled the hall like an aged and furious Gloria Swanson, would then decide whether you were to be relieved, or had to try to force down more.

Even worse than the ersatz roasts were the puddings, which came with colour-coded sauces composed overwhelmingly of corn flour. Puddings might have been expected to be the sweet relief at the end of the torment for children, but not these. They were nothing like sumptuous tinned sponge puddings, or indeed Mum's own, but sat like unexploded ordnance in their bowls, surrounded by pink custard or yellow custard, and sometimes further garnished, in a touch of Grimod de la Reynière, with some heat-treated white substance squirted from a can. After one particularly agonising session of alternating refusal and self-*gavage*, the pudding one day involved something like puff pastry with a pineapple ring on top of it, sitting in a lake of yellow, topped with squirty. I managed a single mouthful of it before tipping it into the adjacent boy's dish. Amid the mangily constituted nay-sayers like me, there were kids who stuffed everything down with gruesome relish, inhaling each mouthful off their forks with furrowed brow, raising their determined chewing faces from their plates just long enough to see what anybody else might be intending to leave. I can't remember who it was relieved me of the pineapple pudding. He hated it too, but ate it regardless, like a real man. It was an enforced bit of heroism, but one that wasn't quite sufficient to prevent a bilious afternoon in the classroom, at the end of which I went home and vomited for England. A better England.

As the years went by, nothing revived my appetite. While the rest of my family ate their Sunday roast, I set about a packet of crisps, sometimes two if I was hungry. If I was invited over to tea with friends, I had to announce that I wouldn't eat anything. Every family holiday, in hotels and guest-houses the length and breadth of England and Wales, began on the first evening with my mother explaining to whoever brought the dinner round that I wouldn't eat anything. The soup was usually fine, but after that, I sat politely and watched the others eat, until proceedings arrived at the cheese-and-biscuits stage. I did eat chocolate and sweets to some extent, but I never had a pronounced sweet tooth, and besides, puddings often came with bits of whole fruit hovering around them, or under layers of floury grit, or topped with squirty. So while others devoured those gratefully, I unwrapped my portionettes of Cheddar and balanced them on buttered crackers, like a pint-sized connoisseur.

This silly nonsense went on until I left for university at eighteen. It was only when, in the course of my first term there, I started being invited over to dinner by fellow-students that I finally decided that declaring that I wouldn't eat anything was becoming a childish liability. Purely as an act of adult volition, I began to eat anything that was offered (mostly either spaghetti bolognese or lasagne, but some students were freakishly vegetarian and ate things like couscous and buckwheat). The long food strike was over, along with whatever it was that had started it, sixteen under-nourished and parent-maddening years earlier.

A child psychologist examining this scenario now would almost certainly point to the fact that, when it began, my mother was pregnant with my sister. Since I was the firstborn, could the refusal to eat represent a manifestation of classic sibling jealousy, breaking out on cue when the first child realises he is no longer the undivided centre of his parents' attention? What undermines this theory in my case is that it hadn't yet been explained to me that there was a sister or brother on the way, and it seems a leap too far to claim that I had somehow divined it. No doubt the actual arrival of my sister only helped to reinforce my obstinacy over food, but I doubt she could have acted as some sort of intuitive trigger. At about the same time, there was an incident when my grandmother was looking after me for the afternoon, and had suddenly been unable to get me to eat. All that was different from anything either she or my mother had given me before was that the gravy, instead of being smooth, had sliced onion in it. It might have been the first thing I'd ever been presented with that I didn't like. But why wouldn't order have been restored by the next mealtime? Could a single attempt to eat something that I didn't like have been so traumatic that I was subconsciously reminded of it every time I tried to eat something more familiar?

A child's refusal to eat in the expected way represents his first exercise of control. In a world where everything flows from the provision of parental nurture, he is a helpless and almost entirely passive being, far more so than is the case with any other species of mammal. And while eating is not something that the infant can entirely forgo, it becomes apparent to him that he can become choosy about what exactly he is prepared to consume, and how much of it. Research conducted in the UK and Ireland in 2005-6 found that eating disorders were to be found in just 0.003 per cent of under-thirteens, with 82 per cent of identified cases being girls. Nearly half of all cases are a non-anorexic eating disturbance, occurring in children who are not underweight. Only a tiny handful of these cases affect children as young as five. An eating disorder at two is virtually unheard of. Regina Casper, in a 2000 paper for the American College of Neuropsychopharmacology, points out that '[c]hildren refuse food for all kinds of reasons, aversion to the sight, taste, or form of food, little appetite, or distractions with more interesting activities, such as play. However, this kind of food refusal seldom lasts long.'[1] The period between the ages of six months and three years has been termed by child psychologists the separation or individuation phase. At some point during this stage of life, the infant begins to realise his own physical and cognitive identity, and if his mother doesn't respond in quite the ways he is expecting, the refusal of food can become an alternative way of insisting on his nascent individuality. When a child will only eat very selectively (often with a predilection to carbohydrates), parents naturally worry that he isn't receiving a balanced nutritional intake. The efforts of paediatricians can sometimes alleviate this, but if his overall growth is adequate, there is no lack of energy, and the child isn't suffering from any other type of emotional malady, there may be no harm in leaving well alone. A slight tendency to poor social functioning in later life, first observable when the child reaches school age, is the only remaining risk to consider. If you don't eat properly, you will quickly become aware that you are not like the others. How much that matters then varies from one child to the next.

A scene that plays itself out with monotonous regularity in negotiating with selective eaters, adults as well as children, is the attempt to induce them to try something they have never had before, an attempt that fails when they insist that they already know they don't like it. 'How do you know if you won't try it?' is the apparently rational challenge, answered if at all with the assurance that you just know. Though it doesn't seem so to the cajoler, this is hardly less rational than the enquiry itself. It is possible to look at an item of food and not be able to overcome the aversive impulses it awakens in you. Perhaps if you didn't know what it was, it wouldn't matter, but you do. To take an example, I don't particularly want to eat snails. I don't like the look of them. I don't like the thought of them as food. The idea that they may have been cooked alive fills me with ethical horror, and it often turns out that the amount of determined rumination they require in the mouth is scarcely proportionate to their degree of taste. There are at least a hundred more appealing vehicles for garlic butter. I will eat one or two, however, if occasion demands, just as my schoolmate ate the appalling pineapple pudding. What is required here is a willed suspension of aversion, a mental discipline that makes it possible to set aside the fact that you don't like something for as long as it takes to consume it. To most people, in most circumstances, there is no earthly reason to do this, which is why people who obstinately won't try the morsel of delicious goat's cheese, or the glistening plump vinegared whelk, are not being irrational in letting the tempter know they won't like it. What could be more infuriating than being fooled into trying something that then turns out to be at least as horrible as you knew it would be, and in precisely the pungently slimy way you knew it would?

On the other hand, my own refusal to try things until I had started living away from home for the first time has had a wholly benign effect on my subsequent working life. So interested did I eventually become in food and drink that they were the consuming interests of my earliest journalistic career. I became a restaurant critic and wine writer. Nobody, observing my sixteen-year cheese diet, or for that matter my fastidious refusal of alcohol when I first started going out in my teens, could have seen that coming. It was about as likely as an acrophobic becoming an airline pilot. The explanation I have always preferred, however, is that it was precisely because I was unused to the taste of so many things that discovering them as an adult was so productive. At eighteen years old, I had a more or less virgin palate. I had gone into reverse at the age of two, and put off learning to eat till another time, when the whole enterprise would be full of wonder, and I would be equipped with a more finely honed set of analytical capabilities than even the most precocious two-year-olds have.

At just past forty, I underwent an endoscopy, which established that I have a probably congenital hiatal hernia. Although I can't recall suffering regularly from gastric reflux until I had turned twenty – after I had started eating properly, in other words – could it have been that it first manifested itself at two years old, and that the narrow range of foods I would eat, in their mostly loose-textured mushiness, were ones that wouldn't aggravate my digestive frailty? Although I will nowadays eat practically anything out of professional interest, I still get full-up far sooner than anyone else, and any straying over a very defined line can make me positively ill.

Recent developments in medical science have identified the existence of a condition called Hypersensitive Taste Bud Syndrome (HTBS), which has been posited as explaining some instances of finicky eating in children. The theory suggests that in some individuals, the taste receptors are over-developed, resulting in an innate ability to sense every last dimension in the taste of a food, and making it more likely that they will identify something in it that they don't like. On this reading, the rest of humanity is munching away in a state of blissful ignorance, consuming plenty of food that they don't really like because they aren't tasting it with any accuracy. It is now thought that this condition, far from being a peripheral rarity, may affect around 25 per cent of the population and – like many another newly defined condition – it is on the increase. Being a supertaster is not, as it might at first appear, to be enviably gifted, but to be at risk through one's constant choosiness of not getting sufficient nutrients. HTBS sufferers particularly object to bitterness, which makes them reject all kinds of green vegetables. To counter-balance that, they are generally averse to too much fat as well, and they find the taste of alcohol unbearably astringent and off-putting. Which last point, to some considerable relief, would appear to rule out the possibility of such a diagnosis in my own case.

Acknowledgements

The author would like to thank the following people, who have helped during the writing of this book in various ways, from advising on interpretation, chasing down references and copy-editing to offering the least tangible and most valuable forms of solidarity: Jackie Bonham, Fr Dexter Bracey, Gillian Carney, Sarah Cave, Rose Collis, Denise Cording, Janice Darkes-Sutcliffe, Shoya Koshimizu, Kaho Lee, Sally Marden, Max Moroz, Daniel Pavlovits, Tracey Steele, Lucie Tobin, John Wang, Fr Robert Ward, Lesley White, Tim Winter, Sergey Zalesov, Zhong Houchun and Mateusz Zielsdorf.

A grant from the Althorpe Foundation was crucial in assisting the completion of the book.

Notes

Preface

1. Theodor W Adorno, *Negative Dialectics*, trans EB Ashton, London, 1973, p xx.

Part One: Theory of the Senses

1. David Hume, 'Of Refinement in the Arts', in *Political Writings*, eds Stuart D Warner and Donald W Livingston, Indianapolis, 1994, p 239.
2. Michael O'Shea, *The Brain: A Very Short Introduction*, Oxford, 2005, p 64.
3. René Descartes, *Meditations on First Philosophy*, ed and trans John Cottingham, Cambridge, 2013, p 25.
4. Walter Dill Scott, *The Psychology of Advertising: A Simple Exposition of the Principles*, London, 2013, pp 78-79.
5. Aristotle, *De Anima (On the Soul)*, trans Hugh Lawson-Tancred, London, 1986, II:12, p 187.
6. Ibid.
7. Barry Stroud, *The Quest for Reality: Subjectivism and the Metaphysics of Colour*, New York, 2000, p 49.
8. Jonathan Sawday, *The Body Emblazoned: Dissection and the Human Body in Renaissance Culture*, London, 1995, p 147.
9. Gottfried Wilhelm Leibniz, *New Essays Concerning Human Understanding*, trans Alfred Gideon Langley, New York, 1896, bk II, p 111.
10. Ibid, p 109.
11. Karl Marx, 'Private Property and Communism', *Economic and Philosophic Manuscripts of 1844*, marxists.org/archive /marx/works/1844/manuscripts/comm.htm, all emphases original.
12. Ibid.
13. Ibid.
14. David Howes, *Sensual Relations: Engaging the Senses in*

Culture and Social Theory, Ann Arbor MI, 2003, p 225.

15. Martin Heidegger, *Being and Time*, trans John Macquarrie and Edward Robinson, Oxford, 1962, §34, p 207.
16. Jean-Luc Nancy, *Corpus II: Writings on Sexuality*, trans Anne O'Byrne, New York, 2013, p 26.
17. Thomas Mann, 'Tonio Kröger', in *Death in Venice and Other Stories*, trans David Luke, London, 1998, p 186.
18. Sigmund Freud, 'Id, Ego, Super-Ego', *New Introductory Lectures on Psychoanalysis*, trans WJH Sprott, New York, 1933, p 106.
19. Ibid, p 108.
20. Ibid, p 112.
21. Paul Verlaine, 'Ariettes Oubliées III', *Romances sans Paroles*, 1874.
22. Henrik Ibsen, *Peer Gynt*, V:v, trans Robert Farquharson Sharp.
23. Walter Benjamin, 'Theses on the Philosophy of History', XVI, *Illuminations*, ed Hannah Arendt, trans Harry Zohn, New York, 1969, p 262.
24. Walter Benjamin, 'Berlin Toy Tour I', *Radio Benjamin*, ed Lecia Rosenthal, trans Jonathan Lutes, London, 2014, p 43.
25. Immanuel Kant, 'On Stupefying Oneself by Excessive Use of Food or Drink', *The Metaphysics of Morals*, ed and trans Mary Gregor, Cambridge, 1991, pp 222-223.
26. Ibid, p 223, emphasis original.
27. Ibid, emphases original.
28. telegraph.co.uk/finance/newsbysector/banksandfinance/9641806/Occupy-protesters-were-right-says-Bank-of-England-official.html, accessed 31 January 2015.
29. Aristotle, op cit, II:5, p 169.
30. Ibid, p 170.

Part Two: Application of the Senses

Chapter 1: Sight

1. Georg Simmel, 'On the Psychology of Money', *Simmel on Culture*, eds David Frisby and Mike Featherstone, trans Mark Ritter and David Frisby, London, 1997, p 242.
2. Nicolas Malebranche, *Dialogues on Metaphysics and Religion*, trans Morris Ginsberg, London, 1923, p 69.
3. Ibid.
4. Ibid, p 71.
5. GWF Hegel, *Science of Logic*, trans AV Miller, London, 1969, p 93.
6. Malebranche, op cit, p 71.
7. René Descartes, *Meditations on First Philosophy*, ed and trans John Cottingham, Cambridge, 2013, p 49.
8. Philo, *Questions and Answers on Genesis*, trans Ralph Marcus, Cambridge MA, 1961, p 22.
9. René Descartes, *The Philosophical Writings of Descartes*, vol II, trans John Cottingham, Robert Stoothof and Dugald Murdoch, Cambridge, 1984, p 22.
10. Martin Buber, *Eclipse of God: Studies in the Relation between Religion and Philosophy*, trans Maurice S Friedman, London, 1953, p 56.
11. Aristotle, *De Anima (On The Soul)*, trans Hugh Lawson-Tancred, London, 1986, II:7, p 173.
12. Ibid, III:2, p 193 (emphases original).
13. Hannah Arendt, *The Life of the Mind*, New York, 1978, pp 110-111.
14. This argument is persuasively put by P Christopher Smith, 'From Acoustics to Optics: The Rise of the Metaphysical and Demise of the Melodic in Aristotle's *Poetics*', in *Sites of Vision: The Discursive Construction of Sight in the History of Philosophy*, ed David Michael Levin, Cambridge MA, 1997, pp 69-91.

15. Aristotle, *The Basic Works of Aristotle*, ed Richard McKeon, trans WD Ross, New York, 1988, p 689.
16. Simmel, op cit, 'Sociology of the Senses', p 118.
17. Thedor W Adorno, *Negative Dialectics*, trans EB Ashton, London, 1973, pp 206-207.
18. Thedor W Adorno and Max Horkheimer, *Dialectic of Enlightenment*, trans John Cumming, London, 1979, p 123.
19. Guy Debord, *Society of the Spectacle*, trans Fredy Perlman and John Supak, 1983, §28.
20. Immanuel Kant, *Critique of Pure Reason*, trans JMD Meiklejohn, London, 1993, II:ii, §16, p 99 (emphases original).
21. Ibid, II:ii, §27, p 117.
22. Ibid, p 69.
23. Franco Moretti, *The Way of the World: The Bildungsroman in European Culture*, trans Albert Sbragia, London, 1987, p 210, quoting SFC Milsom, *Historical Foundations of the Common Law*, London, 1981, p 89.
24. Alain Badiou, *Cinema*, trans Susan Spitzer, Cambridge, 2013, p 154.
25. British Museum Sieveking cat., Palart 551.
26. Stefan Andriopoulos, *Ghostly Apparitions: German Idealism, the Gothic Novel and Optical Media*, New York, 2013, p 157.
27. Carl du Prel, *Die Magie als Naturwissenschaft. Erster Theil: Die magische Physik*, Jena, 1899, p 23, cited and translated in Andriopoulos, loc cit, p 157.
28. Diane Ackerman, *A Natural History of the Senses*, New York, 1990, p 229.
29. Sophie von La Roche, *Tagebuch einer Reise durch Holland und England*, Offenbach, 1788, extracted in *Sophie in London, 1786*, trans Clare Williams, London, 1933, p 141.
30. Ibid, p 87.
31. Theodor W Adorno, 'Prologue to Television', *Critical Models: Interventions and Catchwords*, trans Henry W Pickford, New

York, 1998, p 53.

32. Pierre Bourdieu, *Distinction: A Social Critique of the Judgement of Taste*, trans Richard Nice, Abingdon, 2010, p xxvi.
33. Friedrich Nietzsche, *The Gay Science*, trans Josefine Nauckhoff, Cambridge, 2001, §110, p 110.
34. Ibid, pp 8-9, emphases original.
35. Adorno, *Negative Dialectics*, p 15.
36. Ibid.
37. Nietzsche, *Basic Writings of Nietzsche*, 'Ecce Homo', ed and trans Walter Kaufmann, New York, 1968, p 103.
38. Nietzsche, *The Anti-Christ, Ecce Homo, Twilight of the Idols and Other Writings*, eds Aaron Ridley and Judith Norman, trans Judith Norman, Cambridge, 2005, p 144.
39. Henry James, *The American Scene*, Bloomington IN, 1968, p 169.
40. Vladimir Nabokov, *Speak, Memory*, New York, 1989, pp 124-125.
41. Peter Hohenstatt, *Leonardo da Vinci*, Cologne, 1998, p 79.
42. Jacques Lacan, *The Seminar of Jacques Lacan, Book XI: The Four Fundamental Concepts of Psychoanalysis*, ed Jacques-Alain Miller, trans Alan Sheridan, New York, 1981, pp 102-103.
43. Pliny, *The Elder Pliny's Chapters on the History of Art*, trans Katharine Jex-Blake, London, 1896, p 111.
44. Theodor W Adorno and Max Horkheimer, *Towards A New Manifesto*, trans Rodney Livingstone, London, 2011, p 71.
45. Ibid.
46. Adorno and Horkheimer, *Dialectic of Enlightenment*, pp 120-167.
47. Aristotle, *Politics*, trans Benjamin Jowett, Oxford, 1885, VIII:5, p 252.
48. Henry David Thoreau, *The Portable Thoreau*, ed Carl Bode, New York, 1964, p 266.
49. Lewis Carroll, *Alice's Adventures in Wonderland and Through the Looking-Glass*, London, 1998, pp 222-223.

50. Sophocles, *Oedipus the King*, in *The Three Theban Plays*, trans Robert Fagles, London, 1984, ll 359-360, p 176.
51. Theodor W Adorno, *Minima Moralia*, trans EFN Jephcott, London, 1974, §146, 'Toy shop', p 228.
52. Immanuel Kant, *Religion and Rational Theology*, 'What does it mean to orient oneself in thinking?', trans Allen W Wood, Cambridge, 1996, p 15.
53. Ibid, p 16.
54. Ibid, p 15.
55. Ibid, p 17, emphasis original.
56. Rebecca Comay, 'Materialist Mutations of the *Bilderverbot*', in *Sites of Vision*, op cit, p 352.
57. Anthony M Coniaris, *Introducing the Orthodox Church: Its Faith and Life*, Minneapolis, 1982, p 174.
58. Friedrich Nietzsche, *Beyond Good and Evil*, trans Walter Kaufmann, New York, 1966, §146, p 89.
59. Walter Benjamin, 'On Some Motifs in Baudelaire', *The Writer of Modern Life: Essays on Charles Baudelaire*, ed Michael W Jennings, trans Harry Zohn, Cambridge MA, 2006, p 204.
60. Debord, op cit, §12.
61. Ibid, §30.
62. Adorno, *Negative Dialectics*, op cit, p 167.
63. Ibid, p 82.
64. Simmel, op cit, p 117.
65. Orrin NC Wang, *Romantic Sobriety: Sensation, Revolution, Commodification, History*, Baltimore MD, 2011, p 99.

Chapter 2: Hearing

1. Michel Serres, *The Five Senses: A Philosophy of Mingled Bodies*, trans Margaret Sankey and Peter Cowley, London, 2008, p 134.
2. Aristotle, *De Anima (On the Soul)*, trans Hugh Lawson-Tancred, London, 1986, II:8, p 176.
3. George Eliot, 'Notes on Form in Art', *Selected Essays, Poems*

and Other Writings, ed AS Byatt and Nicholas Warren, London, 1990, p 234.

4. Immanuel Kant, *Anthropology from a Pragmatic Point of View*, trans Robert B Louden, Cambridge, 2006, p 47.
5. Jean-Luc Nancy, *The Sense of the World*, trans Jeffrey S Librett, Minneapolis MN, 1997, p 85.
6. Pte Fred Ball, in *Everyman at War*, ed CB Purdom, London, 1930.
7. Luigi Russolo, *The Art of Noises*, New York, 1986, accessed at unknown.nu/futurism/noises.html.
8. G Elliot Smith and TH Pear, *Shell Shock and Its Lessons*, Manchester, 1917, pp 8-9.
9. Hillel Schwartz, *Making Noise: From Babel to the Big Bang & Beyond*, New York, 2011, p 243.
10. James Sully, 'Civilisation and Noise', *Fortnightly Review*, vol 24, no 143, November 1878, pp 704–720.
11. *Spectator*, 2 November 1878, pp 10-11.
12. Sully, op cit.
13. Theodor W Adorno and Hanns Eisler, *Composing for the Films*, London, 2007, p 13.
14. Walter Benjamin, *Radio Benjamin*, trans Jonathan Lutes, Lisa Harries Schumann and Diana K Reese, ed Lecia Rosenthal, London, 2014, p 372.
15. Ibid, p 364.
16. Hadley Cantril and Gordon W Allport, *The Psychology of Radio*, New York, 1935, p 20.
17. David Hendy, *Noise: A Human History of Sound and Listening*, London, 2013, p 290, emphasis original.
18. Ibid, p 292.
19. Ibid, p 293.
20. Adorno and Eisler, p 14.
21. Serres, op cit, p 99.
22. Ibid, p 86.
23. Schwartz, op cit, p 330.

24. Günther Stern, 'Spuk und Radio', *Anbruch*, XII, February 1930, pp 65-66.
25. Walter Benjamin, 'L'oeuvre d'art à l'époque de sa reproduction mécanisée', *Zeitschrift für Sozialforschung*, V: 1, 1936.
26. Michael O'Shea, *The Brain: A Very Short Introduction*, Oxford, 2005, p 80.
27. Agatha Christie, 'Wireless', *The Hound of Death and Other Stories*, London, 1933, pp 101-102.
28. Hendy, op cit, p 239.
29. Ibid, p 240.
30. BBC Radio 4, *The Sound of Fear*, 18 October 2011.
31. George Steiner, *In Bluebeard's Castle: Some Notes towards the Redefinition of Culture*, New Haven CT, 1971, p 115.
32. Ibid, p 114.
33. Ibid.
34. Ernst Cassirer, *Language and Myth*, trans Susanne K Langer, New York, 1953, p 98.
35. 'Great Preface' to the *Book of Poetry*, in Ruan Yuan ed., *The Thirteen Classics with Annotations*, cited in Zhang Longxi, *From Comparison to World Literature*, Albany NY, 2015, p 161.
36. Diane Ackerman, *A Natural History of the Senses*, New York, 1995, p 205.
37. Richard Leppert, *The Sight of Sound: Music, Representation, and the History of the Body*, Berkeley CA, 1995, p 44.
38. Oliver Strunk ed., *Source Readings in Music History: The Renaissance*, New York, 1965, p 97.
39. William Congreve, *The Mourning Bride*, 1697, I:i.
40. Veit Erlmann, *Reason and Resonance: A History of Modern Aurality*, New York, 2010, p 133.
41. Ibid, pp 144-145.
42. Christian Friedrich Michaelis, *Über den Geist der Tonkunst*, Chemnitz, 1997, p 160, cited and translated in Erlmann, op cit, p 167.
43. Plato, *The Republic*, III, trans AD Lindsay, New York, 1957, p

118.

44. Leppert, op cit, pp 84-85.
45. Jean-Luc Nancy, *Listening,* trans Charlotte Mandell, New York, 2007, p 53.
46. Ibid, pp 57, 58.
47. Georg Simmel, 'Sociology of the Senses', *Simmel on Culture,* ed David Frisby and Mike Featherstone, trans Mark Ritter and David Frisby, London, 1997, p 114.
48. Guy Debord, *Society of the Spectacle,* trans Fredy Perlman and Jon Supak, Detroit MI, 2010, §18.
49. Nancy, *Listening,* p 12, translation modified.
50. A full account of the incident is available at ufoevidence .org/documents/doc408.htm.
51. 'On the Infinite Universe and Worlds', Dialogue 3:9, in Dorothea Waley Singer, *Giordano Bruno: His Life and Thought,* trans Dorothea Waley Singer, New York, 1950, p 240.
52. Michael J Crowe, *The Extraterrestrial Life Debate: 1750-1900,* Mineola NY, 1999, pp 52-53.
53. Immanuel Kant, *Critique of Pure Reason,* trans JMD Meiklejohn, London, 1855, p 500.
54. GWF Hegel, *Hegel's Philosophy of Nature, Being Part Two of the Encyclopaedia of the Philosophical Sciences,* trans AV Miller, Oxford, 1970, § 268 Z.
55. Michael E Zimmerman, 'Encountering Alien Otherness', *The Concept of the Foreign: An Interdisciplinary Dialogue,* ed Rebecca Saunders, Lanham MD, 2003, p 164.
56. Walter Benjamin, 'Paris, Capital of the Nineteenth Century', cited in Supervert, *Extraterrestrial Sex Fetish,* New York, 2001, p 167.

Chapter 3: Smell

1. Immanuel Kant, *Anthropology from a Pragmatic Point of View,* ed and trans Robert B Louden, Cambridge, 2006, p 50.
2. Thomas Aquinas, *Commentary on Aristotle's De Anima,* lectio

20, 493-495.

3. John Burnet, *Early Greek Philosophy*, 2nd edn, London, 1908, p 150.
4. John Sallis, *Delimitations: Phenomenology and the End of Metaphysics*, 2nd edn, Bloomington IN, 1995, p 191.
5. Ibid, pp 190-191.
6. In Plutarch, *On the face in the moon*, 28.
7. Johann Wolfgang von Goethe, *Faust*, Prologue in Heaven, trans Anna Swanwick, ll 45-50.
8. George Steiner, *The Poetry of Thought: From Hellenism to Celan*, New York, 2011, p 38.
9. Henry Thornton Wharton, *Sappho: Memoir, Text, Selected Renderings, and a Literal Translation*, New York, 1920, p 90.
10. Jonathan Reinarz, *Past Scents: Historical Perspectives on Smell*, Urbana-Champaign IL, 2014, p 33.
11. '[Culture] abhors stench because it stinks – because, as Brecht put it in a magnificent line, its mansion is built of dogshit.' Theodor W Adorno, *Negative Dialectics*, trans EB Ashton, London, 1973, p 366. The line remains unlocatable in any of Brecht's writings. For all that Adorno refers in the next sentence to the line having been 'written', it seems to me the best conjecture that it was said in conversation, as indeed was much else of what Adorno quotes from Brecht.
12. *Ancient Christian Writers: St Gregory of Nyssa, The Lord's Prayer and the Beatitudes*, trans Johannes Quasten and Joseph C Plumpe, Mahwah NJ, 1954, p 64.
13. 'On the Making of Man' VI, *Nicene and Post-Nicene Fathers, vol V, Gregory of Nyssa, Dogmatic Treatises*, ed Philip Schaff and Henry Wallace, trans HA Wilson, New York, 2007, p 391.
14. Gregory of Nyssa, *The Lord's Prayer*, op cit, p 66.
15. Susan Ashbrook Harvey, *Scenting Salvation: Ancient Christianity and the Olfactory Imagination*, Berkeley CA, 2006, p 159.
16. *'Commentarius in Posteriorum Analyticorum Libros'*, I:14, in AC

Crombie, *Robert Grosseteste and the Origins of Experimental Science 1100-1700*, trans AC Crombie, Oxford, 1953.

17. Catherine Pickstock, 'Liturgy and the Senses', in John Milbank, Slavoj Žižek and Creston Davis, *Paul's New Moment: Continental Philosophy and the Future of Christian Theology*, Grand Rapids MI, 2010, pp 129-130.
18. David Hume, *A Treatise on Human Nature*, I: pt 4, sect ii, 'Of scepticism with regard to the senses'.
19. Ibid.
20. Ibid.
21. Ibid.
22. Ibid, I: pt 4, sect iv, 'Of the modern philosophy'.
23. Robley Dunglison, *Human Physiology*, 3rd edn, 2 vols, Philadelphia, 1838, vol 1, pp 126-127.
24. Thomas Jefferson, *Notes on the State of Virginia*, Richmond VA, 1853, p 150.
25. Ibid.
26. Ford Madox Ford, *The Soul of London: A Survey of a Modern City*, London, 1905, pp 26-27.
27. Ibid, p 28.
28. Aromatherapy, University of Maryland Medical Center, umm.edu/health/medical/altmed/treatment/aromatherapy#ixzz3EnGXaawI, accessed 30 September 2014.
29. Richard L Doty, *The Great Pheromone Myth*, Baltimore MD, 2010, pp 2-3.
30. GWF Hegel, *Philosophy of Right*, trans William Wallace, §244, Addition.
31. Georg Simmel, 'Sociology of the Senses', *Simmel on Culture*, ed David Frisby and Mike Featherstone, trans Mark Ritter and David Frisby, London, 1997, p 118.
32. Karl Marx, 'Estranged Labour', *Economic and Philosophic Manuscripts of 1844*, trans Martin Milligan, Moscow, 1959, p 73.

Chapter 4: Taste

1. Paul Valéry, *The Collected Works of Paul Valéry, vol 13: Aesthetics*, trans Ralph Manheim, New York, 1964, pp 80-81.
2. Valéry, *Collected Works, vol 14: Analects*, trans Stuart Gilbert, Princeton NJ, 1970, p 185.
3. Carolyn Korsmeyer, *Making Sense of Taste: Food and Philosophy*, Ithaca NY, 2002, p 44.
4. Joanne Finkelstein, *Fashioning Appetite: Restaurants and the Making of Modern Identity*, London, 2014, p 121.
5. *El Porvenir de las Naciones Hispano-Americanas* [*The Future of the Hispanic-American Nations*].
6. Cindy R Lobel, *Urban Appetites: Food and Culture in Nineteenth-Century New York*, Chicago, 2014, pp 142-143.
7. Ernst Bloch, 'Sich Mischen', *Spuren* [Traces], Frankfurt, 1969, p 12, my translation.
8. EC Spary, *Eating the Enlightenment: Food and the Sciences in Paris 1670-1760*, Chicago, 2012, p 295.
9. Ibid.
10. Finkelstein, op cit, p 182.
11. George Eliot, *Adam Bede*, Oxford, 2008, pp 196-197.
12. Claude Lévi-Strauss, *Introduction to a Science of Mythology 1: The Raw and the Cooked*, trans John and Doreen Weightman, London, 1970, p 336, translation modified, emphasis original.
13. E Breck Parkman, 'Community and Wilderness in Pomo Ideology', *Journal of California and Great Basin Anthropology* 16:1, 1994, p 26.
14. Jason König, *Saints and Symposiasts: The Literature of Food and the Symposium in Greco-Roman and Early Christian Culture*, Cambridge, 2012, p 139.
15. Rachel Laudan, *Cuisine and Empire: Cooking in World History*, Berkeley CA, 2013, p 249.
16. Ibid, p 273.
17. Antoine Le Camus, *Médecine de l'esprit*, 2nd edn, Paris, 1769, quoted and translated in Spary, op cit, p 205.

18. Spary, p 206.
19. Laudan, op cit, p 223.
20. Eliza Smith, *The Compleat Housewife*, London, 1727, preface, unpaginated.
21. Cited in Spary, op cit, pp 250-251, italics original.
22. Cited in Spary, p 251.
23. Jean-Jacques Rousseau, *Emile, or On Education* II, trans Allan Bloom, New York, 1978, p 151.
24. Cited in Spary, op cit, p 261.
25. GWF Hegel, *Phenomenology of Mind*, trans JB Baillie, Mineola NY, 2003, p 330.
26. A concise account of this process is given by C Fernando Valenzuela, 'Alcohol and Neurotransmitter Interactions', *Alcohol Health and Research World*, vol 21 no 2, 1997.
27. Giorgio Samorini, *Animals and Psychedelics: The Natural World and the Instinct to Alter Consciousness*, Rochester VT, 2002.
28. Ronald K Siegel, *Intoxication: Life in Pursuit of Artificial Paradise*, New York, 1989.
29. Slavoj Žižek, *Less Than Nothing: Hegel and the Shadow of Dialectical Materialism*, London, 2012, p 389.
30. Theodor W Adorno, 'Morals and Criminality', *Notes to Literature II*, trans Shierry Weber Nicholsen, New York, 1992, p 40.

Chapter 5: Touch

1. Aristotle, *De Anima (Of the Soul)*, trans Hugh Lawson-Tancred, London, 1986, II:3, p 162.
2. Ibid, II:5, p 171.
3. Ibid, II:11, p 184.
4. Ibid, II:11, p 185.
5. 'Research on Communication by Touch', in *Touch in Psychotherapy: Theory, Research, and Practice*, eds. Edward WL Smith, Pauline Rose Clance and Suzanne Imes, New York,

1998, pp 59-73.
6. Gabriel Josipovici, *Touch*, New Haven CT, 1996, p 59.
7. Immanuel Kant, *Anthropology from a Pragmatic Point of View*, trans Robert B Louden, Cambridge, 2006, p 126, emphasis original.
8. Ibid, pp 127-128, emphases original.
9. Ibid, p 129.
10. Ibid, p 133.
11. Ibid, p 134.
12. Ibid.
13. Ibid, p 135.
14. Ibid.
15. Aristotle, op cit, III:2, p 194.
16. Thomas Aquinas, *Commentary on Aristotle's 'De Anima'*, trans Kenelm Foster OP and Silvester Humphries OP, rev edn, Notre Dame IN, 1994, p 187.
17. Ibid.
18. Jean-Luc Nancy, 'Elliptical Sense', trans Jonathan Derbyshire, in *A Finite Thinking*, ed Simon Sparks, Stanford CA, 2003, p 110, emphasis original.
19. Kant, op cit, p 47.
20. Ibid, p 46, emphases original.
21. Jacques Derrida, *On Touching – Jean-Luc Nancy*, trans Christine Irizarry, Stanford CA, 2005, p 47, emphases original.
22. Jean-Luc Nancy, *The Sense of the World*, trans Jeffrey S Librett, Minneapolis, 1997, p 83.
23. Ibid, p 194, n 135.
24. Samuel Pepys, *The Diary of Samuel Pepys*, eds Robert Latham and William Matthews, Berkeley CA, 1976, vol IX, p 457.
25. John Dart, *Westmonasterium; or The History and Antiquities of the Abbey Church of St Peter's Westminster*, 2 vols, London, 1723.
26. Michel de Montaigne, 'On the Cannibals', *The Complete*

Essays, I:31, trans MA Screech, London, 1991, p 241.
27. William Langland, *Piers Plowman*, ll 99-101.
28. Georg Simmel, 'The Sociology of Space', *Simmel on Culture*, ed David Frisby and Mike Featherstone, trans Mark Ritter and David Frisby, London, 1997, p 143.
29. Ibid, p 153.
30. 'The Holy Oil' by S, *The Royal Lady's Magazine, and Archives of the Court of St James's*, vol I, London, 1831, p 234.
31. Leo Tolstoy, *What is Art? and Essays on Art*, trans Aylmer Maude, London, 1930, p 260.
32. Theodor W Adorno, *Philosophy of New Music*, trans Robert Hullot-Kentor, Minneapolis MN, 2006, p 55.
33. Theodor W Adorno, 'Sexual Taboos and Law Today', *Critical Models: Interventions and Catchwords*, trans Henry W Pickford, New York, 1998, p 73.
34. Ibid, p 76.
35. William Gerhardie, *The Polyglots*, London, 2008, p 284.
36. Adorno, *Philosophy of New Music*, p 87.
37. Hugh Aldersey-Williams, *Anatomies: The Human Body, Its Parts and the Stories They Tell*, London, 2013, p 212.
38. Sigmund Freud, 'Inhibitions, Symptoms and Anxiety' (1926), *The Standard Edition of the Works of Sigmund Freud*, ed James Strachey, London, 1953-66, vol 20, p 122.
39. Freud, 'Civilisation and Its Discontents' (1930), *Standard Edition*, loc cit, vol 21, p 105.
40. Ibid, p 106.

Appendix B: When Would You Like To Eat?

1. Regina C Casper, 'Eating Disturbances and Eating Disorders in Childhood', *Psychopharmacology: The Fourth Generation of Progress*, Brentwood TN, 2000, acnp.org/g4/GN401000162/Default.htm, accessed 8 November 2012.

zero books

Contemporary culture has eliminated both the concept of the public and the figure of the intellectual. Former public spaces – both physical and cultural – are now either derelict or colonized by advertising. A cretinous anti-intellectualism presides, cheerled by expensively educated hacks in the pay of multinational corporations who reassure their bored readers that there is no need to rouse themselves from their interpassive stupor. The informal censorship internalized and propagated by the cultural workers of late capitalism generates a banal conformity that the propaganda chiefs of Stalinism could only ever have dreamt of imposing. Zer0 Books knows that another kind of discourse – intellectual without being academic, popular without being populist – is not only possible: it is already flourishing, in the regions beyond the striplit malls of so-called mass media and the neurotically bureaucratic halls of the academy. Zer0 is committed to the idea of publishing as a making public of the intellectual. It is convinced that in the unthinking, blandly consensual culture in which we live, critical and engaged theoretical reflection is more important than ever before.

ZERO BOOKS

If this book has helped you to clarify an idea, solve a problem or extend your knowledge, you may like to read more titles from Zero Books. Recent bestsellers are:

Capitalist Realism Is there no alternative?
Mark Fisher
An analysis of the ways in which capitalism has presented itself as the only realistic political-economic system.
Paperback: November 27, 2009 978-1-84694-317-1 $14.95 £7.99.
eBook: July 1, 2012 978-1-78099-734-6 $9.99 £6.99.

The Wandering Who? A study of Jewish identity politics
Gilad Atzmon
An explosive unique crucial book tackling the issues of Jewish Identity Politics and ideology and their global influence.
Paperback: September 30, 2011 978-1-84694-875-6 $14.95 £8.99.
eBook: September 30, 2011 978-1-84694-876-3 $9.99 £6.99.

Clampdown Pop-cultural wars on class and gender
Rhian E. Jones
Class and gender in Britpop and after, and why 'chav' is a feminist issue.
Paperback: March 29, 2013 978-1-78099-708-7 $14.95 £9.99.
eBook: March 29, 2013 978-1-78099-707-0 $7.99 £4.99.

The Quadruple Object
Graham Harman
Uses a pack of playing cards to present Harman's metaphysical system of fourfold objects, including human access, Heidegger's indirect causation, panpsychism and ontography.
Paperback: July 29, 2011 978-1-84694-700-1 $16.95 £9.99.

Weird Realism Lovecraft and Philosophy
Graham Harman
As Hölderlin was to Martin Heidegger and Mallarmé to Jacques Derrida, so is H.P. Lovecraft to the Speculative Realist philosophers.
Paperback: September 28, 2012 978-1-78099-252-5 $24.95 £14.99.
eBook: September 28, 2012 978-1-78099-907-4 $9.99 £6.99.

Sweetening the Pill or How We Got Hooked on Hormonal Birth Control
Holly Grigg-Spall
Is it really true? Has contraception liberated or oppressed women?
Paperback: September 27, 2013 978-1-78099-607-3 $22.95 £12.99.
eBook: September 27, 2013 978-1-78099-608-0 $9.99 £6.99.

Why Are We The Good Guys? Reclaiming Your Mind From The Delusions Of Propaganda
David Cromwell
A provocative challenge to the standard ideology that Western power is a benevolent force in the world.
Paperback: September 28, 2012 978-1-78099-365-2 $26.95 £15.99.
eBook: September 28, 2012 978-1-78099-366-9 $9.99 £6.99.

The Truth about Art Reclaiming quality
Patrick Doorly
The book traces the multiple meanings of art to their various sources, and equips the reader to choose between them.
Paperback: August 30, 2013 978-1-78099-841-1 $32.95 £19.99.

Bells and Whistles More Speculative Realism
Graham Harman
In this diverse collection of sixteen essays, lectures, and interviews Graham Harman lucidly explains the principles of Speculative Realism, including his own object-oriented philosophy.

Paperback: November 29, 2013 978-1-78279-038-9 $26.95 £15.99.
eBook: November 29, 2013 978-1-78279-037-2 $9.99 £6.99.

Towards Speculative Realism: Essays and Lectures Essays and Lectures
Graham Harman
These writings chart Harman's rise from Chicago sportswriter to co founder of one of Europe's most promising philosophical movements: Speculative Realism.
Paperback: November 26, 2010 978-1-84694-394-2 $16.95 £9.99.
eBook: January 1, 1970 978-1-84694-603-5 $9.99 £6.99.

Meat Market Female flesh under capitalism
Laurie Penny
A feminist dissection of women's bodies as the fleshy fulcrum of capitalist cannibalism, whereby women are both consumers and consumed.
Paperback: April 29, 2011 978-1-84694-521-2 $12.95 £6.99.
eBook: May 21, 2012 978-1-84694-782-7 $9.99 £6.99.

Translating Anarchy The Anarchism of Occupy Wall Street
Mark Bray
An insider's account of the anarchists who ignited Occupy Wall Street.
Paperback: September 27, 2013 978-1-78279-126-3 $26.95 £15.99.
eBook: September 27, 2013 978-1-78279-125-6 $6.99 £4.99.

One Dimensional Woman
Nina Power
Exposes the dark heart of contemporary cultural life by examining pornography, consumer capitalism and the ideology of women's work.
Paperback: November 27, 2009 978-1-84694-241-9 $14.95 £7.99.
eBook: July 1, 2012 978-1-78099-737-7 $9.99 £6.99.

Dead Man Working

Carl Cederstrom, Peter Fleming

An analysis of the dead man working and the way in which capital is now colonizing life itself.

Paperback: May 25, 2012 978-1-78099-156-6 $14.95 £9.99.

eBook: June 27, 2012 978-1-78099-157-3 $9.99 £6.99.

Unpatriotic History of the Second World War

James Heartfield

The Second World War was not the Good War of legend. James Heartfield explains that both Allies and Axis powers fought for the same goals - territory, markets and natural resources.

Paperback: September 28, 2012 978-1-78099-378-2 $42.95 £23.99.

eBook: September 28, 2012 978-1-78099-379-9 $9.99 £6.99.

Find more titles at www.zero-books.net